HEARTLAND
Family Child Care Handbook

Author:
Lesia Oesterreich

Contributing authors:
Sally Clausen
Brenda Cude
Bess Gene Holt
Kerry Moore Kroneman
Shirley Karas
Carolyn Clawson Langill
Ruth Litchfield
Suzanne Secor Parker
Kathy Reschke
Sandra J. Ryan
Elisabeth A. Schafer
JaneAnn Stout
Carol Volker
Mary Yearns

Illustrator:
Lonna Nachtigal

PM 1541 Revised September 2007

Copyright: © 1986, 1993, 1995, 1999, 2007 Iowa State University.
All rights reserved.

ISBN 0-9700528-6-3

Legislation and legal parameters can change the application of the material in this book. No endorsement of companies or their products mentioned is intended, nor is criticism implied of similar companies or their products not mentioned.

Reprint information

Permission is granted to reprint individual articles of this document for noncommercial (STRICTLY NOT FOR SALE) purposes, provided the author and Iowa State University Extension receive acknowledgment and the following notice is included:

Reprinted with permission. Oesterreich, L. (2007). Heartland Family Child Care Handbook, Iowa State University Extension, Ames, Iowa.

Individuals or organizations wishing to adapt and distribute versions of this document or copy and distribute whole chapters from this book must request permission from:

Permissions Editor
Extension Communications and Marketing
Iowa State University Extension
3630 Extension 4-H Youth Bldg.
Ames, IA 50011-3630
(515) 294-9915
Fax: (515) 294-7767

Ordering information

Copies of the Heartland Family Child Care Handbook may be ordered from
http://www.extension.iastate.edu/store
or
Extension Distribution Center
119 Printing and Publications Bldg.
Iowa State University
Ames, IA 50011-3171
(515) 294-5247
Fax: (515) 294-2945
E-mail: pubdist@iastate.edu

Edited by Barb Abbott
Graphic design by Jane Lenahan
Illustrations by Lonna Nachtigal

File: Family Life 2

. . . and justice for all
The U.S. Department of Agriculture (USDA) prohibits discrimination in all its programs and activities on the basis of race, color, national origin, gender, religion, age, disability, political beliefs, sexual orientation, and marital or family status. (Not all prohibited bases apply to all programs.) Many materials can be made available in alternative formats for ADA clients. To file a complaint of discrimination, write USDA, Office of Civil Rights, Room 326-W, Whitten Building, 14th and Independence Avenue, SW, Washington, DC 20250-9410 or call 202-720-5964. Issued in furtherance of Cooperative Extension work, Acts of May 8 and June 30, 1914, in cooperation with the U.S. Department of Agriculture. Jack M. Payne, director, Cooperative Extension Service, Iowa State University of Science and Technology, Ames, Iowa.

Author:
Lesia Oesterreich,
Family Life Extension Specialist,
Department of Human Development and Family Studies,
Iowa State University.

Contributing authors:
The original content prior to 1993 of the Iowa Family Child Care Handbook was developed by Bess Gene Holt and Shirley Karas, Department of Child Development, Iowa State University. Since that time, much of the content has changed due to the outstanding contributions of many professionals dedicated to supporting and improving the quality of family child care. Lesia Oesterreich has served as primary author for the 1993 edition and all subsequent editions. In addition, the following individuals have made contributions to the handbook: Sandra J. Ryan (former Families Extension Nutrition Assistant), Elisabeth A. Schafer (former Extension Nutrition Specialist and Associate Professor), Ruth Litchfield, Assistant Professor and Extension Nutrition Specialist, Department of Food Science and Human Nutrition, Iowa State University, and Suzanne Secor Parker, Education Program Consultant, Bureau of Nutrition, Iowa Department of Education made significant contributions to the nutrition chapter. Brenda Cude (Extension Specialist and Associate Professor, University of Illinois) and Carol Volker (former Extension Family Resource Management Specialist and Associate Professor, Iowa State University) are the original authors of the information on liability insurance. Sally Clausen, ARNP, BSN Healthy Child Care Iowa Department of Public Health and Kerry Moore Kroneman, MS, gave their generous time and expertise to update the health and safety information. Kerry Moore Kroneman also spent extensive time revising and updating the resource section included on the CD and painstakingly reviewed every chapter in the book. Appreciation also is extended to JaneAnn Stout (Associate Dean and Director of Iowa State University Extension to Families) for her art curriculum contributions and administrative support, and to Mary Yearns (Associate Professor and Extension Housing Specialist) for significant contributions on home safety issues. Kathy Reschke, Early Development & Care Consultant ChildWise Resources wrote and contributed original fingerplays. Carolyn Clawson Langill, PhD, contributed to the information on disabilities.

Reviewers:
We especially wish to thank the following individuals for their time and effort as reviewers: Grace Aiton, Joyce Howard, Mary Hughes, Michele Kostelecky, Kerry Moore Kroneman, Gayle Luze, Betsy Meyers, Liz Novak, Suzanne Secor Parker, Janet Peterson, Joy Rouse, Melissa Thorson, and Masha Wolfe.

Funding support:
Partially funded by the Federal Child Care Development Block Grant. Administered by the Iowa Department of Human Services.

Acknowledgments

The authors of the Heartland Family Child Care Handbook wish to thank Iowa child care providers, training professionals, and state agency staff members for their tremendous efforts to review, critique, and suggest material for this handbook. Appreciation also goes to: Iowa Department of Human Services; Iowa Department of Education, Early Childhood Iowa, Iowa Department of Public Health, Healthy Child Care Iowa, Iowa State-wide Child Care Resource and Referral System; Iowa Family Child Care Association; and Iowa State University Extension.

The efforts and commitment of these individuals have truly contributed to the development of a resource that reflects the very best of the family child care profession. It is our hope that the Heartland Family Child Care Handbook will continue to be a source of information and inspiration for child care providers everywhere.

A special thanks goes to our extremely gifted illustrator, Lonna Nachtigal, as she captures the spirit of young children everywhere and brings the text to life. Her illustrations bring delight to our hearts and renew our enthusiasm for the important work we do.

Finally, I wish to thank my family for their continued patience and support, Wolfgang Oesterreich, Annamarie Oesterreich, Cara Dennis, and Beth Wyatt.

Seventh Edition changes

- **New name**—*Heartland Family Child Care Handbook*—formerly *Iowa Family Child Care Handbook*. This change was made to reflect the growing use of the handbook in many other states across the nation.

- **National audience**—Iowa specific resources and licensing/registration requirements have been removed from the text. Web site links to Iowa specific information can be found at: www.extension.iastate.edu/childcare

- **Available in Spanish.** The full handbook text also is available in Spanish, PM 1541(S).

- **Updated and improved content.**
    1. Includes a CD with articles and forms that may be shared with parents
    2. Reflects changes in national health and safety performance standards and emerging state early learning standards
    3. Aligns with the newly revised Family Child Care Environment Rating Scale – Revised (FCCERS-R) by Thelma Harms, Debby Cryer, and Richard M. Clifford

Lesia Oesterreich
September 2007

Table of contents

1. Welcome to family child care 1
2. Together with families 11
3. Places and spaces: How to organize your home 39
4. The right tools: Toys, books, and equipment 57
5. Planning your day: Routines and schedules 79
6. Creative play and learning 97
7. Understanding children: Ages and stages 143
8. All together now: Multi-age groups 171
9. Guiding behavior 191
10. Business matters 219
11. Health and safety for active kids 279
12. Nutrition power: Choices with kid appeal 321
13. Children with disabilities 357
14. Child abuse and neglect 377
15. Taking care of yourself 397
16. Growing as a professional 415

Welcome to family child care

Contents

Providing high quality child care for children in your home 3
What is a good family child care home? 4
Is this for you? 5
Seven success stories 5
Skills and knowledge—Make all the difference 8
Registration and licensing 8
How can the *Heartland Family Child Care Handbook* help you? 8
Heart of the Matter 9

Chapter 1

Welcome to family child care

Providing high quality child care for children in your home

All over the country, child care providers open their homes to care for children each day. These caregivers may be friends, family members, or neighbors. Often they are individuals who have joined a growing profession called family child care.

Family, friends, and neighbors

If you are a friend, family member, or neighbor who is just beginning to care for children in your home, you may have chosen to care for just one or two children. Your decision to care for children may be short term. And you may not be interested in many of the business aspects of the family child care profession. Nevertheless, you will find a great deal of useful information in this book. There are many fun activities to do with children and helpful ideas for preparing snacks and dealing with troublesome behaviors. You also will find useful tips to help you organize your time and save you energy.

Family child care professionals

If you are someone who has a growing interest in the family child care profession, you will find this book is a great way to get started. It is full of information that will allow you to earn a reasonable income by providing high quality child care.

The effort you put into becoming a professional will have great rewards. Improving your knowledge and skills will make your job easier and more enjoyable. As you learn more, you will be able to offer higher quality care and your services will be in demand. Families want high quality care for their children. Growing more knowledgeable as a business person also will allow you to earn a higher income.

Family child care benefits you, the provider, by offering:
- an opportunity to work at home
- meaningful work that can make a difference in the lives of others
- a way to earn income while caring for your own children
- an opportunity to learn more about children's growth and development
- an opportunity to grow professionally as an early childhood educator
- an opportunity to operate a personal business

Families value family child care because it provides:
- care in a home-like setting
- the ability to keep brothers and sisters together during the day
- small family-like groups of children
- flexible schedules
- consistent, year-after-year care from the same familiar caregiver
- support and connection with another family
- care that's close by in the local neighborhood or community

What is a good family child care home?

High quality care, the kind all parents want for their children, is warm and caring. The home is clean, children eat nutritious food and are kept safe. There are great books, toys, and activities for play and learning. A great deal of time each day is spent helping children learn new skills and how to get along with each other.

Good child care is NOT "just baby sitting"

A good family child care home does much more than keep children busy, under control, and out of trouble.

A nurturing place. A quality family child care home is a place where a family child care professional understands and responds to children, takes care of their physical needs, and nurtures them. Caregivers in a good family child care home know how to show children love and acceptance, and at the same time, strengthen the bond that children have with their own home and family members.

A learning place. The family child care home is a place where children not only play but learn through play, using toys and materials that are interesting and just right for their age. Care is given by a provider who knows how children grow and develop.

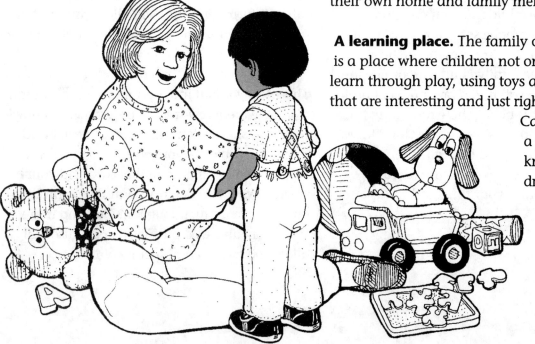

4 Heartland Family Child Care Handbook — Chapter 1

A family child care home can provide rich opportunities for children's learning. Young children learn best when they are actively involved with things and people. They also learn well when they are comfortable, in a familiar setting, and when the experiences fit in easily with what they know already. The kitchen is one of the world's best places to learn. Preparing food can teach science, math, and language as a child watches steam rise from a tea kettle, helps measure the flour into the muffin batter, and talks about the white and yolk of an egg.

A natural part of the community. Natural happenings and neighborhood events contribute to a child's learning in a home. When it "looks like rain," there is time to search the sky and talk about clouds. If a city crew starts to fix a pothole in the street or a neighbor invites the children to see a litter of kittens, this event becomes the activity of the moment. For young children, daily happenings are important educational events.

A small family-like group of children. Family child care makes it possible for children to get the attention they need, when they need it, and promotes understanding between children. A family child care home usually cares for a small group of children, but a wide range of ages—just like a family. The range in ages allows an infant to enjoy the closeness and activity of a 5-year-old's play while giving the 5-year-old a chance to learn about babies.

A secure, positive place. Early development is the basis for all later development. Children's feelings of self-worth, their attitudes toward other people and the world are all shaped through early experiences. A quality child care home fills many hours with meaningful experiences and activities that help children grow and learn.

Is this for you?

Successful family child care providers truly enjoy children and find helping children grow and learn very rewarding. But loving children is sometimes not enough to carry providers through this demanding profession. Providing the very best for children often means learning some new skills.

There are many important factors to consider in making the decision to become a family child care professional. The following real-life stories share some of the reasons individuals become family child care providers and decide to continue in this important profession.

Seven success stories

Beth—started as a stay-at-home mom (15 years experience). "I began caring for children in my home because I wanted the opportunity to earn income while caring for my own children. I didn't want to miss their preschool years. I grew up in a large family and liked the idea that my child care children could provide my own two children with playmates. I thought I would quit when my children reached school age, but by then I realized that I also wanted to be there for them when they came home from school.

"Of course there have been drawbacks. My own children have to share my time and attention with the child care children. Sometimes they must also share toys and their rooms for play and napping space. All of us have had to adapt to having toys, cribs, and other equipment around the house for years.

"All in all though, I'd say my children have really benefited. They have grown up to be very responsible and know how to share and appreciate others. They also have a real understanding of what I do for a living. My kids are very proud of me and often tell friends about what I do. That makes me feel great!"

Bernice—began as mom of a child with a disability (4 years experience). "I had planned to stay home with my children, but when we found out that my son Toby had cerebral palsy it became a sure thing. But I needed to bring in some income too. My neighbor is a teacher who works across town and I began by caring for her kids before and after school. And well, it sort of grew. I now care for five school-age children and it works out great. I have time during the day for Toby and myself and then can provide care for the children before and after school. Because all of the children are teachers' kids, I have my summers off. This is ideal for all of us."

Rosa—cares for grandchildren (7 years experience). "I only care for my five grandchildren. I have two granddaughters from one son and two grandsons and a granddaughter from my daughter. So they are all cousins. I think it is great that they all can grow up together in this way. I teach them about the importance of family. I teach them to respect each other, their parents, and themselves. I want the best for them. I want them to learn and to give back to this world. So I go to training to find out about things I can do to help them learn.

"I do enjoy visiting with other providers. Sometimes I have good advice for them. But I have learned a lot too, especially about health and safety. When I think about the way I raised my own kids, it's a wonder they survived to adulthood! I have always been a good cook, but I now have learned a lot about nutrition too. My motto is 'You are never too old to learn.'"

Lois—loves being her own boss (3 years experience). "I never dreamed that becoming a family child care provider would help me grow so much as a person. I also never realized that I would actually be running a small business. I have learned how to keep accounting records, do taxes, advertise, and draw up a budget. I've also learned a lot about food and nutrition by being on the child care food program. The best part of it all is that I am my own boss!

"On the down side of things, the pay is somewhat limited. I realize that I am not going to get rich doing child care. But I do bring in a respectable income, and I like the tax advantages that I can take to decrease my mortgage and other home expenses. Managing all of this is a challenge, but I really like the independence it gives me."

Mei—wanted to help her neighbor (4 years experience). "My mother lives with us. I provide some care for her as well as two little girls who live next door. It is good to have young children around. I enjoy watching the children listen to my mother as she tells stories to them each day. She is a very good storyteller. It reminds me of my own childhood—only I think my mother is even better now. I guess it comes with age.

"My husband enjoys listening to the girls play as he works in the garden. Sometimes they help him. We both try to teach them things they should know. I want them to be able to read well and be successful in life.

"Their mother sometimes must work evenings or weekends so we work things out each week. It means a great deal to me to care for these children. And I also like supporting their mother in this way. She is young and a good person. They bring great joy to our lives and have become a part of our family."

Aretha and Ryan—made a husband and wife career change (7 years experience).
Aretha: "We made a career change – for the better. I got laid off and decided that providing child care at home might be a good option. Our kids were in elementary school and could have stayed home alone, but we just weren't thrilled with the idea. Sometimes I think the older kids need more supervision than the younger ones.

"Anyway, family child care worked out really well—in fact it was great. Two years later we had a heart-to-heart talk about Ryan's job. He was in a high pressure sales job. He was exhausted from traveling so much and missed not being home with our family. So after seeing how happy I was and looking carefully at our family budget, he decided to join me in providing child care.

"Our life is busy, but much more relaxed. Ryan is great with the kids and does things with them that I normally would not do. He loves to cook and plays more games with them outdoors. I really think it is wonderful for the children to have a man around. He is a great role model."

Ryan: "We now care for 11 children together. Fortunately we live in an older, big house—but it still gets a little crowded sometimes. It was a little tough for me at first—still is—because there aren't many men in child care. It feels awkward sometimes when we go for training. I hesitate when I explain to people what I do. It has its ups and downs just like anything else, but it is much more important work than my sales job and I get to watch my kids grow up."

Vicki—values the relationships with families (6 years experience). "The first years were a bit rough. I loved being at home, but the hours were long and I craved adult conversation. I also found that this job could be really confining. I longed to just be able to go out to eat with a friend or take off an afternoon for shopping. After a while I linked up with other providers and found support. Now we talk to each other almost every day by phone. We share menu ideas, talk about discipline problems, and give each other a pat on the back. I learned that it was okay to get a substitute occasionally so I could have a special lunch with a friend.

"I've attended a number of training workshops and have learned a lot about child development and child care. Much of what I've learned has really benefited my own family. I am much more careful about cleanliness and safety now, and I have learned a lot about how to discipline children.

"The best part of family child care for me has been the children and their families.

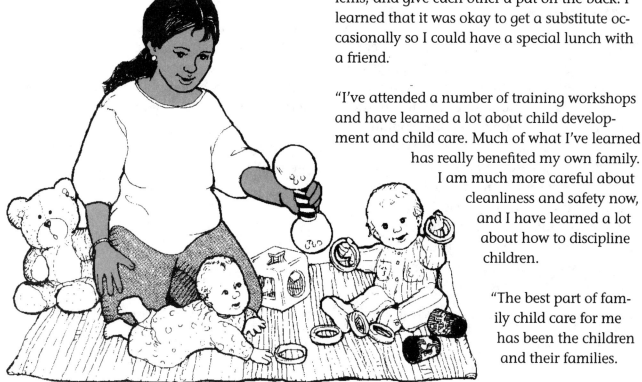

I have loved watching them grow from year to year, and I have developed real friendships with parents that will last forever because we shared in the raising of their children."

Skills and knowledge—Make all the difference

Caring for children in your home can be very rewarding, but it also requires skill and great commitment to children and their families.

This is true for family, friends, and neighbors and for individuals who wish to make family child care their chosen profession.

You may find that your life experiences as a parent, teacher, or professional in another field have prepared you well. On the other hand, you also may discover that you have a lot to learn.

Registration and licensing

In most states when you care for a number of unrelated children, you will need to be certified, registered, or licensed with the state. The requirements vary from state to state, but are generally very minimal regulations put in place to ensure the health and safety of children. Being registered or licensed is a good idea and offers you some benefits. For example, you can get linked up with a network of providers, just like you, for help and support. You can get useful training that will help you in the day-to-day care of children. In some states you also can receive extra funds or bonuses.

More information about registration and licensing is in chapter 10.

How can the *Heartland Family Child Care Handbook* help you?

- A **skills and knowledge checklist** (Where am I now? What can I improve?) is listed on the first page of each chapter. Take a few minutes to check out your skills and think about areas for improvement. A complete list of all skills is included on the CD accompanying this handbook.

- There are **FamilyShare** ideas for strengthening relationships with families.

- **Heart of the Matter** sections share the author's personal stories and reflections.

- **Experience Talks** lists tips and suggestions from experienced providers.

- **Resource** materials and handouts are included on the CD to share with families and other providers.

The more you read and learn, the more you will enjoy your work with children and families. Whether you choose to care for children for just a few years or for a lifetime, you can feel very proud of the work you do.

The memories you create and share with children will remain in their hearts forever.

Heart of the Matter

I have always enjoyed hearing the many stories from child care providers discussing how they got into the business of child care. Many seem to have stumbled into the profession. Usually it was somehow tied to the need to care for their own children. Sometimes the decision was made with the first child; sometimes it was made later after a second or third child was born. At other times, it came about from a sense of duty to care for family or to help out a friend. For some, it was a way to make a living while continuing to live in a community that offered few other jobs. And sometimes young people who receive degrees in early childhood education choose family child care as their chosen profession. This of course is a wonderful thing.

A common experience for many providers who have shared their stories is the surprise of discovering they really do enjoy the job. Many who fell into this profession did not expect to love it—or even like it. Our society does not offer much respect for those who care for young children.

A second surprise was that it takes real skill and knowledge to help children grow and learn. And when you care for other people's children you also need "people" skills and business "know-how" skills.

It is the children that make child care wonderful, but it is not all fun and games. Like any job there are problems and hassles. And there are some who grow weary of this demanding career and decide to move on. Regrettably there are also those who feel they must leave because they need to earn a greater income or have more stable health care insurance. Often this is a tremendous loss for children and their families. It is also a loss for our society.

In recent years, I have been delighted to see several good friends return to the family child care profession. After many years of providing care, they took other positions working in other professions. They felt they needed a change and left family child care feeling like they had closed the door to that time in their life. Yet now, several years later, they have returned. They realized how much caring for children had meant to themselves personally. And perhaps for the first time truly understood the tremendous impact they had made on shaping a child's future.

Sometimes you see things more clearly when you look back at the path you have traveled.

Lesia

Together with families

Chapter 2

Contents

Where am I now? 12
Introduction 13
Family, friends, and neighbors 13
Your own family 14
Accepting a new family 15
Welcoming a new child 19
Respecting family values and lifestyles 20
Family relationships 21
"Great News" notes 22
Family meetings 23
The art of giving advice 25
When things get personal 27
Speak no evil 27
Confidentiality 27
Involve families in their children's learning and development 28
A parent's point of view 28
Handling complaints and solving problems 30
FamilyShare 36
Heart of the Matter 37
Experience Talks 38

Together with families—
Where am I now? What can I improve?

	Seldom 1	Sometimes 2	Often 3	Most Often 4
1. I know what questions to ask and what information to give over the phone to families interested in child care.				
2. I know how to share information and provide a good follow-up interview in my home.				
3. I share policy and fee information with families in writing.				
4. I help new children and families feel welcome.				
5. I speak and listen respectfully to families.				
6. I greet families each day and share information.				
7. I use a variety of ways to communicate with families (bulletin board, e-mail, phone calls, written notes, newsletter, handout, notebook).				
8. I involve families in their child's learning and development by providing suggestions and learn-at-home ideas.				
9. I provide opportunities for families to share skills and talents.				
10. I use problem-solving steps to effectively resolve problems with parents.				
11. I recognize stress factors influencing families.				
12. I respect and support families of different structures and cultures.				
13. I protect and maintain confidentiality for children and families.				
14. I meet with families once or twice a year to discuss their child's growth and development.				
15. I refer families to other resources or professionals for help and information.				

Chapter 2

Together with families

Sharing the responsibility for young children requires a great deal of trust and respect between providers and families. The relationship you have can have a tremendous impact on those first early years.

When you care for children in your own home, they become a part of your life. Children may start coming as a baby and continue on through elementary school for after school care. You will come to know families very well. In some cases, you will develop relationships that will last a lifetime.

A long-term relationship offers children and families great security and stability. The opportunity for a child to remain with the same quality caregiver over several years is a real benefit. It gives you the opportunity to get to know a child well and to really make a difference in that child's life. It is an important reason that many parents seek out family child care rather than center care.

A positive relationship with families is an essential ingredient to helping children grow and learn. Children thrive when all the adults around them are supportive and caring. Since this is likely to be a long-term situation, there are a few things to think about to make sure this new relationship goes smoothly.

Family, friends, and neighbors

You may be asked to care for a child of a friend, neighbor, or family member. In this situation, you will already have begun a relationship. Most likely you have already had some experience caring for this child and so have some idea about what you are agreeing to do. But there is a difference between caring for children occasionally and caring for them for many hours each week.

Consider your interest and skills. Children need both nurturing and opportunities to learn. We know that children learn a tremendous amount in the first years of life. Children need adults who are willing to read to them and teach them new skills every day.

Consider your energy level and interest. A child in your care from 7:30 a.m. to 5:30 p.m. for at least five days will be with you for 50 hours a week. That is a lot of together time for both you and the child. You want to provide the very best care so you need to be at your best.

Consider the cost. You may feel awkward asking friends or family for money. Yet you will have expenses. Children need to be fed lunch, snacks, and sometimes breakfast or dinner. To provide really good care, toys and books will be needed as well.

Discuss values and expectations. Rules for discipline will need to be shared. If you are a grandparent or family member you may find the child's parents have certain expectations that you are not prepared for. All of this needs to be discussed openly.

Consider a trial period. Relationships with families, friends, and neighbors can be wonderful. But sometimes they also can get complicated. Before you agree to care for a child for a long time period, agree to try it for a short time. Then you can evaluate how well things are working.

Your own family

If you are just now considering offering child care to other families, you will want to think about the impact this will have on your own family. There are many advantages, but there are trade-offs as well.

Consider the advantages. You will be home more for your family and that will be a big plus. There is also the big advantage of bringing in extra income. You will probably spend less money on work clothes and gas to take you to and from work—not to mention the driving time you will save.

But there are disadvantages as well. Child care can be confining. It may be hard to make it to family events or appointments during the day. Your children will probably need to share space, toys, and equipment with your child care children. Sharing personal items can be hard for some children. Child care requires a lot of extra equipment and toys that can get in the way of everyday living. And there will be wear and tear on your house. Walls will need to be painted more frequently. Spills and stains will happen more often too. All of this needs to be discussed openly with your family.

Accepting a new family

Agreeing to care for children from a family you don't know requires some thought. They will have many questions to ask you and you will have questions for them as well. Plan the steps you will go through before you say "yes" or "no" to a new family.

The phone interview

Your first contact with a new family is generally over the phone. Information you share will help each of you decide whether to get together face-to-face to find out more.

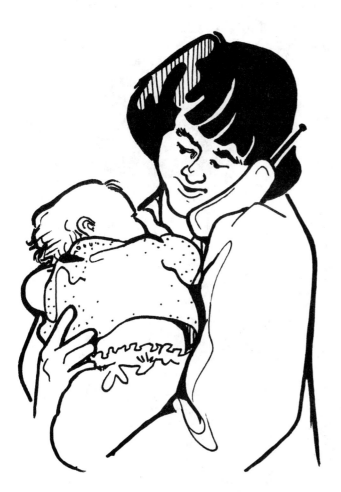

Polish up your answering machine message. A family may connect with your answering machine before reaching you in person. Make sure your answering machine message is friendly, professional, and easy to understand.

Gather information you will need to answer parents' questions. Many parents will have questions about fees, available openings, and the number of children in your care. Have the following information near the phone when you talk to interested parents. Add to this list any information that is specific to your situation.

- fees and payment dates
- hours of service
- ages of children in your program
- information on routines and activities
- information about your years of experience and education
- other _____
- other _____

Make a list of questions to ask parents. Most likely you also will have questions you would like to ask families. For example, you would want to know the age of the child, previous child care experience, and if the child is older, where he or she would be attending school. Keep it brief, more detailed information can come when they visit your home later.

Practice how you will handle requests for information over the phone. Conducting a phone interview is a little different than visiting with a friend on the phone. It may help to practice what you might say ahead of time.

The home interview

Set up a face-to-face interview and visit to your home. Encourage parents and their children to visit you at a time when you can have plenty of time to talk with them. Successful interviews take time. You should expect to visit with the family for an hour.

Many providers prefer that parents visit in the evenings or on weekends so they can give the interview their full attention. Other caregivers feel it is important for parents to see them "in action" as they interact with the children. Often it is a good idea for families to do both.

A typical interview might include:

- Doing introductions – greet parent and child.
- Giving a brief tour of your home and outdoor play area.
- Making time for adults to talk. Involve the child or children in an interesting activity such as play dough or a puzzle.
- Asking about family needs and expectations for care.
- Having parents talk about the child (likes, dislikes, etc.).
- Sharing your experience and qualifications.
- Discussing your daily schedule and activities.
- Explaining your beliefs and practices regarding discipline.

- Discussing your policies on meals, toilet learning, television, and illness.
- Giving parents time to review a copy of your policy statement and parent-provider agreement (contract). See chapter 10.
- Explaining the terms of your mutual agreement (contract).
- Providing time for questions from both sides.
- Giving parents references—names and phone numbers of past and current families in your program.

Questions parents may ask

Family child care providers often complain that all parents want to know about are fees. But in reality, many parents know very little about quality child care and just don't know what else to ask about.

Child care resource and referral agencies are located in many communities. These agencies help families find child care and encourage parents to ask the following questions. Look over this list before meeting with families and determine how you will respond. If it appears that a family has not received help in knowing what questions to ask, you may want to go ahead and share some of the following information with them anyway.

- What background or special training in child care do you have?
- If you hire assistants to help out or give you a leave time for appointments, what is their background or special training?
- How will you communicate with me? Phone? Newsletter? E-mail?
- Is there an open parent visitation policy? Can parents visit at any time?
- How will you discipline my child?
- What meals and snacks are provided? What nutritional guidelines are followed?
- Do you participate in the Child and Adult Care Food Program?
- How would you handle a medical emergency?
- Have you or your assistants taken pediatric CPR or first aid training?
- What insurance coverage do you carry?
- What do you do when you are unable to care for children due to illness or some other emergency?
- What is your schedule for a typical day?
- Are children required to take naps?
- Do you go outdoors with children? How often and how long?
- Do you take children with you on errands? Do you have car seats or will I need to provide one?
- What type of learning activities do you have? How will I find out about what my child does each day?
- How often do you read to children?
- Do you have a policy on television and video viewing?
- Do you allow children to use computers?
- Is there a written parent agreement or contract?
- What does it include?
- What are your fees?
- What are your long-term plans in regard to your child care business?
- Are you registered or licensed?

HFCCH Chapter 2 — Together with families

Saying "yes" or "no"—it's your decision

Caregivers sometimes feel they automatically have to accept families who wish to place a child in their program. However, both caregivers and parents have a right to choose.

As a child care professional owning and operating your own business, you are responsible for making the final decision. If the interview goes well, you may immediately offer to provide care. However, if parents indicate that they may not respect your policies regarding program activities, fees, or methods of discipline, it is appropriate to refuse service and refer them to another caregiver or your local child care resource and referral agency.

Saying no can be a bit awkward so you may want to practice ahead of time. Here are some ideas about how to handle such a situation.
- "I have interviews with two more families before I make my decision. Why don't I give you the name of another child care provider to interview or better yet the number of our local child care resource and referral so you also have several choices?"
- "I try very hard to balance my children with same-age playmates. Right now I have an opening for a child who is at least 2 years younger. If I accepted your son into my program, he wouldn't have anyone close to his age to play with."
- "I appreciate your need to have extended (or weekend) care that meets your work schedule. However, I am unable to do that. Like any other professional, I have set hours for my services. This policy helps me have time for my own family and personal interests."

Sometimes family child care professionals will agree to a trial period. Parents and providers sometimes agree to try the arrangement for 2 to 3 weeks and then come to a more formal decision. You may agree to do this for any number of reasons. Sometimes parents are unsure if a child will do better in a family child care home or a center program. Other reasons could involve a parent's schedule, or access to a nearby after school program for older siblings. Be cautious and ask parents to pay for fees up front or on a weekly basis, so you don't risk losing income if the family decides suddenly to go elsewhere.

It is often easier to say no in the beginning. Providers who accept a family even when they have misgivings may actually be doing the family a disservice. It is not helpful to start a child in a program and then pull him or her out after only a few months when things do not work out. Remember, your primary responsibility is to yourself and to the children already in your care.

Be aware that you cannot discriminate against a family. You may not refuse to care for a child on the basis of race or ethnic origin nor can you refuse service to a child with disabilities. In some cases, if caring for a child with a specific disability would create an "undue burden" for your program, you would be legally allowed to decline service. More information about this issue can be found in chapter 13, Children with disabilities.

Welcoming a new child

Before coming to your home, a child may have been home with a parent or staying with a grandparent or another provider. Joining you in your home can be a big step for a little one.

Imagine what it must feel like for a young child to come into your home. The furniture and rooms are not familiar. And everything seems so big to someone who may be only a few feet tall. You do things at different times and in different ways—not like at home. And there are many new faces—children and adults. It can be overwhelming.

Introduce a new child to the other children. You can help a new child remember the older children's names by repeating the names throughout the day. Tell the child something special about each new playmate. For example, you might say, "Ernesto loves to draw and paint. Maya has great fun playing with blocks."

Spend a little more time with a new child. Extra attention can help a new child feel welcome and comfortable. Ask parents to give you ideas about favorite toys or activities. Encourage the child to bring a favorite stuffed animal from home.

Help your other child care children adjust to the new child. It may take a little time for the other children to know how to play with the new child. Stay close by, so you can gently make suggestions and guide their play.

Create a picture book with pictures of all the children in your care and their names. A small photo album works well for this. If there is room, you can write a sentence underneath each picture such as "Nathan enjoys apples at snack time." The new child can take home the picture book to read or share with other family members. Be sure to add the child's picture to the book as well.

Have children bring a picture of Mom, Dad, or their family. Children often find comfort and enjoy looking at pictures of family members. A picture of a favorite pet is a good idea too.

HFCCH Chapter 2 — Together with families

Respecting family values and lifestyles

Families come in all shapes, sizes, and colors. Professional caregivers respect and honor different family values and lifestyles. Caring for a child from a different ethnic culture can be a very enriching experience.

Be respectful and open to different kinds of families. Family customs, traditions, and food preferences can add new life to everyday activities. Children may live with one parent, both parents, grandparents, foster parents, or adoptive parents. You can help children best by being supportive of each family situation. This means accepting that families live in different ways and helping children share their experiences and feelings about their family life.

Ask families to help you understand their culture and background. When interviewing a family that may have cultural beliefs different from your own, you will want to carefully explain your routines and practices.

You might say, "I enjoy caring for children from different cultures or backgrounds. Are there any family customs or practices that would be helpful for me to know so I can make your child feel more comfortable?"

Key areas where families may have different beliefs or practices include:

- **Personal space:** some cultures prefer to stand very close to each other when talking, and some prefer to stand farther away.
- **Eye contact:** some cultures feel that looking directly at a person is the proper way to give attention. Other cultures feel this is a sign of disrespect.
- **Touching:** some cultures view touching as a sign of warmth or friendliness. Other cultures view touching as an insult or sign of superiority.
- **Time:** all cultures have rules and priorities about time and what it means to be "on time" or late.
- **Eating:** some cultures have strong views about the type of food children should eat and how and when they should receive it.
- **Discipline:** some families believe in rather strict discipline, while others are much less strict.
- **Toileting:** some cultures advocate very early toilet learning with intense adult involvement and others expect toileting to happen much later.

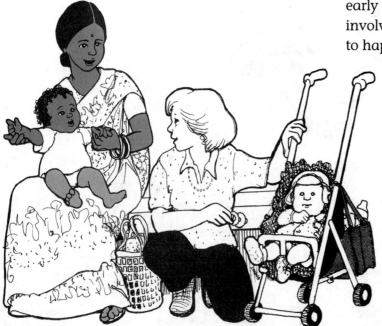

Remember that within each culture every individual and every family is unique. Expectations of a family who has newly immigrated may be very different than those of a family who is actively embracing more traditional "Americanized" culture. It is always wise to respectfully ask families to share information with you.

Family relationships

Greet parents and children every day. Ever notice how good it makes you feel to be noticed and made to feel special? The truth is that greeting families may be the single most important thing you do to foster good communication. Make it a point to greet parents and children every day at drop-off or pick-up time. A friendly smile, a "Great News" note, goes a long way in laying the foundation for a good relationship. It is much easier to work out problems with someone you already have a good relationship with than with someone you barely know.

Send home "Great News" notes. Your days will be busy. Often you will see something you would like to share with a parent, but then later forget to mention it. Children also don't often remember what happened during the day. "Great News" notes help parents remind children of the good things that happened and they can talk about them more at home. For parents of older children, it also may help to list a question for the parent to ask the child. For example, you might write, "Ask Jason about the block building he built today." This will help foster communication between parents and children.

Use the telephone. If parents are in too much of a hurry to stop and talk at drop-off or pick-up time, try calling them at home in the evening. Phone calls are also a great way for parents and children to talk with each other. Encourage parents to call from work to speak with their children, and ask parents if they would appreciate an occasional call from their children. To make this work, you may want to ask about appropriate times to call and suggest to parents that they avoid calling at nap or lunch time.

Have a meal together. Once or twice a year, have a "family dinner." Children can make their invitations or help prepare part of the meal. Parents enjoy having a dinner prepared when they get off work and appreciate the chance to meet other parents and their children.

Make a movie. Have a yearly movie night. Videotape the children throughout the year and then invite parents to come and see home movies of their children. It is amazing how much children can change in a year's time. Parents will enjoy seeing their children and will gain a new appreciation and understanding of the special work you do with them.

"Great News" notes

Make copies of this page. Cut on the dotted lines. Write the child's name on the top line. On the bottom lines, tell the parents something special their child did today. Give "Great News" Notes to parents each day when they come to pick up their children.

_____

had a great day!

_____
_____
_____
_____

Today was a super day for

_____
_____
_____
_____
_____

It's terrific to tell you what

_____

did today!

_____
_____
_____
_____

Guess what

_____

did today!

_____
_____
_____
_____

Remember to ask. We work hard to teach children to ask for help, but we often forget that it is OK for us to ask for help, too. Parents can't help with supplies or assistance if they don't know what you need. Post a "wish list" or send home a "Wish upon a Star" note occasionally. Parents often can donate old dress-up clothes, toys, or boxes or lend time to paint or repair. Remember, under the right circumstances, most of us truly enjoy helping others, especially when it makes us look good in the eyes of our children.

Celebrate family traditions. Encourage communication and understanding between families by asking them each year to share something about their family with the other children. It can be a meal, a favorite song, or photos of their last vacation. Almost anything will do. The point is to make each child feel that his or her family is special.

Consider a newsletter. Newsletters take a lot of time to write, but if you enjoy writing it can be a good way to share information. Keep it simple—one or two pages is fine. It can be every month, quarterly, or even once a year.

Use a family bulletin board. A bulletin board can help families know about your daily schedule, menus, and special projects. Have the board where families can see it easily, perhaps near the door. Parents love to see pictures of their children. Post a few pictures on your bulletin board with a sentence about what the children are doing. Watch the smiles.

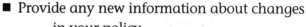

Family meetings

It is often helpful to have a longer period of time to chat. Parents have many questions about their child's development and value your knowledge and expertise. It is a good idea to set aside some time once or twice a year to share notes about how a child is developing and to ask parents if they have any concerns.

To set up a meeting:
- Identify a place and time when you can speak uninterrupted.
- Notify parents at least two weeks ahead of time so they can get this on their schedule.
- Set a time limit of no longer than an hour.
- Serve light refreshments.

During the meeting:
- Share general information about how the child is developing.
- Share photos of the child playing and learning.
- Focus on positives.
- Listen to parents' concerns.
- Respond to questions.
- Identify any challenges or upcoming changes—toilet learning, getting ready for kindergarten, etc.
- Provide some written information (see FamilyShare resources).
- Provide any new information about changes in your policy.

Sample letter to set up a family meeting

Dear Family,

Once a year I like to set aside some time to visit with you about your child. Although we chat briefly each day, there are things I would like to share with you that deserve a little more time.

During our visit I will share some photos of your child playing and learning. I also will have ages and stages information and other resources to share.

But most importantly, I want to hear from you. I have learned that family members can teach me a great deal about caring for and teaching their children.

So let's get together. We will have a light snack and chat a bit. The children can be with us. I know they will love seeing their photos. I will have a fun activity for them while we continue to talk.

I have the following times available to meet with you. Please let me know if any of these will work for you.

Date:	Time:
Date:	Time:
Date:	Time:

Sincerely,

The art of giving advice

Advice-giving is an art. Some parents actively seek advice. Other parents just want someone to listen to their feelings and concerns. Listening, suggesting a few ideas, and more listening is generally the best form of advice-giving. You have a great deal to offer parents about your knowledge of child development and about the experience their child has had while he/she has been in your care. It is important to share that knowledge with families.

Advice goes both ways. Parents also have a great deal of knowledge. They know what their child is like in a home setting. Parents have a history with their child and have a better understanding of how their family members interact with their child.

Avoid giving one-solution—"do it this way" advice. The most effective advice usually comes in the form of suggestions that focus on parents as the decision makers. Problem solving should be a team approach. You may assume the role of a coach, but the parent is the real-life player, and it is hard to know for sure what will really work best. Respect the right of the parent to be the final decision maker.

Support parents as decision makers. For example, you might say, "some ideas I have heard of for dealing with this situation are . . . but of course you are Rachel's parent and have a better understanding of what will work for your family. What do you think would work best?"

HFCCH Chapter 2 — Together with families

Make your communication helpful, not hurtful

- Words can be very powerful. Think about how you talk with families in everyday conversations. Choose words that support children and parents in positive ways.

    One of these phrases is a good example of how to assure a parent that she or he is still loved and needed by the child.

    Instead of: "Gabriel has adjusted so well. He plays so hard with the other children that he doesn't miss you at all during the day."

    Say this instead: "Gabriel told the other children about your plans to take him to the zoo. He really is looking forward to going with you."

- Consider which response will best alert parents to a child's progress without spoiling their joy at discovering the special moment.

    Instead of: "Oh, it was so cute today. Jesse took his first steps. I wish you had been here to see it. He pulled himself up against the side of the couch and wobbled for a while and then took three steps."

    Say this instead: "You might want to watch Jesse pretty carefully during the next few days. He looks like he is getting ready to start walking."

- One of these responses lays blame. The other is an example of a positive approach to use when complaining to a parent.

    Instead of: "I wish you'd feed Bonny breakfast. She's always cranky and hungry in the morning."

    Say this instead: "Bonny seems really hungry well before snack time. Has she been eating her breakfast okay at home?"

- One response is a positive approach to changing parents' expectations about their children; the other is an "I know more than you do" approach that is sure to turn a parent off. Remember you are not competing for authority but are sharing the responsibility for caring for the child.

    Instead of: "You said Tina doesn't like raw vegetables. But you were wrong! Today she ate some raw broccoli and some carrots."

    Say this instead: "Here's a recipe for a really nice vegetable dip that Tina likes. You may want to try it at home."

When things get personal

On occasion we may find ourselves needing to ask for personal information. For example, you may need information so you can respond to a child's worries or concerns about something that happens at home. Start by telling parents why you need the information and how the information will be used. Reassure parents that information will be kept confidential. Remember also to show your appreciation for their willingness to share.

Finally, respect parents' rights to not share such information with you. Some parents will make this choice.

Speak no evil

Never bad mouth a child's parents to your friends, neighbors, or relatives or to the child. This is important for the welfare of the child you care for and for the sake of your business. You may not always agree with the lifestyle chosen by a child's parents or with the way they care for their child. But if the children hear you make negative remarks about their parents—even when those comments are meant as a joke—the youngsters may be left unhappy or confused.

In one case, a child overheard his child care provider complain that the child's mother seemed to be able to afford a new car but never paid her child care bills. The remark left the child feeling that he meant less to his mother than her new car. Bad mouthing the parents also is a fast way to lose them as clients—and to lose other potential clients as well. After all, would you want to leave your children with a person you couldn't trust to be helpful rather than hurtful?

Confidentiality

Just as children and families become a part of your lives, you also will become a part of their lives. As your relationship grows, parents often will ask you for advice and will share personal family information with you. And children may tell you very personal things about their home life. Make a commitment to keep this information confidential.

Keeping parents' remarks and concerns confidential builds respect. The greatest marketing tool a child care provider has is a happy, appreciative parent. Keeping things confidential, however, is not always easy.

Remember to stop and think before you talk. When you are frustrated, it is often tempting to blow off steam with colleagues or family members. A good guideline to follow is to not discuss anything about a child with anyone other than his or her parents.

Avoid revealing names whenever possible. At times you may struggle with the need to share information because you are concerned about an issue with a particular family and need help or resources. Often you can ask for help or resources without revealing a child's name.

Break confidentiality if you suspect abuse or neglect. If you suspect a child is being harmed or seriously neglected you will need to report your concerns. For more information about how to identify and report child abuse see chapter 14.

Involve families in their children's learning and development

Share resources with parents. You are a valuable source of information and support to many families. Clip articles or publications on specific topics that you can share with parents. A small file of articles on topics such as toilet learning, guidance and discipline, self-esteem, or sleeping problems will be useful.

Use trusted resources. Free or low cost information on many topics can be found at your child care resource and referral, your county Extension office, or the local library. You also may wish to search online. For all information, be sure that you use a reputable, trusted resource. There is a great deal of inaccurate information available in both print and online. The resources included on the CD give suggested links for online searches.

Invite parents to share knowledge or skills. Parents often enjoy reading a story or sharing a skill with children. Invite them to visit or share a meal.

Use FamilyShare ideas. Review the FamilyShare section in each chapter for other ideas on how to reach out to parents. You are welcome to photocopy information from this handbook to share with parents. Parent fact sheets and information also are included on the accompanying CD.

A parent's point of view

One of the greatest challenges of working with families is understanding what they need and expect. If you could listen in on a private conversation between parents, you might hear comments like these:

■ **"I sometimes feel guilty about working.** I love my job and we need the money. I mean we really do need it—it doesn't go for extras. My paycheck goes to feed and clothe my children. But I worry that I am not spending enough time with them."

■ **"Sometimes, I'm very envious of my child care provider.** She gets to see my children at their best. I get stuck with the morning rush and dinner time crankiness."

■ **"Leaving my child is so hard.** Sometimes I just push her in the door and run. I know it looks awful—like I don't care—but really it's just too painful to hear her cry."

- **"We live hundreds of miles from any of our family.** I guess I really see my child care provider as sort of an extended family member. It helps to have someone who cares, someone who can tell me what is normal for children this age, and someone who can give me an occasional pat on the back."

- **"I have mixed feelings about child care.** My child care provider is my neighbor and a good friend. I really see her as a second parent, and I'm glad that she cares a great deal about my daughter. But sometimes I'm just a little jealous. It's hard to share your children."

- **"Child care costs so much.** In our family we pay as much for child care as we do for groceries or rent. The cost is a real hardship. The irony is that even though child care is costing us an arm and a leg, she tells me she really is not making much money. I resent having to pay so much, and she resents getting such a poor salary. Nobody wins."

- **"It really helps to know that my child is happy and well cared for.** It means that I can focus on my work and do a good job. I'm not sure that my provider will ever know how much I appreciate her."

- **"I worry sometimes about what my child care provider thinks about me.** Things are not going so great at home and I know my kids may sometimes say things about their dad and me fighting. I really hope she isn't talking to others about this."

- **"My provider wants us to drop off our children at a certain time and pick them up at a certain time.** I understand the reasons but it is so tough. It is all I can do to make it through the day. I just feel exhausted all the time."

- **"I miss my children so much.** Sometimes I would like to just drop in and watch them play for a few moments. But I don't know how my provider would feel about that. It's not that I'm checking up on her, it's just that I want to see my children play. I feel like I am missing all those special moments."

- **"My mother takes care of my children.** It's good for us because I trust her, but it can be a bit awkward. I worry that she spoils them too much and doesn't discipline like she should."

- **"We live in a small community and my provider is a neighbor.** I really like her, but you know our kids tell her everything. It can get a little embarrassing. I really don't want the whole town to know every detail of our family life."

Be respectful and understanding. The decision to leave a child day after day in the care of another adult requires a tremendous amount of trust. It is natural for parents to struggle with different emotions.

HFCCH Chapter 2 — Together with families

Handling complaints and solving problems

Complaints and disagreements with parents are bound to happen every so often. But problems can be solved if the relationship between you and the parents is good and communication is open.

If you have a complaint or a problem

Choose a good time to talk. Bring it to the attention of the parent at a time when neither of you is tired and when you both have a free moment. If that time never seems to happen, set up an appointment.

Begin with something positive. It will be easier for parents to listen to your concern if they know that you truly value their child. Parents also need to feel valued. Remember to comment sincerely on helpful things they do for their child. If you let the parents know you think they are doing a good job, they may be more open to hearing your suggestions.

Talk in a respectful, helpful manner. For instance, if Carlos always seems to be tired, it doesn't do any good to blame his parent for keeping him up too late. Instead, phrase your comments more positively and ask for the parent's help or advice. "Carlos seems more tired than usual today. Has he had trouble sleeping?"

Try to find out more. Parents know their children better than anyone else does. If you listen respectfully, you can learn a lot about the child's needs and situation. For example, you may discover that Carlos is going to bed on time but a baby sister who cries all night is creating sleep problems for everyone in the family.

Work closely with families to solve problems. If you support parents, they usually will support you. Together you can work as partners to come up with a workable solution.

Consider the following two scenarios. The first is a single parent mother who is struggling with a difficult job situation. In this case, the provider works with the mother to help her come up with several workable solutions. In

---

Get it in writing

Right from the start, it is important for you and parents to sit down and talk about expectations. That way, you will better understand what they want in terms of child care, and you can explain the time and financial commitments that you expect the parents to meet.

It is generally helpful to gather information about a child and to outline responsibilities that are to be met by you and by the child's parents. A parent-provider agreement and policy statement will help you explain expectations. See chapter 10 for more discussion and examples.

The formal written approach shows the parents that you really are concerned about providing responsible child care. A written agreement can help you avoid potential problems about child care costs and drop-off and pick-up times.

the second situation, a father has been very irresponsible about picking up his daughter on time, and does not seem to be very willing to explore options or change his habits. In this case, the provider uses the same problem solving steps, yet when the father continues to be uncooperative, she must firmly state what the consequences will be.

Solving Problems I— Laura, the late mother

Step 1
State the problem.

Provider: Laura, I noticed that you picked Thomas up late every day this week. If you will remember the agreement you signed when Thomas began coming here, you agreed to pick him up by 6:00 p.m. This is a real problem for me, because I have other responsibilities after that time.

Step 2
Listen to the parent's explanation.

Mother: I'm sorry, but things have been so crazy at work. They are talking about layoffs, and I'm really trying to put in a little extra effort so that I don't lose my job.

Step 3
Check your understanding.
Repeat or summarize what you think you heard the parent say to you. Ask more questions if you need clarification.

Provider: I see. So you are putting in extra time because you are worried about your job? How long do you think you will have to be staying late like this?

Mother: I wish I could say it would only be a few more weeks, but it could go on for longer—maybe a few months.

Step 4
Share your thoughts and feelings about the problem.

Provider: I understand your problem. However, I really need to spend time with my family. Also we have evening activities like softball practice and church that we need to get to. When you pick Thomas up so late, it really is hard for my family.

Step 5
Brainstorm some solutions.

Provider: Let's try to think of some solutions.

Mother: Well, I guess I could arrange for someone else to pick Thomas up. My mother could do it on some evenings, I think.

Provider: You might also hire a teenager to watch Thomas for about an hour. There are two teens next door who might be interested in the job. I'd be happy to introduce you.

Mother: What if I brought Thomas early—around 6:15 in the morning? Would that be as much of an inconvenience for you? I would be willing to pay extra.

Provider: I would be willing for you to bring Thomas early, but it might be hard on him.

Step 6
Try to reach an agreement. Be as specific as possible.

Mother: I guess you're right. Mornings are hectic enough already. So I guess we're back to having someone else pick him up.

Provider: Why don't you check with your mother tonight and give me a call. If she can't do it, then I'll make plans to introduce you to one of the teenagers next door tomorrow afternoon. If that doesn't work out we will look at the early morning arrival idea again.

Solving Problems II—Frank, the late father

Step 1
State the problem.

Provider: Frank, you picked Josie up late twice this week and twice last week. If you will remember the agreement you signed when Josie began coming here, you agreed to pick her up by 6:00 p.m.

Step 2
Listen to the parent's explanation.

Father: Yeah I know, time just seems to slip away. I know she's a good kid. She won't cause you any trouble if you need to go ahead and fix dinner. You are really good with Josie. I'll bet she could be a lot of help to you while she's waiting.

Step 3
Check your understanding.
Repeat or summarize what you think you heard the parent say to you. Ask more questions if you need clarification.

Provider: I see. So the reason you are late is because you don't notice the time. And you think I shouldn't mind keeping her around during my personal time.

Father: Well, she is a good kid and she thinks of you like a second mother. I know you take good care of her.

Step 4
Share your thoughts and feelings about the problem.

Provider: Frank, Josie is a great kid and I really care about her. However, at the end of the day I need to spend time with my family. We have evening activities like our granddaughter's softball practice and church functions that we need to get to. When you pick Josie up so late, it really is hard on me. And Josie really wants to be with you.

Step 5
Brainstorm some solutions.

Provider: Frank what can you do to get here on time?

Father: Well, I don't know. I am just forgetful. It's just the way I am.

Provider: Would it be possible for your wife to pick Josie up?

Father: No, she has to work the evening shift at the hospital.

Provider: Perhaps there is someone at work who could remind you when it is time to come pick Josie up.

Father: Well I guess I could ask a coworker—but he is just as forgetful as I am. (Chuckle)

Provider: Perhaps you could get a watch with an alarm or learn to set the alarm on your cell phone as a reminder.

Father: I guess, but I am not very good with that technical stuff.

Provider: You will need to find something that will remind you to get here on time, or I will be forced to charge you more. In situations like this when parents are often late, I charge an extra $5.00 for every 15 minutes a parent is late. It can add up very fast.

Father: That's crazy—why would you do that? Josie is a good kid!

Step 6
Try to reach an agreement. Be as specific as possible.

Provider: Frank, Josie is a wonderful child and I like you as well. But I have to be firm about this. Find a way to pick her up on time. If you are late again, I will charge you an extra $5.00 for every 15 minutes.

Father: But what if my car breaks down, or I have some other emergency?

Provider: Then you can call me and I will consider waiving the fee. But emergencies don't happen every day. Josie and I both need you to come on time every day. Be prepared to pay a $5.00 fee if you are late tomorrow.

Father: I can't believe you are doing this to my little girl. I may have to find someone else to care for her.

Provider: That would make all of us very sad. But you will find that other providers will want you to pick Josie up on time too. And many have the same late fee charges. This won't have to happen at all if you come on time to pick her up. I am sure you can do this. I know you really care about Josie and want to be a good father.

When a parent comes to you with a complaint or disagreement

Listen carefully, not just for the words, but for the feelings. Try not to react defensively or be hurt or angry. And never resort to name-calling or blaming. That only makes it more difficult to reach an agreement.

Hear parents out. Remember, as your customers, they have a right to complain. Their comments may help you improve the quality of your services.

Sum up what you've heard. Once the parent has finished talking, summarize what he/she has just said so you can be sure you understood the concern.

Share your thoughts and feelings about the problem. Calmly sharing your thoughts will help parents understand your point of view. If you are too upset by the complaint to be able to have a calm discussion, suggest a discussion at a better time.

You might say:
"You have a valid concern. I would like to think about that and talk more with you. But now is not a good time. When could we get together to discuss this further?"

"That is an interesting point that I have not considered. I need some time to think about your suggestion. Let me get back to you on that tomorrow."

"I am a little surprised by your complaint, but honestly, it has been a very difficult day and I would prefer to discuss this when we have a little more time. Let's step back a bit and talk about this tomorrow."

Try to reach an agreement. Together each of you can propose several solutions and try to reach an agreement. Try to be as specific as possible about what you will do to remedy the problem.

Be flexible. Every problem is different and you will need to adjust your approach with each situation.

The third scenario shows how a provider might handle a complaint from a parent. The steps for resolving the situation are very similar. Notice how the provider relies on her policy statement when explaining what she will and will not do. Having a written policy statement to back you up can help a great deal when trying to reach an agreement.

Solving Problems III— Swear words at home

Step 1
Listen to the parent's complaint without interrupting or becoming defensive.

Father: I am very upset. Yesterday, Jessica called her brother a very bad word. We do not allow swearing and name calling in our home. We spanked her and sent her to her room. I know she has not heard that kind of language at home, so she must have picked it up here.

Step 2
Check your understanding and summarize.
Acknowledge the parent's feelings and ask for more information.

Provider: I can see you are very concerned about this. That must have been upsetting! You must have been shocked to hear Jessica say such a word.

Step 3
Explain your policy and thoughts about the problem.

Provider: I can assure you that I don't believe that kind of language is okay. But you know, children hear language everywhere they go, and it's not always the kind of words we want them to repeat. It's hard to tell where Jessica heard that particular word and you probably won't be able to keep her from hearing other words like that every now and then. But we can certainly talk about how both you and I can react if Jessica repeats them.

Father: I am glad to hear that we agree. I didn't think you allowed that kind of language, but I was very upset.

Step 4
Discuss possible causes for the problem. Brainstorm solutions.

Provider: So let's talk about what to do if it happens again. It will benefit Jessica the most if we can be consistent between your home and here.

Father: As I said before, I spanked Jessica and sent her to her room. I will not tolerate that kind of language in my home.

Provider: As you know from the parent handbook that explains my policies, I don't use physical punishment when I discipline children. I also need to keep all the children within my sight while they are with me, so I won't send her to a room alone.

Father: I don't want her getting away with this. She needs to know she can't use that kind of language. And I want to know that any other children using that kind of language will be punished too.

Provider: I agree that we do need to do something if it happens again. You know, sometimes I find that children Jessica's age don't have any idea what swear words mean and they use them more out of curiosity than out of anger. Maybe if it happens again, we could talk to her about how those words are used to hurt other people's feelings.

Father: Well she wasn't using it because she was angry. It seemed to be quite a joke to her and her brother. I guess that's one reason I got so angry about it. It certainly wouldn't be a joke if she said it to the wrong person!

Provider: Maybe we need to talk about that to her too—what usually happens when people do say those words to each other.

Step 5
Try to reach an agreement. Be as specific as possible.

Father: Well okay, but I still think she should get some kind of punishment.

Provider: We may need to compromise on this point. Here's what I can tell you that I will do. If Jessica uses a swear word while she is here, I will talk to her about the reasons to not use that kind of language. If I feel that she is saying it purposely to hurt someone's feelings or make them angry, I will discipline her. What usually works well is to have a child stop playing for a few minutes and have a "cooling off" time away from the rest of the children. I will continue to talk with her and teach her what words are okay and what words are not okay.

Father: Well, all right, but I want to know if this happens again!

Step 6
Follow up.
Keep track of progress, and discuss any changes with parents later. If there is no change, brainstorm with the parent again. Maintain an attitude of working with the parent as a team.

Provider: Why don't we plan on talking again in a few days to see if this is still a problem. You know this actually happens quite often with young children. In fact, I have an article on swearing that you can take home. It really helped me understand why it happens and how to deal with it. I'd like to know what you and your wife think about it.

If problems cannot be solved

Sometimes things don't work out. It may result from a personality clash, differences in beliefs about childrearing, or unrealistic demands. This doesn't mean that you're not good for the child—but that you and the family are mismatched. Refer the parent to the child care resource and referral agency and keep your complaints confidential.

Sharing the care of children with parents has more ups than downs. Developing a good working relationship early on often leads to a close personal friendship that may last for years. Parents recognize that their child care provider is a special person who brings skill, professionalism, and love to each family and child that they serve.

FamilyShare...
Supporting your partners

It is often helpful to share written information with parents when discussing a problem.

Be sure to keep on hand articles and publications that deal with common problems that you can share with parents. Hearing the same opinion from another source, especially if it's an "expert," may help to persuade parents to trust your judgment on issues on which they disagree. For some problems, it may also help to refer them to another professional that they trust, such as their pediatrician.

The CD that accompanies this handbook offers many parent fact sheets that you can print off and share with parents. A list of publications from Iowa State University Extension and other trusted resources also can be accessed online at http://www.extension.iastate.edu/childcare or http://www.extension.iastate.edu/store.

Heart of the Matter

When you really think about it, it is absolutely amazing. A family briefly visits your home and then the next morning leaves you with their treasured child. Few relationships begin so suddenly and so intimately. Within minutes, you are holding and rocking this child. Within hours you provide the most basic of necessities: food, water, hugs, and laughter. It is all so deeply personal and involves such a huge leap of trust.

Over the years, I have worked with many families. All have entrusted me with their children and with the details of their lives. I have seen their hardships and struggles. I have shared in their joys. I have grown close to many families and yet others have remained distant. They are all different. Some relationships form quickly and some take time—a lot of time.

These relationships get under your skin and become a part of your very being. I still have very vivid memories of children I cared for 30 years ago. In my mind, I can still see faces, smiles, and well worn teddy bears. And I can still hear that special giggle of one dear little girl, and a mother's words as she shared her grief after learning her son was profoundly deaf. If I close my eyes, I can still feel the fear I experienced when dealing with an angry father who had been drinking too much. And I also can remember the pride and respect for that same man after he stopped drinking because he didn't want to lose his son.

It was not all so very romantic. There were dirty diapers and smelly bottoms. And I had more than my share of biting toddlers and kids with temper tantrums. But to get through it all I learned to look for the small everyday pleasures. Who could forget dancing in the grass with bare feet or the excitement of rescuing earthworms after a spring rain? And the incredible peace of holding a sleeping baby in my arms—that perhaps is the ultimate memory. It is a shared memory experienced by millions of parents and caregivers all over the world and it binds our very souls.

This kaleidoscope of memories has become one of the great treasures of my life.

I know of no other profession that gives you a chance to make such a meaningful difference to children and families.

Lesia

Experience Talks

Conversations with other providers

■ **I make it a point to greet parents every day at pick-up time with a good news item, even if it means I have to sandwich in a little explanation about wet pants.** I keep a little note pad by the refrigerator and jot down something positive about each child during the day.

■ **One easy way to remind parents to bring diapers is to give them a little note with a diaper coupon attached.** Parents appreciate thoughtful touches like this.

■ **I have a soup supper the second Monday of each month.** I keep it simple—a crock pot of soup and bread. Parents enjoy having a dinner with us and enjoy visiting with other parents. We all look forward to it.

■ **I ask parents to save items that we can use for art projects or pretend play.** One parent who worked at a local department store was very willing to bring me a refrigerator box for a pretend spaceship. Other parents bring an assortment of other things like squirt bottles, dress-up clothes, old wallpaper books, and magazines.

■ **During the year I collect sample drawings from each child.** At the end of the year, I put them together in a book format to give to parents as a memento.

■ **I make short audio recordings of children's conversations, songs, and storytelling to give to parents.** An easy way to do this is to simply turn on the recorder when we are eating lunch. The results are hilarious, and parents love listening to them.

■ **Often I send an art recipe home with parents.** They can make play dough or finger paint with their children just like we do in our child care program.

■ **I used to take pictures of the kids and give them to parents every so often.** However in the chaos of going home, they would often get lost. Now I save the pictures and put them in a small pocket-sized photo album that I give to families at the end of the year. Parents tell me these small albums are among their most treasured possessions.

■ **When working with difficult parents, I try to use some of the same positive techniques that I use with children.** I always try to find something positive to comment on every day, and I reinforce positive behavior by saying things like "I really appreciate you being on time today" or "You really made my day by bringing that check this afternoon."

Places and spaces: How to organize your home

Chapter 3

Contents

Where am I now? 40
Introduction 41
Think it through—create a general plan 41
Make your home say welcome 42
Space for greeting and departing 42
Space for eating 44
Space for toileting and washing 45
Space for napping 46
Space for storage 47
Space for play and learning 49
Space for business matters 53
FamilyShare 53
Heart of the Matter 54
Experience Talks 55

Places and spaces—How to organize your home

Where am I now? What can I improve?

	Seldom 1	Sometimes 2	Often 3	Most Often 4
1. I maintain a pleasant, orderly space to greet children and families each day.				
2. I have areas to post photos, notes to parents, and children's art work.				
3. I provide individual space for children to keep their personal belongings.				
4. I organize my space to maintain good visual supervision of all children.				
5. I provide a safe, protected space for infants to kick, roll, crawl, and pull up.				
6. I arrange space so the children and I can eat together family style.				
7. I keep supplies for toileting and washing hands within easy reach.				
8. I arrange space to be respectful of children's different needs for rest and sleep.				
9. I arrange space so children can play and work individually or in small groups.				
10. I organize space so that children can easily use and put away toys and materials.				
11. I provide space for books and reading.				
12. I provide space for art and creative play.				
13. I provide space for sand and water play.				
14. I provide space for pretend play.				
15. I provide space for table toys (games, puzzles, small blocks).				
16. I provide space for block play.				
17. I provide space for active indoor play.				
18. I provide areas for active outdoor play.				
19. I have specific work space to plan and organize my child care business records.				

Places and spaces: How to organize your home

Chapter 3

One unique advantage of family child care is that children are cared for in a home away from home. Homes offer children a rich environment filled with textures, patterns, aromas, and sounds that are hard to find in other settings.

Homes are wonderful places to learn. Children learn best by hearing, seeing, tasting, smelling, and touching. The smell of a lilac outside the back door, the feel of sofa cushions, the sound of the mail carrier's footsteps, or the unique view from sitting underneath the dining room table all enrich the lives of children in a family child care setting.

Homes are good working places for adults. Family child care providers can decorate their "place of business" to suit their individual tastes and needs. Comfortable furniture and personal belongings are a plus for most caregivers.

The challenge is to organize your home for child care, yet keep it a comfortable, enjoyable place for your family. It is unfair to expect children to spend their day in a "hands off," "don't touch," "don't make a mess" setting. It is equally unfair to expect providers and their families to always live in a child's world.

Think it through— create a general plan

Arranging space for child care takes creativity, planning, and organization. Children will need areas to play, learn, eat, rest, wash, and use the toilet. Your first step should be to take a thoughtful look at your home.

You will have many adults and kids moving through your home. Parents will come and go in and out of your house every day. Children will come to know your home as well as they know their own home.

Choose rooms or areas that will work well for child care and identify those that will be off limits. Many providers have at least one room that is set up for child care all the time, while other rooms are used for limited purposes, such as eating or sleeping.

Space can be divided and organized for particular activities. A part of the kitchen, living room, or hallway or corners of any room can be made into learning areas. The space behind a couch may be a quiet reading space. A basement family room could be an area for active play.

Play and learning areas can be as permanent or as temporary as your home allows. Putting on a special tablecloth can signal that this table is now a game area. A sign, a blanket, or a quick turn of a chair can signal a change to children. Pillows in a corner or carpet samples on the floor can mean a group activity. A coat rack with dress-up clothes can turn the same corner into a dramatic play area.

Make your home say welcome

Families often say they like family child care because of the smaller, cozier atmosphere. They want their children to feel comfortable and welcome. As you walk through your home, pretend you are a parent or child and consider how each area can be more welcoming.

Consider the appearance of your home. Curb appeal counts. The first glance at your home tells families a lot. Peeling paint, a broken fence, or a cluttered front porch are signs that tell parents to look elsewhere. A well cared for home gives parents the message that their children also will be well cared for.

Create childhood memories. A pot of flowers on the front porch or a funny clay frog will delight children and make your home say welcome. Wind chimes, a tank of colorful fish, or a window prism that sparkles in the light are also good additions. Children often will remember these small touches well into adulthood.

Help children feel like they belong. In today's rapidly changing world, it's very important to find ways to help children feel secure and safe. Posting familiar photos of family members or pets can be very comforting. Finding a special place for a treasured teddy bear or blanket also will help children feel at home.

Space for greeting and departing

This is the space that children and families see first and last each day. Often this is the area where children separate from their parents, say a tearful good-bye, or wave cheerfully at the window. Within this small space you will conduct business, accept payment for your services, get to know families, and share heartfelt stories.

Keep your entrance clean, orderly, and inviting. This area gets high use and a lot of wear and tear. A fresh coat of semi-gloss paint will make fingerprints and scuff marks wash off easily. Invest in high quality rugs that will trap mud and debris. Door openings should be at least 32 inches wide. A low threshold (1/2 inch or less) will make it easier for wheelchairs, strollers, or the occasional broken leg to enter.

Get organized. Think about creative ways to store coats, shoes, and hats so they don't clutter the entrance. A chair or bench encourages parents to help out with removing snow boots or tying shoes. You also will need a place for children's art work and treasures. Plastic tubs, shelves, or baskets located near the door are good choices.

Make room to chat. You will want to greet children and connect with families as they arrive and leave each day. Make sure there is room to stand or sit briefly as you talk about the day's activities.

Keep families informed. A bulletin board to post your daily schedule or notes about the children is a nice addition. It is also a wonderful place to post photos or drawings to show parents what you do during the day. You can place a bulletin board on the door or a wall and remove it in the evening to make your home feel more home-like during your time off.

> **Remember all spaces need:**
> - Good lighting
> - Good air flow
> - Easy-to-clean surfaces
> - Soft, comfortable places
> - Sound absorbing materials
> - Good temperature control
> - Pleasant or neutral smell
> - Balance—active and quiet areas

HFCCH Chapter 3 — Places and spaces: How to organize your home   43

Space for eating

You will spend much of your day preparing food and feeding children. Mealtime is a regular routine, but it is also a time for learning and for building relationships.

Find space for quiet activities in or near the kitchen. You will need to keep a watchful eye on children while you are preparing snacks or lunch. Sometimes children can help you with snack or meal preparation, but other times they will need to play quietly nearby.

Make it kid-friendly. A kitchen cabinet drawer for paper and crayons is a good idea. A basket of books or puzzles that can be carried in from another room also works well. Children love to cut out food coupons and ads so keep some newspapers or magazines on hand.

Make it personal. Because children will spend a great deal of time with you in the kitchen, consider posting some of their artwork on a kitchen bulletin board or on the refrigerator at their eye level. Photos of favorite foods, play activities, or pets from home are also great conversation starters.

Make mealtime comfortable and enjoyable. Serving food "family style" with everyone seated around a table encourages children to talk and help each other. At times this can mean that everyone sits around the family table with booster chairs and high chairs to assist younger children. Or you may prefer to have children sit at a child-sized table with child-sized chairs. Child-size chairs and tables can be purchased inexpensively at discount stores, garage sales, flea markets, and school sales.

Save a place at the table for you. It is always a good idea for you to sit and eat with the children. Children can learn a lot at mealtime. Foods come in many shapes, sizes, and colors. This is a great time to encourage them to try different foods and learn new words. You also can help them learn about good manners and how to talk with each other.

Make cleanup easy. Eat in the kitchen over a washable floor for easy cleanup or use floor mats or a large piece of vinyl flooring to protect carpeted surfaces. Keep a sponge, hand broom, and dustpan handy so children can help clean up spills. A nearby sink to wash hands before and after eating also is important.

Space for toileting and washing

You will quickly discover that you spend a lot of your time washing hands, changing diapers, and helping children learn to use the bathroom. This is certainly not the most glamorous part of your job! You will want to organize your space so you can complete these tasks in the most comfortable and efficient way possible.

Make it clean. Changing a wiggly infant's diaper on the floor or the sofa is never a good idea. Using a sturdy diaper changing table is a cleaner, safer option and is much easier on your back. Use a surface that can be washed easily and sanitized after each diaper change. Avoid using safety straps or padded surfaces made from cloth that can trap bacteria. A trash can with a step pedal also will help you reduce the spread of germs. Locate your changing area close to a bathroom sink where you can easily clean up afterwards and wash hands. Using a kitchen counter and sink as a changing area is not sanitary and can contribute to serious illness.

Make it reachable. Children need to wash their hands frequently. Provide a short and sturdy stool or wooden box for children to stand on to reach the sink safely. Place disposable towels, cups, and tissues within reach as well. Hang combs or toothbrushes on cup hooks, or store them upright in slots in a shoe box. Label personal items with the child's name or an easy-to-recognize symbol or color. Store diapers, wipes, and bleach water sanitizer within easy reach of the diapering area.

Make it comfortable. If you care for children who will be learning to use the toilet, you may choose to use a potty chair or potty attachment for the toilet. A potty attachment is preferred because a potty chair will need to be emptied and sanitized after each use.

Make sure that children can reach toilet paper while sitting on the toilet or potty chair. The American Academy of Pediatrics suggests avoiding urine deflectors because they can cut a child who is climbing on or off a potty chair. Learning to use the potty can sometimes take time and children may get lonely. A nearby stool will allow you to sit comfortably as you wait to help out.

HFCCH Chapter 3 — Places and spaces: How to organize your home

Space for napping

Most children will need to nap or at least rest for a while. Choose areas for napping that will be quiet, safe, and easily supervised.

Create personalized sleeping areas. Toddlers and preschoolers should have their own mat, sheet, blanket, and pillow. Consider giving each child a special color of sheet or blanket to reduce mix-ups. Some providers use two large swim towels for each child, one to sleep on and the other as a blanket. Sleeping areas should be spaced at least 36 inches apart. Farther apart would be better. This helps children to avoid spreading germs through coughing, and reduces the temptation to giggle and play.

Keep watchful eyes and ears. Many providers view naptime as a time to take a break. It is true that you will be less busy, but you will still need to keep sleeping infants within sight. A baby monitor is helpful for letting you know when the baby is awake and stirring, but is not a substitute for being able to see if the baby is breathing and safe. Toddlers and preschoolers need close supervision too. Keep within listening distance and check on them frequently.

Keep naptime safe. Infants should always nap in cribs or bassinets. Allowing an infant to sleep on a family bed is not safe, because the child could roll off, get stuck between the bed and the wall, or smother against a pillow. Cribs should have a snug-fitting mattress, be painted with lead-free paint, and have slats that are no more than 2-3/8 inches apart so the infant's head does not get stuck between the slats. Remove posts or cutout designs (often found on older cribs) that could catch a cord or a piece of baby's clothing. Use regular mattress covers that fit snuggly around the mattress; plastic bags or loosely covered sheets can cause suffocation. Lambskin coverings also are hazardous. If you have more than one crib, space them 36 inches apart to reduce infections from coughing.

Make naptime spaces flexible. Some children need less time to sleep and others need more. Provide space for quiet, restful activities for children who become tired before naptime or who wake up early.

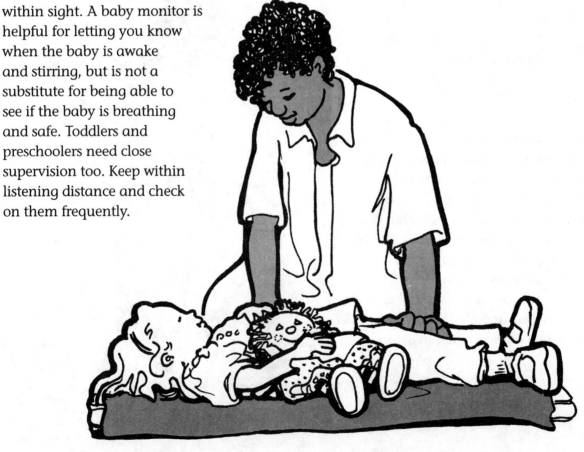

Infants need space too!

It is tempting to put infants in cribs, infant seats, or swings to keep them from getting run over by active toddlers and preschoolers.

But infants need many opportunities to move, kick, roll over, crawl, pull up, and learn to walk.

Look for ways to provide infants with protected space so they can develop these important skills.

Space for storage

It is amazing how many toys, materials, and supplies you need for child care. Finding a place for it all can be a real challenge. The following ideas will help you stay organized and reduce clutter.

Personalize it. Provide a box, divided shelf, or drawer for each child to keep personal belongings like pictures and toys. Label the area with the child's name or picture. When a child is in another home all day and has to share almost everything, having a personal space is important. Provide a low coat rack or hooks where children can hang coats and sweaters.

Shelve it. Storing items in clear plastic storage boxes on low shelves makes it easy for kids to find toys on their own and to put things away. They can put similar things together in the same container if you label cartons with pictures of the objects to be stored inside. You can draw pictures, use pictures of toys from the box you purchased them in, or cut out pictures from newspaper ads or catalogs. Cover pictures with wide, clear adhesive tape or clear adhesive shelving paper. Every so often, switch out toys on the shelf with others that have been stored for awhile so children don't tire of them. An old toy can seem like a new toy if it has not been played with for awhile.

Stash it. At cleanup time the floor can be quickly cleared by stashing things in a gigantic toy box. The trade-off is that toys often become tangled or damaged. Little fingers also can be hurt from heavy lids that fall. Kids have a tendency to crawl into small, enclosed spaces so if you use a toy box be sure it has air holes. It's a good idea to remove latches or locks too. A better idea would be to use an open box or low shelves inside a closet with an easily closed door. A closet also can act as a "garage" for small push and pull or riding toys.

Stack it. Use lightweight clear plastic boxes to store and stack items along a wall. Keep stacks low to the ground and make sure the boxes are not heavy enough to hurt children if they should take a tumble.

Roll it. Consider using a sturdy cart to move frequently used toys and materials from room to room throughout your day. Good choices for a cart would include everyday items such as paper and drawing supplies, puzzles, and

HFCCH Chapter 3 — Places and spaces: How to organize your home   47

books. A wagon also provides good storage. Children love to pull the wagon around as they help clean up.

Slide it. If toys need to be set up for a period of time, like a train or auto racing set, put them up on large pieces of plywood or cardboard. When the toy isn't being used, slide it under a sofa or bed to keep it from being stepped on or taken apart by younger children. Rubber dishpans and shallow clothing boxes also are handy for wooden blocks, flat toys, or dolls. They also can be slid out of sight during clean-up time.

Hang it. On a doorknob, hang a cloth bag for crayons or other small objects that otherwise might be crushed underfoot. An open mesh bag that can be hung over a sink or bathtub is a great idea for storing water toys. Mesh bags also are great for storing balls of different sizes, Frisbees, and jump ropes.

Cluttered space or grimy space?

Busy, happy children are always playing and learning—and that means things can get messy. A reasonable amount of clutter is certainly okay. However, every so often do a quick check to see if the clutter has moved to the crazy stage. If so, it's time to clean up.

Comfortable clutter—the room is scattered with toys that children are actively playing with or will come back to shortly. It is still fairly easy for children to move through the room and find places to play. There are few squabbles over toys.

Crazy clutter—toys are no longer easy to find and are stepped on or broken. It is hard to walk through the room and there is no place left for children to play. Children are bumping into each other or fighting over toys.

Grimy unclean—don't confuse clutter with grime and filth. It is one thing to have toys scattered across the room, it is another to have dirty floors, spills on the furniture, grimy fingerprints, and a house that smells like diapers. Keeping things clean is easier if you do a little each day. Spending five minutes each morning and afternoon to sweep the floor and wipe up smudges can make a big difference. Often children will be eager to help you with these tasks.

Basket it. Storing things in baskets is a popular option for a home. Baskets with books near a cozy arm chair encourage children to read. Baskets with drawing supplies or small building blocks near the kitchen table are also very handy. Baskets with handles are also good choices for moving items from room to room easily.

Space for play and learning

Play and learning come naturally for young children. Walk through your home and look for areas that can be used for a specific type of play such as reading, art, puzzles, or blocks. Often we call these play areas "learning centers" because children learn best through play.

Use home spaces to create learning centers. Quiet areas for reading books can be small cozy spaces. Your kitchen table can become a learning center for art work and cooking. A chair can be pushed aside in the living room to make room for children to play with blocks. Or you may choose to group most learning centers in one room such as a den, basement, or remodeled garage. Either way is okay, as long as children have several learning center areas to choose from every day.

Locate quiet activities away from noisy activities. To make learning centers work smoothly, it is best to locate noisy activities such as blocks and art together. Quieter activities like reading or a place to work on puzzles can be in another area.

Learning center boundaries can be flexible. Learning and play often will flow naturally from one area to another. Paper and markers from the art area may drift over to the pretend play area to create pretend money or signs. Small blocks may become "pretend cornbread." It's okay to let some items flow across boundaries.

The ages and interests of children should always shape how you use space. As children grow older in your program, you may find they develop different interests. One year you may need a large area for active play, the next year you may find yourself needing more room for games and puzzles.

HFCCH Chapter 3 — Places and spaces: How to organize your home

Reading. Every home should have several places for reading and looking at books. A basket of books near a comfy chair works well. A soft rug and pillow behind a sofa works well too. Children need many books to look at, so they should be placed in different areas throughout your home. At least one reading space should be large enough so that one child can read or share a book with another child. Older children may like to listen to books that are taped or recorded so a space for a CD player and head phones is a good idea too. This area should be away from noisier, more active play areas.

Art and creative play. It is a good idea to always have several play spaces for art and creative play. A child-sized table or a wood coffee table at the right height is a good place to cut or draw. The table in the kitchen or on the patio can be a creative area for messier art work with play dough and finger paint. Save one shelf in a low cupboard for paper, paint, crayons, and glue so children can help themselves.

Sand and water play. Math and science skills develop naturally as children pour, measure, squeeze, shape, swirl, and mix water, sand, and gravel. Water play also is very calming for children who are stressed or anxious. Water—plain, soapy, or colored—and funnels, cups, pots, egg-beaters, and measuring cups can be played with in a bathtub, dishpan, plastic wading pool, or an old washtub placed on a drop cloth to minimize mess. Water play should be located where you can always closely supervise it.

Pretend play. Children love to pretend and act out real life situations. Successful pretend play requires space for both large and small items. Set the stage with large items such as a child-size table, toy stove, refrigerator, and doll bed.

Children become more involved in pretend play if they have many smaller items to use. Find space for pots, pans, dishes, toy phones, and cash registers. Dress-up items such as shoes, pants, hats, shirts, dresses, and aprons are nice additions.

Monday's store could be Tuesday's hospital, Wednesday's house, and Thursday's gas station. You can collect materials for each type of theme play in its own "prop box." And store them in a closet. When children are interested in camping, for example, you can bring out the box with a canteen, backpack, and old pots and pans.

Obvious clues that a space is not working.
- Children wander around aimlessly.
- Children run too much.
- Children find it hard to reach items.
- Children can't find things.
- Children argue, fight, and misbehave.
- One activity or goal continually interferes with another.
- You find yourself saying "NO" constantly.
- Your stress level hits the ceiling.

How to make space work better—a few things to try.
- Change its purpose.
- Change its size.
- Adjust the lighting.
- Adjust the temperature.
- Make it easier to clean.
- Reduce distractions.
- Make it more interesting.
- Arrange materials differently.
- Provide better storage.
- Add different toys.
- Add more toys.
- Reduce the number of toys.
- Make it more age appropriate.
- Make it more comfortable.
- Add softness—pillow, carpet, etc.
- Block or open up a pathway.
- Ask the children for their ideas.
- Protect it with a barrier.

Small muscle play. Children need to learn how to use their hands and fingers well. Infants need space for busy boxes and cradle gyms they can grasp, push, turn, and pull. Toddlers and preschoolers need space to sort and string beads, work puzzles, stack small blocks, and cut with scissors. School-agers will need space for more complex puzzles, marble games, and larger, more involved arts and crafts projects.

Store materials in containers or on an open shelf so children can see them and reach them easily. This also will help with clean up. Remember that infants might choke on smaller play items, so it is a good idea to keep some areas closely supervised and protected with a baby gate.

Block play. Finding room for blocks can be a bit of a challenge, but it is well worth it. Children will willingly spend hours playing with blocks and building structures. Learning about size, shape, balance, and number of blocks to use are important math skills. A protected corner of a room provides a good space for block play. Blocks can be stored on low shelves, or in shallow tubs that can slide under a bed or sofa.

Music and active play. Children need space to crawl, run, skip, dance, jump, balance, and climb in-and-out. Indoor space could include areas in the family room for scarf dances or circle games. Hallways make great places for push and pull toys. Larger basement spaces can be used to set up an obstacle course or play a game of tag.

Outdoor play. Children need to play outside every day for at least an hour. Almost anything you can do indoors also can be done outdoors. You can read a book under a tree, use play dough on the picnic table, draw chalk pictures on the patio, and set up a pretend car wash. Children can measure rainfall and snow, chase butterflies, collect rocks, and feed the birds. A good outdoor play area will offer lots of different options and will have some shelter from

HFCCH Chapter 3 — Places and spaces: How to organize your home

wind, rain, or sun. A protected driveway or path can be used for balls, push-pull toys, and wagons. Grassy areas are great places to throw large and small balls or set up running games. Other options include mats for tumbling, large cardboard boxes for tunnels, a low basketball hoop, jump ropes, and hula hoops. Sand and water play and gardening also are good outdoor activities.

Swings and climbing equipment are very expensive, take up a lot of space, and can often be quite dangerous. If you use this type of playground equipment, you will need to make sure you have surfacing that can cushion a fall. Experts recommend at least 12 inches of bark mulch or pea gravel beneath equipment. Many states have strict rules about playground equipment safety standards. Check on this before you buy.

When children are outdoors, they move around a lot and can quickly slip out of sight. Ideally, it is best to have a fenced-in yard that will keep children in and wandering neighborhood animals out.

You also may choose to walk to a nearby park. If so, be sure to do a quick check each time to make sure equipment is in good repair. Check also for broken glass or unsafe items. Supervise children closely as they play.

Quiet "all-by-myself" play. Playing with a group of children all day can be hectic and very tiring for a young child. Most children will need a space to break away from active play and recharge.

Provide a quiet place where a child can sit and draw, read, or talk to a favorite doll. When children have opportunities to work quietly on a puzzle or special project, they learn more about themselves as individuals. And they learn that they can be comfortable when they're alone.

A quiet area may be no more than a child-sized table or a cozy pillow in a corner. Children love little nooks and alcoves. Semi-hidden spaces can be created with an empty cardboard box or by covering a table with a blanket to create a personal tent for reading, thinking, or relaxing.

Space for business matters

You will discover that you also need a place to organize your business records. At a minimum, you should have a box or cabinet for file folders, and a paper shredder. As you become more interested in your new profession, it also will be helpful to have access to a computer and the Internet. An inexpensive printer that makes photocopies and prints photos also is helpful to have.

FamilyShare...

Supporting your partners

Parents looking for child care often say they want to find a place that is nurturing, educational, and clean. Generally, a quick look at your home will tell them whether your home is clean or not. By talking with you they will make a quick decision about your ability to be nurturing. However, determining if you have an educational program may be a bit more challenging. When you give your parents a tour take the time to share your knowledge with them.

Explain that you offer a wide range of activities that help children learn. Be sure to mention the following skills:

- block play = math skills
- books = reading
- pretend play = creativity, language, and social skills
- cooking = math and science skills
- water and sand play = math and science skills
- art = creativity
- puzzles and games = math and social skills

Heart of the Matter

Years ago, I was hired as a very inexperienced, new teacher in a child care center. My co-workers showed me how to arrange my room with different "learning center" areas for blocks, art, puzzles, books, and pretend play and toys with materials displayed on shelves, so children could select them easily. Learning centers were new for me, but I was willing to give this a try and eager to see how it would work.

To my dismay, the next morning when the children arrived, they just ran around the room like wild animals, jumping on and off the loft ladder, playing with the water in the sink, whining, hitting and—out of control. This new way of doing things was not working. I was at a loss and near tears.

About that time, my director walked in and saw my distressed look. She smiled sympathetically and quickly surveyed the room. She moved to the art area and placed some paper and crayons out on the table. Next she moved to the block area, put a few blocks on the floor and some wooden barn animals. In the book area, she selected a book and placed it with a teddy bear on the floor pillow. She then moved to the pretend play area, set the table with dishes, placed a coffee pot on the stove, and sat down. She said, "Oh my, I am so thirsty. I wonder if someone would make me a cup of coffee?"

I watched a miracle happen before my very eyes. Several children quickly ran to prepare her a "pretend" cup of coffee and busily began to make muffins. One girl noticed the paper and crayons in the art center and began drawing pictures. One child sat down with the blocks and began building a barn. Another child snuggled down to read a book to the teddy bear.

These wild, out-of-control children quickly became happy, busy children. I also was happy and relieved. I learned the importance of making each play area more inviting by setting out a few interesting items to get children started. I also learned that I had an important role to play. I could "step into" children's play for a few moments, just as my director had done to ask for a cup of coffee. I could also move about the room, just as a good hostess at a party would do, to briefly talk with children and make sure they had what they needed for play and learning.

Most of all I learned that it is very important to make each space very welcoming and inviting each day. This approach works well for family child care too. Just a few simple touches can make all the difference.

Lesia

Experience Talks

Conversations with other providers

■ **I like to keep a bulletin board by the door to post notes, pictures, and other things.** However it is not my favorite thing to look at on the weekends! So I simply remove it, slip it into a closet, and hang a picture on the same hook.

■ **We eat our snacks in the downstairs play room, which is carpeted.** To protect against spills, I purchased a large 5'x5' scrap piece of vinyl flooring to put under the table and over the carpet. It works great.

■ **I like to use different colored vinyl table cloths on my kitchen table.** I use an inexpensive red vinyl table cloth for art activities. Play dough is easily cleaned off, and a slip of a pen or marker is no big deal. School-age kids get to play games on the blue table cloth. For lunch I try to change things up and use different patterns throughout the year. Poinsettias, pumpkins, watermelons, and spring flowers help children understand a change in the seasons.

■ **Folding card tables are great for so many things!** Toss a sheet over it, and the kids have a great hide-away place—indoors or out. Stick a toy cash register on one and it becomes the checkout lane in a store. If the school-age kids want to spend several days working a large puzzle, I can set them up a temporary space over in the corner. Use it outdoors with a vinyl table cloth for messy finger paint and I can hose it down. And best of all—at the end of the day, I can fold it, store it in the garage, and enjoy my regular furniture.

■ **I have a special blanket that I use just for story time.** The children know when I place it on the living room floor, it's time to gather around to read a book and sing a song. We use it only for that special time.

■ **I have a special reading quilt that we keep in a cozy comfortable chair.** It actually is an old teddy bear crib quilt. The children enjoy climbing up into the chair, snuggling under the quilt, and pretending to read a book with their favorite doll or stuffed animal.

■ **All the wonderful plastic boxes and crates that are available now are lifesavers.** I'm big into color coding. Blocks go into red containers, balls into green, dolls into yellow. This idea makes it easier to clean up and find things later. Children love to sort things into different colored containers.

■ **I like clear containers to store things in, because it makes it easier to see and find things.** Whenever possible I choose containers with clear tops too. If I need to color code anything, I used a colored label, which I tape on to the front of the box with clear packaging tape.

HFCCH Chapter 3 — Places and spaces: How to organize your home

- **Whenever I purchase a toy, I keep the packaging and cut out several pictures for labels.** I tape one label onto a plastic storage container, and file another label in a folder. This way when the first label gets worn, I can replace it with a fresh one.

- **Plastic containers are okay, but I think there is value in storing things in different types of containers.** Children need to experience different materials and textures. I use baskets and cloth sacks to store many items. I also use shiny copper pots and gift wrapped cardboard boxes.

- **I am a big believer in wheels. They are a real necessity for hauling stuff back and forth.** I use a wagon to move snack items to the patio in summer. A large wheelbarrow is a terrific storage place for outdoor equipment. I just whisk it in and out of the garage. And year around, I have my supply cart with everything you could need to use for art projects. Wheels are great!

- **I was very upset when we realized we didn't have the money to replace our old and unsafe outdoor swing set and climber.** But actually it was the best thing that could have happened. The children really seem to play better using other things. I bring out balls, hula hoops, and gardening tools. We do art projects on the picnic table. My husband put up a low basketball hoop next to the patio. We created a tricycle car wash by attaching the water hose to a fence post. Every day during the summer we sip lemonade and read books under a shady tree. Life is good.

- **In the wintertime, I have families enter through the garage because it gives them more shelter.** I place long carpet runners for the entire length of the garage to cut down on muddy feet. I also place two chairs just outside the door for sitting down to take off boots.

- **I have an old church pew just inside the door.** This is a great place for parents to sit as they are helping their children put on their coats. I have three large baskets that slide under the seat to store mittens, hats, and scarves.

- **We spend a lot of time in the kitchen cooking and eating.** I put photos of the kids and their families and pets on the refrigerator. I also ask families to share vacation pictures. This makes the children feel like they belong. It also makes for some interesting discussions as we eat.

- **I am not a big TV fan but children see it in the room and ask to watch it.** To help prevent this, I drape a small quilt over the TV each morning. Of course the kids know the TV is behind it, but putting the quilt over it somehow keeps them from paying much attention to it.

The right tools: Toys, books, and equipment

Contents

Where am I now?	58
Introduction	59
Toys and supplies to help children learn	60
Toys to build skills	61
Toys to choose for each age	62
Before you toss—unusual uses for ordinary materials	64
Materials from your home	65
Before you buy—quiz yourself	68
Toys and equipment safety—avoid these items	69
FamilyShare	70
Toys you can make	71
Great books for children!	74
Heart of the Matter	75
Experience Talks	76

The right tools: Toys, books, and equipment
Where am I now? What can I improve?

	Seldom 1	Sometimes 2	Often 3	Most Often 4
1. I have 12-20 books with at least 2-3 books for each age group.				
2. I enrich my collection of children's books with regular visits to the public library.				
3. I select books that help children learn about families of different races, cultures, ages, abilities, and lifestyles.				
4. I select books that help children learn about nature and respect for the environment.				
5. I select non-violent books that encourage positive social skills.				
6. I have a good selection of basic toys for each age child.				
7. I purchase toys and equipment that are safe, non-toxic, and in good repair.				
8. I have toys and equipment that help children learn to use small muscles.				
9. I have toys and equipment that help children develop large muscles.				
10. I have toys that help children learn about math and science.				
11. I have toys that help children pretend and be creative.				
12. I have toys that help children develop language skills.				
13. I have child-size furniture for children.				
14. I have a variety of soft toys and soft furniture.				
15. I have adult furniture that allows me to be comfortable when I am teaching, supervising, and caring for children.				

Chapter 4

The right tools: Toys, books, and equipment

Good quality toys, books, and equipment can make child care much easier to manage. But knowing what works best and deciding what to buy can be challenging. Before you head off to the store or local yard sale, decide what items you really need. You'll invest your money more wisely and be less likely to wind up with unsafe or unusable equipment.

Make a list of toys that you have. Make a wish list too. Often it works better to buy or acquire equipment gradually than to go out and purchase everything at once. Focus first on getting a few of the basics and learn what works best for you.

Stock, restock, and restock again. Remember to set aside funds to purchase paper, crayons, markers, glue, and other items that children need to be creative. Children use up these items quickly, so this will be an ongoing expense.

Understand a toy's purpose. Commercial toys often are designed for a particular purpose. Understanding that purpose can help you find substitutes, often in your own home. For instance, stacking toys or nesting cups teach relationships, shapes, or size concepts. A set of plastic measuring cups from your own kitchen cabinet can teach the same thing. Professional caregivers of young children have a proud tradition of turning "junk" and everyday items into creative play for children.

Choose the right toy for the right age child. The toys you choose for child care will depend a great deal on the needs and interests of your children. If the children you care for are mostly infants and toddlers, you may need toys that squeak, rattle, push, and pull. Preschoolers will need building blocks, puppets, and sturdy tea sets. School-agers will be most interested in board games, magnets, and printing or stamp sets.

If it is well loved, buy several. It's also a good idea to get several sets of popular toys. Young children often have difficulty sharing. Toddlers simply do not understand the whole idea of sharing, and preschoolers have very limited skills in trading or negotiating. Having several play telephones and a ball for each child can make the day go more smoothly.

Larger equipment you may need

You don't need to purchase a lot of larger equipment or furniture. Consider first what age children you will be caring for and then start with a few of the following items.

Infants and Toddlers	■ Crib ■ Play pen or travel crib ■ Diaper changing table ■ Stroller ■ Baby gates ■ Infant carrier seat ■ Sheets, blankets, pillows ■ Car seats—if you will be driving with children
Preschoolers	■ Child–size table(s) and chairs ■ Pretend play stove, sink, and refrigerator ■ Wagon ■ Sleeping cots or mats ■ Sheets, blankets, pillows ■ Car seats—if you will be driving with children
School-agers	■ Table and chairs ■ Large floor pillows

Toys and supplies to help children learn

The best toys help children learn and play in many different ways. Almost all toys help children develop language skills as they learn to talk, trade, and share with other children. Most toys also allow for creativity and muscle development.

Toys to build skills

	Small Muscles	Creativity	Language Skills	Math and Science	Large Muscles
Books	■	■	■	■	
Play dough, crayons, paint, scissors	■	■	■	■	
Pretend play, hats, scarves, shoes	■	■	■		■
Shape sorters, nesting cups, stacking rings, beads for stringing, peg boards	■			■	
Board games	■		■	■	
Dolls, soft animals	■	■	■		
Puppets and puppet theater	■	■	■		■
Musical instruments	■	■	■		■
Toy dishes, cash register, telephones	■	■	■	■	
Blocks—wooden, plastic, foam	■	■	■	■	■
Interlocking blocks	■	■		■	
Balls	■				■
Puzzles	■		■	■	
Magnets, magnifying glass, binoculars, funnels, tape measures	■		■	■	
Wagon		■	■		■
Push and pull and riding toys					■
Hula hoops, jump ropes					■

HFCCH Chapter 4 — The right tools: Toys, books, and equipment

Toys to choose for each age

Newborn to 1 year

Choose
- brightly colored objects
- pictures within view but out of reach
- mobiles that have objects attached with cords less than 12 inches long
- unbreakable toys that rattle or squeak
- washable dolls or animals with embroidered eyes
- stacking ring cones
- tapes or CDs with gentle music

Avoid
- toys with parts smaller than 1 1/4 inches, (about the size of a half dollar)
- toys with sharp edges
- toys with toxic paint
- toys with cords more than 12 inches long
- stuffed animals with glass or button eyes
- balloons
- push and pull toys

1 to 2 years

Choose
- books with cloth or stiff pasteboard pages
- non-glass mirrors
- take-apart toys with large pieces
- blocks—foam, plastic, or cardboard
- nested boxes or cups
- musical and chime toys
- floating tub toys
- pounding and stacking toys

Avoid
- small toys that can be swallowed
- toys with small removable parts
- stuffed animals with glass or button eyes
- toys with sharp edges
- balloons

2 to 3 years

Choose
- play dough
- large crayons
- pegboards with large pieces
- low rocking horses
- sandbox toys
- soft balls of different sizes
- cars or wagons to push
- simple musical instruments
- simple dressup items like hats, scarves, shoes
- sturdy riding toys
- books with rhymes, pictures, jingles

Avoid
- toys with sharp edges
- toys with small removable parts
- small objects such as beads, coins, or marbles
- electrical toys
- lead soldiers
- tricycles with seats higher than 12 inches
- riding toys used in hilly or inclined driveways
- balloons

3 to 4 years

Choose
- dolls with simple clothes
- balls of all sizes
- nonelectrical trucks, tractors, trains
- building blocks
- toy telephones
- sturdy tea sets
- plastic interlocking blocks
- blunt scissors
- play dough
- washable markers, large crayons
- sewing cards
- simple board games
- books

Avoid
- electrical toys (unless battery operated)
- lead soldiers
- flammable costumes
- toys with sharp edges or small, removable parts
- riding toys used in hilly or inclined driveways

4 to 5 years

Choose
- building blocks
- simple construction sets
- modeling clay
- nonelectrical trains, battery operated toys
- puppets and puppet theaters
- finger paints
- stencils
- board and card games
- simple musical instruments
- small sports equipment
- bicycles for 4- to 7-year-olds with 20-inch wheels and training wheels (all should wear bike helmets)
- books

Avoid
- toxic or oil-based paint sets
- flammable costumes or ones that can be easily tripped over
- kites made of aluminized polyester film (this material conducts electricity)
- electrical toys (unless battery operated)
- shooting toys and darts with pointed tips
- fireworks of any kind
- lawn darts

5 to 8 years

Choose
- construction sets
- sleds, roller skates
- sewing materials
- simple cameras, film
- printing and stamp sets
- paints, colored pencils
- sketch pads
- kites
- battery powered electrical toys
- jigsaw puzzles
- dominoes
- board games
- simple tool sets
- dolls
- magnets, magnifiers
- simple calculator
- bicycle (24-inch wheels)

Avoid
- kites made of aluminized polyester film (this material conducts electricity)
- shooting toys and toys with loud noises like cap guns
- fireworks of any kind
- sharp-edged tools
- electrical toys run on household current
- bike or skateboard riding without helmets

8 to 12 years

Choose
- hobby materials
- arts and crafts materials
- musical instruments
- sports equipment
- camping equipment
- construction sets
- electric trains
- bicycles (26-inch wheels for kids 10 and older)
- models

Avoid
- fireworks of any kind
- air rifles, chemistry sets, darts, skateboards, and arrows (unless used with parental supervision)
- bike or skateboard riding without helmets

HFCCH Chapter 4 — The right tools: Toys, books, and equipment   63

Before you toss—unusual uses for ordinary materials

You will be surprised at how many items on the toy list can be found in your own home, yard sales, flea market, or even the regular garbage! Understanding the idea behind a particular toy (what it teaches), taking inventory of ordinary material in your yard and home, and some creative thinking can save you money and space.

Keep in mind that for children, a toy is anything fun to play with. The box may be a better toy than the shiny, expensive item inside.

Ideas for free material

- **Butcher paper or freezer wrap:** Useful for finger painting, painting long murals by several children, and gift wrap. Merchants may charge a fee for it.

- **Paper rolls:** Ends of newsprint can be obtained from most newspaper or paper companies. Merchants who use wrapping paper are a good source too.

- **Wood scraps:** Most lumberyards and some construction companies have scrap piles filled with odd materials that you sometimes can have for the asking. Plywood is difficult for children to work with. Woods such as white pine, cedar, or spruce are especially desirable for young children's woodworking.

- **Wallpaper books and color chips:** These might be obtained from stores that sell paint, wallpaper, or floor coverings. Use for making collages, placemats, etc.

- **Display pictures:** Grocery stores often will give away used pictures of food displays. Photography, sporting goods, and drug stores have interesting displays.

- **Magazines and catalogs:** Companies, clinics, and agencies often have magazines and catalogs they will donate when they are outdated.

- **Carpet remnants or samples:** Carpet and rug companies usually sell these at low cost. Use for sitting mats, floor coverings, and play.

- **Telephones:** Telephone companies or telephone stores sometimes have junk phones to give away. They can be used for dramatic play as well as for learning how telephones work.

- **Steering wheels:** Automobile wrecking companies may give extras away. Use in dramatic play.

- **Three-gallon ice cream containers:** Obtain from ice cream stores and use for storage, as space helmets, waste paper baskets, or as individual storage bins for children's belongings.

- **Cardboard boxes:** These are among the best of the free play equipment. A diagonally-cut cardboard box makes a good tabletop easel. Boxes can be stacked, rearranged, used as cities or costumes, or made into a play car or boat. Make a clothespin-drop or bean bag target using a sealed shoe box or cardboard carton with a hole or holes on top. Small boxes make good doll beds and can be used to store "kits" of materials that go together. Many such cartons, taped shut, become building blocks. Large crates from furniture and appliance stores stimulate creative outdoor play. They can make a playhouse, hospital, ambulance, moving van, store, or puppet theater. Holes large enough for children to crawl through can be cut on the sides of the carton for play. Most cardboard box activities provide excellent large muscle development play.

Materials from your home

Here are some ideas for things around the house that you might wish to save and ways to use some of these materials.

From the kitchen:

Materials	Possible Uses
Beans and seeds	Bean bag to toss, growing experiments
Plastic napkin rings	Teething rings
Plastic salt shakers	Rattles
Plastic shaker spice jars	Sprinkle crafts, sand play
Plastic bowls and tumblers	Nesting toys
Plastic sponges	Bath toys, painting
Wooden bowls and spoons	Banging toys, sand play
Milk cartons	Rattles, blocks, bowling game
Cereal cartons	Drums, stacking toys, playing store
Plastic meat trays	Sewing cards, crafts
Cooking pans	Domestic play
Flour sifter	Cooking activities, sand play
Funnels	Water play
Plastic squirt bottles and pump bottles	Water play
Soap flakes	Bubbles
Paper bags	Hats, masks, puppets
Muffin tins	Counting games, play store, sorting

From the kitchen (continued):

Materials	Possible Uses
Egg cartons	Counting games, play store, planting seeds, craft activities
Food coloring	Cooking, paint
Paper plates	Hats, sewing, pasting
Corks	Animals, boats to float
Straws	Sorting, pasting, blowing bubbles
Popsicle sticks	Boats, paste sticks, construction
Plastic lids	Key chains, bracelets, glue or paint dishes

From the bedroom or clothes closet:

Materials	Possible Uses
Jewelry	Dangle toys, dressing up
Cotton socks	Balls, dolls
Shoelaces	Stringing beads, practicing lacing shoes, sewing cards
Pieces of fur	Animals, hats, texture games
Gloves	Puppet heads, dress up
Men and women's clothing	Dress up play
Scarves	Dancing, doll clothes
Feathers	Hats, bird games, collages
Handbags	Doll bags, dress up
Nylon stockings	Wigs, doll hair, stuffing
Lipstick, rouge, etc.	Playing grown-up, circus

From the sewing room and laundry:

Materials	Possible Uses
Plastic needles	Sewing cloth or cards
Elastic	Dangle toys, doll clothes
String, yarn, etc.	Sewing, collages, stringing games
Buttons	Sewing, stringing, sorting, counting, play money
Fabric pieces	Touching, sorting, doll clothes, pasting collages, making roads
Plastic bleach jug	Scoops, buckets for sand play, bird feeders
Tape measure	Measuring children, furniture
Clothespins	Manipulative play, small dolls, target games
Spools	Dangle toys, stringing, counting, sorting various sizes and colors

From the home in general:

Materials	Possible Uses
Paper clips	Necklaces, manipulative toys
Tissue and wrapping paper	Paint, collages
Poker chips	Stacking, building, counting
Cellophane tape	Crafts, hats, pictures
Playing cards	Building, card games
Pipe cleaners	Animals
All art media: crayons, glue, pencils, markers, paper, scissors	Creative activities, construction
Towels	Cuddly toys, washcloth
Holiday cards	Cutting, small puzzles
Magazines and catalogs	Scrapbooks, designs, collages
Brushes	Water play, painting
Cardboard rolls	Counting games, telescopes, talking tubes
Small tools, bolts, nuts	Counting, sorting, construction
Rope and wire	Knots for climbing, mobiles, sculpture
Clocks	Numbers, mechanical experimentation
Stones, rocks, pine cones, acorns	Games, collections, science exploration

Before you buy— quiz yourself

You will be spending money and time choosing and buying toys and equipment. Here are some questions that can help you get going on the right track.

Is it good for children?
- Is it safe?
- Will children of different ages enjoy it?
- Can it be used in a variety of ways?
- Does it encourage children to get along and play well together?
- Will it create conflict and encourage fighting or violence?
- Is it harmful to the environment?
- Do I need more of this item for the number and ages of children in my home?
- Do I have something at home that is similar and for the same type of play?
- Will using this toy take too much time away from other things children need to learn?
- Is this item essential? Can it wait?

Can I take care of it easily?
- Is it durable—will it last?
- Is it easy to clean?
- How often will I need to clean it?
- Is it easy to connect, fasten, or put together?
- Can I store it easily?

Is it worth the cost?
- Should I buy books or borrow them from the local library?
- Are there community programs that loan out toys and equipment (e.g. child care resource and referral)?
- Can I borrow it from a friend until I am sure it is what I need?
- Can I make it for less money than I will pay for it?
- Can I buy a more useful item for the same money?
- Should I buy this new or look at secondhand stores, auctions, yard sales, and flea markets?
- Can I find some of the things I need online or in the local paper?
- Will it help to place an ad "Wanted by child care home—infant crib"?
- Can I explain the purpose to local merchants and get them to give some of the materials free?
- Can I get parents involved in making or purchasing toys or equipment?

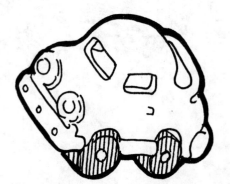

Toys and equipment safety—avoid these items

Whether you purchase toys or make them at home, think carefully about safety. The same is true for purchasing equipment at yard sales. Many yard sale items no longer meet safety standards—this is especially true for infant equipment.

The U.S. Consumer Product Safety Commission issues recalls for unsafe equipment and toys. If you have a question about the safety of an item, you can see a list of recalls at www.cpsc.gov.

When you care for children of different ages, you need to be especially careful. What is okay for older children can sometimes be very dangerous for young infants and toddlers. Curious children often play with toys in ways that were not intended. They also delight in placing small parts in their mouth, ears, and nose.

Here are some safety precautions to remember.

Avoid sharp items.
- Toys with glass parts, such as toy cars with glass windows or glass dishes
- Toys with sharp edges
- Toys with brittle or breakable parts
- Loose screws, bolts, or other hardware

Avoid items that can choke.
- Toys less than 1 1/4 inches (about the size of a half dollar) can be swallowed easily
- Larger toys, with small loose parts smaller than 1 1/4 inches.
- Stuffed toys and puppets with button-type eyes that could fall off or be removed
- Caps or plugs that could be removed easily

Avoid items that can strangle or suffocate.
- Toys with strings or cords longer than 12 inches
- Pacifier with ribbons or wrist cord
- Wooden play pens, cribs, or baby gates with slats greater than 2 3/8" wide
- Mesh netting with a large weave (should be less than 1/4 inch)
- V-shaped or diamond-shaped openings between slats (e.g., old accordian style baby gates)
- Cutouts in crib headboards or footboards
- Toy chests with heavy lids and no ventilation holes

Avoid broken, missing, or cracked items.
- Cribs or gates with missing or broken slats
- Travel cribs with mesh sides that are torn
- High chairs with broken or missing restraining straps

Avoid loud items.
- Toys that produce loud noises, such as cap pistols, can damage hearing
- Equipment or head phones that allow music to be played too loudly

Avoid hard to clean items.
- Toys that can't be machine washed or placed in the dishwasher
- Toys with textures that must be scrubbed by hand
- Toys and materials that stain easily

Avoid items that can burn or explode.
- Electrical toys or objects that must be plugged into an outlet
- Fireworks or sparklers
- Arts and crafts items such as a glue gun or soldering iron

Avoid toxic materials.
- Toys painted with toxic paints or glaze
- Toys with lead parts
- Diaper pails with deodorizers

Avoid items that can collapse or tip easily.
- Play pens or travel cribs that have frames or top rails that do not lock into place
- Travel cribs that have collapsible sides
- Tables, shelves, or furniture that is unstable

Avoid items that could be a fall hazard.
- Walkers for infants without safety features
- Back carriers, swings, high chairs, or strollers with leg openings that might allow a child to slip out
- Swings that could be tipped over easily
- Changing table without safety strap
- High chairs without both waist and leg restraining straps
- Shelves that are not anchored to the wall
- Climbing equipment placed on hard surfaces
- Hook-on high chairs

FamilyShare...
Supporting your partners

Parents often struggle with deciding which toys to buy for their children. Advertising can be misleading and the choices can be overwhelming. Sometimes young parents purchase things on impulse that really don't work well for the age of their child. This can happen too, when they receive things from friends, grandparents, or other family members.

You can help parents by sharing information with them about favorite toys and books. You may photocopy some of the charts and book recommendations in this handbook to share with parents. Giving parents a suggested booklist from your public library will remind parents that the gift of reading is free.

Toys you can make

Making wooden blocks. If you're handy with woodworking or know someone who is, you can make the blocks rather than buy them at the store. If you don't have the equipment to do the wood cutting yourself, you could have this done at the lumber yard and finish the blocks yourself. Either way, you save money.

To make blocks, use one board 2 inches by 4 inches by 8 feet. (See illustration below for cutting suggestions.) Then sand the blocks well and rub in mineral oil as a finish that won't hurt children if they chew on the blocks.

If you keep the wood's natural tone, you'll encourage creativity play. But if you prefer color, be sure to use nontoxic paints.

White pine is recommended because it has fewer splinters than other wood.

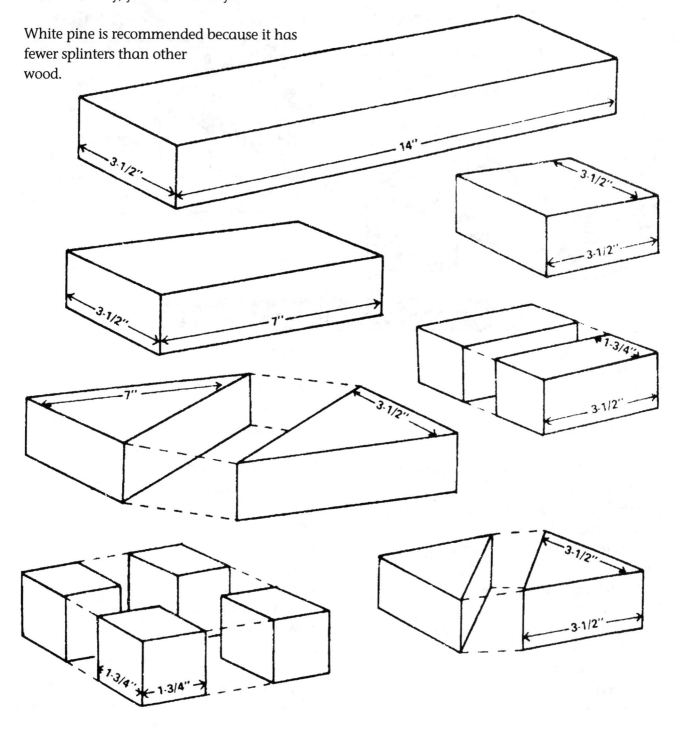

HFCCH Chapter 4 — The right tools: Toys, books, and equipment

Milk cartons blocks

First, take any 2 cartons of equal size, and cut them to the same height. Slit the corner edges of one carton. Fit the two cartons together, open sides together to form a block.

Secure the edges with duct tape or with heavy plastic mailing tape. To make the blocks more attractive, you can cover them with adhesive paper.

Nail art

Take a well-sanded piece of plywood. Hammer nails into the board leaving about one inch of the nail above the board. Create several rows of nails about 1 1/2 inches apart. Older children, if supervised, can help hammer the nails. The children can stretch colored rubber bands or yarn over the nails to form designs.

Art recipes

Play dough
Mix:
2 cups flour
1 cup salt
2 tablespoons oil
1 cup water
1 tablespoon cream of tartar or alum
Few drops of food coloring

Mix together, cook over low heat until it thickens, knead well, and store in a plastic bag or container in the refrigerator.

Play dough (will harden)
Mix:
2 cups cornstarch
1 cup baking soda
1 cup water
Food coloring

Finger paint
Mix:
3 tablespoons sugar
1/2 cup cornstarch
2 cups cold water

Cook over low heat until the mixture thickens. Cool, and add a few drops of food coloring. Refrigerate.

Modeling clay
Mix:
1 cup salt
1 1/2 cups flour
1/2 cup warm water
2 tablespoons oil
Food coloring

(See chapter 6 for more art recipes.)

Folk toys

Some toys seem to pop up again and again, generation after generation. These are folk toys—proven in popularity—like the hobby horse, the bean bag, or the button whirling on a string. They're all easy to make, using scraps from other household projects.

One of the most popular toys is the cuddly sock doll. Like most folk toys, there is no right or wrong way to make it. All you need are:
- one sock
- scissors, needle, and trim
- stuffing (polyester, cotton, or cut-up nylon hose)

1) Fold the sock (as shown) so the heel is flattened.
2) Cut the ankle portion in half lengthwise.
3) Cut into the ankle. Use each half of the ankle for arms. Sew up the rest of the ankle to create legs.

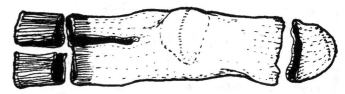

4) Cut off the toe of the sock to make a stuffing hole. Start to stuff.
5) Sew ribbon or string securely halfway up the foot of the sock to form a neck, and sew on the arms. Stuff the rest of the doll. (The heel of the sock will bulge out to form the doll's bottom.)

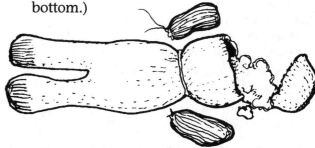

6) Reattach the toe as a cap for the doll. Add features, too, and, if you like, add clothes.
Caution: Do not use buttons or other items that could be pulled off and swallowed.
To clean: Hand wash.

HFCCH Chapter 4 — The right tools: Toys, books, and equipment

Great books for children!

Borrow books from your public library and begin to build your own collection of favorites. Children should be able to select from at least 12 to 20 books every day. At a minimum, you should have at least 2-3 books suitable for each age.

The best selection of books will be found at a bookstore or online. Select both fiction and non-fiction books about animals; familiar experiences; and people of different races, ages, and abilities.

Books for children—0-12 months
Baby's Faces, Ben Argueta
The Rock-A-Bye Collection (audio tape and book), J. Aaron Brown & Associates, Inc.
Teddy In The House, Lucy Cousins
Touch and Feel: Baby Animals, DK Publishing
Grow! Babies!, Penny Gentieu
Animal Babies, Harry McNaught
Hide and Seek Puppies, Roy Volkmann

Books for children—12-24 months
Baby! Talk!, Penny Gentieu
Baby's Colors, Neil Ricklen
Baby's First Words, Lars Wik
Farm Animals, Phoebe Dunn
Goodnight Moon, Margret Wise Brown
Moo, Baa, La La La, Sandra Boynton

Books for children—2 years
All About Baby, Stephen Shott
Animal Time, Tom Arma
Bunny and Me, Adele Aron Greenspun
The Little Quiet Book, Katharine Ross
Trucks, Byron Barton

Books for children—3 years
Brown Bear, Brown Bear What Do You See?, Bill Martin Jr.
Mouse Paint, Ellen Stoll Walsh
The Little Red House, Norma Jean Sawicki
When I Was A Baby, Catherine Anholt
Sounds My Feet Make, Arlene Blanchard
Harold and The Purple Crayon, David Johnson Leisk
Mr. Little's Noisy Truck, Richard Fowler
Peter's Chair, Ezra Jack Keats
The Very Hungry Caterpillar, Eric Carle

Books for children—4 years
Blackboard Bear, Martha Alexander
Harriet, You'll Drive Me Wild!, Mem Fox
Bedtime for Frances, Russell Hoban and Lillian Hoban

Snowballs, Lois Ehlert
What Do You Do With A Kangaroo?, Mercer Mayer
If You Give A Mouse A Cookie, Laura Joffe Numeroff
The Quilt Story, Tony Johnston and Tomie De Paola
May I Bring a Friend?, De Regniefs and Beatrice Schenk
Imogene's Antlers, David Small
How Do Dinosaurs Say Good Night?, Jane Yolen

Books for children—5 years
Ira Sleeps Over, Bernard Waber
Feathers for Lunch, Lois Ehlert
Little Bear, Else Holmelund Minarik
Whistle for Willie, Ezra Jack Keats
Alexander and the Terrible, Horrible, No Good, Very Bad Day, Judith Viorst
Are You My Mother?, Philip D. Eastman
Harry and the Terrible Whatzit, Dick Gackenbach
The Art Lesson, Tomie De Paola

Books for children—6-8 yrs
A Chair for My Mother, Vera Williams
Anna Banana and Me, Lenore Blegvard
Arthur and the Dog Show, Marc Brown
Everybody Needs A Rock, Byrd Baylor
The Garden of Abdul Gasazi, Chris Van Allsburg
The Kid Next Door and Other Headaches: Stories About Adam Joshua, Janice Lee Smith
Little House in the Big Woods, Laura Ingalls Wilder
Ramona, Beverly Cleary

Books for children—9-11 years
Chocolate Fever, Robert Kimmel Smith
How It Feels to Be Adopted, Jill Krementz
How To Eat Fried Worms, Thomas Rockwell
The Indian in the Cupboard, Lynn Banks
Nothing's Fair in Fifth Grade, Barthe DeClements
The Oxford Book of Poetry for Children, compiled by Edward Blishen
Ramona's World, Beverly Cleary
Tales of a Fourth Grade Nothing, Judy Blume

Heart of the Matter

One of my favorite things to do when working with a group of parents is to help them understand how children learn through play. I've found the best way to do this is to let them play with toys that their children use every day.

I will give one team of parents some play dough. Another team will get some blocks. A third team will get to experiment with toys that float and sink in a tub of water. A fourth team will be assigned to make the whole group a yummy snack.

Parents find this experience very enjoyable. They mix, roll, stir, pour, float, and have a great time. And they listen closely as I point out how all four activities teach basic math, science, and language skills.

What fascinates me the most, however, is that when the activity is over, they just don't want to stop playing. They are far worse than any group of children I've ever worked with. The water play and play dough groups are especially hard to rein in. Fathers are particularly challenging and will continue to knead and roll the dough into snakes and other shapes. Often they will pull me aside and sheepishly ask if they can take the play dough home. A few will stuff play dough in their pockets and try to sneak off with it.

After some good natured teasing, I point out to them that the sensory nature of these items is tremendously appealing. Even as adults, they too need to see, touch, taste, and smell as they are learning. I also remind them that this inability to stop playing shows that they believe play is important and very meaningful. I wrap things up by giving all the play dough away and by encouraging them to go home and play with their children.

Some adults are able to capture the playfulness of their childhoods and to build upon it. They become devoted gardeners, creative quilters, and gifted musicians.

Lesia

Experience Talks

Conversations with other providers

■ **I always post a toy and book wish list on a bulletin board for parents.** Sometimes their children have outgrown toys, and they are just collecting dust at home. Other times they like to make a special gift to our child care program at holiday time. Parents want their children to have interesting things to do, and it's amazing how often they come through when I really need another toy telephone or something.

■ **The best book I've found for infants and toddlers is a photo album.** The pages are heavy and don't tear easily. I insert photos of the children and magazine pictures of familiar items. Sometimes I can even add flat objects like a brightly colored leaf. Often one of the older children will draw a picture and want to add that to our book. I add that too.

■ **Toy guns are a pet peeve of mine.** I don't like violent play and I don't allow toy guns. Children will still pick up a block and pretend to shoot, but I've learned that a block easily turns back into a block and can be used for other types of play. A gun is always a gun. It can only be used for one thing.

■ **I have about ten prop boxes that I keep for dramatic play.** Each box has all sorts of props that children like to play with. My pizza prop box has a red checked table cloth, placemats, coupons, delivery boxes, an old pizza pan and pretend money. Our "delivery person" makes deliveries on his tricycle.

■ **My son sometimes has difficulty sharing his toys and his room with my child care children.** We finally decided that it would help if I paid him rent each week. He saves his rent money in a special bank and then can use that to purchase additional toys that he wants. This solution has really worked for us.

■ **Toys are so expensive!** I realized early on that I would need to use some of my children's toys in my program because I just couldn't afford to purchase a whole new set. I also realized that my kids needed to have a few toys that were theirs alone. Both kids have a special place in their room for toys that are off limits to everyone else. Occasionally they will bring these things out for other children to play with, but it is their decision.

■ **When collecting toys, stick with the tried and true basics.** Dolls, a toy cash register, play dishes, pretend stove, toy phone, grocery cart, toy table and chairs are absolute musts. Push toys seem to be better for toddlers than toys they can pull. My toddlers have pushed our toy grocery carts for hundreds of miles around my house. You can create pretend food by washing and saving real food containers. I wash out small orange juice containers and butter tubs. Empty pasta boxes work well too.

■ **I can't afford hardback books, so I use clear plastic shelf adhesive paper to protect the covers of paperback books.** It works well. The books tear less, and the covers are easier to keep clean.

■ **Each time I read to children, I talk to them about the importance of books.** They have learned from me that books are special. They can choose a book from the book basket and read it on their own any time, but they know they need to do this in the book corner or on the sofa. Even the toddlers have learned to take care of books, and not drop them on the floor.

■ **My husband made me a set of blocks from scrap lumber.** They are made of pine, and not as durable as hardwood blocks, but they have been a wonderful addition to our toy selection. The preschoolers play with them all the time, and the school-age kids do too. I have a large area in the basement corner for blocks, and they will spend hours playing with them. Over time, my husband has added more blocks to our set. I also have some toy trucks and animals on the shelves in this area for them to use as props. The kids do amazing things. I take pictures with my digital camera and give these to parents.

■ **I love to go to yard sales, but I am very choosy about buying toys.** Sometimes I will discover a great find like a doll cradle or toy high chair. Board games for school-age kids are fairly easy to pick up too. But there is so much junk out there. I have to look things over carefully to make sure there are no sharp edges. I avoid buying toys that have tiny parts because I just can't risk having the infants and toddlers choking on them.

Planning your day: Routines and schedules

Contents

Where am I now?	80
Introduction	81
Family, friends, and neighbors	81
Establishing a routine	82
Cleanup time	83
Creating a schedule	89
Heart of the Matter	93
FamilyShare	94
Experience Talks	94

Planning your day: Routines and schedules—
Where am I now? What can I improve?

	Seldom 1	Sometimes 2	Often 3	Most Often 4
1. I use a daily schedule and follow regular routines each day.				
2. I allow some flexibility in my schedule to adjust for individual needs of children.				
3. I follow a schedule for each infant that meets his or her individual needs (e.g., nap in morning).				
4. I plan weekly play and learning activities.				
5. I share information about schedules, activities, and routines with families.				
6. I closely supervise everyday routines.				
7. I schedule transitions so that children never have to wait longer than 3-4 minutes as they are moving from one activity to another.				
8. I use routines to teach important self-help skills and habits such as hand washing and cleaning-up.				
9. I use routines to help children with everyday learning (colors, counting, problem-solving, sharing, and getting along with others).				
10. I balance our daily schedule to include both indoor and outdoor play and learning.				

Chapter 5

Planning your day: Routines and schedules

Good family child care homes are orderly places. Daily schedules provide times for eating, resting, playing, and learning. Children feel more comfortable if they know what happens when, and what comes next. You also will feel more relaxed and confident if your day is manageable. A regular and dependable routine makes for a smooth day for everyone.

Family child care homes can be flexible places too. Caring for a small group of children means you can be more thoughtful about meeting a child's individual needs. Rather than making everyone fit into a rigid schedule you can stop and share the excitement of the arrival of a baby bird or spend a little more time reading another favorite book.

The key is to establish a schedule that will work for you and the children—one that provides a sense of order and yet allows for some flexibility.

Family, friends, and neighbors

Even if you are caring for just one or two children, you will find many of these ideas useful. Children seem to behave better when they have a regular routine. And planning simple learning activities for them will help your day be more interesting. Watching children learn is especially rewarding when they are like family. Years later you will feel a special pride in how you helped them grow and develop.

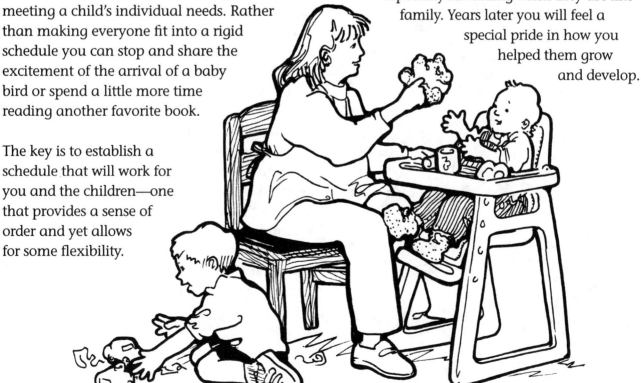

Establishing a routine

Arrival

Arrival time sets the tone for the rest of the day. Some children will arrive fresh and eager to play. Others will be tired and cranky. Often parents will be in a rush to get to work. This important time of moving from home to child care can be made easier for everyone with a regular routine.

Greet each child and parent. Encourage parents to arrive early enough so they can come in, help their children with coats and boots, and say goodbye. For children who have difficulty saying goodbye this practice is especially important. You also will want to visit briefly with parents to determine if there is any information you need to know about changes in schedule, medications, or family events.

Encourage children to bring a favorite stuffed animal, doll, or blanket from home. Children feel more comfortable and secure when they can have something familiar with them both at home and in the family child care setting. It also is helpful for children to have a special place of their own to store their things while they are with you. A drawer, cabinet, or closet shelf labeled with the child's name works well.

But set some limits. A "special something" from home does not mean that children need to bring every toy they own, because that can lead to squabbles and tears. You also may want to draw the line on certain types of toys. For example, many providers do not allow children to bring pretend guns or violent toys. Decide your policy about bringing toys from home and share it with children and parents when they join your program.

Cleanup time

Encourage children to clean up throughout the day; this will make the job easier later on and keep things flowing smoothly. Cleanup is more effective when it is part of every activity. Teach children to pick up and return toys when they are done playing. Do this before too many toys are scattered on the floor and play becomes chaotic and crazy. When children cannot find the toys they need, toys are stepped on and broken, and the general disorder of the room leads to frustration for everyone.

Make it fun. Children love games. Help them view cleanup time as just another activity. You might consider the following ideas.

- Play a song on the piano or CD player, and see if the children can clean up before the song ends.

- Play "I spy." "I spy something that is blue with orange stripes. Who can find it and put it on the shelf?"

- Assign children different areas to clean up and let them race as you count out loud.

- Encourage children to jump like a bunny or fly like a plane as they clean up.

- Assign children different colors. One child picks up everything red. One child picks up everything blue.

- Count everything in sight. "I see two balls. I see four dolls. I see one, two, three, four blocks still on the floor."

- Sing nursery rhymes or songs during cleanup.

- Put your hands over your eyes and ask children to surprise you. Ask the children to tell when you should "peek" and see the clean room.

- Sing the following to the tune of "I'm a Little Teapot."

I'm a little helper
See me clean
I can pick up
With my team
When we are finished
You will see
A nice clean room
for you and me.

Tell children what activity is coming next. "After the toys are picked up, we will be going outside." Or "after we eat our lunch, we will lie down for a nap."

HFCCH Chapter 5 — Planning your day: Routines and schedules

Play and learning time

A big part of your day will be centered on play time. This also will be an important learning time, because children learn best through play.

Set out familiar play activities for children's arrival. After children arrive each morning, they often are eager to join their friends and play with favorite toys. Set toys and other play material out so children can get involved in something right away while you visit briefly with parents. Some paper and crayons on a table, blocks on the floor, and a few books by the sofa can help children make the transition smoothly.

Reconnect with children. After all the children arrive, you may want to bring children together in a group to sing a song or read a book. This is also a good time for children to share news from home and for you to discuss any special events of the day. If you have a wide range of ages, you may prefer to do this with 2-3 children at a time, rather than the one large group. Keep this time very brief. Remember, toddlers cannot sit still quietly for more than a few minutes.

Find the right activities for the right child. Teaching young children is different than the way you may have been taught in elementary school. Young children learn best through hands-on play. Worksheets and lengthy group activities do not work well for young children and limit learning. Instead, take your cue from the children. Consider age, interests, and skills of your children when choosing activities. Providing several activities for children to choose from at any one time generally works very well.

Choose activities for all types of learning. Children need time each day to read books, sing songs, learn fingerplays, count objects, work puzzles, observe nature, run, and leap. We all have our favorite activities to share with children. It is very easy to find ourselves focusing only on arts and crafts or pretend play. Or perhaps your special interest is cooking with kids. On the other hand we may find ourselves avoiding outdoor play or math and science activities. But children need opportunities to experience all types of play and learning. So strive for balance. You will find many ideas for successful activities throughout this book.

Snacks and mealtimes

A great deal of your time with children will be spent preparing and eating food. Eating is an important part of our culture. Enjoying food, visiting with friends, and developing good eating habits are important parts of the early childhood experience.

be like to have someone hovering over you as you eat. It is also a good idea to eat with children for health and safety reasons. Young children choke easily, and you may not see them choking unless you are facing them. A child who is truly choking is a silent child. It is best to keep your attention focused on the children when they eat.

Use mealtime to teach self-help and social skills. Children can help set the table with napkins, utensils, and plates. When food is served and eaten family style, children can learn how to share and help each other. Older children also can help you teach good manners.

Wash hands first. Germs and children go together. They often eat with their fingers and they share food. Help children develop a regular habit of washing hands before every snack or meal.

Make snacks and mealtimes enjoyable. Eating is a social activity and children enjoy sitting around the table together. Some providers find it helpful to provide a child-sized table for children to eat around. Other providers use their own dining room table with booster chairs and high chairs arranged around it. Allow plenty of time for children to eat because young children eat slowly at times.

Insist that children sit down when they eat. Toddlers who carry snacks around are likely to stumble and choke. A trail of food across your home also can present cleanliness problems. It is not very pleasant to find a moldy peach under the sofa or a squishy carrot behind the TV. Besides, it could present a health hazard if another child finds it before you do.

Eat and visit with children. You will find that children are much more willing to sit down and eat if you join them. This may seem unnecessary to you, but consider what it would

Teach children about food. Mealtime is also a great time to discuss colors and shapes of food. Older children will want to know more about where food comes from and can share stories about shopping for groceries or cooking at home. You also can encourage them to help you with snack or meal preparation.

Teach children that cleaning up is everyone's responsibility. Finish up snack or mealtime by asking children to help you clean up and clear the dishes. Washing hands, brushing teeth, and using the toilet should be routine habits after lunch. Supervise children and make sure they are using proper hand washing steps. See chapter 11. Most child care providers now require children to brush their teeth as well. For some children this may be the only time during the day that they brush their teeth.

Rest time

Everyone—young or old, needs time to rest. Sometimes this means a nap, sometimes this just means taking time to slow down and relax.

Having a regular rest time routine can teach children the importance of balancing their active lives with a rest and relaxation time.

Keep a watchful eye on very young children. Most infants and some toddlers will take a morning nap and an afternoon nap. Lay infants on their backs to avoid sudden infant death syndrome (SIDS). Infants will let you know when they wake up, but if they should begin to choke or have trouble breathing, you won't be able to hear them on a baby monitor. Watch infants closely to make sure they are sleeping comfortably on their backs and breathing well.

Help children calm down. Learning how to relax and calm down is a skill everyone should have. In today's rushed and stressful world, many families don't know how to help children learn this important skill. You can help by showing children how to set aside some time to relax each day. Begin by playing soft music during mealtime. Afterwards spend a few minutes talking and reading a book together. Many children will respond well to a gentle back rub. If older preschoolers seem to have difficulty sleeping, it is not unreasonable to insist that they lie quietly and look at books.

Give school-agers some quiet time too. Even school-age kids need time to get away from it all. Provide some space for them to read quietly, do homework, or busy themselves with a hobby. If school-agers arrive before younger children get up from rest, spend some time with them to hear about their day. They also may want to help you prepare an afternoon snack.

Outdoor time

Children who are with you all day need to be outdoors for at least an hour each day. When the weather is nice, you may want to consider going outside both in the morning and in the afternoon. Encourage active play, but allow time for quiet activities too. Play dough on the picnic table, chalk drawing on the sidewalk, and water play in a shallow plastic tub are favorite activities.

Supervise closely.
Even if you have a fenced-in yard, it is important for you to be outside with the children as they play. This is especially true if children are climbing or swinging on playground equipment. Children can slip and fall in a blink of an eye. You need to be within arms reach whenever they might be at risk. If you think your backyard equipment is too risky or takes too much supervision—get rid of it. There are many other wonderful things to do outside.

Help children explore nature. Families spend a great deal of time indoors and children often have very little opportunity to be outside and explore nature. As they grow older much of their outside time will be limited to sport activities. Early childhood is a wonderful time to introduce children to the wonders of nature. Chasing butterflies, growing a garden, and splashing in puddles should be a part of every child's experience.

Transitions—going from here to there

It can be a challenge at times to take children from one activity to another or from an activity to a routine, like mealtime. Children can get very involved in an activity and not want to stop. Or the block structure they have just built is too precious to tear down at cleanup time.

Cleanup is not always a favorite activity. It is also a challenge to get six children to use the toilet, wash hands, and sit at the table for a snack. Dressing multiple children for outdoor play—coats, boots, hats, or sunscreen—can be overwhelming too.

It isn't always necessary for everyone to do everything at the same time. You may find it easier to start one or two children toward the sink to wash up before you gather the rest of the children. After all, few family providers have a sink large enough for more than two children at a time anyway.

Remember to ask older children to help you with younger children. Taking responsibility for helping little ones wash their hands or zip a jacket can help them feel very grown up.

HFCCH Chapter 5 — Planning your day: Routines and schedules

Departure

When children have been with you all day they may need some help shifting gears and going home.

Children who are involved in an activity may resist leaving. Parents often are tired, exhausted, and in no mood for a conflict with their child. At times, they also may view their child's actions as personal rejection.

Bring active play to a close. It helps if children have some wind down time before they leave. Providers often enjoy reading a book or playing a quiet game with children as they wait for parents. Some providers like to wait outside with the children when the weather is good.

But keep children busy. Take into consideration that parents will arrive at different times. For some children this can be a bit unnerving, especially if their parent happens to arrive later than the others. Young children do not have a good understanding of time, and "soon" is a difficult concept to understand. Reassure the child that his/her parent will come after " cleanup time." Children understand that better than "soon."

Consider a light snack. Children often are hungry at the end of the day. It's been a while since snack time, and dinner may be a long way off. A light snack of crackers or juice helps. Check with parents to make sure they are okay with this.

Use a regular end-of-the-day activity as a signal that it is time to go home. A logical one would be to get jackets, artwork, and other personal items together and put them by the door. A quick snack and a trip to the bathroom also help. Take time to greet each parent and share a positive comment or story about their child. Parents want to hear about their child's day.

Encourage parents to put items in the car before they actually leave with the children. This is especially helpful if families have large bulky items such as car seats and diaper bags. It also helps to keep children safer as cars come and go.

Creating a schedule

Daily and weekly planning

It may be helpful to plan on a weekly basis and post your schedule on a bulletin board where families enter each day. Parents think about their children during the day and want to know what their children are doing and learning.

Planning also makes your day more manageable. Children also benefit because you are more likely to plan learning activities that meet their needs and interests.

Why a schedule?
- Parents want to know what their children are doing and learning.
- Your day becomes more manageable.
- It is easier to build learning activities into the day.

Your planning can be simple or detailed. When routines are well established, all you may need is a general reminder of the main activities for the day. Your *Daily Schedule* shows your routine activities each day and may not change a great deal from day to day. Your *Weekly Learning Activity Schedule* should change from week to week.

You also may choose to complete a more detailed *Weekly Activity Schedule* that shares snack and menu choices and shows specific times for play and learning activities. Or if you prefer, snacks and menus could be posted on a separate chart.

Consider setting individual goals for children each week. For example, you might want to help one child learn how to drink from a cup. Another may need some guidance on how to cut with scissors. Your goal for others might be to teach a new song or fingerplay.

Observe what children are learning. If you spend a few minutes each day observing children, you can identify learning areas they may need help with. For example, a preschool child who has difficulty working puzzles might benefit from playing quietly with more simple "toddler" puzzles. Over several weeks, you may choose to slowly introduce harder puzzles.

Meeting children's individual learning needs should be the foundation of your daily activities. The Ages and Stages chapter 7, in this handbook will help you identify skills that children should be developing at each age.

HFCCH Chapter 5 — Planning your day: Routines and schedules

Use themes to recognize special events in children's lives. Sometimes it is helpful to plan activities around a theme for the week and tie all your activities to that theme. This works best if children are familiar with the topic. For example, if several of your children went to the circus with their parents, the following week you might choose to have a parade, read books about a circus, make animal collages, and visit a neighbor's new kittens. These types of activities can help enrich and build upon children's experiences.

Include both new and familiar activities. When you plan activities, remember that children like variety but they also like to do some things over and over again. Avoid doing too many new things in one day; spread new activities throughout the week. It is important to have basic activities like books and block play available all the time, although you can vary book titles and block accessories.

Make realistic plans. It is better to make reasonable plans that you can fulfill than ambitious ones that frustrate you. If you find yourself feeling frazzled or observe that you are pushing children through too heavy a schedule, it may be time to change your plan. Remember, daily schedules are supposed to make the day easier, not more difficult.

Sample Daily Schedule

Time	Activities
7:30 – 8:30	Children arrive, early morning learning activities
8:30 – 9:00	Story time. Discuss plans for the day
9:00 – 10:00	Blocks, art, and dramatic play
10:00 – 10:30	Snack
10:30 – 11:30	Outdoor play and learning
11:30 – 12:00	Clean up and prepare for lunch
12:00 – 1:00	Lunch
1:00 – 1:30	Story and music time
1:30 – 3:00	Rest and naptime
3:00 – 3:30	Snack
3:30 – 4:30	Outdoor play and learning
4:30 – 5:00	Story and music time Prepare to go home
5:00 – 5:45	Departure

Sample Weekly Learning Activity Schedule

Special Activities for the Week (in addition to regular learning activities)					
Dates:					
	Mon.	Tues.	Wed.	Thurs.	Fri.
Morning	Book: *Curious George Goes to the Circus*	Make circus posters and tickets	Play dough with animal cookie cutters	Wagon parade	Animal collage
Afternoon	Pretend play circus	Pretend play circus	Walk to playground	Make muffins	Visit neighbor's new kittens
Special snack or treat			Kristen's birthday cupcakes for snack		

Sample Weekly Schedule (detailed)

Dates:					
	Mon.	Tues.	Wed.	Thurs.	Fri.
Arrival 7:30 – 8:30	Books and blocks	Drawing with crayons	Play dough	Drawing with markers	Books and puzzles
Welcome activity 8:30 – 8:45	Welcome Friends song / Book: *The Very Hungry Caterpillar*	Welcome Friends song / Book: *All Kinds of Babies*	Welcome Friends song / Book: *If You Give a Mouse a Cookie*	Welcome Friends song / Book: *Caps for Sale*	Welcome Friends song / Book: *Harold and the Purple Crayon*
Play and learning activities 8:45 – 9:45	Plant seedlings Cut coupons Pretend play grocery store	Wash baby dolls Pretend play house with new dolls	Block play Help make cookies for snack	Pretend play hat shop Monkey puzzle	Pretend play hat shop Monkey dance with hats
Clean up Prepare for snack 9:45 – 10:00					
Snack 10:00 – 10:30	Apple juice Muffin	Milk Cinnamon toast	Orange pineapple juice Oyster crackers	Milk Dry cereal	Orange juice Toasted raisin bread

Sample Weekly Schedule (detailed) continued

Dates:					
	Mon.	Tues.	Wed.	Thurs.	Fri.
Outdoor play and learning 10:30 – 11:30	Scarf dance Chalk drawings Plant tomato plants	Sand play Collect bugs Water garden	Paint rocks Bean bag toss Wash baby dolls	Wagon parade Chalk drawings Water garden	Tricycle car wash Measure shadows Water garden
Clean up Prepare for lunch 11:30 – 12:00					
Lunch 12:00 – 1:00	Milk Ham cubes Boiled potatoes Pineapple chunks Green beans Roll	Milk Tortilla with refried beans and cheese Bell pepper pieces Pineapple chunks	Milk Spaghetti (ground beef) Peas Diced pears Garlic bread	Milk Baked chicken Mashed potatoes Peas Carrot stick Roll	Milk Peanut butter and jelly Bell pepper pieces Sliced peaches Cottage cheese
Nap and Rest time 1:00 – 3:00					
Snack 3:00 – 3:30	Milk Oatmeal cookie	Apple juice Celery sticks with peanut butter	Apple juice Soft pretzel	Milk Peanut butter cookie	Fresh fruit cup Bran muffin
Play and learning 3:30 – 4:30	Dramatic play circus	Dramatic play circus	Walk to playground	Make muffins	Visit neighbor's new kittens
Quiet time, music, reading, prepare to go home 4:30-5:15					

92   Heartland Family Child Care Handbook — Chapter 5

Heart of the Matter

Some time ago, I spent a year working with another provider to care for a group of children in a home setting. I was very proud of my knowledge about child development and worked very hard to have exciting activities for the children. I spent a lot of time organizing, planning, and gathering materials. I busied myself at the beginning of each day with getting activities and snack ready and worked hard to keep everything on schedule.

To my dismay, I seemed to be the only one that was really concerned about these things. The other provider seemed very content to let me deal with these important matters. Instead, she seemed more focused on talking with families as they arrived. She also spent a great deal of time moving from activity to activity, and talking with children throughout the day.

As I watched my friend work with the children, my frustration with her "style" changed to one of respect. She really connected with the children and their parents in a way I did not. I found myself talking "at" the children as I gave directions or explained an activity. Instead she talked "with" children. She had a knack for really observing each child and knowing how to gently ask questions that would help each child think and learn.

And the children adored her. They liked me, but they really adored her. They connected with her on a very personal level.

Over the year I learned a lot. I learned from my friend how to slow down and really get in tune with each child. I also learned how to visit with parents at the end of the day, and really listen to them.

I still believe that planning and organization is important. I know all too well that a day without planning can create chaos. But planning it is just one part of child care. Connecting with each child on a deeply personal level and gently guiding daily learning experiences is the real goal of quality child care.

Lesia

FamilyShare...

Supporting your partners

You may want to give families a copy of your daily schedule to keep at work or at home. You can suggest times for parents to call to talk with children if they wish during the day. Knowing about daily activities also will help parents know when to schedule doctor's appointments or a special lunch with Mom or Dad. Also be sure to ask about family summer or holiday vacation plans. This will help you be more flexible with your planning.

Experience Talks

Conversations with other providers

■ **I really love talking with families each day as they arrive.** It helps me understand more about the children if I know their parents well. I think it is a shame that teachers in elementary schools do not have this opportunity. It really helps you connect with the child.

■ **I have a selfish reason for wanting to visit with parents each day as they arrive and leave.** Frankly, in this job you get a little starved for adult conversation and it is nice to chat with a parent. On a professional level I share information about their child, but it also is okay to discuss other things. This helps me get to know families at a deeper level.

■ **I have a few toys and activities that I only use at arrival time.** I have a wooden train set that the children just love. They always run to it right away. This gives me a chance to say hello to Mom and for her to leave without a lot of tearful goodbyes.

■ **Bringing toys from home is always an issue because children have a hard time sharing favorite toys.** I tell families that children may bring one thing and only one thing. And I suggest that it not be their most favorite toy in the world. It is better to bring something that is comforting but not so special that they can't bear to share it at all.

■ **If children need a "comfort" toy from home, I have found that what works well is to ask parents to choose a stuffed animal or doll as a special "child care" toy.** In other words, this would not be their treasured teddy bear that they sleep with at night, but a special friend that journeys with them to child care each day. It seems to be easier to share a special child care "friend." And if by chance the favorite toy gets left at child care accidentally, it is not such a crisis.

■ **Life skills are important. Learning how to prepare food and eat like a civilized human being is a part of growing up.** I really try to help children learn to value food and learn the art of conversation. It breaks my heart when I hear families jokingly say they only eat in front of the TV. And I agonize when I think about how one of my child care children could develop an eating disorder later in life. I want to show children how eating healthy food can be a wonderful part of their everyday lives.

■ **Snacks and meals should be wholesome and simple.** It's fun to do some of those complicated things like making a boat out of a pear, but most of the time kids really get a kick out of just helping to set the table and spread jam on bread.

■ **Ah-h-h rest time—one of the true benefits of this job.** I love rest time. Before doing child care, my work life was rush, rush, rush. I barely had time for a quick bite to eat, and often worked through breaks. But caring for children has changed all of that and has brought balance back to my world. I truly believe that if the rest of the world had an enforced rest or naptime we could achieve world peace.

■ **I believe in music!** I have collected a variety of really soothing music to use at naptime. Most of the music is not children's music—it is much too lively. Soft piano or classical music seems to work well. Some music stores now have listening stations set up, so you can listen to the music before you purchase. You can also do this online. Music really helps children relax and rest comfortably.

■ **We have a cleanup wagon.** At cleanup time one child pulls the wagon around and the other children toss everything in. After the wagon is loaded, everyone helps to unload the toys into the storage closet.

■ **I really make use of the older children as "helpers."** It can be as simple as asking them to bring me the baby's cap or get the crayons out of the cupboard. Not only does this help me as we move from one activity to another, but it makes them feel very grown up and valued.

■ **I only care for my two grandchildren, but I still feel it is important to stick to a routine.** They behave better and our day goes more smoothly.

■ **I care for my twin niece and nephew and my eight-month-old baby.** I must admit it is tempting when I am busy with the baby to just stick them in front of the TV. But I know better. I try to plan at least one or two interesting activities each day. I keep it simple and fun. It helps all of us have something to look forward to.

■ **You really can teach an old dog new tricks!** Even though I just care for my grandchildren, I love learning tips and techniques from regular child care providers. The cleanup ideas alone are great. I wish I had these ideas when my own children were little.

■ **We have special songs that we only sing at the end of the day.** Children can't tell time, but they have learned that these songs come just before their parents arrive. It helps bring the day to a close.

■ **Often just before time to go home, I gather the children and we talk about what they will do when they get home at the end of the day.** Often they will talk about going home to see a pet, or supper time. Talking about this helps them look forward to going home and makes leaving more pleasant.

■ **I make a point of sharing with parents at least one thing every week that their child has learned.** Parents sometimes have a hard time understanding all the learning that happens in a family child care home. Sometimes they feel their children would be learning more in a preschool or center. I work hard to teach families that I provide a lot of learning opportunities that their children might not get elsewhere.

Creative play and learning

Chapter 6

Contents

Where am I now?.	98
Three basic ways to help children learn.	99
You are a special teacher in children's lives.	99
Children learn in different ways.	100
Set goals for individual children.	101
What children are learning when they play.	102
Creating learning centers in your home.	103
Pretend play.	103
Art.	108
Table toys and board games.	112
Block play.	114
Sand and water play.	116
Books.	119
Food and cooking.	121
Music and movement.	125
Outdoor play.	133
Explore the community.	136
Use themes to plan activities.	138
Heart of the Matter.	139
FamilyShare.	140
Experience Talks.	140

Creative play and learning—
Where am I now? What can I improve?

	Seldom 1	Sometimes 2	Often 3	Most Often 4
1. I understand how children of different ages play in different ways.				
2. I recognize individual differences in learning styles.				
3. I provide many activities and experiences that encourage active, "hands-on" play and learning.				
4. I plan activities to include many types of learning: blocks, books, art, pretend play, music, movement, etc.				
5. I provide at least three interesting activities or play areas for children to choose from daily.				
6. I select books, toys, and other materials that are appropriate for children of different ages.				
7. I set and enforce rules and limits on TV, video, and/or computer time.				
8. I listen and talk with children about many different topics that interest them.				
9. I use my observations of children's skills and interests to set goals and plan activities that will help them grow and learn.				
10. I ask many who, what, why, when, where, and how questions to help children learn and problem solve.				
11. I add to children's learning by giving them new information or adding new materials to their play.				
12. I know how to choose a theme or topic of interest for children and plan topic-related activities in all learning areas.				
13. I introduce activities and experiences that will recognize and honor children's different cultural backgrounds.				
14. I involve families in their children's learning by sharing ideas and activities they can do at home and by inviting them to visit and share their interests and skills.				
15. I introduce children to community resources through library story time, field trips, and neighborhood walks.				

Chapter 6

Creative play and learning

Three basic ways to help children learn

Children are learning all the time, but there are ways you can "turn on" the learning to make it much more fun and interesting.

Learning happens when you talk and interact with children. Your routine, daily conversations are important teaching tools. Talk with children about colors, shapes, sizes, how things work, and how things don't work. Listen to their responses.

You can observe children's individual skills and provide activities that will help them develop new skills or knowledge. For example, if Gabriella is interested in butterflies, you may want to read books about butterflies, grow a butterfly garden, and watch a cocoon hatch. If 4-year-old Adam is beginning to develop good finger skills, it is time to help him learn how to use scissors. Other good suggestions for how to develop activities that meet children's developmental needs can be found in chapter 7, Ages and Stages.

Create play areas or "learning centers" in your home. Child care is different from elementary school. You do not have to directly "teach" a "group" of children all day long—in fact this is not at all desirable for young children. They do best in individual and small group activities. And they learn a lot from each other through everyday play. Offering several learning centers such as art, pretend play, or table toys every day will give children choices and make your job easier.

You are a special teacher in children's lives

Talk "with" children—not "at" children. It is very easy to spend most of your time talking "at" children—telling them to clean up, wash hands, eat lunch, and so on. But what children really need is someone to talk "with" them. Children need to see you smile, listen, and have a conversation with them. Even infants need to have these important conversations with you. They are learning to understand language long before they can speak.

Listen and observe. You can help children learn if you know what their skills and interests are. Take time to watch them play. Often just a few minutes of observing will give you great ideas for activities they might be interested in.

Have "tell me about . . ." conversations. Let children know that you are interested in what they play and learn. For example, you might begin, "I notice that you have set up a yummy pizza shop here. Tell me about . . ."

Encourage learning by asking questions. Who, what, when, where, how, and why questions encourage children to think and problem solve. Try asking questions that begin with:
"Have you ever felt . . . ?"
"Can you find . . . ?"
"I wonder what would happen if . . . ?"
"Why do you think . . . ?"
"What else would . . . ?"

Avoid questions that only encourage one word responses like yes or no. The goal is to encourage children to think about what they are doing and talk about it.

Children learn in different ways

Children learn through play. When children work a puzzle they learn about size, shape, and space—basic math skills. When they pretend to play "house" they learn about relationships and how to get along. Singing songs, doing fingerplays, and playing with puppets enrich language skills. And cooking with you in the kitchen is early science at its best.

Children have different learning styles. Some children learn best through active play, touching, doing, and moving around. Other children seem to learn best by listening, talking, and asking questions. Some children are very cautious and hesitant to try new things. Other children are very impulsive and ready to jump right into a new activity. Too much noise and activity can upset some children; they do better when play is calm and low key. Some children seem to need a lot of touching and hugging; others will pull back and resist. Some children will stay focused on a play activity for a long time; others are more easily distracted. Paying attention to learning styles will help you choose the right activities for children.

Children of different ages play differently.
- **Solitary play**—Infants watch others, but play alone. They may hold an object and explore it by tasting, touching, smelling, and looking at it.
- **Parallel play**—Toddlers play alongside each other. They like to watch and be close to other children, but don't have the skills to interact well with others yet.
- **Cooperative play**—Older preschoolers and school-agers play with each other. They will take on pretend play roles, assign tasks, and negotiate.

Children love to do the same activity over and over again. They learn from repetition and enjoy finding new ways to use toys and materials. When the children arrive, you may notice that some will head to a space where they can play with blocks and others will want to curl up with a book. As children develop new skills, they will look for ways to make the same activity more complex and interesting.

Children love to play with everyday objects. Coats that zip, drawers that pull open, toilet paper that rolls, clocks that chime, ceiling fans that whirl, tea kettles that whistle, dishwashers that gurgle, and door knobs that twist are fascinating for young children. Homes are full of everyday items that children can explore.

Set goals for individual children

If you want to really make a difference in children's lives, you should plan activities to match their individual needs and interests. This also will make your work easier and more meaningful. This is a much better approach than coming up with a grab bag of ideas that may or may not work for your group of children.

Plan each week to focus on some specific skills children are developing. Children have a lot to learn. You can teach children colors and shapes, their first and last name, simple words, how to hop and skip, how to cut, how to share and negotiate, and so much more.

Make it a habit to watch and observe individual skills. Notice each child's physical, thinking, social, and emotional skills. Compare what you observe with what you know about normal ages and stages. You may want to look in chapter 7 to learn more. Choose at least one skill or interest each week for each child that you would like to encourage.

Notice any special interest in other subjects. Children always have unique interests. One child may be interested in trucks, another may delight in cooking. One child may be obsessed with dinosaurs. Note these special interests and plan for them in your weekly activities.

HFCCH Chapter 6 — Creative play and learning

What children are learning when they play

	Skills	Knowledge
Blocks	counting, sorting, classifying, measuring, estimating, planning, problem solving	balance, strength, gravity, shapes, patterns, cause and effect, quantity (more, less, same)
Art	developing small muscle skills, coordinating eye-hand movement, expressing emotions, making choices, planning, organizing, representing ideas visually	cause and effect, color, line, patterns, shape, size, balance, vocabulary
Books	reading, writing, listening, talking, coordinating eye muscles	alphabet basics; vocabulary rhymes and word patterns; word recognition; language; ideas and information about people, places, and things
Table toys and games	counting, estimating, problem solving, planning, making choices, negotiating	number recognition, quantity, patterns, cause and effect
Sand and water	measuring, estimating, predicting, problem solving	quantity (more, less, same), density, textures (smooth, rough, soft, gritty)
Music and movement	listening, singing, moving, developing small and large muscles	rhythm, pitch, sense of space, body awareness, physical skills, ideas and information
Cooking	planning, organizing, counting, measuring, predicting, estimating	quantity (more, less, same), cause and effect, word recognition, vocabulary
Pretend play	talking, listening, sharing, cooperating, negotiating, problem solving, creating	word recognition, vocabulary, language, self-awareness, awareness of others

Creating learning centers in your home

You can set up learning centers by being creative with the space you have. A space behind the sofa can be a quiet area for playing games or building with blocks. An arm chair or an empty closet with a few pillows can be a cozy place to read and look at books.

Water play can happen in the kitchen sink or in plastic tubs on the kitchen floor. Children can work puzzles on a wood coffee table. Art activities can happen at the kitchen table.

Children need a variety of places and spaces to explore. Being confined to one room is difficult. Fortunately, homes have bedrooms, kitchens, living rooms, family rooms, hallways, closets, bathrooms, and generally some type of outdoor play area. As long as these areas can be made safe and are easily supervised, they can provide a wonderful diversity of comfortable spaces to play and live.

Play spaces should be flexible. Ideally, spaces should be set up so they work for children during the day, but transform back into a regular home at the end of the day. If you have an extra room or basement, you may wish to set up play areas that are more permanent.

Pretend play

Pretending is something that young children do every day. At mealtime, Eric may pretend to be an alligator as he eats his fish sticks. During a walk to the park, Trisha may pretend to be a bus driver as she pulls two children in the wagon. Active imaginations help children explore their world and try on "roles" of special people.

Setting up a pretend play area

Children love to play house and pretend to cook, clean, care for babies, and take on the roles of mama, daddy, grandma, grandpa, sister, and brother. Family life is what young children know most about, so this is a good place to start.

HFCCH Chapter 6 — Creative play and learning

Choose a space. A corner works well. A large non-slip area rug on the floor can help define the space. The idea is to create a cozy, home-like area.

Choose basic props. A refrigerator, stove, sink, table, doll bed, full length mirror, and some type of shelf to hold dishes, pots, and pans are important. These items can be purchased or made from sturdy cardboard boxes. Place them like you would in any kitchen, across from each other or on separate walls.

Add accessory props. Use throwaway containers from your kitchen instead of pretend or plastic food. It looks more real. Also make sure you have good storage for these items so children can find them easily. Low shelves are preferable to baskets because children can see items better.

- broom and dustpan
- baby blankets
- a small table cloth
- a phone
- empty cracker boxes
- margarine tubs
- hats
- plastic milk bottles
- egg cartons
- paper sacks
- empty cans without sharp edges
- lunch boxes
- scarves
- purses
- wallets
- shoes
- jackets
- gloves
- dresses
- grocery receipts
- pretend money
- coupons
- pretend cash register

Simple ideas for pretend play prop boxes

Children want to play doctor, teacher, or grocery store. Put together prop boxes or bags based on themes and watch the fun!

- **Pizza restaurant:** Include pizza coupons, cardboard pizza box, old pizza cutter (dull blade), placemats covered with clear plastic or red checked table cloth, paper plates and cups (from local pizza vendor), play money, cash register, phone, and old billfold or purse.

- **Painter:** Painter's cap, painter's stick, old paint can with paint washed out, paint brushes, water, food coloring to tint water, measuring tape, sponges, and rags.

- **Mail carrier:** Hat, old stamps, mailbag (old purse), mailbox, old canceled envelopes, packages, play money, rubber stamps, cash register, raincoat, and rain boots.

- **Fishing:** Hat, net, tackle box, rubber boots, box for boat, cardboard oars, poles with strings, spools, cardboard fish, bucket, packing chips for worms (attach magnets to spool and fish), and spray bottles (for pretend rain).

- **Shoe store:** Assorted old shoes, mirrors (2 x 2 feet or long mirror laid on its side), play money or pretend credit cards, cash register, phone, keys, shoe boxes, sacks, shoehorn, and tape measure or ruler.

- **Car wash:** Buckets of water, rags, sponges, spray bottles, tricycles or wagons to wash, keys, and play money.

- **Camping:** Tent (or card table with blanket over it), binoculars, canteen, pots and pans, firewood, sticks, flashlight, jackets, kerchief, backpack, and compass.

- **Pet shop:** Stuffed animals, baskets and other cages, cash register, fish bowl, pet toys, pictures of pets, books about pets.

Other favorite themes are: barber shop or hairstylist, circus, hospital, office, supermarket, gas station, fire fighter, police officer, airplane, bus, and farm.

Playing house— not for girls only!

Learning about family life is important for boys too. They need to learn roles of father, cook, and housekeeper as they grow older. Be sure to help boys feel comfortable in the house area by providing dressup clothes that are appropriate for a male such as a man's hat, sneakers, tie, or overalls. A fix-up kit with a paint brush, tape measure, and pretend tools is also a helpful item. Boys often enjoy dolls and cooking items. Finally, watch what you say to children as they play. Adults can unknowingly say or do things that reinforce stereotypes. It is perfectly okay for a girl to pretend to mow the lawn and a boy to rock the baby to sleep.

Puppets

Puppets can be a comfortable go-between for painfully shy children. When a child uses a puppet, all attention is directed toward the puppet, leaving the child free to deliver his or her own message.

Puppets can help children sort out feelings. Strong emotions are hard for children. Puppets can help children act out feelings and get their message across. For example, puppets allow a child to gently nudge and push without hurting other children.

Puppets can help reduce childhood fears. By using a puppet to act out the part of the big dog or boy down the block, that fear may seem more controllable.

Puppets can quickly capture children's attention. When children seem to ignore your reminders to clean up, a puppet can come to the rescue and make things more fun.

Puppets can be decision makers. When children are begging to be first to play a game—let the puppet decide by drawing names out of a hat or bowl.

What pretend play looks like for children . . .

Infants and toddlers	Preschoolers	School-agers
Infants enjoy watching other children play "pretend." They are fascinated as older children change themselves by putting on a floppy hat and pretend sunglasses. **Infants try to explore pretend play props by touching, tasting, smelling, and hearing.** Check for small object playthings that can lead to choking in infants. **Toddlers play alongside others.** They spend a lot of time just carrying props around, often one in each hand. **Toddlers imitate and copy others.** A toddler watching preschoolers having a tea party may approach the table, pick up a cup, pretend to drink, and then walk off. Toddlers are not yet ready for complex play scenarios. **Toddlers need simple and realistic props.** They are likely to choose a hat rather than an elaborate costume.	**Preschoolers have vivid imaginations.** They can spend a good part of their day focused on pretend play and are likely to develop elaborate play scenarios with other children. **Family life is a favorite theme** because home life is what children know best. Other favorite play themes include shopping, visiting the zoo, camping. **Imaginations can be confusing.** Sometimes imaginations can get in the way of understanding the difference between reality and "pretend." **Imaginary playmates and fear of monsters are common.** Preschoolers are likely to scare themselves. You can tell a child there are no monsters living under the bed, but don't expect him or her to believe it.	**A favorite theme is school**, where preschoolers and toddlers get to be the "students." TV game shows are also a popular item. **School-agers' pretend play is more complex.** They may spend considerable time planning skits and plays and creating props. **School-agers prefer real props rather than toy ones.** For example, an old broken camera or flashlight would be a much more suitable prop for a school-ager than a toy camera. School-agers like to design background scenery, too. **School-agers are very project oriented.** However they often do not have a realistic idea of their capabilities and what is possible. **Frustration over props or skits that don't work well are common.** You will need to work with school-agers and help them set realistic goals.

Art

Art activities are a favorite with children. Supply materials that children can use in a variety of ways, and encourage their creativity.

Focus on the process rather than the end product. Coloring books, worksheets, or precut projects that are supposed to look a certain way stifle creativity. Young children have difficulty staying within the coloring book outlines and may have very different ideas about how to make a mask or puppet. Provide materials that let children be creative without having to do something "the right way" or "the same way." For example, avoid having the children make "look-alike" orange pumpkins.

Setting up for art activities

Make cleanup easy. A washable floor and a nearby sink are extremely helpful. Provide old shirts or children's aprons to protect clothing.

Basic art materials for children to choose from every day:
- paper
- crayons
- water-based markers
- play dough—cookie cutters, plastic knives, small rolling pin
- clay
- blunt-ended scissors
- collage materials—magazines, ribbons, fabric scraps, cotton balls, yarn
- paints
- brushes
- glue or paste
- cleanup items—sponges, brooms, mops, paper towels

Art recipes for play dough, clay, and finger paint can be found in chapter 4.

Make art materials easy to find and reachable. Low storage shelves or drawers work well. Use clear plastic boxes, juice cans, margarine tubs, old coffee cans, or ice cream tubs as storage containers. Group items of the same type together. Label each container with the name and picture of the item.

Consider an art easel. Children love to paint or draw pictures on an art easel. An easel can be set up for a good part of the day, and children can come and go as they choose.

What art play looks like for children . . .

Infants and toddlers	Preschoolers	School-agers
Infants and toddlers are interested in looking at colors and patterns and feeling textures. They observe and enjoy the art around them in everyday objects like pictures on the wall, patterns in the upholstery, and designs on the curtains or the floor. **Infants also enjoy sitting on your lap and watching other children paint.** They love to hear you talk about or describe what you are seeing. **A toddler will delight in playing with colorful scarves.** They also enjoy swatches of fabric or tearing paper. **Early attempts at drawing are random marks and scribbles.** Large crayons are easier to hold. Tape paper to the table to keep it from moving.	**Preschoolers enjoy experimenting with art materials.** They like to make different colors, patterns, and swirls. **Three-year-olds just like "doing" art.** They like to paint and draw just for the sake of painting and drawing. Usually, they do not intend to draw something that is recognizable. **Five-year-olds, however, will draw something and ask you to label it.** They also enjoy displaying the art with their name on it. **Preschoolers enjoy playing with other children.** They often like group art projects such as shadow tracing or a large mural.	**School-agers like to make things and are very interested in "real" crafts.** They will no longer be content to string wooden beads or play with play dough. They will want to make real jewelry with real beads and real pots or sculpture with self-hardening clay. **School-agers have high expectations.** They may become very frustrated because their drawing of a cat does not look like a real cat. **School-agers like to plan big projects.** Help them by joining in on the planning process. Guide them in making decisions and in polishing their skills.

30 simple art activities

Simple art activities are generally the best. All you have to do is vary the materials you offer and let the children take the lead.

Drawing
- Paper sacks or newsprint with markers
- Colored chalk on sidewalk
- Rock art—color or design with markers
- Placemats—cover drawing with clear adhesive shelf paper

Painting
- White paper with watercolors
- Yellow paper with orange and black paint
- Black paper with white tempera paint
- Sponge print paintings—paint sponge shapes and print
- Footprint paintings—paint feet and walk across paper
- Paint snow
- Coffee filters or paper towels with water colors
- Printing with paint—kitchen utensils, cookie cutters
- Printing with paint—combs, corks, spools, nuts, bolts

Collages
- Felt ribbon and fabric swatch collage
- Holiday wrapping paper collage
- Magazine picture collage
- Seed and bean collage
- Wood scrap collage
- Leaf collage—press autumn leaves

Sculpting
- Red and green play dough
- Play dough with cookie cutters
- Junk sculpture (glue or tape together recycled "junk")
- String necklaces with spools
- Rock sculptures—glue different rocks together
- Foil sculptures
- Pipe cleaner sculptures

Weaving
- Paper strips
- Pipe cleaners
- Ribbon and lace
- Paper chains

Art recipes

There are several sensory activities that can be done with young children. Try some of the following recipes to give young children hours of fun.

Squeeze-bottle glitter
   1 part flour
   1 part salt
   1 part water

Mix equal parts of flour, salt, and water. Pour into plastic squeeze bottles, such as those used for mustard and ketchup. Add liquid coloring for variety. Squeeze onto heavy construction paper or cardboard. The salt gives the designs a glistening quality when dry. The resulting pictures can be mounted and framed.

Gunk
   1 part cornstarch
   1 part water

Mix cornstarch and water together. This mixture can be colored by adding food coloring or dry tempera paint.

Silly putty
   liquid starch
   glue

Add equal amounts of liquid starch and glue.

Salt dough
   2 cups flour
   1 cup salt
   1 cup water

Add water slowly. Knead until smooth. Roll out, cut with cookie cutters, and poke a hole or insert a paper clip for hanging. This dough also can be used for sculpting. Bake at 275–300 degrees for about 45 minutes.

Colored bubbles
   1 cup granulated soap or soap powder
   1 quart warm water
   food coloring
   plastic straws
   small juice cans

Dissolve soap in warm water; stir in food coloring. Give each child a can about 1/3 full of soap mixture and a plastic straw. (Be sure to teach the children to blow out and not suck in.)

Additional art recipes can be found in chapter 4.

Table toys and board games

Children learn to sort, classify, and count with table toys and games. They also learn how to solve problems and play well with others.

Setting up for table toys and games

Basic supplies*: Puzzles, Legos™, Fisher-Price sets™, lotto, Tinker Toys™, Bristle Blocks™, stringing cards and beads are favorite learning toys. Favorite board and card games are Old Maid, Go Fish, Memory, Bingo, Candyland, Chinese checkers, and dominoes.

You also can use materials found around the house. Children can sort buttons and colored pebbles. They can match silverware, different-sized jars and lids, nuts and bolts. Many household items can be used to help children learn important concepts like big and small, in and out, up and down, over and under, and before and after.

Use a flat surface for table toys and games. A low table works well. You can store a large piece of vinyl flooring under a bed or sofa and pull it out when children want to play. Trays will help children keep small pieces together. Store items in separate containers on low shelves for easy cleanup.

Rotate toys. If you have a large number of puzzles, table toys, and games, set out a few of each at a time. Put away the rest in a closet. Children become overwhelmed when they have too many choices for play.

Keep things safe. Remember to look for and eliminate pieces less than 1 1/4 inches, because they present a choking hazard to infants and toddlers. When you do have games that include small pieces, put them out of reach and let children request them. This will allow you to supervise their use more closely.

*No endorsement of products or firms is intended, nor is criticism implied of those not mentioned.

What table toys play looks like for children . . .

Infants and toddlers	Preschoolers	School-agers
Infants and toddlers like to use their senses. They are most interested in objects that they can see, smell, touch, taste, feel, and explore. **Infants like to explore different textures.** They like to play with large wooden spoons, lids, and plastic blocks. **Toddlers like to stack, dump and fill.** They enjoy playing with nesting or stacking cups. They also spend a lot of time dumping and filling containers with small objects.	**Preschoolers enjoy solving problems.** Working puzzles and playing with pegboards or plastic blocks help children learn important problem-solving skills. **Children under 5 have a hard time understanding games with rules.** For preschoolers, choose simple games that involve a series of actions rather than a set of rules. For example, count and match the dots on dominoes, play Memory with matching picture cards. **Young children are focused more on the fun of playing rather than the end result.** They are more interested in rolling the dice and counting the number of spaces to move than in deciding who is winning the game.	**School-agers enjoy more complex jigsaw puzzles.** A puzzle set up on a card table can provide ongoing fun for many days. **Card games and dominoes are favorites.** Both help children develop math and problem-solving skills. **School-age children will have their own ideas about how a game should go.** Even though they have a better understanding of rules and competition, older children sometimes become frustrated and want to change the rules when they do not suit their situation. **They may need a referee when the rules and competition get hard.** Be prepared to support the hurt feelings of "losers."

HFCCH Chapter 6 — Creative play and learning

Block play

Building with blocks helps children learn basic math concepts. Discovering how many small blocks can be laid end to end to equal one long block introduces addition and the idea of fractions. Balancing blocks to construct a tower illustrates some basic principles of physics. The world of young builders is a fascinating place and one you can help develop.

Setting up for block play

The key to success in block building is plenty of blocks. There are many kinds of blocks: hardwood, cardboard, plastic interlocking blocks, hollow blocks, and soft sponge blocks. You may want to have several types available for children, but if money is limited focus on one type first. Ideas and plans for making blocks can be found in chapter 4.

Provide enough space. If you have a large living room or basement you have an advantage when it comes to block play. An ideal place, of course, is an out-of-the-way corner, where block structures will be protected from foot traffic and vice versa. Store blocks on low shelves for easy cleanup. Good props to use with blocks include toy animals, people, trucks or cars, and small colored blocks. If a low shelf is not available, you may want to store blocks on a movable cart and use the cart to transport blocks outdoors too.

Establish boundaries. If you find that children are expanding too far into other indoor play areas, you may need to set some boundaries. One easy way to do this is to use masking tape and tape a boundary line on the floor. This seems to work well for many children. In fact, they will sometimes step high as they walk over a line, much like they would over a higher boundary.

What block play looks like for children . . .

Infants and toddlers	Preschoolers	School-agers
Infants like to hold and drop blocks. They also like to explore textures and may try to taste. **Toddlers like to carry and push down blocks.** Toddlers also will spend a great deal of time dumping blocks in a pile, picking them up again, and moving them elsewhere. **They begin to learn about size and weight.** They understand how many blocks they can carry and how one block can be heavier or lighter than another.	**Children first learning to use blocks will stack or line them up.** Sometimes they make patterns. **Next they learn to build fence-like enclosed structures or bridge-like structures.** They learn to balance one block on top of two other blocks. **Older preschoolers will build more complex structures.** They are also likely to seek out pretend props such as a fire truck or farm animals to make their structure more complete.	**School-agers often test the extremes of balance or height.** They like to create complex structures. **School-agers like to work with others to plan and design.** They enjoy problem solving together. **They may resist taking apart their structure at cleanup time.** They like to take pictures of their block structures to show to family members.

Sand and water play

Playing with sand and water is tremendous fun! Many providers will tell you there is something almost magical about sand and water. Children experience life less verbally and intellectually than adults, and touch takes on added importance. An environment that allows children to "mess around" with many different substances is rich in learning opportunities.

Splashing, swirling, and pouring can be very soothing. Children who are overly distressed or anxious benefit a great deal from sand and water play. They learn by exploring the qualities of materials by pouring, sifting, mixing, and measuring (and avoiding spills).

Children also learn how substances go together. Water can be colored or soapy. Sand can be dry or wet. Children also may add things that they find around them such as sticks, stones, and leaves. Older children may get involved in designing dams, diggers, makeshift construction equipment, or a whole marina of boats.

Setting up for sand and water play

Sand and water play can happen both outdoors and indoors. Use the outdoor sandbox in the warm months, and plan for a "day at the beach" indoors for those winter months. A plastic wading pool with sand or water, a few beach towels, and a picnic lunch on the kitchen floor can provide relief from cabin fever.

Choose a space. The kitchen or bathroom floor, the sink, bathtub, or plastic tubs all work well for indoor sand and water play. Use an old tablecloth or shower curtain to protect the floor.

Supervise closely. When using the kitchen or bathroom, lock or childproof cabinets, cover electrical outlets, and never leave children alone with water. Children can burn themselves if they turn on a hot water faucet, and a very young child can drown in just a few inches of water.

Basic supplies:

Sand: Buckets and shovels, measuring cups and spoons, sifter, colander, muffin tins, pretend dishes, rolling pin, sea shells, pebbles and rocks, funnels, small pretend people, dinosaurs, trucks or cars.

Water: Plastic dolls, wash cloths, soap bubbles, egg beater, turkey baster, eye dropper, food coloring, buckets, funnels, measuring cups and spoons, squirt bottles, sponges, corks, squeeze bottles, whisks, and paint brushes.

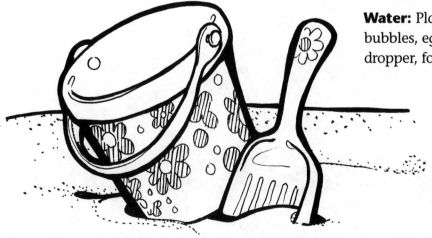

What sand and water play looks like for children . . .

Infants and toddlers	Preschoolers	School-agers
Infants and toddlers love to feel sand and splash water. They also enjoy the sensory experiences of wet, dry, cool, and hot. **Toddlers practice using their hands and fingers.** They can spend a lot of time swishing, scooping, pouring, and stirring. **A frustrated toddler finds water or sand play very soothing.** Sand and water can be a great preventive tool for behavior problems.	**They like to experiment.** They discover that some items sink while others float. **Preschoolers like to pretend.** They enjoy adding props to sand and water play. Plastic dinosaurs, jungle animals, fire trucks, and dolls are special favorites. **They like to interact with friends.** They may help each other pour water or sand and trade buckets or shovels.	**School-age children are very project oriented.** They will build complex sand structures such as tunnels or castles. **They like things to look realistic.** They may bring in rocks or make designs with colored sand. **They enjoy planning and problem solving together.** At times they may draw sketches and assign tasks.

HFCCH Chapter 6 — Creative play and learning

TV time

Children who watch TV at home may expect to watch it at child care too. Adult programming is not appropriate for children. Children often watch commercials, because they are attention grabbers. Many commercials promote risky behaviors, show inappropriate sexual content, and contribute to obesity.

Studies show that TV has many negative effects for children.
- Children who watch TV a lot are more likely to be overweight.
- Children who view violent events, such as a kidnapping or murder, are more likely to believe that the world is scary and that something bad will happen to them.
- Children are more likely to be influenced by gender-role and racial stereotypes.

Even educational TV leaves a lot to be desired. It is better for children to learn from "hands-on" experimenting, reading, pretending, and interacting with other children. Active play is healthier than time spent sitting on the sofa.

The American Academy of Pediatrics (AAP) recommends that children under age 2 should have no "screen time" at all. Children older than 2 should watch no more than 1 to 2 hours a day of quality programming. Most likely children will get this 1-2 hours at home. So that leaves no place for it in child care.

Resist the temptation to turn on the TV.

Books

Children learn about people, places, and events through books. An area for books allows children to relax quietly and get away from it all.

Reading books every day sets the stage for later learning. Children who are read to early in life are likely to enjoy books and become good readers later on.

Setting up a reading area

A reading or rest area is one of the easiest places to set up. A sofa or comfy chair works well. Children can use a quiet, out-of-the-way place, like the space behind a chair or sofa, under a table, in a large cardboard box, or in a corner with soft pillows. Provide natural or soft lamp light, and store books on a low shelf or in a magazine holder.

Tips for reading

Reading, listening, and writing are important skills that you can foster early in a child's life. The following are some suggestions to help children love to read.

Establish a regular time every day for reading books. Better yet, read several times a day. Books give children a sense of what reading and writing are all about.

Ask parents to get a library card for their child. Make regular visits to the library. Take advantage of library story times and special events.

Preschoolers enjoy hearing the same story over and over again. Reading books with repeat phrases such as "The House That Jack Built," gives young children an opportunity to participate by letting them read the repetitive parts with you.

Preschoolers love to "pretend" to read by telling a favorite story they have memorized. Allow children access to books throughout the day.

Ask questions or talk about what is waiting for them at the turn of a page. Questions like "How many pigs are there? Let's count them together," "Why is the puppy dog sad?" "Can you show me everything in this picture that is red?" and "What do you think will happen next?" all help children develop important language skills.

Encourage older children to tell stories or read aloud to the younger children. They also may read aloud a dramatic piece from a play or a poem. Older children often love to put on a good performance.

Help children understand the structure of a book. Stories have a beginning, a middle, and an end. We read from the top of the page to the bottom of the page. We read from left to right—the front of the book to the back of the book. We read words. Words are different from pictures and tell us different things.

Help children recognize simple words. Show children how pictures can give us a clue about what the words might say.

Make an "US" book using a photo album. Use pictures of children in your care, routine activities like eating and napping, other learning activities, your house exterior, friends, favorite animals, toys, etc. Albums with magnetic pages are sturdy and easy to keep clean and allow you to change pictures easily. You also can use snapshots, post cards, magazines, and catalog pictures.

Explain the joy and importance of reading regularly. Before children can become readers, they must learn why people read and what people do when they read.

Invite children to help you read a recipe as you cook. Read cooking instructions out loud. Point out measurement markings on measuring cups and spoons.

Provide other types of reading materials. Use TV schedules, junk mail, old catalogs, and magazines for pretend play and art projects. When you are outdoors, read out loud traffic signs, road signs, and billboards.

Choosing books

Whether purchasing books or borrowing them from the library, it is important to look for quality. Use the following guidelines to select books that children will be sure to love.

Select different books for different ages. Infants and toddlers need durable cardboard or cloth books with simple pictures. Drawings or pictures of familiar objects are best. Preschoolers like books that have simple but predictable stories. School-agers like beginning reader and nonfiction books.

Look for books with clear, colorful illustrations. Because young children cannot read well yet, they spend a great deal of time looking at and learning from pictures. The illustrations should follow the story line.

Select books that match children's interests and concerns. If a toddler likes trucks, try to find several books about trucks. If a preschooler will soon have a new baby sister, seek out books about a new baby. If your children are eagerly awaiting the first snow, check out a book about winter time.

Choose books that involve children. Stories that encourage children to count, rhyme, sing along, or guess the ending are great favorites.

Avoid books with pictures or text that reflect gender, race, age, or disability bias. Look for books that portray women and minorities in positive ways. Seek out books that include characters from different cultures or individuals with disabilities.

Avoid books that promote commercialized products or advertisements. These books are usually of poor quality.

Avoid books that promote violent behaviors. Children may try to imitate behaviors. They have a hard time understanding the difference between reality and make-believe.

Look for language in books that is respectful of different lifestyles, cultures, and life situations. For example, avoid books that suggest that children from divorced parents come from "broken homes." Language that depicts certain ethnic groups as "lazy," "backward," or "savage" also should be avoided.

Suggested books for children
Try to have a few of your own books for children to read. Trips to the public library can add variety. Children also may like to bring books from home to share at story time. Ideally you should have at least 12-20 books for children to choose from, with 2-3 books suitable for each age group. See book list in chapter 4.

Food and cooking

Cooking does not have to be something you need to accomplish with a baby perched on one hip, a toddler crawling into the pantry, and two preschoolers coloring at the kitchen table.

Children of all ages can help with cooking. The baby may be content to watch and mouth a wooden spoon, but a toddler would love to stir the batter. And the preschoolers can set the table, sift flour, measure, and pour milk. Children enjoy scrubbing carrots and whipping no-cook pudding. School-agers may be ready to make some food all by themselves.

Children learn to appreciate food if they have helped prepare it. Picky eaters also may eat new foods more willingly.

Cooking teaches children about science and math. They learn about how eggs cook, and about counting and measuring.

Cooking teaches basic reading skills. Children learn that words and writing are found on food labels and recipe cards. Learning to read may start with a favorite recipe.

HFCCH Chapter 6 — Creative play and learning 121

Cooking teaches life skills. Cooking and eating are a part of life. Everyone needs to learn the basics of preparing food and about good nutrition.

Setting up for cooking

Setting up a child-friendly kitchen takes a little planning. The following suggestions may help.

Use child-size tables and chairs. Another option would be to purchase wide, sturdy stools for children to stand on.

Color code utensils. Purchase red serving spoons and red vinyl tape to mark utensils. (Vinyl tape stays on well in the dishwasher.) Teach children that the red utensils are for serving, mixing, and measuring; no licking or tasting allowed!

Use clear bowls and measuring cups. Food will be easier to see and measure.

Use child-sized utensils. Bend the metal handles of measuring spoons so that children can measure liquids easily. Plastic measuring spoons and cups also work well.

Serve food in shallow bowls rather than on plates. Little hands can scoop food up more easily.

Use small pitchers filled only half-way for pouring juice or milk. Pitchers with adjustable spouts or lids help to regulate the amount of liquid poured.

Learning new words and ideas through food experiences

Children learn about colors, shapes, temperature, sizes, and quantities. Discuss red and green apples, round oranges, square cheese cubes, warm bread, and cold juice. Talk with children about the round shapes of bananas or tomatoes as they are sliced. Children can compare a "short" celery stick with a "long" one. Count out "2 eggs," or note that there are "a lot" of grapes on a "bunch," but only "1" plum "per" person.

Children learn about sequences—that one thing happens after another—as they help prepare muffins. They begin to understand ideas of time and change as they wait for muffins to come out of the oven.

Children learn about science. They watch dough rise, soup boil, and ice melt.

Children learn about their world. Talk about where fish comes from, how butter is made, or how corn grows. Consider making butter or visiting a farm. Talk about food from different cultures.

What cooking activities look like for children . . .

Infants and toddlers	Preschoolers	School-agers
Infants like to smell, taste, and touch food. Infants participate in the kitchen by smelling foods warming on the stove, tasting a tiny bit of spaghetti sauce, or poking their finger in the oatmeal. **Infants learn that eating is a comfortable social activity,** especially when held during feeding time or seated next to other children around the table. **Toddlers like to experiment.** They like to taste, touch, crumble, shake, squish, and drop food off the edge of the table. **Toddlers are learning to use a spoon and fork.** Finger foods work well for toddlers, but they also need to practice eating at least one item with a spoon.	**Preschoolers like to be independent and love to help.** They like to set the table and prepare simple food items. **Preschoolers need to practice basic cooking tasks.** Stirring orange juice or spreading jam on toast are activities that preschoolers can handle well. Spreading, tearing, stirring, and pouring help children develop small muscles and eye-hand coordination. **Preschoolers need lots of practice learning to use a fork and spoon.** Canned green beans and meat loaf are great items to eat with a fork. **Preschoolers are more interested in trying new foods.** Now is a good time to introduce tasting games so children can sample different foods.	**School-agers can cook using simple recipes.** They can make fruit salad, bake muffins, or prepare spinach dip. **School-agers like to print recipes and share them with family members.** School-agers also like to collect recipes or make cookbooks. **Many school-agers enjoy planning weekly menus.** They enjoy making a shopping list of needed items and looking through cookbooks.

22 Simple cooking activities

- slice bananas (with sturdy plastic knives)
- cut cheese with a wire cheese cutter
- stir orange juice
- spread butter on muffins
- peel hard boiled eggs
- spread jam on toast
- tear lettuce
- hull strawberries
- stir muffin batter
- spread refried beans on a tortilla
- cut bread or cheese with cookie cutters

Tasting games—Offer sample bite-size pieces of all the items.

- **Fresh fruits**—Apple, pear, banana, peach, apricot, grapes, strawberries, raspberries, pineapple, kiwi, orange, nectarine, blueberries, and grapefruit.

- **Vegetables**—Tomato, peas, celery, grated carrot, zucchini, lettuce, cabbage, onions, cucumber, turnip, broccoli, cauliflower, radish, and spinach.

- **Breads**—Sourdough, whole wheat, French, rye, pumpernickel, raisin, and oat.

- **Cheese**—Cheddar, Swiss, Monterey Jack, Muenster, Roquefort, Mozzarella, and cottage cheese.

- **Beans**—Red beans, garbanzos, black-eyed peas, navy beans, lima beans, and black beans.

- **Milk**—Whole milk, nonfat milk, powdered milk, chocolate milk, buttermilk, pudding, custard, and yogurt.

- **Condiments**—Salsa, ketchup, mustard, relish, tartar sauce, soy sauce, sour cream, and mayonnaise.

- **Juices**—Apple, orange, lemonade, grape, pineapple, cranberry, tomato, grapefruit, and apricot.

- **Strawberries**—Fresh, frozen strawberries, strawberry jam, strawberry icing, strawberry popsicle, and strawberry milk shake.

- **Carrots**—Grated, cooked, carrot cake, carrot juice, and frozen carrots.

- **Bananas**—Frozen bananas, fresh, banana chips, and banana nut bread.

Music and movement

Children enjoy music in many ways. It offers them a way to move and be active.

Setting up for music and movement

Basic equipment:
- tape or CD player
- tapes or CDs (from library)
- radio
- musical instruments (cymbals, maracas, bells, chimes, wooden sticks or blocks)
- Dancing props: scarves, banners, paper streamers, or pom-poms.

Space for movement and dancing can be found just about anywhere. Wide open spaces are great but so is a long hallway. At times, children prefer to snuggle up in a corner with a pillow and listen to music quietly.

Create homemade instruments. Old aluminum pots and pans are great to bang on with a wooden spoon. The lids make great cymbals. Plastic salt shakers or spice jars with a few pebbles make good rattles or maracas. Tape pie tins or paper plates together to make a tambourine. Make drums from coffee cans or oatmeal containers. Beans or seeds in margarine tubs or film canisters make great shakers. Children also love to clap hands and snap their fingers to create a rhythmic sound.

"How to Walk Like an Elephant"... and other body movement rhymes

Body movement rhymes and exercises are great favorites with kids. Rhymes can be used to teach children directions, concepts, and simple counting.

To the tune of "The Mulberry Bush"
Here we go to the zoo in the park, the zoo in the park, the zoo in the park. Here we go to the zoo in the park so early in the morning.
(Join hands and swing arms like an elephant's trunk)
This is the way the elephant walks, the elephant walks, the elephant walks. This is the way the elephant walks so early in the morning.
(Hop like a kangaroo)
This is the way the kangaroo hops, the kangaroo hops, the kangaroo hops. This is the way the kangaroo hops so early in the morning.
(Continue with other animals—hopping rabbits, walking penguins, etc.)

Two little feet
Two little feet go tap, tap, tap.
Two little hands go clap, clap, clap.
A quick little leap up from the chair,
two little hands fly up in the air.
Two little fists go bump, bump, bump.
Two little feet go jump, jump, jump.
One little body turns round, round, round,
And one little child sits quietly down.

Taller, Smaller
When I stretch up, I feel so tall;
When I bend down, I feel so small.
Taller, taller, taller, taller;
Smaller, smaller, smaller, smaller,
Into a tiny ball.

High, Low, Around We Go
We clap up high, we clap down low,
We jump, jump, jump and around we go.
Up and down, up and down,
Clap your hands and turn around.
or... Clap your hands and sit right down.

All Sizes
As high as a house;
(reach up high)
As small as a mouse;
(crouch down low)
As wide as a barn;
(feet apart, arms spread wide)
As thin as a pin.
(stand straight)

One More
One child stands up,
One child turns around,
One child claps hands,
And then sits down.
Two children stand up,
Two children turn around,
Two children clap hands,
And then sit down.

(Continue adding children.)
We all stand up,
We all turn around,
We all clap hands
And then sit down.

To the tune of "London Bridge"
(point to the body parts mentioned)
Head and shoulders, knees and toes, knees and toes, knees and toes. Head and shoulder, knees and toes. Eyes, ears, chin, and nose.

I Spy
I spy someone wearing red;
Stand up, turn around,
Touch that red.
   (Repeat with other color names.)
I spy every color I know;
Stand up, turn around,
We're a rainbow!

Fingerplays and Rhymes

When children repeat fingerplays and rhymes, they are learning and practicing many important language skills: building vocabulary, rhyming, rhythm, memory, matching words with actions—just to name a few. Verses also can help develop children's muscle coordination and listening skills. Their understanding of concepts such as counting, colors, and space (up, down, behind, etc.) also is strengthened.

Little, Bigger, Biggest
A little ball,
(make ball with finger and thumb)
A bigger ball,
(make ball with two hands)
And a great big ball I see.
(make a ball with arms)
Now help me count them,
One, two, three!

(repeat gestures for each size)
[Variations: Use cut-out paper shapes or real objects to show the three sizes. Create additional verses with other shapes of differing sizes.]

Favorite Foods
I like watermelon, how about you? Let's eat and eat 'til the day is through!
(eating motions)
Oh, I think I've had enough,
(hands on tummy)
Let's try something different. . .
(substitute other foods that are children's favorites)
(Last verse, last line. . .)
Let's go out and play!

HFCCH Chapter 6 — Creative play and learning

Funny Bunny
Here is a bunny
(raise two fingers)
With ears so funny
And here is a hole in the ground.

(make hole with fingers of other hand)
At the first sound she hears,
She pricks up her ears

(straighten fingers)
And pops right into the ground.
(put fingers in hole)

Tool Time
Peter works with
1 hammer, 1 hammer, 1 hammer

(one fist moving up and down)
Peter works with one hammer, now he works with 2.
Peter works with 2 hammers, etc.
(two fists)
Peter works with 3 hammers, etc.
(two fists and one foot)
Peter works with 4 hammers, etc.
(two fists and two feet)
Peter works with 5 hammers, 5 hammers, 5 hammers
(two fists, two feet and head nodding)
Peter works with 5 hammers,
Now his work is done.

[Note: Substitute any name for Peter. You also can make the fingerplay longer by counting backwards from 5 down to no hammers before saying, "Now his work is done."]

Home Sweet Home
A nest is a home for a robin;
(cup hands to form a nest)
A hive is a home for a bee;
(turn cupped hands over)
A hole is a home for a rabbit;
(make a hole with hands)
And a house is a home for me.
(make roof with peaked hands)

[Note: If these animals are not common in your geographic area, substitute other animals that are. Consider other types of people homes as well. Also, encourage children to help lengthen the poem by adding more animals and homes to make additional verses.]

Dancing Fingers
Thumbs are up;
Thumbs are down;
Thumbs are dancing
All around the town.

Pointers up;
Pointers down;
Pointers dancing
All around the town.

(additional verses)
Tall fingers up, etc.
Ring fingers up, etc.
Little fingers up, etc.
All fingers up, etc.

Quiet Cats
(use hands, crawl, or tip toe)
We are little pussy cat.
Walking round and round.
We have cushions on our feet *(whisper)* And never make a sound.

Amazing Fingers
I have ten fingers and they all belong to me; I can make them move—would you like to see? I can shut them tight, I can open them wide, I can put them together, I can make them hide, I can make them jump high, I can make them jump low, I can fold them quietly and hold them just so.

Opposites

Roll your hands so slowly,
As slowly as can be;
Roll your hands so slowly,
And fold your arms like me.

(additional verses . . .)
Roll your hands so quickly, etc.
Clap your hands so softly, etc.
Clap your hands so loudly, etc.

Big Fat Hen

1,2, buckle my shoe,
3,4, shut the door,
5,6, pick up sticks,
7,8, lay them straight,
9, 10, a big fat hen!

Spring is coming

Spring is coming,
Spring is coming,
How do you think I know?
I saw the green grass growing,
I know it must be so!

Spring is coming,
Spring is coming,
How do you think I know?
I heard a robin singing,
I know it must be so!

(additional verses . . .)
. . . I felt a warm wind blowing . . . I smelled a blooming flower . . .
[Make up additional verses for other seasons.]

The Field Trip Rhyme

[You will need to do the "before" activity below before trying the rhyme.]

Going on a field trip,
Leaving right away.
If we could, we'd stay all day!

Going to the [name of destination]
What will we see?
Use your imagination;
Now tell me.

We might see a _____ and we might see a _____. And we might see a _____ and a __ _____. We might see a _____ and we might see a _____. And we might see a _____ and a _____.

Hello, Neighbor!

Hello, [child's name], how do you do?
Who is the person next to you? [child says next person's name] [Continue until all the children and adults in the group have had a turn.]

Picnic Time

Going on a picnic,
Gotta pack a lunch.
What should we bring to munch, munch,munch? [list children's ideas of food for a picnic]
[You read from list. . .]
Let's bring sandwiches, [children echo. . .] sandwiches, sandwiches.[continue with all the foods listed]
Ready for a picnic,
Ready with a lunch,
Now we're ready to munch, munch, munch!

[Variation #1—Give each child a picture of a food item. Then, for the second verse, you say: "Who'll bring (sandwiches)?" and the child with that food item answers, "I'll bring (sandwiches)".
Variation #2—Hold up pictures of food items one at a time and, for the second verse, everyone say, "Let's bring (sandwiches, sandwiches, sandwiches)."]

The Apple Tree

Way up high in the apple tree,
(point up high)
Two little apples smiling at me;
(make two circles with hands)
I shook that tree as hard as I could;
(wrap hands around "trunk" and shake)
Down came the apples and
(two circle hands come down)
Mmmm, they were good!
(rub tummy)

Names

Names, names, we all have names;
Here is a friend to tell hers/his:_____
[choose a child]
Names, names, we all have names;
Let's join in and spell hers/his:_____
[Continue until everyone has had a turn.]
[Variation #1—Give each child a card with his or her name printed on it. Each child should hold it so it is facing everyone else when it is his or her turn.
Variation #2—You keep the cards with children's names printed on them. Hold them up one at a time, having the child identify her or his name by saying it out loud on the second line of the rhyme.]

What music and movement looks like for children . . .

Infants and toddlers	Preschoolers	School-agers
Babies are calmed by lullabies and gentle music. Rocking and swaying have similar effects too. Some studies even indicate that infants respond to music and movement in the womb. **Lively music can excite babies.** They may kick and wave their arms. **Toddlers love music and respond to it with their whole bodies.** They may bounce slightly, turn around in circles, or clap hands. **Toddlers love to copy or imitate.** They love to hear nursery rhymes, imitate gestures, and echo key words.	**Preschoolers are full of energy and creativity.** They will dance wildly to music or bounce around the room. They also love to dance with scarves and streamers or march with percussion instruments. **Preschoolers like to practice different creative movements.** Teach and encourage children to move their bodies in a variety of ways like tiptoeing, creeping, wiggling, galloping, twirling, swaying, shaking, and rolling. **Preschoolers love to pretend.** They love to move like animals or special objects. Try flying like a bird, bouncing like a kangaroo, or shaking like a leaf.	**School-age children enjoy creating songs and dances.** They also like to make or play instruments. **School-agers like to teach younger children.** They enjoy doing fingerplays with younger children and teaching them popular dance steps. **School-agers enjoy listening to their own music.** They may ask to bring CDs or tapes of their own and either share them or listen to them with headphones. **School-agers use music to relax and unwind.** They may wish to listen for a few minutes after school.

30 simple movement activities

Creative movement
- Move like a balloon losing air
- Move like a falling leaf
- Move like a melting snowman
- Move like a slippery snake
- Move like a hopping frog
- Move like a large elephant
- Tip toe, hop, skip, roll, walk backward—from here to there
- Dance with scarves
- Dance to different types of music: rock and roll, blues, classical
- Dance to music of different cultures

Action songs and rhymes
- "Row, row, row, your boat"
- "London Bridge is falling down."
- "If you're happy and you know it"
- "Old Mac Donald had a farm"

Action games
- Bowling with balls and milk carton blocks
- Balloon chases
- Flashlight beam chases
- Obstacle course
- Follow the leader
- Bean bag or sponge toss
- Bean bag crawl—(bean bag on child's back)
- Potato on a spoon race

Fingerplays
- The Apple Tree
- Big Fat Hen
- Amazing Fingers

Learning games
- Marching band with real or pretend instruments
- March in a line, circle, square, triangle
- Measure distance in steps, hops, skips
- Move arms in alphabet letter shapes
- Walk in alphabet letter shapes: C, D, J, L, M, N, O, S, U, V, W, Z

Outdoor play

The great outdoors offers tremendous opportunities for children. Being outside gives children a chance to run, jump, play, discover nature, and learn about the environment.

Almost anything that can be done indoors also can be done outdoors. On a beautiful day, you may want to move regularly scheduled activities like snack and reading time outside. Once outside, dramatic play often moves to themes like mail carrier, camping, or car wash. The different sizes and shapes of rocks, flower petals, and leaves offer children hundreds of opportunities to sort, match, and classify. Sand and water play are also natural activities for outdoor time.

Basic supplies: buckets, large paint brushes, baskets, shovels, scoops, funnels, wagon, small wheelbarrow, child-size gardening tools, watering can, trucks, cars, balls, wheel toys, spray bottles, blanket, sidewalk chalk, pretend play items.

What active outdoor play looks like for children...

Infants and toddlers	Preschoolers	School-agers
Infants and toddlers use their senses to learn. They love to explore, taste, touch, smell, and hear. They learn from the smell of a flower, the touch of tree bark, the feel of hot pavement, or the sound of a passing car. **Infants like to watch other children play and to crawl on different surfaces.** They can sometimes get in the way of older children's play, so they need to be watched closely. **Toddlers can wander off easily.** It is a good idea to have a fenced area to play. **Toddlers love to fill and dump.** A bucket and a few rocks can keep them entertained for a long time.	**Preschoolers have a lot of energy.** Being outdoors gives them a chance to run, jump, bounce, and yell. **Preschoolers spend a lot of time observing and experimenting outdoors.** They learn by watching a twig float in a puddle, a frog hop across the garden, or a tree shed its leaves. **Preschoolers like to pretend.** They will often bring pretend play outdoors. Super hero play and camping are popular themes.	**School-agers need a break.** Outdoor play provides the needed release for school-agers, who are in school all day. **School-agers like challenging projects.** They may be interested in planning and organizing elaborate projects such as building a clubhouse or selling lemonade. **School-agers take risks.** They like to test their physical abilities. They may be older, but they still need close supervision. **School-agers often participate in team sports.** You may want to provide a variety of balls, bats, gloves, or tennis rackets to allow them to practice their skills.

30 simple ideas for outdoor play

- Paint a fence with buckets of water and large paint brushes
- Wash tricycles and wagons
- Build a fort, castle, or spaceship with boxes
- Plant a garden
- Make snow angels
- Blow bubbles
- Sprinkle or spray colored water on the snow
- Wash doll clothes and hang them out to dry
- Have a picnic
- Bathe plastic dolls
- Play hopscotch
- Play hide-and-seek
- Toss bean bags at a target
- Roll balls down the sidewalk
- Roll hula hoops
- Play follow the leader
- Go for a hike
- Stomp barefoot in puddles
- Read a book under a shady
- Collect bugs
- Set up a tent and play camping
- Wash rocks
- Color with chalk on the sidewalk
- Dig for worms
- Set up a lemonade stand
- Draw shadow outlines with chalk
- Collect leaves, acorns, or pine cones
- Rake leaves
- Make an obstacle course
- Walk like different animals

HFCCH Chapter 6 — Creative play and learning

Explore the community

Children can learn a lot from everyday experiences with people, places, and things. All it requires is some planning and watching. Children enjoy watching a truck getting loaded or unloaded, the mail carrier at work in the neighborhood, a house painter at work, or the neighbor's roof being repaired.

Field trip supply kits

Car supplies
- Large water jug for drinks and hand washing
- Cups
- Liquid soap
- Paper towels
- Lightweight blanket
- Car seats
- Strollers
- Portable potty chair
- Extra clothing
- First aid kit
- Books, puppets, bubbles
- Plastic bags for trash

Backpack supplies
- Emergency cards—with parent permission signature and emergency contact information
- Cell phone
- Whistle
- Camera
- Small zipper-like plastic bags (for treasures)
- Sunscreen
- Bug spray
- Hand sanitizer
- Diapers
- Wipes and tissues
- Diaper changing pad

30 simple ideas for field trips or community visitors

- **Police officer**—Police departments encourage police officers to explain their work in the community to children. They may bring a police car or motorcycle to your home for the children to see.
- **Fire fighter**—Fire departments are happy to have children come to the fire station to see the engines, ladders, and other equipment. Fire fighters may even bring a fire truck to your home.
- **Nurse**—Many hospitals or nursing schools have student nurses who will come to private homes and give demonstrations as well as talk about what nurses do.
- **Hair stylist**—Children will enjoy watching a hair stylist shampoo and cut a child's hair.
- **Pilot**—An airplane pilot has an interesting job, and one may come to your home to explain it. If you live close to an airport, you might arrange to have the children go on board an airplane.
- **Plumber**—Invite a plumber to show children how wrenches and other tools are used to fix clogged drains.
- **Zookeeper**—Visit a local zoo with the children, and maybe arrange a personal visit with the zookeeper. Zoos sometimes have animal trainers who will bring animals to child care homes.

Other people to see
- chefs
- truck or bus drivers
- doctors
- mail carriers
- teachers
- musicians
- restaurant workers
- artists

Places to see
- ice cream shop
- hardware store
- post office
- park
- library
- bakery
- pet store
- farm
- candy shop
- florist shop
- garden center
- bicycle shop
- recycling center
- music store
- apple orchard

HFCCH Chapter 6 — Creative play and learning

Tips for an enjoyable outing

Plan trips. Consider the children's needs for snacks, meals, using the bathroom, naps, etc. Do not plan trips to places where they are required to be still or quiet for long.

Keep it simple. A trip to the grocery store can be very enjoyable. Children can walk around, touch the cans on the shelf, look at the meat, smell the bread baking, see the fruits and vegetables, push the cart, and feel the cold air in the refrigerator case.

Involve children in the action. Children do not learn well by just hearing and looking; they learn best by touching, smelling, tasting, and handling real materials.

Keep neighborhood outings and trips short. Children tire if the trip stretches out too long, particularly if naps and eating times are delayed.

Take along supplies. Include snacks, toys for children to play with, extra clothing, and dry diapers. Wet wash cloths in individual plastic bags for quick cleanups can be handy. Prepackaged moist towelettes are also a good idea. When you go on walks, give each child a bag to collect "treasures."

Do not take more children on a trip than you can supervise safely. There should be an adult responsible for every 3 to 5 children, depending on their ages. If young babies and toddlers are included, an adult is needed for every 1 or 2 children. You may need to ask a friend to go along. It's a good idea also to bring along your emergency phone numbers and medical release forms.

Prepare the children for the trip. Tell them where you are going and what you will be doing. Read a book about the subject of your trip.

Follow up with more learning. After the trip is over, let children talk and draw pictures about what they saw. Discuss the trip with them.

Use themes to plan activities

It is often fun to plan activities around weekly themes or projects. You might choose circus, insects, trains, or winter. Activities for each theme should be introduced in each learning center area.

Planning activities around a certain theme can teach children important information about a subject. You will still need to pay close attention to children's individual learning needs and integrate those into play as well.

Sample Theme: Zoo	
Blocks	plastic animals and berry basket cages
Art	animal collages
Books	"Caps for Sale," "Curious George Goes to the Zoo"
Cooking	Cookie cutter animal sandwiches
Pretend play	stuffed animals and cardboard cages, pretend animal food
Music and movement	"animal" fingerplays and action verses
Outdoors	Pretend camel rides, child-size cardboard cages, buckets for zoo food, animal races

Heart of the Matter

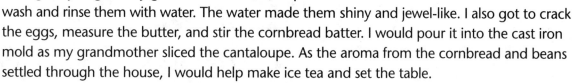

When I was a child, my grandmother often cared for my brother and me while my mother worked. Much of our time together was spent in the kitchen. One of my favorite activities was to sort dried red beans.

I loved the texture and feel of the beans as they ran through my fingers. My grandmother would help me wash and rinse them with water. The water made them shiny and jewel-like. I also got to crack the eggs, measure the butter, and stir the cornbread batter. I would pour it into the cast iron mold as my grandmother sliced the cantaloupe. As the aroma from the cornbread and beans settled through the house, I would help make ice tea and set the table.

After lunch we would pick tomatoes and black-eyed peas from the garden. I was taught very early as a child to know which peas were ready and which were to be left on the vine. We would also pick squash. I didn't like yellow squash, because it was bumpy and made me feel "itchy." But baby rabbits often hid under the large green squash leaves and I delighted in discovering them. The ripe, juicy tomatoes often had worms, but we took them anyway because my grandmother would cut those out. They went in the top of the basket, so they wouldn't get squished.

These experiences in my grandmother's kitchen are among my most treasured childhood memories. Today, when I talk with children who spent their early years in family child care, the experiences they seem to remember most often are about eating and cooking together.

All children should have positive "real life" everyday living experiences with caring adults. And in family child care this is a real possibility. Children can learn about colors, textures, math, and science in the kitchen and the garden. Daily conversation and stories that "happen" during this time will naturally influence language development. There is a richness in these "home" learning experiences that is hard to duplicate.

Adult who share their life in this way and take the time to teach children everyday skills will have a lasting impact.

Lesia

FamilyShare...

Supporting your partners

When you talk with families each day, be sure to point out play and learning activities. And give them suggestions for "talking points" or questions they might ask children on the way home about their day.

You also will want to ask families to let you know if an important event or trip is coming up. If you know ahead of time, you can select books or plan activities about that topic. Parents will appreciate how you are meeting the individual learning needs of their children.

Experience Talks

Conversations with other providers

■ **When I first started child care, I thought I had to do completely different activities every day.** I quickly learned that children really preferred to do many things over and over. For example if we played circus on Monday, the children also wanted to play circus on Tuesday, Wednesday, and Thursday. I might add a few new props to keep things interesting, but it is not really necessary to do a different activity every day.

■ **I have a "good works" file for each child.** I collect drawings, photos, and writing samples throughout the year, and show them to parents when we have our parent meeting.

■ **I teach children skills by giving them real jobs.** They can set the table, feed the fish, and water the plants.

■ **I try to connect most of our activities to weekly themes.** We have weekly activities for circus, restaurants, zoo, shoe store, camping, castles, farm, etc. This idea helps me stay creative.

- **When toddlers want to draw, I tape paper to the table.** Their arm movements can be a little wild sometimes and this helps keep the paper stable.

- **I give "cafeteria-like" trays to children when they are stringing beads.** The tray helps keep beads from rolling off onto the floor. This works great for other activities with small pieces, like puzzles and small blocks.

- **I use my husband's old shirts as paint smocks.** They are large, easy to get on, and cover most of a child's clothing. I cut the sleeves down to size and they work great. I can easily throw them in the wash.

- **I buy extras of favorite toddler toys.** I have two toy cash registers, two toy phones, two shopping carts. My toddlers love to talk on the phone and don't want to give it up. It takes time for toddlers to learn to share and this prevents a lot of problems.

- **I sometimes put dolls and doll furniture in the block area.** The boys sometimes try to take that area over and this is my way of helping the girls feel like they belong there too.

- **I take pictures of block structures and send them home with children.** With a digital camera it's easy to do and I can make as many copies as I need. I often print them out on regular paper rather than photo print paper, because this is cheaper. Often I will print them out in black and white.

- **I print out pictures of the children playing on regular paper and then write words all over it.** I may write, "Rosa's pizza shop" or "Charlie feeds the fish." I also label other things in the picture, like animals or trucks. The children tell me what to write and sometimes help me print the words.

- **I ask children to help me repair well-worn books.** We use clear tape on torn pages and on the spine of the book. This helps them last a little longer and encourages children to be a little more careful with books.

- **I give children different sizes of crayons to choose from.** Fat crayons are recommended for toddlers, but I have found that some 2-year-olds prefer the regular ones. And some older kids like to turn the fat ones on their side so they can cover large areas.

- **I use clipboards a lot.** We don't have a lot of table space. Often a child will like to sit down and "write" or draw on the clipboard.

- **I keep a child care writing notebook.** When children have an idea for playtime, we write it down in the notebook. When we need to remember something for our walk later in the afternoon, we write it down. This way they get a basic understanding of what writing is all about.

- **I use magnetic letters on my refrigerator.** I spell out new words each day and talk about them during snack time.

- **I talk about words and writing all the time.** If the phone rings and I take a message, I show children what that looks like. If I take a can of soup out of the cupboard, I show children the label and talk about that too.

- **I make signs for block buildings— "Annie's bridge."** Before the blocks come down, I may have children hold the sign and kneel down beside their block structure so I can take their picture. Children often want to help make the sign.

Understanding children: Ages and stages

Chapter 7

Contents

Where am I now?	144
Introduction	145
Individual differences	145
Cultural, family, and community influences	146
Typical ages and stages	146
Newborn to 1 year	146
By 4 months	147
By 8 months	147
By 12 months	148
12 to 18 months	150
18 to 24 months	152
Two-year-olds	154
Three-year-olds	156
Four-year-olds	159
Five-year-olds	162
Six- through eight-year-olds	165
Nine- through eleven-year-olds	167
Heart of the Matter	169
FamilyShare	170
Experience Talks	170

Understanding children: Ages and stages—
Where am I now? What can I improve?

	Seldom 1	Sometimes 2	Often 3	Most Often 4
1. I recognize individual temperament differences in children (e.g., activity level, thinking style, need for security, and response to change).				
2. I recognize cultural, family, and community influences on development.				
3. I recognize and understand developmental stages for infants.				
4. I recognize and understand developmental stages for toddlers.				
5. I recognize and understand developmental stages for preschoolers.				
6. I recognize and understand developmental stages for school-agers.				
7. I share information with families about children's growth and development.				
8. I note concerns about a delay or unusual change in development and suggest families seek evaluation and assessment.				

Chapter 7

Understanding children: Ages and stages

Children of the same age are both different and alike in many ways. If you know how children grow, develop, and learn, you will be better able to respond to children, plan your day, and arrange your house for play and learning. It helps to know that toddlers have trouble sharing or that swear words and "bathroom humor" are common for a 4-year-old.

Individual differences

Even though children go through the same ages and stages, there will be some differences. Children learn in different ways. They have different personalities and are influenced by other events in their lives. A move to a new home or the birth of a new brother or sister can sometimes delay or speed up a new skill.

Children sometimes develop at different rates. Most children learn to crawl, walk, and talk at about the same time as other children, but this can vary somewhat. Some children begin to walk at 10 months, some at 15 months. Some toddle along quickly and smoothly, getting the "hang of it" right away. Others fall down a lot, hesitate, or even give up for a few days. Some children talk before they are 2, others talk very little before they are 3 or so.

Personality influences development

Some children tend to be quiet and shy. Others never seem to stop talking! Some abilities become clear in one child, but may never be very strong in another. Look for children to differ in the following ways:

■ **Some children need more security.** They need more consistency, more reassurance, and more confidence and trust-building than others. Insecurity sometimes can cause a child to withdraw or behave aggressively.

■ **Some children are more active.** They need the opportunity to move around, jump, run, and bounce many times throughout the day. Other children need more quiet time or more rest.

HFCCH Chapter 7 — Understanding children: Ages and stages   145

- **Some children are easily distracted or frustrated.** Children are all different in how they tolerate noise, activity, or changes around them. A provider who is sensitive to this need in children will have interesting activities as well as a quiet place to get away from the action.

- **Some children approach things in different ways.** Some children think quietly through possible solutions to a problem; others push in and try the first thing they think of. Some children are interested in experimenting to find out how objects work; others choose to ask for help.

Cultural, family, and community influences

Cultural values and practices influence development. In middle-class American culture, a child's growing independence is viewed very positively. In fact, most early childhood programs provide many activities that encourage self-help and problem-solving skills. However, other cultures may value dependence and obedience as more important.

Asian American children often are not expected to make direct eye contact with adults when speaking because it is viewed as disrespectful. African American children often will look directly at an adult while speaking, but may look away when listening. In Native American cultures, silence is generally viewed as a sign of respect. Mexican American culture places great value on children's good behavior. And in some cultures, cooperation, rather than competition, is greatly valued.

All of these cultural differences may vary from family to family. It is often best to respectfully ask family members to help you understand more about their culture. You also may find it helpful to seek out training or other resources.

Typical ages and stages

The ages and stages in this chapter should be used as a general guide. In your work with children, do not confuse earlier or faster development with better development. Early talking by a 1-year-old does not mean that the child will be a chatterbox or a brilliant conversationalist at age 10. Later talking may mean that a toddler is putting more energy into learning how to walk and move around.

If you notice that a child is not developing a skill within the normal range of time that most children do, this may mean there's a problem that needs attention. You may need to help parents recognize possible problems and special needs, such as poor vision or hearing. If you are familiar with how children normally develop, you can help parents seek community resources or professional advice about developmental concerns. See chapter 13 for more information on possible concerns about children's development.

Newborn to 1 year

Throughout the first year, infants grow at a very fast rate. In fact, by the end of the first year they will have tripled in birth weight. Length can be expected to double. By their first birthday, most infants will be crawling and even may be taking a timid first step! Infants need warm, responsive, and dependable caregivers. Try to spend lots of time holding, cuddling, and playing with the infants in your care. You will be richly rewarded with babbles, smiles, and squeals of laughter.

By 4 months

Physical development
- weight: 10-18 pounds
- length: 23-27 inches
- sleeps about 6 hours before waking during the night
- averages 14-17 hours of sleep daily
- lifts head and chest when lying on stomach
- holds both eyes in a fixed position
- follows a moving object or person with eyes
- grasps rattle or finger
- wiggles and kicks with arms and legs
- rolls over (stomach to back)
- sits with support

Mental development
- explores objects with mouth
- plays with fingers, hands, toes
- reacts to sound of voice, rattle, bell
- turns head toward bright colors and lights
- recognizes bottle or breast

Social and emotional development
- cries (with tears) to communicate pain, fear, discomfort, or loneliness
- babbles or coos
- loves to be touched and held close
- responds to a shaking rattle or bell
- returns a smile
- responds to peekaboo games

By 8 months

Physical development
- weight: 14-23 pounds
- length: 25-30 inches
- first teeth begin to appear
- drools, mouths, and chews on objects
- needs at least 3-4 feedings per day
- reaches for cup or spoon when being fed
- drinks from a cup with help
- enjoys some finely-chopped solid foods
- closes mouth firmly or turns head when no longer hungry
- may sleep 11-13 hours at night although this varies greatly
- needs 2-3 naps during the day
- develops a rhythm for feeding, soiling a diaper, sleeping, and being awake
- true eye color is established
- rolls from back to stomach and stomach to back
- sits alone without support and holds head erect
- raises up on arms and knees into crawling position; rocks back and forth, but may not move forward
- uses finger and thumb to pick up an object
- transfers objects from one hand to the other
- hair growth begins to cover head

Mental development
- cries in different ways to show pain, hunger, discomfort, or loneliness
- makes noises to voice happiness or unhappiness
- recognizes and looks for familiar voices and sounds
- learns by using senses like smell, taste, touch, sight, hearing
- focuses eyes on small objects and reaches for them
- looks for ball rolled out of sight
- searches for toys hidden under a blanket, basket, or container
- explores objects by touching, shaking, banging, and mouthing
- babbles expressively as if talking
- enjoys dropping objects over edge of chair or crib

Social and emotional development
- responds to own name
- shows fear of falling off high places such as table or stairs
- spends a great deal of time watching and observing
- responds differently to strangers and family members
- imitates sounds, actions, and facial expressions made by others
- shows distress if toy is taken away
- squeals, laughs, babbles, smiles in response
- likes to be tickled and touched
- smiles at own reflection in mirror
- raises arms as a sign to be held
- recognizes family member names
- responds to distress of others by showing distress or crying
- shows mild to severe distress when separated from parent

By 12 months

Physical development
- weight: 17-27 pounds
- length: 27-32 inches
- sleeps 11-13 hours at night
- some babies will stop taking a morning nap; others will continue both morning and afternoon naps
- begins to refuse bottle or weans self from breast during day
- needs 3 meals a day with a snack in between
- enjoys drinking from a cup
- begins to eat finger foods
- continues to explore everything by mouth
- enjoys opening and closing cabinet doors
- crawls well
- pulls self to a standing position
- stands alone holding onto furniture for support
- walks holding onto furniture or with adult help

Mental development
- says first word
- says da-da and ma-ma or equivalent
- "dances" or bounces to music
- interested in picture books
- pays attention to conversations
- claps hands, waves bye, if prompted
- likes to place objects inside one another

Social and emotional development
- imitates adult actions such as drinking from a cup, talking on phone
- responds to name
- likes to watch self in mirror
- expresses fear or anxiety toward strangers
- wants caregiver or parent to be in constant sight
- offers toys or objects to others but expects them to be returned
- may become attached to a favorite toy or blanket
- pushes away unwanted items

Ideas to encourage growing and learning

Respond to baby's cries. Help babies develop a sense of trust and security by responding to their cries. Infants need to feel safe and secure before they are ready to learn and try new things. Be consistent so they know what to expect.

Help babies be "people watchers." Babies learn by watching and you are their favorite thing to look at. Place babies in new places and new positions so they can see you and others from different angles.

Hold and cuddle infants when feeding them. Even infants who hold their own bottle need to be held. Being held and cuddled frequently is extremely important in the development of baby's sense of self-worth and security. Holding and cuddling a baby is also a great stress releaser for an adult. Do not prop infants drinking from a bottle because it may cause choking.

Respect a baby's natural schedule. Most babies will settle into a regular routine for eating, sleeping, and soiling their diapers, but the schedule will vary depending on the baby. Some babies need to eat more frequently than others. Some will sleep more and take longer naps.

Baby-proof everything! Store toxic substances such as dishwasher detergent, make-up, paint, or medicine up high. Put safety latches on cabinets and covers on electrical outlets. Lower crib mattresses so older infants can't fall over the rail. Cover sharp corners of tables or shelves that infants might bump into.

Provide many different sounds. Help infants learn to recognize common household sounds such as a vacuum cleaner, a radio, a clock, a whistling tea kettle, or a doorbell. Talk to them about the sounds they are hearing.

Provide interesting objects for babies to feel, touch, mouth, and explore. Very young babies can't move very far to explore their world. They depend on you to introduce them to interesting things and everything is interesting to a baby! Square nylon scarves, cold metal bowls, plastic measuring cups, large wooden spoons, and wet washcloths are favorite household toys. Keep easy-to-swallow objects out of infants' reach. Babies should not be allowed to play with anything smaller than a half dollar (about 1 1/4 inch).

Provide opportunities for infants to smell different smells. Lemon, vanilla, and apple juice are wonderful kitchen smells. Babies also enjoy smelling tree bark, dirt, grass, and other natural things.

Introduce older babies to a variety of tastes and temperatures in food. Babies love to learn by using their senses. Tasting new things can be great fun. Offer cold sherbet, warm oatmeal, mashed peaches, and chopped cooked carrots.

Help babies develop a sense of movement and balance. Hold baby close as you rock, dance, sway, or move across the room. Gently bounce baby on your knee.

Talk with infants as you go through the day. Face babies when talking to them so they can see you and smile with you. Talk about what you are doing, familiar objects, or people. You may even want to babble back or echo sounds your baby makes much as you would in a regular conversation. Infants cannot understand everything you say, but will start to learn how words are used.

Read to infants. Babies enjoy cuddling on your lap, looking at colorful picture books, and hearing the rhythm of your voice. With time they begin to understand that words have meaning and can be used to identify objects.

Encourage older infants to feed themselves. Offer pieces of banana and soft bread sticks. Give babies a spoon with some mashed potatoes or other sticky food, and let them practice eating with a spoon. Yes, it will be messy! Be patient. Learning this skill takes lots of practice.

Play peekaboo. Hide your face behind a blanket and then peek out at the baby. Older babies will learn to do this themselves and will enjoy this game for a long time.

Give babies the freedom to move around. Young infants enjoy being on their backs so that they can kick, wiggle, and look around. Older infants need space and time to practice crawling, creeping, pulling up, and walking. Spending too much time in a walker, playpen, or infant swing may slow down their development.

Stay with infants when someone new is around. Encourage strangers to approach slowly. Introduce an infant by name. Help the infant to open up to someone new in the safety of your presence.

12 to 18 months

One-year-olds are delightful. Babies this age are developing a real personality and will reward you with laughter, funny faces, and affectionate hugs. First steps and first words are exciting events.

Growth during this time is still rapid, but height and weight gains are not as dramatic. As growth slows, appetite decreases and children may eat less.

Physical development
- weight: 17-30 pounds
- height: 27-35 inches
- crawls well
- stands alone, sits down
- gestures or points to indicate wants
- likes to push, pull, and dump things
- pulls off hat, socks, and mittens
- turns pages in a book
- stacks 2 blocks
- likes to poke, twist, and squeeze
- enjoys flushing toilets and closing doors
- enjoys carrying small objects while walking, often one in each hand
- holds crayon and scribbles, but with little control

- waves bye-bye and claps hands
- walks without help
- enjoys holding spoon when eating, but experiences difficulty in getting spoon into mouth
- rolls a ball to adult on request

Mental development
- says 8-20 words you can understand
- looks at person when talked to
- says "hi" or "bye" if reminded
- uses expressions like oh-oh
- asks for something by pointing or using one word
- identifies object in a book

Social and emotional development
- becomes upset when separated from parent
- likes to hand objects to others
- plays alone on floor with toys
- recognizes self in mirror or pictures
- enjoys being held and read to
- imitates others, especially by coughing, sneezing, or making animal sounds
- enjoys an audience and applause

Ideas to encourage growing and learning

Enjoy some "floor time" with one-year-olds each day. Crawl around together, play peekaboo behind the sofa, or roll a ball back and forth. Young children will love having you down on their level.

Review your baby-proofing. Children's increasing growth and mobility make it possible for them to reach unsafe heights and play with dangerous material. Get down on your knees in each room and look at things from a child's perspective. Put toxic items like paint, dishwashing detergent, medicine, and make-up in high cupboards, preferably with a safety cabinet latch.

Put together an "everyday junk box." Include safe items that are fun to feel, poke, and squeeze. You might include plastic margarine tubs, an old sock, tissue paper to crumple, measuring cups of different sizes, a turkey baster, a nylon scarf, an egg carton, and paper cups. Remember, items smaller than a half-dollar can cause choking.

Stand or sit with a child before a mirror. Talk together, make funny faces, and encourage movement. Encourage other children to play with baby in this way as well.

Provide a variety of simple picture books. Children can point at objects, animals, and people as you name them. Encourage them to name items and talk about the activities in the pictures.

Provide items that children can practice dropping into containers. For example, let them drop clothespins into a plastic bottle. Provide containers with loose-fitting lids, and encourage children to open and close them.

Relax and have fun dancing to music.
Encourage children to bounce, sway, and wiggle. Hold baby close to you as you dance. Try different kinds of music.

Carry on conversations throughout the day. Babies love to hear you talk. They learn a lot from the words you say, the tone of your voice, and your facial expressions. All of this strengthens their understanding of language.

Use diapering time to talk with baby.
Changing a diaper is not a favorite task, but a good conversation can take your mind off this unpleasant job. Point to some body parts and say them with an infant. Nose, ears, arms, legs, tummy, toes....

Teach new words at dressing time. Point to and name clothes or body parts. For instance, "See this warm, red coat? Your arms go into the sleeves. See this soft, blue cap? It goes on your head!"

Reduce time apart. Around 18 months a child may get anxious and clinging about being separated from parents and other familiar caregivers. This behavior is normal. If possible, minimize separations during this time and stick to consistent routines.

18 to 24 months

Children this age are truly on the go. A greater sense of independence begins to develop as children begin to walk, run, and climb with greater skill. You also may notice that toddlers this age love to imitate everything. Pretending to talk on the phone is a favorite activity.

Physical development
- weight: 20-32 pounds
- height: 30-37 inches
- walks well
- likes to run, but can't always stop and turn well
- drinks from a straw
- feeds self with a spoon
- helps wash hands
- stacks 2-4 blocks
- tosses or rolls a large ball
- opens cabinets, drawers, and boxes
- bends over to pick up toy without falling
- walks up steps with help
- enjoys sitting on and moving small-wheeled riding toys
- takes steps backwards
- begins to gain some control of bowels and bladder—complete control may not happen until around age 3 (boys often do not complete toilet learning until age 3 1/2)

Mental development
- has a vocabulary of several hundred words, including names of toys
- uses 2-3 word sentences
- echoes single words that are spoken by someone else

- talks to self and "jabbers" expressively
- prefers some favorite toys
- likes to choose between two objects
- hums or tries to sing
- listens to short rhymes or fingerplays
- points to eyes, ears, or nose when asked
- uses the words "please" and "thank you" if prompted
- enjoys singing familiar songs

Social and emotional development
- likes to imitate actions of others
- begins to show signs of independence; says "no"
- has trouble sharing
- is very possessive
- finds it hard to wait and wants things right now!
- gets angry sometimes and has temper tantrums
- acts shy around strangers
- comforts a distressed friend or parent
- refers to self by name
- uses the words "me" and "mine"
- enjoys looking at picture books
- tries to do many things "by myself!"
- enjoys adult attention
- enjoys simple pretend play like wearing hats and talking on phone
- enjoys exploring, gets into everything, and requires constant supervision
- generally unable to remember rules
- often gets physically aggressive when frustrated—slaps, hits
- shows affection by returning a hug or kiss
- may become attached to a toy or blanket

Ideas to encourage growing and learning

Enjoy dancing with children to music with different rhythms. Provide simple musical instruments such as a rattle or an oatmeal box drum. Now is a good time to teach children simple fingerplays such as "Eensy Weensy Spider."

Talk out loud about the everyday things you do. Children need to hear language so they can learn how to put words together. For example, instead of just quietly making lunch, you could say, "It is time to make lunch. Since it is cold outside, I think I will make some warm chicken soup today. I'll set our bowls and spoons on the table so we can eat our soup. I think we should have some green peas too."

Name, describe, and compare everyday objects. Talk about a red apple and a green apple, a cold piece of ice, wet water, a pink flower, green leaves, a soft blue rug, a hard floor, a shiny mirror, or a loud door bell.

Bag it or sack it. Toddlers love to carry "special" items around in paper sacks or small buckets. Give them a few simple items, such as a green sock, a shiny spoon, a piece of red yarn. Name and describe the objects they carry in their bag. Ask them to repeat these names during the day.

Teach children the name of common objects. After 18 months, language skills seem to explode. Children now learn new words at a very rapid rate. Understanding words comes first. Often they can point to an object before they can say the name of the object.

Read simple books with children every day. Choose books made of cardboard or cloth pages. Stories that have familiar objects are best. Hold toddlers on your lap and show them how books are used. Encourage them to gently turn the pages. Make playful noises as you read about different things; bark like a dog, purr like a kitten, make a noise like a train.

Make a sturdy toddler book. Include magazine pictures of objects or photos of people your toddlers know in a small, sturdy photo album. Hold children on your lap as you introduce them to "their book." Teach them to be gentle and careful with the book. Soon they will be able to look at this book and other books on their own.

Add a few more words. When your toddler talks, add a few more words to show how words link to one another. For example, if a child says "kitty," you can say, "yes, the kitty is little and soft."

Play a simple game of "find." Place three familiar toys in front of a toddler and say, "Give me the ——." See if your toddler tries to find it and hand it to you.

Encourage a toddler to play dress-up. Toddlers are very interested in learning how to use their body. Provide a full-length mirror on the wall and a "pretend box" filled with caps, scarves, and old shoes.

Two-year-olds

Two-year-olds like to be independent! Favorite words are "Mine" and "No" and "I do it!" Emotions take on a roller coaster-like quality as 2-year-olds can go from excitement to anger to laughter within a few moments. A great deal of time is spent exploring, pushing, pulling, filling, dumping, and touching.

Two-year-olds are surer of themselves and of what they can do as they grow. Their bodies stretch out, and most will lose the potbellied look during this third year of life. Their appetites lessen, and they may be choosy about food. They are still growing fairly rapidly.

Toddlers are very attached to their caregivers. You may find them trying out new ideas and exploring their surroundings, but still staying close to you as they need a base of support and trust. Two-year-olds are usually interested in other children. However, social interest and physical abilities sometimes collide as a hug becomes a tackle and a gentle pat becomes a whack. You will need to teach children how to express affection in an helpful way.

Physical development
- weight: 22-38 pounds
- height: 32-40 inches
- has almost a full set of teeth
- walks up and down stairs by holding onto railing
- feeds self with spoon
- experiments by touching, smelling, and tasting
- likes to push, pull, fill, and dump
- can turn pages of a book
- stacks 4-6 objects
- scribbles quickly with crayons or markers
- many children (but not all) will learn to use toilet
- walks without help
- walks backwards
- tosses or rolls a large ball
- stoops or squats
- opens cabinets, drawers
- can bend over to pick up toy without falling

Mental development
- enjoys simple stories, rhymes, and songs
- uses 2-3 word sentences
- says names of toys
- hums or tries to sing
- enjoys looking at books
- points to eyes, ears, or nose when asked
- repeats words
- interested in learning how to use common items

Social and emotional development
- plays alongside others more than with them
- acts shy around strangers
- likes to imitate parents
- easily frustrated
- affectionate—hugs and kisses
- insists on trying to do several tasks without help
- enjoys simple make-believe like talking on phone, putting on hat
- very possessive—offers toys to other children but then wants them back
- needs lots of time to change activities
- capable of frequent tantrums, which are often a result of an inability to say or ask for something in words
- can show aggressive behavior and the intent to hurt others
- can be extremely demanding and persistent
- may smash or break objects when frustrated and angry
- possessive about caregiver's attention; shows feelings of jealousy
- has fears and nightmares
- has sense of humor; capable of laughter
- shows interest in dressing, brushing hair and teeth
- cannot sit still or play with a toy for more than a few minutes

Ideas to encourage growing and learning

Baby-proof your house again! Once safe, is not always safe. Two-year-olds are taller and more skillful at opening doors and getting into mischief. Look at your home with the eyes of a 2-year-old and make things safe.

Read aloud to children every day. Snuggle with toddlers to look at books with large pictures and sturdy pages. Show them how to handle books and turn the pages. Encourage them to point to pictures and name objects as you read. Simple story lines are best.

Help children develop listening skills by identifying familiar noises. Play games and try to recognize sounds with your eyes closed. Try common sounds such as a vacuum, tap water, dogs barking, thunder, airplane, and car.

Let toddlers help you with simple chores. Young children love to help you put fruit in the refrigerator or put clothes in the laundry basket. Encourage them to name things that you are using.

Continue to add new information to what a child is saying. Say or repeat the correct words, but don't expect the toddler to copy you right away. For example, if a child says "more juice," say "Anna wants more orange juice." If a child says "blankie" say "Yes that's a blanket, a soft, warm blanket."

Give toddlers clear and simple choices. "Do you want to drink milk or juice? Do you want to wear green or blue socks?"

Know how to handle a temper tantrum:
- don't yell or hit the child
- talk in soothing tone
- remain calm

Introduce toddlers to drawing and painting. Children need practice to learn how to hold crayons, markers, and brushes. Scribbling is actually good practice for later writing skills. Provide inexpensive newspaper and flattened grocery sacks for drawing and painting. Taping paper to the table helps hold it in place.

Do not expect toddlers to share or take turns. Right now they are focused on learning how to physically handle themselves and on learning to talk. Learning to share will come later.

Provide spaces where toddlers can spend time away from others. A corner space behind a sofa that you can easily see behind is ideal. An old cardboard box or a blanket over a card table works great too.

Avoid pressuring children to be right or left handed. A few 2-year-olds will begin to show preference for one hand, but many children will continue to use both hands for a few years.

Strengthen physical skills by providing small steps, boxes, pulling and pushing toys, ride-on and ride-in toys.

Help children learn about the science of "what happens when?" Give toddlers many opportunities to fill, dump, collect, gather, give, hide, and seek.

Play "parade" or "follow the leader." Sing songs that repeat like "Old MacDonald."

Teach children to follow simple directions. Help children learn new language skills by giving simple directions like "Close the door, please." or "Would you pick up the doll?" Older toddlers can learn to repeat the directions for others.

Encourage a toddler's love to "copy" you. Teach simple fingerplays. Play "copy cat." Stand or sit facing the children and have them copy everything you do. Reverse roles and let the child lead while you copy the actions.

Encourage sand, mud, clay, and water play. Toddlers enjoy messy play and learn a great deal from mixing, sifting, pouring, stirring, and shaping. Kick off your shoes and roll up your sleeves. You'll have fun with this too!

Three-year-olds

Three-year-olds are full of wonder, and spend a lot of time watching and imitating. Their days are filled with exploring their world.

Three-year-olds are interested in perfecting physical skills, and it is common for them to spend the entire morning going down the slide or riding a favorite tricycle.

Three-year-olds have very little memory for past events and do not understand "yesterday" and "tomorrow" the way adults do. They often repeat activities or may do and undo actions such as putting a puzzle together. This helps them begin to understand how things change or stay the same.

Physical development
- weight: 25-44 pounds
- height: 34-43 inches
- develops a taller, thinner, adult-like appearance
- develops a full set of baby teeth
- needs approximately 1,300 calories daily
- sleeps 10-12 hours at night
- sleeps through most nights without wetting the bed (occasional accidents are still quite common)
- uses the toilet with some help (many boys may not be ready for toilet learning until sometime during their third year)
- puts on shoes (but cannot tie laces)
- dresses self with some help (buttons, snaps, zippers)
- feeds self (with some spilling)
- tries to catch a large ball
- throws a ball overhead
- kicks a ball forward
- hops on one foot
- walks short distance on tiptoes
- climbs up and down a small slide by self
- pedals a tricycle
- walks on a line
- can stand, balance, and hop on one foot
- jumps over a 6" barrier
- can feed self with spoon and small fork; often butters bread with knife
- can brush teeth, wash hands, get a drink
- interested in preparing and cooking food

Mental development
- talks so that 75 to 80 percent of speech is understandable
- talks in complete sentences of 3-5 words. "Mommy is drinking juice. There's a big dog."
- stumbles over words sometimes—usually not a sign of stuttering
- enjoys repeating words and sounds
- listens carefully to short stories and books
- likes familiar stories told without any changes in words
- enjoys listening to stories and repeating simple rhymes
- is able to tell simple stories from pictures or books
- enjoys singing and can carry a simple tune
- understands "now, soon, and later"
- asks who, what, where, and why questions
- stacks 5-7 blocks
- enjoys playing with clay or play dough (pounds, rolls, and squeezes it)
- can put together a 6-piece puzzle
- draws a circle and square
- recognizes common everyday sounds
- matches an object to a picture of that object
- identifies common colors such as red, blue, yellow, green
- can count 2-3 objects
- can solve problems if they are simple, concrete, real, and immediate, and if wants to
- interested in similarities and differences
- can match and name colors
- interested in features of animals that make them unique
- has good self-knowledge; can understand difference between self and younger children, but not between self and older children
- can say his/her age

Social and emotional development
- seeks attention and approval of adults
- sometimes shows preference for one parent (often the parent of the opposite sex)
- accepts suggestions and follows simple directions
- enjoys helping with simple household tasks
- can make simple choices between two things
- enjoys making others laugh and being silly
- enjoys playing alone but near other children
- spends a great deal of time watching and observing
- enjoys playing with other children briefly, but still does not cooperate or share well
- enjoys hearing stories about self
- enjoys playing "house"

- enjoys imitating other children and adults
- answers whether a boy or a girl
- expresses interest in ethnic identities of self and others if exposed to a multicultural setting

Ideas to encourage growing and learning

Be patient with toileting. Many children (especially boys) will not be ready for toilet learning until after age 3. Accidents will happen for a while; treat accidents calmly. Avoid shaming a child.

Help children learn to use their fingers to do small tasks. Provide large buttons, wooden beads or used sewing spools to string on a shoe lace. Show them how to stack small blocks.

Play ball—show children how to roll a ball to each other. Next practice throwing or kicking balls of different sizes toward a large net or target.

Teach children how to use their bodies in different ways. Show them how to hop like a rabbit, fly like a bird, waddle like a duck, slither like a snake, and run like a deer.

Talk frequently with children; use short sentences and listen. Add new information to what they say. Ask who, what, when, where, and how questions.

Teach children to remember first and last names. This strengthens a child's sense of identity and is also a good safety practice in the event a child is lost. Practice saying both first and last names of children and parents. Write names on paper and post it on the wall or refrigerator.

Ask parents to bring baby pictures. Talk about "When you were a baby." Read stories about families. Talk about brothers, sisters, aunts, uncles, grandparents, and friends.

Encourage reading. Provide books for children to look at, and read the same books to them. Read poetry and nursery rhymes. Show children that words are everywhere. Point out words on cereal boxes, street signs.

Teach reading skills. As you read to children, teach them that books have titles, authors, and illustrators. Help them learn that you read books from left to right. Ask them to turn the pages. Show them that the words on a page connect to the pictures on a page. Ask them to predict what will come next in the story. Encourage a child to repeat or retell the story and discuss the ideas and events.

Encourage interest in writing. Encourage children to watch you write as you prepare a grocery list or note for parents. Write words on cards of their favorite toys and place them on shelves as labels. Post words on everyday items such as chair, table, or door. Provide paper, small notebooks, and markers for pretend play.

Teach children how to count 3-4 objects. Count everyday objects such as cookies, cups, napkins, or dolls. When possible, move one object at a time as you and the children count together. Ask children to help you count the eggs needed for a recipe.

Sing simple songs. Make simple rhythm instruments: oatmeal box or coffee can drums, rattles of dry beans in a box, etc. Encourage a variety of body movements and dance to music of many kinds. Play musical games such as "London Bridge," "Ring-around-the-Rosie," and "Farmer in the Dell."

Encourage creative art. Provide lots of blank paper, crayons, and markers and collage materials. Avoid asking "what" children are drawing. Three-year-olds may not know or care, but simply enjoy the process of creating. Instead comment on colors and shapes, etc.

Make simple puppets. Draw a face on an old sock and show children how to "talk" or sing with puppets. Keep it simple. A small piece of fabric can be used to make a scarf or a hat. Read a book to children about different kinds of puppets.

Talk about colors, numbers, and shapes in your everyday conversation. "We need ONE egg. That's a RED car. The butter is in this SQUARE box."

Show children how to help with very simple household tasks. Ask children to help you put napkins by each plate, put socks in a drawer, water plants, or stir the muffin batter.

Four-year-olds

"Energetic" and "imaginative" best describe the 4-year-old. Often impatient and silly, they discover humor and spend a great deal of time being silly and telling you "jokes." A 4-year-old's language may range from silly words such as "batty-watty" to swear words. Loud, rowdy laughter may accompany such language.

Imagination suddenly becomes greater than life for the 4-year-old, who often confuses reality and "make-believe." Wild stories and exaggerations are common.

Four-year-olds feel good about the things they can do, show self-confidence, and are willing to try new adventures. They race up and down stairs or around corners, dash on tricycles or scooters, and pull wagons at full tilt. You still need to watch them closely because they can overestimate their own abilities and are capable of taking some outlandish and dangerous risks.

Physical development
- weight: 27-50 pounds
- height: 37-46 inches
- uses a spoon, fork, and dinner knife skillfully
- needs 10-12 hours sleep each night
- dresses self without much assistance (unzip, unsnap, unbutton clothes; Velcro®, lace but not tie shoes)
- can feed self, brush teeth, comb hair, wash, dress, hang up clothes with little assistance
- walks a straight line
- hops on one foot
- pedals and steers a tricycle skillfully
- jumps over objects 5-6 inches high
- runs, jumps, hops, and skips around obstacles with ease
- stacks 10 or more blocks
- forms shapes and objects out of clay or play dough, sometimes human and animal figures
- threads small beads on a string
- catches, bounces, and throws a ball easily
- likes to gallop, turn somersaults, climb ladders and trees

Mental development
- can place objects in a line from largest to smallest
- can recognize some letters if taught, and may be able to print own name
- recognizes familiar words in simple books or signs (STOP sign)

HFCCH Chapter 7 — Understanding children: Ages and stages

- understands the concepts of "tallest, biggest, same, more, on, in, under, and above"
- counts 1-7 objects out loud—but not always in the right order
- understands the order of daily routines (breakfast before lunch, lunch before dinner, dinner before bed time)
- speaks in fairly complex sentences. "The baby ate the cookie before I could put it on the table."
- asks a lot of questions, including ones on birth and death
- enjoys singing simple songs, rhymes, and nonsense words
- adapts language to listener's level of understanding. To baby sister: "Daddy go bye-bye." To Mother: "Daddy went to the store to buy food."
- learns name, address, and phone number, if taught
- asks and answers who, what, when, why, and where questions
- continues one activity for 10-15 minutes
- names 6-8 colors and 3 shapes
- follows two unrelated directions (put your milk on the table and get your coat on)
- has basic understanding of concepts related to number, size, weight, colors, textures, distance, position, and time
- understands immediate passage of time as in what happened yesterday, but does not understand calendar time
- has long attention span and finishes activities
- understands and remembers own successes
- may add "ed" to words. "I goed to the door and put-ed the cat outdoors. He hurted me."

Social and emotional development
- enjoys playing with other children
- takes turns and shares (most of the time); may still be rather bossy
- seeks out adult approval
- understands and obeys simple rules (most of the time)
- makes many changes to rules of a game during everyday play
- likes to talk and carries on elaborate conversations
- capable of feeling jealous
- asks why—a lot
- boastful—enjoys showing off and bragging about possessions
- fearful of the dark and monsters
- begins to understand danger—at times can become quite fearful
- has difficulty separating make-believe from reality
- lies sometimes to protect self and friends, but doesn't truly understand the concept of lying—imagination often gets in the way
- may name call, tattle freely
- likes to shock others by using "forbidden" words
- expresses anger verbally rather than physically (most of the time)
- still throws tantrums over minor frustrations
- imitates parent of the same sex, particularly in play
- enjoys pretending with playmates
- pretending goes far beyond "playing house" to more elaborate settings like fire station, school, shoe store, ice cream shop
- loves to tell jokes that may not make any sense at all to adults
- can feel intense anger and frustration
- has vivid imagination and sometimes imaginary playmates
- enjoys dramatic play and role playing

Ideas to encourage growing and learning

Read aloud each day. Encourage 4-year-olds to look at books on their own. Provide other types of reading material such as outdated coupons, junk mail, newspaper ads, and old cereal boxes.

Say nursery rhymes and fingerplays together. Encourage 4-year-olds to tell stories to younger children. For fun, change the words to a familiar song or rhyme. For example, "Row, row, row your boat gently down the stream" can become: "Skip, skip, skip and play all around the room . . ."

Encourage interest in writing and words. Provide children with paper and notebooks for writing. Print letters and numerals on art work, and label toy shelves with pictures and words that describe objects.

Provide a variety of art experiences. Make play dough. Create collages from magazine pictures, fabric, wallpaper, and newsprint. Encourage children to experiment with new media like wire and cork, soda straws, string, or yarn. Teach children to mix different colors with paint.

Teach important number and space concepts. Sort and count everything in sight, like silverware, socks, rocks, leaves, etc. Talk about things being in, on, under, behind, beside, before and after, larger than, too far, etc.

Teach children the correct use of the telephone. Teach children how to answer the phone, how to say hello and good bye. Arrange for children to call a parent at work or to receive a call from a grandparent.

Four-year-olds have a strong need to feel important and worthwhile. Provide opportunities for them to help you with everyday tasks. Thank them for helping other children, praise each little success.

Take fears seriously. Children are often fearful for surprising reasons. Reassure children that you will make sure that nothing bad will happen to them.

Help children understand and cope with strong feelings by giving them words to use when they are upset. "I can see you are 'sad' about going home, 'angry' at your friend, 'frustrated' that you can't open the box, 'irritated' by the baby's crying . . ."

Explain why and how things happen. Use books to show how things work. Help them do simple science activities like using magnets, freezing water, planting seeds, making a terrarium, and flying kites on a windy day.

Provide opportunities to experiment. Provide old faucets, tools, light switches, knobs, latches, and toys that come apart. Ask "why" and "what if" questions.

Teach the use of landmarks to find their way around your neighborhood. Take short walks and point out familiar trees, signs, and houses. For fun, see if children can tell you how to get back home.

Strengthen physical skills. Pretend to walk like various animals. Set up an obstacle course indoors with challenges such as crawling, climbing, leaping, balancing, and running across stepping stones. Walk and balance a small beanbag on the head.

HFCCH Chapter 7 — Understanding children: Ages and stages   161

Promote respect for life and living things. Build a bird house or a bird feeder. Record the kinds of birds you see, and teach them to identify birds by color or markings like the red male and green female cardinals, the black caps and white cheeks of the chickadee.

Encourage 4-year-olds to help you plan and plant a garden. They will love to water plants daily and will enjoy measuring plant growth.

Encourage children to be aware of different cultures. Provide dolls, puppets, pictures, and books that show children of different color and backgrounds. Teach children about recipes, songs, and customs used in different cultural celebrations.

Make pretend play more interesting by adding different materials. Provide a variety of props for themes like grocery store, pizza place, birthday party, and firefighter.

Be patient with the untidiness and clutter. Allow plenty of time to clean up. It helps to store and organize materials on low, open shelves so they can be found and put away easily.

Five-year-olds

Five-year-olds are cheerful, energetic, and enthusiastic. They enjoy planning, and spend a great deal of time discussing who will do what. They especially enjoy pretend play, usually with other children.

Five-year-olds are more likely to notice the needs and feelings of others around them. It is less difficult for them to wait for a turn or to share toys and material. "Best friends" become very important.

Many 5-year-olds will be going to kindergarten. Be sensitive to the needs of a 5-year-old returning from school who may be tired, talkative, hungry, or wanting to share the day's happenings.

Physical development
- weight: 31-57 pounds
- height: 39-48 inches
- requires approximately 1,700 calories daily
- sleeps 10-11 hours at night
- may begin to lose baby teeth
- is able to dress self with little assistance
- learns to skip
- throws ball overhead
- catches bounced balls
- rides a tricycle skillfully; may show interest in riding a bicycle with training wheels
- balances on either foot for 5-10 seconds
- uses a fork and knife well
- cuts on a line with scissors
- prefers to use either left or right hand

- walks down stairs, alternating feet without using a handrail
- jumps over low objects
- can run, gallop, and tumble
- can skip and run on tiptoe
- can jump rope
- interested in performing tricks like standing on head, performing dance steps
- capable of learning complex skills like swimming, ice or roller skating, and riding bicycles
- may be able to tie shoelaces
- may be able to copy simple designs and shapes

Mental development
- understands about 13,000 words
- uses 5-8 words in a sentence
- likes to argue and reason; uses words like "because"
- knows basic colors like red, yellow, blue, green, orange
- is able to memorize address and phone number
- understands that stories have a beginning, middle, and end
- is able to remember stories and repeat them
- enjoys creating and telling stories
- understands that books are read from left to right, top to bottom
- enjoys riddles and jokes
- draws pictures that represent animals, people, and objects
- enjoys tracing or copying letters
- can place objects in order from shortest to tallest
- can understand and use comparative terms like big, bigger, or biggest
- sorts objects by size
- identifies some letters of the alphabet and a few numbers (if taught)
- understands "more," " less," and "same"
- counts up to 10 objects
- recognizes categories ("These are all animals; these are all toys.")
- understands before and after, above and below
- builds more complex block structures
- has good attention span and can concentrate well
- is project minded—plans buildings, play scenarios, and drawings
- is interested in cause and effect
- can understand time concepts like yesterday, today, and tomorrow

Social and emotional development
- invents games with simple rules
- organizes other children and toys for pretend play
- still confuses fantasy with reality sometimes
- often fears loud noises, the dark, animals, and some people
- expresses anger and jealousy physically
- likes to test muscular strength and physical skills, but is not emotionally ready for competition
- carries on conversations with other children and adults
- often excludes other children in play—"best friends only"
- uses swear words or "bathroom words" to get attention
- sometimes can be very bossy
- likes to try new things and take risks
- likes to make own decisions
- notices when another child is angry or sad—more sensitive to feelings of others
- prefers company of 1 or 2 children at a time; may become bossy or sulky when others join in
- likes to feel grown up; boasts about self to younger, less capable children
- begins to have a very basic understanding of right and wrong
- is content to spend some time playing alone
- takes turns and shares (sometimes)
- understands and respects rules— often asks permission

- understands and enjoys both giving and receiving
- enjoys collecting things
- sometimes needs to get away and be alone
- can understand relationships among people and similarities and differences in other families
- seeks adult approval
- is sometimes critical of other children and embarrassed by own mistakes
- is less fearful of the world than toddlers because understands the world better
- has a good sense of humor and enjoys sharing jokes and laughter with adults

Ideas to encourage growing and learning

Encourage body skills and balance. Play "Follow the Leader" with skipping, galloping, and hopping. Skip to music, teach simple folk dances and games. Show children how to walk or balance on a board. Teach children how to throw a ball into a lowered basketball net or basket.

Play games that can teach right and left directions, like "Hokey-Pokey," "Looby-Loo," and "Simon Says." "Follow the Leader" can help with this too.

Help children learn to use scissors well. Let them cut out newspaper coupons or make paper money for pretend play.

Help children learn to use their hands to do everyday tasks. Show children how to repair toys and books. Provide carpentry, take-apart, and put-together experiences with junk clocks and old small appliances.

Make story time fun. Use different voices for different characters. While reading a familiar story, stop before the end and ask children to add their own end to the story. Ask 5-year-olds to tell you a story. Write it down and post it on the wall or refrigerator.

Ask "what if" questions. What if there were 5 little pigs instead of 3? What if Little Red Riding Hood saw a rabbit instead of a wolf?

Involve children in writing. Help them write "thank-you" notes, holiday greeting cards, and letters. Cut off the pictures from old greeting cards and let children write their messages on the back. Some children can tell you what they want to say, watch you write it on a separate piece of paper, and then copy the message down on their own card.

Give 5-year-olds time to sort, group, match, count, and put things in order. These are important math skills. Use real life tasks such as setting the table, counting the number of turns, and sorting out socks by size, color, and fabric. Lotto games and card games such as "Go Fish" are fun ways to help children sort and match.

Help children learn to make rules and play simple games. Provide opportunities for them to play board and card games with simple rules. Let them be the leader and give directions in the "Follow the Leader" game.

Teach "getting along" skills. Teach children the words to use when they ask for something, trade a toy, or join others in play. Show them how to bargain and reach an agreement. Teach them the words to use to say thank you and I am sorry.

Take questions seriously. Listen to children and try to understand what they are asking. Talk to children about what happens and why. Give answers they can understand.

Make your praise specific and give details. Specific praise helps children understand the true value of their actions. Say "I like the way you stacked the toys neatly on the shelf" rather than "You did a good job!"

Provide a comfortable place to have some alone time. A large cardboard box makes a wonderful hideaway. You can still see and supervise children, but give them some private space.

Allow 5-year-olds some privacy in the toilet. Remind them to wash their hands until it becomes a habit.

Strengthen math skills. Five-year-olds will show an increasing interest in numbers. Encourage them to count anything of interest—cups, leaves, drums, bells, number of children absent, meters, etc. Let them measure children's height, the length of the sofa, or water in the rain gauge.

Encourage interest in jokes, nonsense, and riddles by reading humorous stories, riddles, and nonsense rhymes. Join them in jokes from school, books, and TV.

Help children use their bodies in creative ways. Teach children how to move their bodies to act out the opening of a flower, falling snow, leaves, or rain; wiggly worms and snakes; and laundry blowing in the wind.

Continue to teach telephone skills. Practice having a conversation with children on a pretend phone. Use a play phone to teach how to call 911 or an operator for help. Arrange for them to call a family member on a real phone.

Six- through eight-year-olds

Six-, seven-, and eight-year-olds build on the important developments of the first 6 years of life and seem to settle down to a steadier pace of growing and learning. Young school-age children are interested in real life tasks and activities. Pretend and fantasy play happen less often. School-agers want to make "real" jewelry, take "real" photographs, and create "real" collections.

School-age children have longer attention spans. They are more likely to stick with things until the project is finished, the problem solved, or the argument resolved. Doing things together with friends, teamwork, and following rules become very important. This age group is fascinated by rules and can develop games with extensive rules and rituals.

Physical development
- skilled at using scissors and small tools
- develops permanent teeth
- enjoys testing muscle strength and skills
- has a good sense of balance
- can catch small balls
- can tie shoelaces
- enjoys copying designs and shapes, letters, and numbers
- can print name
- long arms and legs may give a gawky, awkward appearance

Mental development
- may reverse printed letters (b/d)
- enjoys planning and building
- uses and understands more complex words
- reading may become a major interest
- has increased problem-solving ability
- is interested in magic and tricks
- has longer attention span
- enjoys creating elaborate collections
- is able to learn difference between left and right
- can begin to understand time and the days of the week

Social and emotional development
- being with friends becomes more and more important
- is interested in rules and rituals
- girls want to play more with girls; boys with boys
- may have a best friend and an enemy
- has strong desire to perform well, do things right
- begins to see things from another child's point of view, but still very self-centered
- finds criticism or failure difficult to handle
- views things as black and white, right or wrong, wonderful or terrible, with very little middle ground
- seeks a sense of security in groups, organized play, and clubs
- generally enjoys caring for and playing with younger children
- may become upset when behavior or school work is ignored

Ideas to encourage growing and learning

Encourage active play. Children coming from school may need to move around and release some energy. Throwing at targets, running, jumping rope, tumbling, and aerobics may be of interest. Older children can lead other children in play and teach them new skills.

Provide ways to learn about rules and written directions. Provide a variety of table games: cards, dominoes, checkers, tic-tac-toe, etc. Read through directions together and stay close by to help children resolve problems.

Encourage activities that teach children how to work together. Completing a jigsaw puzzle or planting a garden requires children to plan, think, and work together. Everyday tasks such as preparing snacks are good too.

Help children feel capable. Build children's confidence by providing opportunities to build models or cook. They may also enjoy making crafts, practicing music, or working with wood.

Support children's collections. Check out books from the library that would interest children in collections. Favorites are books about rocks, coins, or butterflies. Provide materials for children to make special boxes to store their collections in.

Encourage reading and writing by allowing children to produce stories with scripts, create music for plays and puppet shows, produce a newspaper, record events, go on field trips, or conduct experiments.

Help children explore their world. Take children on trips to museums, work places, and other neighborhoods. Invite people in the community to your home and ask them to talk about what they do. Firefighters, nurses, or mechanics often prefer to talk with small groups of children rather than large school groups and are very willing to drop by for a few minutes.

Nine- through eleven-year-olds

Children of this age develop a sense of self and find it important to gain social acceptance and experience achievement. Friends become increasingly important. Secret codes, shared word meanings and made up languages, passwords, and elaborate rituals are important ways to strengthen the bonds of friendship. Close friends are almost always of the same sex, although children in this age group are usually increasingly interested in peers of the opposite sex.

Be prepared to use all your "patience" skills if caring for children this age, because they tend to think that they do not need any adult care or supervision. Yet, when they are left to care for themselves, they can be lonely, unhappy, and sometimes frightened.

Physical development
- girls are generally as much as 2 years ahead of boys in physical maturity
- girls may begin to menstruate
- body strength increases
- ability to use hands to complete complex tasks increases
- coordination and reaction time improves

Mental development
- is interested in reading fictional stories, magazines, and how-to project books
- may develop special interest in collections or hobbies
- may be very interested in discussing a future career
- fantasizes and daydreams about the future
- is capable of understanding concepts without having direct hands-on experience

Social and emotional development
- begins to see parents and authority figures as human beings with faults
- likes rituals, rules, secret codes, and made-up languages
- enjoys being a member of a club
- has increased interest in competitive sports
- has fewer outbursts of anger
- may resist adult authority

Ideas to encourage growing and learning

Provide ways for older school-agers to help out with real skills. Most children love to cook. Repairing toys and designing dramatic play props also are helpful ways for them to use their skills.

Provide time and space for an older child to have some time apart from other children. Time to read, daydream, or do school work uninterrupted will be appreciated.

Support school friendships. When possible, allow children to make a short call to a school friend. Ask them to tell you about their friends and their day at school while it is still fresh on their mind.

Encourage children to participate in an organized club or youth group. Many groups encourage skill development with projects or activities than can be worked on in your child care program.

Encourage older children to help you with younger children, but don't overdo. Avoid burdening older children with too many adult responsibilities. They can help with younger children, but you are the one who is really in charge. Allow time for play and relaxation.

Provide opportunities for older children to play games of strategy. Checkers, chess, and Monopoly are favorites. Working on a large jigsaw puzzle from day to day is a way for children to relax after school.

Remember to provide plenty of food. Older children have larger appetites than younger children and will need to eat more. This may vary from day to day.

Heart of the Matter

One of the most interesting lessons I've had on child development came as I watched two young boys grow up together in my care. Jason and Alex were the same age. In fact, their birthdays were just three weeks apart. They also had something else in common. They were cousins; their mothers were sisters.

I began caring for Alex when he was about 8 weeks old and Jason just a few months later. Both boys looked a lot alike—dark hair, big brown eyes, and dimples. And they laughed just alike, even as babies. But their personalities were very different. From the very beginning, Jason was the calm and careful one. Alex was his opposite and was very, very active. He never seemed to stop moving.

Jason seemed to master physical skills at a slower rate than Alex. It was almost as if he had to watch and study every little thing before he tackled a new task. However, once he began walking, it was as if he had always been walking. I don't think he fell more than once. Alex, however, was one rough and tumble kid. He began walking early but fell often. I quickly lost count of the many times he hurt himself.

As they grew older, I noticed Jason seemed to learn other kinds of skills more quickly. Because he had more patience, he learned to work puzzles very easily. He was the first to learn to tie his shoes. And as he grew older, he was great at board games. Alex, on the other hand, would become frustrated with these things. Velcro® shoes were invented for kids like Alex. But he learned to ride a tricycle and bicycle with great ease. As a school-ager, he became much more athletic than Jason.

Because they were cousins and so close in age, their mothers often compared notes on how the boys were growing and changing. From time to time, each mother would worry that her son was "falling behind." They seemed to think that because the boys were cousins and the same age that they should develop new skills at exactly the same time. Whenever this happened, I would get out my "ages and stages" information and reassure them. I would also give them tips on how to help their child learn new skills.

I'll admit, caring for two children so close in age really forced me to learn about ages and stages on an everyday basis. I learned so much watching both boys grow from infants, to toddlers, to preschoolers. And then as they grew older it was my great fortune to care for them after school for many years.

I strongly believe that being able to share ages and stages information with the moms helped to strengthen relationships and lessen any competitiveness between the boys and their two families. Years later, the boys are the best of friends.

Lesia

FamilyShare...
Supporting your partners

Parents often appreciate information about their child's development. Ages and Stages publications for parents are available on the CD that accompanies this book. These publications also are available on the web at www.extension.iastate.edu/store. Search on PM 1530. They are in English and Spanish.

Experience Talks
Conversations with other providers

■ **Caring for children of different ages has really helped me appreciate the special qualities of each child.** To watch them grow from year to year is the most amazing thing. I see these children going through the same stages, learning to walk, talk, etc., but each child approaches it in a different way. They are truly unique little beings.

■ **I take pictures of the children as they reach a new skill.** For example, I have a whole set of "crawling and walking" pictures. When one of the babies learns to walk, we celebrate it! I take out the pictures of the other kids and we have a great time looking at them. Children love to talk about when they were a "baby." It is all great fun.

■ **Most of us will confess that we have a favorite age.** Some of us love babies, some of us preschoolers. And for some it is the school-age kids that tug at their heart. It is all okay as long as we strive for a balance in the attention we give the kids.

■ **The big advantage of family child care is having multiple ages; however, it is perfectly okay to narrow your focus.** For example, if you really don't do well with babies, then just focus on preschoolers. Or if you would prefer to take two babies during the day and then a few afterschool kids; that is okay too. You can make your program what you want it to be.

■ **I print off the ages and stages lists in this book and share them with parents.** I want parents to know what to look for and to understand how they can encourage their child's development. It also helps them to understand the importance of what I do with their children.

■ **Physical growth is fairly easy to see, but it is a little harder to see social or emotional changes.** It helps to review the stages from time to time. For example, just knowing that it is normal for 4-year-olds to be boastful and bossy is such a relief, because these characteristics drive me crazy. It helps me to be more patient and understanding.

All together now: Multi-age groups

Chapter 8

Contents

Where am I now?	172
Introduction	173
Benefits	173
Disadvantages	175
Eight rules for working with multi-age groups	176
It looks like this!	179
FamilyShare	187
Heart of the Matter	188
Experience Talks	189

All together now: Multi-age groups—
Where am I now? What can I improve?

	Seldom 1	Sometimes 2	Often 3	Most Often 4
1. I provide many ways for children of different ages to play together.				
2. I show older children how to talk and play with younger children.				
3. I make a special effort to include infants in daily conversations and activities with the other children.				
4. I encourage helpful behavior between older and younger children.				
5. I introduce new words and new skills to both younger and older children.				
6. I value and celebrate children's different ages and personalities.				

Chapter 8

All together now: Multi-age groups

Most of us are familiar with child care centers or public schools. So we know a little about how classrooms with children of the same age work, but child care programs in the home are different. They are more "family" like and may have children that range in age from a newborn to a sixth grader. There are big differences between an 8-week old newborn, a toddler, a 4-year-old, and a school-ager!

Caring for children with a wide range of ages can be delightful, but it also can present some tough challenges. It requires paying close attention to each child's age. It may also call for some new skills.

Benefits

Multi-age groups encourage family-like relationships. Just like a family, children of different ages in home-based care learn to play together and get along. In fact, family child care often includes siblings. In times when families seem to be going many different directions, the opportunity to keep brothers and sisters together can be an advantage.

Children can teach and learn from each other. They usually have someone just a little older to learn from and someone just a little younger to teach. Children often learn best from other children rather than adults, and family child care sets the stage for that kind of learning.

Children have greater freedom to develop at their own rate. A child care center classroom of 3-year-olds is likely to have children who learn very quickly as well as those who learn much more slowly. Often those children are unfairly labeled as being slow or extremely bright. In a family child care home, those differences seem less obvious. A 4-year-old who is a little slow in learning how to gallop or skip is still miles ahead of the game when compared to a 2-year-old.

Younger children benefit from being included in activities they would have been unable to start on their own. For example, a 2-year-old can be part of a pretend circus adventure with older children that she would not be able to create on her own.

Children in small, multi-age groups are often less competitive and more cooperative or helpful. This is particularly true when the children have been together for several years, which is common in home-based child care. Children who grow up playing together get to know each other well. They learn what to expect from each other and how to get along. Older children delight in showing younger children how to master new skills.

Children and caregivers benefit from closer, more long-term relationships. The comfort of growing up with the same familiar caregiver gives children a tremendous sense of security. As one provider remarked, "I used to be in a program where I cared only for 4-year-olds. Each year we would get a new group of kids. It took almost a year to get to know each child well. Just when I learned how to work with a child and had developed a close relationship, off that child would go to the 5-year-old group! I became a family child care provider because I think that relationships are so important for young children, and really good relationships take time."

Children of different ages and abilities add a special richness to play and learning activities. Adults who care for only one age group often get tired of repeating activities. A provider shared this story: "The other day we were playing pizza parlor. Four-year-old Mark ordered the pizza by phone. The 3-year-olds stuffed the "play dough pizza" in the box. Five-year-old Seth made the deliveries on the tricycle to Laura, who is 2. Laura toddled over to the table, plopped the pizza down on a plate and said "EAT!" Seth arrived on the scene and rescued the pizza by asking Laura to help him make deliveries in the wagon. The children played pizza delivery all afternoon, and each time, it was with a new twist."

Multi-age groups offer children opportunities to develop and practice social skills. Because children are usually together for several years they have lots of time to learn about each other. They notice that babies do things differently from 3-year-olds. They notice that one child is often cranky, while another seems to be happy most of the time. They also watch you work with younger children in different ways. You may find them saying the same words that you would say as they try to convince a toddler to join in a pretend play adventure.

Disadvantages

Safety can be an issue. A crawling infant can easily be stepped on. A great activity for school-agers can be dangerous to do around infants and toddlers. For instance, school-agers may find it difficult to decorate a T-shirt using small beads or sharp scissors with a curious toddler hovering about.

Meal and snack choices are a common concern. Carrot sticks, apple slices, and grapes are fine for 4-year-olds and school-agers, but could cause choking in infants or toddlers. Meal planning with children of different ages may mean separate menus. Feeding a bottle to an infant, helping a toddler with a spoon, and providing second servings to hungry preschoolers can become a juggling act.

Same-age playmates are hard to come by. Toddlers and younger preschoolers seem to be happy to play with children of different ages, but older preschoolers may want to play with children of their own age and gender.

Activity planning can be hard. Infants, toddlers, preschoolers, and school-agers have different interests and skills. Caregivers must be careful not to give all their attention to one age group. It is especially important to avoid neglecting infants.

HFCCH Chapter 8 — All together now: Multi-age groups   175

Eight rules for working with multi-age groups

Rule 1

Arrange your play areas to provide a wide choice of activities.

Young children learn in many different ways. One child may like to curl up in a corner and look at a book, an infant may enjoy lying on a colorful quilt and watching the other children play, two other children may be playing house, and a toddler may roll a ball around the room.

Keep in mind that a family child care provider and a grade school teacher are different. Doing one activity at a time with the whole group does not work well with young children. It is best if the provider sets up several activities in the room for children to choose from. You can help children learn by moving around the room, talking, asking questions, and helping them solve problems.

Rule 2

Provide some play areas that are used just for one age group.

For instance, you may want to have a room or special corner that is used only by school-agers for craft projects, to do homework, or play board games. A special corner for toddlers with low climbing equipment, low riding toys, and a washtub filled with colorful scarves also is appropriate. Safety gates, low shelves, or even the back of a sofa serve as good barriers without blocking your view of the children.

Rule 3

Consider the ages of children when you store materials.

Store materials where children can reach them. Work from the bottom up. Store infant and toddler toys on a very low shelf or on the floor. Store preschool toys and materials on a shelf that is a bit higher or in a drawer that can be pulled out safely. School-age toys and materials can be stored even higher. Storing toys at a child's eye level or within easy reach will save you many steps. Children can get and return toys on their own.

Rule 4

Avoid large group activities.

Large group activities don't work well for very young children. Infants and toddlers may disturb group time because they are easily distracted and can't sit still for very long. Reading books or singing songs to 2 or 3 children at a time will be more successful than trying to read to the whole group. If your play area is set up with other things to do, children who are not reading or singing with you will be enjoying some other activity they can do on their own.

Rule 5

Focus on activities that provide experiences rather than products.

Young children don't do well with coloring book pages, "worksheet" activities, or projects that are supposed to "look-alike" when fin-

ished. When children see what the end product is supposed to look like, they often become upset because they may not have the skills to make it look "perfect." They may not cut straight or glue a picture on the "right spot." If the caregiver ends up finishing the project for everyone, the children may feel that they failed.

A better way is to focus on the experience. For example, instead of providing a "pre-designed" Halloween puppet, try providing a paper sack to decorate with an assortment of crayons, stickers, markers, fabric scraps, and magazine pictures.

Rule 6

Provide materials that can be used in different ways.
Some toys can only be used in one way and so children lose interest in them. However, blocks, play dough, or scarves are examples of play materials that can be used in many different ways. Children of different ages use toys like these to explore, build, create, and learn.

A toddler may pound, squish, and squeeze play dough; a 4-year-old may crumble it into a bowl for "pretend" soup; a 7-year-old may coil long "snakes" of dough into a volcano.

An infant may enjoy mouthing and gazing at different colored blocks while toddlers fill and dump blocks into a container. Four-year-olds may gather a bunch of blocks together to build a pretend fire; 5-year-olds may build a fence to house barnyard animals; and a school-ager may use the blocks as ramps for race cars.

An infant enjoys looking at and grasping a colorful scarf. It could be used to play peekaboo by a toddler, as a tablecloth or doll blanket by a preschooler, and as a turban-like hat by a school-ager.

Rule 7

Find simple ways to involve infants and toddlers in everyday activities.
Infants and toddlers learn a lot from watching and listening, so keep them close by and talk with them often. Infants and toddlers learn best by using their senses: seeing, touching, smelling, hearing, and tasting.

You may wonder about what to do with infants and toddlers while you are helping preschoolers with a special project.

children can do for real, as well as pretend. An older child also can help a younger child wash his or her hands, clean up a spill, or "pretend" to read. Preschoolers often love to help feed the baby and with guidance may become quite good at this task. Young children are not very steady or coordinated in their movements, but training and patience can help. It is common for young children to become quite skillful at helping out.

A final note:

Home child care providers do sometimes limit the span of ages they care for. Some caregivers prefer to work only with preschoolers, and others prefer to care for infants and toddlers only. Still others may like to focus on school-age children. Caregivers who choose to care only for school-agers really like this arrangement because it allows them time during normal school hours to run errands and take care of personal needs. Their program cares for school-agers before and after school and during summer vacations and school holidays.

Here are some ideas:

- Choose to do a special activity with preschoolers when younger children are taking their morning nap.

- Place a low barrier around an activity area so that younger children can watch and learn—but not disrupt the activity.

- Talk openly with infants and toddlers and describe what you do and see during the day.

- Let younger children touch, smell, hear, or taste the end result after the older children are finished.

Rule 8

Teach children self-help skills and encourage children to help each other.

Family child care allows children to be involved in day-to-day home life. Children love to help. Washing dishes is real life water play. Setting the table or putting away silverware helps children learn a basic math skill—"sorting." Dusting furniture, vacuuming, going to the store, and washing cars are activities that

It looks like this! Children of different ages playing together

Here are some examples of what quality child care with children of different ages looks like. Notice all the things you can do to help children learn.

	Infant 0-2	Toddler 2-3	Preschooler 3-5	School-ager 5-11
Reading	Listens to sounds of words as you read. Looks at pictures, colors, and objects. Enjoys sitting on your lap while you read.	Identifies and points to different pictures in the book. Names different objects.	Repeats different words, phrases, or rhymes in the story. Names characters in the story. May pretend to read to a younger child.	Reads or retells story to younger children. Asks and answers questions. Likes to read or look at books alone.
You could:	Hold baby on your lap as you read to others.	Repeat and introduce new words.	Ask questions "What do you think will happen next?"	Encourage older child to read to others.
Fingerplay "Eensy weensy spider"	Listens and watches you. Shows interest by laughing, cooing, moving arms and legs.	Listens and tries to make some finger movements.	Works hard to make finger movements and repeat words.	Leads other children in finger movements and words. Makes up new play rhymes and movements.
You could:	Be sure baby can see and hear you do the fingerplay. Encourage an older child to hold baby on his or her lap and help move the baby's arms and hands.	Repeat the fingerplay several times. Repeat and explain new words. "Eensy" means "very little."	Repeat the movements until children can do the fingerplay well. Ask questions to help children think and learn. "What might happen to a spider when it rains?"	Ask older child to lead the children in the fingerplay. Encourage child to experiment with new rhymes and movements.

	Infant 0-2	**Toddler** 2-3	**Preschooler** 3-5	**School-ager** 5-11
Picture story cards	Watches as older children talk about cards. Holds and touches cards. Looks at the cards.	Points to familiar objects. Names some basic objects in the picture.	Describes people, colors, shapes, and actions in the picture.	Interested in the detail of the story and the pictures. Creates a story that tells what may have happened in the picture. Tells what happened before and what happens afterward.
You could:	Hold child on your lap as you look at cards together. Talk with baby, say names of objects and make sounds "Cats go meow."	Ask child to point to different objects. Say and repeat names of objects. Give child chance to say names of objects.	Ask many "who, what, when, where, how" questions. "What color are the boots? When does it snow? Where do you think they are going? How will they get there?"	Give child paper and markers to create own story cards. Encourage child to tell story to other children.
Music/singing/dancing	Listens and sways or bounces to music.	Sings or shouts a few words of the song. Sways, claps, or dances to the music—not always in rhythm. Shakes a tambourine.	Sings song, moves and dances with other children. Can follow rhythm fairly well. Beats a drum or uses another musical instrument.	Sings words by self from memory. Often will begin the song and lead other children.
You could:	Hold baby as you dance and sing together. Give baby a rattle or bell to shake as music plays. Ask older children to sing to baby.	Sing with child. Show how to clap hands. Hold hands and dance together. Clap and cheer for children.	Help child clap in rhythm. Provide musical instrument, bells, drums, shakers, clickers. Change words of song to make it silly and different.	Help child find new words or ways to sing song. Invite child to make up new dance steps or movements. Ask child to lead others in singing or dancing.

	Infant 0-2	**Toddler** 2-3	**Preschooler** 3-5	**School-ager** 5-11
Pretend play/ airplane	Listens and watches children play.

Shows interest by laughing, cooing, moving arms and legs. | Pretends to be a passenger by sitting in a make believe plane with suitcase. | Imitates the role of a pilot or airline attendant.

Seats travelers, takes tickets, serves refreshments. | Organizes the play adventure (makes tickets, etc) and describes what's happening.

Talks about where the travelers are going. |
| *You could:* | Pretend to be a passenger with a baby. Show children how a baby might experience a plane ride. | Sit with child and talk about suitcase, tickets, and other objects. | Ask questions to encourage learning "Where are you going? How long will it take you to get there? Who will you see?" | Provide paper and materials to make tickets and other play items.

Ask child to read a book or show pictures to other children so they can learn about plane rides. |
| **Pretend play/ firefighter** | Listens and watches children play.

Shows interest by laughing, cooing, moving arms and legs. | Holds pretend fire hose, makes water and siren noises. | Plays the role of the firefighter or the resident of a burning house. | Plays a role and organizes the fire fighting event.

Makes up a story with a beginning, middle, and end. Tells other children what to do. |
| *You could:* | Talk with baby about what the other children are doing.

Hold baby and walk around the pretend play area so baby can see better. | Show child how to hold water hose, make siren sounds.

Read books or sing about the topic. | Pretend to be a person that needs to be rescued.

Give children extra props—such as a toy phone to call 911.

Show children what to do during a fire.

Ask questions. "What sounds do fire engines make, why do firefighters wear masks, what would you do if…" | Help child gather extra items needed for pretend play.

Ask child to read or tell a story about fire fighting so other children will know what to do during play.

Ask more questions to help children learn.

Teach fire safety skills (911, stop, drop, and roll). |

	Infant 0-2	**Toddler** 2-3	**Preschooler** 3-5	**School-ager** 5-11
Pretend play/ animal puppets	Listens and watches children with puppets. Touches and feels texture of puppet.	Holds one puppet, makes animal sounds.	Puts puppet on fist, makes sounds and talks with puppet. Sings song with puppet. Follows directions to act out simple story.	Makes puppets from paper sacks or socks and fabric scraps. Tells a story with several puppets with a beginning, middle, and end.
You could:	Use puppet to talk and sing to baby. Let baby touch and feel puppet.	Show child how to use puppet. Make animal sounds with child.	Show child how to tell a simple story with puppets. Help children make simple puppets with paper plates and paint stirring sticks as holders. Turn furniture so children can use the back of sofa or chair as a puppet stage. Ask "who, what, where, why" questions.	Provide materials to make puppets. Help child create a puppet theater from a cardboard box. Ask child to read a simple story such as "The Three Little Pigs" to the children and then act it out with puppets.
Cooking muffins	Watches and listens to children. May taste.	Will want to taste. Can place paper liners into muffin tin.	Names and describes cooking utensils. Helps mix ingredients. Helps spoon mixture into muffin tins.	Follows recipe steps. Measures ingredients. Predicts what will happen in the cooking process.
You could:	Give baby a wooden spoon to hold or paper liners to play with. Put a small amount of sugar or flour on baby's tongue to taste.	Let child taste flour or sugar before mixing batter. Let child smell foods like cinnamon or lemons. Use words like "sweet, sour."	Use new words; "measuring cup, mixer, beaters, stir, whip." Hold bowl as child stirs ingredients. Show children how to spoon mixture into tins.	Show child how to measure ingredients accurately. Ask child to help you follow the recipe. "How much, what comes next?"

	Infant 0-2	**Toddler** 2-3	**Preschooler** 3-5	**School-ager** 5-11
Block play	Holds blocks, feels texture, may try to chew or taste. Listens to children talk about their structures.	Plays fill and dump. Picks up blocks and puts them in a bucket. Takes them out again. Carries them around. May push other block structures over.	Lines blocks up in a row. Stacks blocks in a tower. Arranges blocks to make an enclosed square. Gives a name to block structure—"barn." Counts blocks.	Creates an elaborate block structure and connects it to another child's block structure. Uses lots of small toys with structure such as trucks or animals. Names it and tells a story about it.
You could:	Let baby sit on floor and play with small block. If baby drops block from high chair, ask an older child to play this game—pick it up over and over. Cover block with a scarf and see if baby can find it. Hold baby and watch other children play.	Give child a small bucket of blocks to play with on his/her own. Show child how to stack blocks. Move shelf or sofa so that older children's block structures are protected.	Show child different ways to use blocks: stacking, rows, an open or closed area, a simple bridge. Provide extra pretend items such as trucks, animals, or dolls. Show how to make a simple pattern using two colors of blocks.	Show child how to make patterns from different colors and sizes of blocks. Ask child to show other children how to use blocks to make buildings and bridges. Take photos of child's block structure to show parents.
Footprint hop	Listens and watches children play. Shows interest by laughing, cooing, moving arms and legs.	Jumps from footprint to footprint with both feet.	Steps with alternating feet from footprint to footprint.	Hops on one foot from footprint to footprint.
You could:	Hold baby close to you as you step and hop across footprints.	Demonstrate how to hop. Introduce new words "high, low, far, close."	Encourage child to count steps. Challenge child to try hopping in different ways. Show child how to measure footprints.	Suggest measuring how far each child hops and charting it on a graph.

	Infant **0-2**	**Toddler** **2-3**	**Preschooler** **3-5**	**School-ager** **5-11**
Water play	Watches and listens to you and other children. Enjoys touching and feeling water with both hands and feet. Wants to taste.	Splashes in a tub of water. Fills and empties containers. Can identify "hot" or "cold," "wet." Likes to squeeze sponges.	Pours from one container into another, but often spills. Notices that corks float, but rocks sink. Pretends water is other liquids—orange juice, coffee, dish soap.	Measures water poured into different containers. Fills containers with different amounts and predicts which will float or sink. Interested in how soap or food coloring changes water.
You could:	Hold baby and gently help touch baby's hands and feet in the water. Say, "cold, wet, splish-splash, brrr."	Provide plastic tubs, corks, sponges, measuring cups, small plastic bottles. Introduce words such as "in, out, over, through, full, empty, heavy, sink, float."	Provide extra pretend play items such as plastic baby bottles, a pretend fishing rod, or dolls. Ask questions and help children describe in words what they are doing.	Supply items that can change the water, such as food dye or soap. Ask "What will happen if . . . what happens next?"
Collect leaves	Watches and listens to you and other children. Touches leaves and branches.	Fills a bucket or wagon with leaves and other found objects. Dumps and fills again over and over.	Collects leaves to take home. Notices different shapes and sizes of leaves.	Uses magnifying glass to compare veins of leaves. Makes crayon leaf rubbings.
You could:	Help baby touch and smell leaves. Use words: "shiny, green, soft, smooth."	Introduce new words: "green, red, yellow, small, big, tiny, torn, wet."	Talk about shapes, colors. Show child how to count and sort leaves. Provide bags or small boxes for "collections."	Provide a magnifying glass and a ruler to measure leaves. Show child how to make crayon rubbings of leaves.

	Infant 0-2	Toddler 2-3	Preschooler 3-5	School-ager 5-11
Shadow tag	Watches and listens to children as they move in sunlight and create shadows.	Walks in sun and observes own shadow.	Moves parts of body and talks about how shadow changes. Looks at shadows of other children and objects.	Runs around yard and tries to tag others by stepping onto their shadows. Creates pretend shadow creatures.
You could:	Hold baby and step into sunlight and into shadows. Talk about "bright and dark."	Demonstrate how to make a shadow move by raising arm or leg. Use words like "high, low, dark, bright, up, down."	Ask questions: "What would happen if you did this…?"	Take pictures of imaginary shadow creatures.
Body drawings	Crawls around and over children as they lie down. Watches children as they use crayon or chalk to draw around each others' bodies.	Lies on back for just a few moments to allow body to be traced onto paper.	Identifies parts of the body as adult or older child draws around them. Tries to draw around own hand or foot.	Moves in several ways to get different types of body drawings. Cuts out tracings with scissors. Is eager to trace other children. Colors in body outline to look like themselves.
You could:	Hold baby's feet and show them to other children. Hold baby and help baby watch as children trace each other.	Show child how to lie down on paper or sidewalk as another child traces you. Draw around just a foot or hand of child. Ask child to point to different body parts. Use words "hand, finger, fingernail, foot, toes."	Ask children to name different body parts. Help them trace their own feet or hands. Use new words, "elbow, wrist, thigh, knee, ankle." Write words of body parts on the child's body picture.	Ask child to help other children compare size of hands or feet with each other. Provide a measuring tape or ruler to measure body drawings. Show children how to use footsteps to measure length or distance.

	Infant **0-2**	**Toddler** **2-3**	**Preschooler** **3-5**	**School-ager** **5-11**
Drawing	Holds crayon and waves in air. May try to taste.	Scribbles on paper. May break regular, thin crayons.	Draws shapes and basic objects. Experiments with different colors, names colors. May ask adult or older child to write name of objects or a word on the drawing.	Draws more detailed objects. Names the drawing. May want to write or add words to drawing. Tells story about it.
You could:	Hold crayon in older baby's hand and move across the paper.	Provide "fat" crayons that are easier to hold. Tape paper to table so the paper won't move as child scribbles. Writes child's name on paper.	Point out color words on crayons. Say "tell me about the drawing" rather than ask what it is. Ask child to name colors or shapes he/she might have used. Help child write name or other words on paper.	Ask questions. "How did you decide to use those colors?" "How does your drawing make you feel?" "What would you do differently in your next drawing?" "What would you like to do with your drawing?"
Rock painting	Holds rock, feels texture. May try to taste.	Covers entire rock with water or paint.	Covers sections of rock with different colors.	Draws a design on the rock with paint or markers.
You could:	Hold baby and let him/her touch several different rocks. Use words: "rock, hard, smooth, shiny, rough."	Give child rock with water and wider paint brush. Show how to use brush with water. Show how to use brush with paint. Talk about colors.	Show child how to use one color on rock and then another. Talk about colors and what happens when two colors are combined. Talk about textures, sizes, and shapes of rocks.	Show how to use masking or painter's tape to separate colors from one another. Provide different size brushes and markers.

	Infant 0-2	Toddler 2-3	Preschooler 3-5	School-ager 5-11
Play dough	Watches and listens to children as they play. Feels and pats play dough.	Pats and squeezes play dough. May try to put it in a container and dump it out.	Rolls out into "snake-like" forms. Pats into pancakes, makes balls. Blends two colors together.	Creates an object. Coils snake-like pieces to form a pot.
You could:	Hold baby and put small piece of dough in hand. Use words "smooth, cold, squeeze."	Show child how to squeeze dough and pat it into a pancake shape. At the table, give him/her a small plastic tub to "fill and dump" play dough.	Provide kitchen tools that can help shape or make patterns. Show child how to roll play dough into balls and snakes. Use new words, "round, ball, long, curve, straight, stretch."	Ask questions: "How did you do that? What would happen if…?" Ask child to help you make play dough from a recipe. Provide other types of clay for ornaments and pots.

FamilyShare...

Supporting your partners

Although families often prefer home-based child care, they sometimes have mixed feelings. They worry that their children should be in a more center-like setting in a classroom with children their own age. You can listen to parents and help them identify their concerns.

Remind them of the key advantages to family child care:

- The stability and security of being cared for by one adult over several years.
- Family-like relationships that include an opportunity for siblings to grow up together.
- The opportunity for young children to learn from older children.
- The opportunity for older children to reinforce their own learning and leadership skills by teaching younger children.
- The support for children to develop at their own rate—faster or slower—in a less competitive environment.
- The opportunity to practice and develop social skills with children of many different ages.

You also will want to keep parents informed about the many things you teach children each day and give them examples of photos, artwork, and projects that show their learning. Remind them also of the education and training you have taken to provide quality care and learning.

Heart of the Matter

I had been working with David (age 5) for a long time to control his anger. He could get really angry in a matter of seconds. Usually his frustration was focused on anyone who interfered with his block building, which was his passion. David was a 'master builder' and spent much of each day planning and building elaborate block structures.

I also cared for 2-year-old Amber. Amber had Down's Syndrome. Like most toddlers, Amber was very much into push and pull, fill and dump, and she usually managed to push David's block building over almost every day. David's usual response was to yell at Amber and give her a good whack.

David had watched me handle the problem in different ways. Usually we barricaded his block area off so she couldn't get in, but other times this wasn't practical, so I tried to notice when she was headed his way and would redirect her (usually under protest) to another activity. Amber was very clever about finding ways to break through the barricade. She seemed to love this game. I had to watch very closely to head off disaster.

One day I was very busy with the baby, and Amber again made it through the barricade. But this time David reacted differently. He gently caught her, put his arm around her in a brotherly way, and said, 'No Amber, don't knock over my blocks. Let's go to the piano. You can play there instead.' As he walked away, he looked over his shoulder and said, 'And I'll listen to your beautiful music!' Amber obediently plunked away at the piano and every so often stopped and looked over at David, who would burst into applause.

I was so proud of him for handling the situation like that! I could tell he was also pleased. From that point on, David's anger just didn't seem to be much of a problem anymore. In fact, he became very protective of Amber. And of course she adored him.

Lesia

Experience Talks

Conversations with other providers

■ **I love the fact that brothers and sisters can be together in family child care.** It saddens me to think that siblings in other types of child care often are separated. Are there squabbles?—yes sometimes. But we learn how to get along. Children can't learn how to be a family if they are never together.

■ **I really encourage the children to teach each other.** If one of the younger children comes to me for help, I ask one of the older children to help out also. This teaches the younger children how to ask the older kids for help, and it makes the older children feel special.

■ **I take pictures of the kids playing together and put them in a special album.** They love to look at this book and have a lot of fun talking about how much they have grown. It's a great conversation piece.

■ **I've learned that activities for multi-age groups of children do not have to be complicated.** Children learn so much from just playing house with each other! If I set up my play areas so that they are interesting, then the children really need very little help from me.

■ **I use "tried and true" basic materials that can be used in a lot of different ways.** Forget all the media hype about the latest "razzle-dazzle" toy. I provide loads of books, lots of art materials, different sizes and types of balls, blocks, and great pretend play stuff. We never run out of things to do. It is amazing what children learn just by using and exploring all these materials.

■ **It is easy to neglect infants so I really work hard to include them in our day.** I make it a point to regularly talk and interact with infants as they watch the older children play. I talk, talk, and talk some more. I talk about what each child is doing. I mention colors, shapes, and sizes of the toys. It is a great way to give attention to them and the older kids. The infant gets to hear new words and the preschooler knows I am watching him play, because he hears me telling the baby about what he's doing.

■ **I am a big fan of baby slings or carriers that you can wear.** I care for two infants and try to carry each baby close to me for at least an hour each day. It makes them much less fussy. This also frees me up to respond to the older children. I think babies need the security of being held. Frankly, I enjoy the closeness too. There are so many slings to choose from now that you easily can find one that fits you okay.

- **I support the "casual" model of group activities.** By this, I mean when I read a book or try to have a group discussion with the children, I do not insist that the 18-month-old sit there the entire time. If he gets up and wanders over to another area, I just go on reading. I take comfort in knowing that as he grows older, he will find it easier to pay attention. And just by being in the room, he is getting the idea of a group "story time." Of course, I do read to all the children one-on-one throughout the day also. I think they need both.

- **I purchase two kinds of toys and materials—some everyone can play with and others are specific for each age group.** Infants need mobiles, toddlers need push toys, and preschoolers need tricycles. But all the children love music. It just takes some thought.

- **Collecting children's toys and equipment is a little like building a wardrobe.** You start with the basics, and then add accessories. Basics without accessories can get a little dull. But accessories without the basics – well that is a recipe for disaster!

- **Older children love to help out, but sometimes they need their own space too.** I have an adjoining room in my house where older kids can go "to get away from the babies." We keep small blocks and board games in that room. I can keep an eye on both rooms and I have a gate in the door to block the younger ones from entering.

- **Caring for children of different ages has really helped me to see each child as an individual.** It's easier to notice each stage. We make a point to celebrate each child's successes. When someone learns to crawl or walk, we make a big deal out of it. We take pictures and have a special treat, and the kids tell everyone—even the mail carrier.

- **I don't do large group activities very often.** Young children really need one-on-one attention. It's easier to work with 1 or 2 children for a few minutes and then "float" off to another child. I find I have a lot more interaction with the children this way.

- **For me, the best part is watching the children grow year after year.** I really get to know the children very well and can plan activities that I know they will be interested in. For example, Jason has loved trucks since he was a toddler. So I used different colored trucks to teach him colors. He also learned numbers by counting small blocks that we put into trucks.

- **I am developing tomorrow's leaders!** I have several school-agers and I have them sit down with me weekly and help plan for the next week. They love it. They really enjoy making suggestions for snack and art projects. They know what will work with different age children—because they have lived it. It takes a bit more time on my part, but it is a good opportunity for them to learn decision-making skills. And it is about something that really matters to them.

Guiding behavior

Contents

Where am I now?	192
Begin with your relationship	193
Establish predictable routines	193
Create a safe place to play and learn	194
Understanding infants	196
Understanding toddlers	198
Understanding preschoolers	200
Understanding school-agers	200
Consider yourself a teacher	201
What about rewards and stickers?	204
When all else fails—The problem-solving approach	205
Frequently asked questions about spanking	206
What about temper tantrums?	207
What about biting?	209
Insensitivity to physical, racial, or ethnic differences	211
What about sex-related play?	213
What about toilet learning?	213
FamilyShare	216
Heart of the Matter	217
Experience Talks	218

Guiding behavior—
Where am I now? What can I improve?

	Seldom 1	Sometimes 2	Often 3	Most Often 4
1. I have a secure and supportive relationship with each child.				
2. I understand common behavior problems for children of different ages.				
3. I understand which guidance methods work best for different ages.				
4. I have realistic, simple rules for children.				
5. I remind, explain, and help children understand the reasons for our rules.				
6. I involve children in setting guidelines and limits for their own behavior.				
7. I set a good example with my own behavior.				
8. I set up and organize space and activity areas in ways that encourage positive behavior and reduce conflict.				
9. I reduce stress for children by following routines and a well-balanced schedule.				
10. I alert children to changes in activities or routines and give them enough time to move from one activity to another.				
11. I select books and activities that encourage cooperative play and teach positive social skills.				
12. I supervise children closely and intervene quickly to help children problem solve.				
13. I encourage children's good behavior by praising the positive things they do.				
14. I have self-control and can guide children's behavior calmly without hitting, yelling, or shaming.				
15. I share information with families about rules, limits, and guidance methods.				
16. I encourage families to give suggestions, ideas, and information that will help me understand and guide their children.				

Chapter 9

Guiding behavior

Children are delightful to have around but at times can be quite a challenge! Learning self-control and how to get along with others is part of growing up, but it takes time. You have an important role in teaching children these skills.

Begin with your relationship

Your relationship with children is the foundation for guiding behavior. It will help to know child development and behavior management techniques, but a secure and supportive relationship with each child sets the stage for everything else.

Children sense when you feel confident and secure. Children need to know you feel comfortable with yourself and that you are in control of your own emotions. This helps them feel safe to learn and explore their world.

Children trust you to guide them. When they begin to be fearful or lose control of their own emotions, they need to know they can trust you to set limits and keep everyone safe.

Children need to feel understood. Learning how to behave can be a struggle. For many children, it is sometimes two steps forward and one step back. Children need to know that you value them even when they fail and make mistakes.

Establish predictable routines

Establish consistent times for eating, napping. Children's small stomachs and high energy levels need nutritious snacks and meals frequently. All children need to rest even if they don't sleep. Children whose basic needs are met will be less cranky and whiny.

HFCCH Chapter 9 — Guiding behavior

Balance active times with quiet times. This will help children learn how to pace themselves. Children are full of energy and don't know how to slow down and rest. Planning your daily schedule so there are active play times and quiet play and rest will help children learn how to pace themselves.

Balance group time with time to be alone. Each day children need time to come together as a group, time to play with one or two friends, and some alone time. This teaches them the importance of community, the value of friendships, and respect for individual needs.

Create a safe place to play and learn

Children are natural explorers and risk takers. Children move quickly, they put things in their mouth, they break things, they love to climb, and they love to hide. Take a close look at your home, indoors and outdoors. A safe place to play and appropriate toys to play with can save you from saying "No" too often and make your day easier.

Childproof your home. Make your home safe by locking up dangerous chemicals and medicines, covering electrical outlets, and storing breakable objects up high. Often you can just see an accident waiting to happen. Fix, repair, toss, or lock up anything that might be a danger to children. A fenced-in yard will help keep children away from the street.

Make sure you have enough toys. Problems often arise when children do not have enough toys or materials to play with. Think about what you need for children of different ages and interests. Plenty of paper to draw on; materials to sort, collect, trade, and share; and well-maintained equipment to climb or ride on will keep children busy and interested.

Make sure children have the right toys for the right age. Toddlers need toys they can push, pull, grab, or yank without causing major damage. Getting hit accidentally on the head with a foam block is okay, but a "bonk" on the head with a hard wooden block is not. Toddlers have not yet learned how to share well, so purchasing several favorite toys can help prevent a lot of behavior problems.

Teach children how to handle toys and materials. Children can be taught how to carefully handle books, toys, and other materials. For example, even very young children can learn that we treasure books, that we handle them gently, and that we read them in special places. Children will need to hear this message a number of times, but they will learn it.

Arrange your space wisely. Often the way you organize space can make a difference in how children behave. Many modern homes have open designs where rooms naturally flow into each other. This can be great for supervision because it allows you to easily see children in different parts of the house. However, if space is too open you may find children running wildly. Pay attention to where behavior problems occur. Try arranging space and furniture differently to see if it makes a difference.

Organize toys and supplies to make things easy for children. You will have fewer problems if children can find toys and supplies. Place toys on low shelves and label the shelves with pictures so children will know where to put them back.

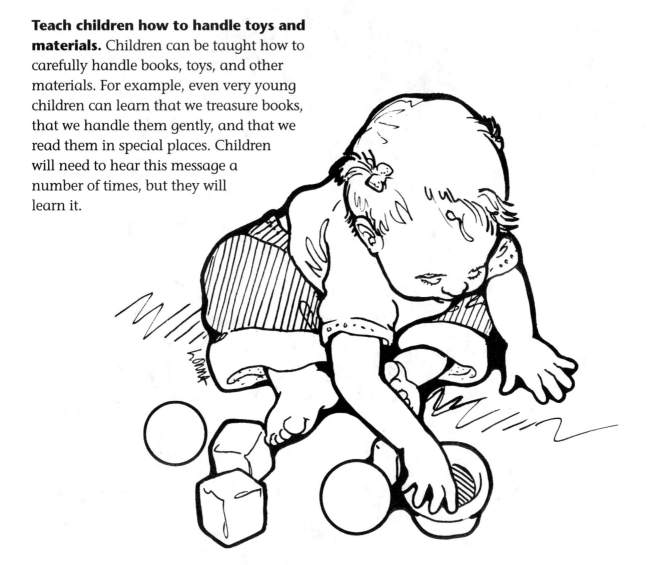

HFCCH Chapter 9 — Guiding behavior

Understanding infants

Infants generally don't pose much of a behavior problem, but they can be a challenge because they are so dependent on adults for their basic needs. The most troublesome behavior for caregivers usually is crying.

Infants cry because they are wet, hungry, cold, hot, or lonely. Crying is their only way of letting adults know they need something. Studies show that infants who have their needs met quickly, and who are held and comforted when they cry, develop a strong sense of security and well-being and actually may cry much less later on.

Sometimes infants have colic. They seem to cry for no apparent reason.

Colic usually begins when a baby is 2-3 weeks old and may continue until an infant is 3-4 months old. Crying may last for 2-3 hours and often reoccurs during the same part of the day. There are many theories about what causes colic but a definite cause has not been found. A baby who continues to cry can be very frustrating for both parents and caregivers.

How to handle a crying baby

It can be exhausting to care for a baby who cries a lot. It is easy to get frustrated and angry. But getting angry and shaking a baby is dangerous.

Never shake a baby! If you shake a baby you can cause permanent damage or death. Babies have large heavy heads and weak neck muscles. When a baby is shaken, the movement bounces the brain back and forth within the skull, rupturing and tearing blood vessels, nerves, and brain tissue. Many babies who are shaken die. Children who survive often have permanent damage including blindness, hearing loss, seizures, developmental delays, speech and learning difficulties, and paralysis.

To calm a baby, try the following.

- **Check to make sure that a baby's basic needs are met.** Crying may be a sign of hunger or a dirty diaper.
- **Try swaddling or wrapping the baby up snugly.** This is comforting and helps babies feel secure.
- **Hold the baby against your chest.** Babies often feel more comfortable if you hold them close.
- **Try feeding the baby more slowly.** Remember to burp often.
- **Rock the baby.** You can do this in a rocking chair or by sitting with baby and swaying back and forth.
- **Go for a walk or ride.** Sometimes a stroller ride in fresh air can work wonders.
- **Give baby a warm bath.** Water can be very soothing.
- **Give baby a gentle massage.** Rub on lotion or a light oil (such as almond oil). Gently massage baby's arms, legs, toes, and tummy.
- **Try singing softly.** Humming works well too.
- **Play a CD with pleasant gentle sounds.** Soft piano music or ocean sounds seem to work well.
- **You can also try using a pacifier** (if parents approve). Sometimes a baby is not hungry, but just needs to suck.

If nothing works, take a break. If you find your frustration level climbing, it is okay to just put the baby down and let him or her cry for short periods (10 – 15 minutes).

Call the doctor. If the crying continues, suggest that parents take the child to a doctor just to make sure there are no serious problems.

Understanding toddlers

Toddlers have trouble telling you what they need. They still express themselves a great deal by crying, shrieking, jabbering, grunting, and pointing. The few words they can say may mean many things. "Cup!" may mean "Hand me my cup!" or "I want more milk," or "The cup just fell off the table" or "The dog just stole my cup!" This limited communication makes it very hard to understand a toddler's needs.

Toddler behavior can be impulsive. They reach out and grab things (like eyeglasses). Sometimes they will scream for a cookie that can't be reached, but at other times they may lead (or drag) you to the jar and point. Learning how to do things in a socially acceptable way is a big step for a toddler.

Toddlers are rather clumsy and awkward with gestures. A well-meant pat can feel like a whack. A spoonful of peas may wind up more on the floor than in the mouth.

"No" and "Mine" are favorite words. Toddlers are very protective of their toys. They are quite willing to hit or bite to get (or keep) a favorite toy. In fact, toddlers may spend as much time carrying around and protecting toys as they do playing with them.

Toddlers are very focused on "moving." They want to drop, carry, push, pull, move around, and climb over. Sitting still for more than a few minutes is very hard to do.

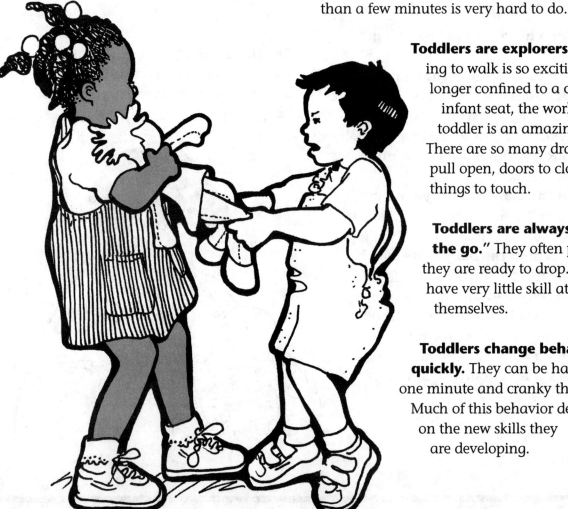

Toddlers are explorers. Learning to walk is so exciting. No longer confined to a crib or an infant seat, the world of a toddler is an amazing place. There are so many drawers to pull open, doors to close, and things to touch.

Toddlers are always "on the go." They often play until they are ready to drop. They have very little skill at pacing themselves.

Toddlers change behaviors quickly. They can be happy one minute and cranky the next. Much of this behavior depends on the new skills they are developing.

Behavior guidance toolbox for infants and toddlers

Remove

Safety is your first priority. When a child is running out into the street or about to get into the household bleach, there is no time for negotiation. Caregivers must remove a child from a dangerous situation. Picking up a child, holding him or her, or putting him or her in the crib for a few minutes until things can be made safe is perfectly okay. A child may protest loudly, but your primary responsibility is to keep him or her safe.

Distract

When a child is doing something unacceptable, try to call attention to another activity—perhaps playing with another toy or reading a book together. The goal is to distract the child from the problem temporarily. For example, if a toddler wants to climb into the dishwasher as you are unloading it, perhaps you can distract him/her with a stuffed toy. A frustrated or cranky child often can be distracted with a song or a fingerplay. Since young children's attention spans are short, distraction often is effective.

Redirect

Sometimes the behavior is okay but it is being done the wrong way. When this happens, you may need to redirect a child. If a child is drawing on books, remove the books and say, "Books are not for drawing on." At the same time, substitute an appropriate material saying, "If you want to draw on something, draw on this paper." If the child is throwing blocks, you can remove the blocks and give him/her a ball to throw. If he/she wants to dance on the coffee table, help the child down and ask him/her to perform for you on the front porch.

HFCCH Chapter 9 — Guiding behavior

Understanding preschoolers

Preschoolers are learning about the world around them. They ask lots of questions, and they love to imitate adults.

They are learning to share, trade, and take turns. There is a lot of give and take as they learn how to cooperate and get along with others.

Preschoolers like attention. They also may try to shock you by using forbidden words. Getting attention is fun; being ignored is not.

Preschoolers are risk-takers. They like to try new things and often take risks they haven't tried before.

Preschoolers like to make decisions. Making decisions helps them feel important. Preschoolers get a little carried away and become rather bossy too.

Preschoolers have lots of energy—often more energy than adults! They play hard, fast, and furious. Sometimes they get tired rather suddenly and become cranky and irritable.

Preschoolers spend a lot of time learning how to get along with others. "Best friends" are very important, but such friendships are brief and may last only a few minutes. Hurt feelings (and sometimes swift kicks from friends) are part of the learning process.

Understanding school-agers

School-age children seem much more grown up—most of the time. They understand the basics of getting along, but they are still learning the finer details. They still need to be taught how to use good manners, how to ask for help, and how to negotiate with others.

School-age children often argue. It is not uncommon for school-agers to argue and fight a great deal with friends. School-agers need considerable help learning social skills like how to make friends, trust others, work in a team, and resolve conflicts.

School-agers want to use "real" things rather than "play" things. They want to use real tools rather than plastic play tools. They want to make real jewelry, rather than play pretend jewelry. They want to cook real food in real pots and pans. All of this takes a different kind of supervision.

School-agers often set standards for themselves that are frustratingly high or unsatisfyingly low. Children this age have not had much experience in setting and achieving goals. They often overestimate what they

Consider yourself a teacher

Children do not grow up on their own; they need adults to teach them. They need to know the rules—what is okay and what is not okay. Your knowledge about how children learn and grow will help you guide children in ways they can understand at each age level. Two-year-olds have limited understanding and need a lot of redirection. Five-year-olds can learn to be good problem solvers.

Keep rules simple and easy to understand. Discuss rules with children and write them down. Consider children's suggestions for rules. Repeat the rules often.

can accomplish. They need you to guide them toward challenging experiences they can be successful at.

School-agers enjoy being "older" but may not like the responsibility that goes with getting older. Often they have to be reminded to carry out homework responsibilities or household chores. Learning self-discipline is an ongoing process that improves each year.

A few rules that work well with children include:
1. We help each other.
2. We take care of our toys.
3. We say please and thank you.
4. We are kind to each other.

Say what you mean; use dos instead of don'ts. Use your words carefully when you teach children. Keep sentences short and simple. Focus on what to do rather than what not to do.

Try saying:	Instead of:
Slow down and walk.	Stop running.
Come hold my hand.	Don't touch anything.
Keep your feet on the floor.	Don't climb on the couch.
Use your quiet voice inside.	Stop screaming and shouting.

Talk "to" or "with" children – not "at" children. Children often don't hear you when you are talking (or shouting) "at" them. You will be much more effective if you get down on their level. Look them in the eyes, touch them on the shoulder, and talk "with" them.

Set a good example. Children watch you all the time. They see how you talk to other children and adults. They see how you cope with anger or frustration. They watch how you deal with sadness and joy. They listen to how you say "I'm sorry." The way you handle the ups and downs of life teaches children a lot about how to behave and get along with others.

Encourage children to set good examples for each other. Children also learn a great deal from each other. Encourage appropriate ways to share, play, and be kind to each other.

Give clear, simple choices. Toddlers can choose between a red cup and a green cup. Preschoolers can choose between playing "airport" and "zookeeper." Give children a choice only when there is a choice. For example, saying "It is naptime, do you want to lie down now?" is not really an option if your rule is that everyone will rest at naptime.

Show respect for children. Talk to misbehaving children in private, remind them of reasons for rules, and talk to them about what they can do.

Catch children being good. All children want attention. It is better to give them positive attention for good behavior than negative attention for misbehavior. Comment on something positive about each child, each day. Better yet, strive for several times a day.

Praise like a good coach instead of a cheerleader. A cheerleader merely shouts general praise: "What a great job!" or "What a beautiful picture." A good coach tells you what you're doing right, uses praise as a teaching tool, and lets you know why he or she is proud of you. If

a child sets the table, you might say, "You did such a good job setting the table! You put the spoons and forks in the right place and remembered the napkins!" When you look at a child's painting, you might remark, "This painting just glows with color. You used blue, green, red, yellow, and orange. Tell me how you did this!"

Share the good news. Remember to share children's good behavior with others. Mention it to other children and to parents.

Teach children how to resolve conflict and problem solve. Help them recognize feelings, identify the problem, come up with ideas for solving the problem, and try possible solutions.

Teach children how to apologize. Learning how to apologize is a skill. Young children have a hard time understanding another child's feelings, but by the time they are 4 years old they should be learning the four steps of this basic skill.

Teach a child to:
1. look at the other child
2. say the child's name
3. say " I'm sorry"
4. say why
Keep it simple: e.g., Lucas, I am sorry I hit you.

With time and practice, children will not have to be prompted and their apology will be more genuine.

Teach children how to correct their misbehavior. If a child throws a bowl of peas onto the floor give him/her a dust pan and show the child how to clean it up. If a child marks on the wall, give him/her a wet cloth to clean it off.

Use play activities to teach children social skills. Use children's books that show how children resolve problems. Play "what if" games. Become a character in children's pretend play and show children how to use good manners and be kind to the baby doll.

HFCCH Chapter 9 — Guiding behavior 203

When is it okay to use time out?

Time outs do not work well with toddlers. They just don't understand what a time out means. It makes no impact and teaches them nothing. Redirecting them to another activity generally works better.

For preschoolers, a time out is better understood as a "cooling off" period. This gives a child a few minutes to settle down and you a few minutes to determine what actually happened. It should be brief, usually no more than 4-5 minutes.

Use "time out" time as teaching time. Young children often don't understand their misdoings. Always follow through by explaining what happened, what they should not be doing, and what they can do instead.

Preschoolers also need the opportunity to practice the correct behavior. Keep such discussions simple. You might say, "It's not okay to hit Tanya. Instead, tell her with words that you want to play with the blocks too." Often you will need to suggest words or phrases to use and model this for them.

Teach school-agers self control. Give them a short time limit for cooling off, but tell them that they need to decide if they are ready to play again. Help them consider if choosing another activity after awhile might be helpful. Let them make the decision for when to come back to their previous activity.

What about rewards and stickers?

Social rewards

Social rewards include smiling, praising, patting, hugging, and listening. These make a child feel special and encourage good behavior. If you smile and nod when a child puts a toy back where it belongs, the child may learn that cleaning up is valued and appreciated.

Material rewards

Material rewards include money, toys, and stickers. These too can be used to support good behavior but present some drawbacks.

Children can become too accustomed to material rewards and refuse to behave properly without them. Frequent use of such rewards also may teach children to bargain or negotiate for more and bigger payoffs.

Children often place more importance on the reward itself than on their "good" behavior. If a child is rewarded with a cookie each time he or she helps clean up, the child begins to place much more importance on the cookie than the feeling of accomplishment or appreciation for a well-organized toy shelf. Overuse of food as a reward may lead to problems with obesity and tooth decay.

When all else fails—
The problem-solving approach

When a problem happens over and over. Take time to sit down and think about the problem. It can help you find a more successful way to handle things.

Try the who, what, when, where, and how method. Ask yourself, "When does the troublesome behavior seem to happen? What happens just before and after? Where does it happen and with whom? How do I usually respond? What could I do to prevent the behavior? What other approaches could I use?"

Finding causes and looking for solutions

	1st incident	2nd incident	3rd incident
What is happening?			
When does it seem to happen?			
What happens just before?			
What happens just after?			
Where does it happen?			
Who seems to be involved?			
How could I respond better to the problem?			
What could I do to prevent the problem?			

Give your solution time to work, and evaluate its success or failure. If you do not find a change in behavior after several weeks, go through the process again, and try another alternative.

Frequently asked questions about spanking

Q: When is it okay to spank a child?

A: It is never acceptable for a child care provider to punish a child by slapping, hitting, or spanking. Pinching, punching, or shaking a child are also not okay. Any of these actions can result in injury and may be in violation of state child abuse protection laws. You also could be legally responsible for injury claims.

Q: But what if the child's parents have given me permission to do so?

A: It still is not acceptable. It is true that parents sometimes try to give child care providers permission to punish children physically. They may encourage you to spank, slap, or even bite their child. Nevertheless, you would still be liable for injury. Parental permission for you to harm a child will not hold up in court.

Q: What is so wrong with spanking? It is the only thing that seems to get some kids' attention.

A: Spanking will get children's attention but doesn't do a very good job of teaching them how to behave. It's hard to reason with a screaming, crying child. Usually, spanking distresses a child so much that explaining or reasoning with a child becomes impossible. Adults who frequently slap a toddler's hands often are dismayed to find the toddler slapping back or worse yet, slapping and hitting others.

There are many other ways to handle misbehavior depending on the situation and the child's age. Redirecting children to another activity, giving a child a brief time out or "cooling-off" period, and teaching problem-solving skills are all more effective than spanking.

Most providers find it more successful to focus on teaching a child what "to do" rather than what "not" to do. It may help to think of behavior problems as an opportunity to teach children new skills.

Q: So does this mean I can never touch a child? What can I do instead?

A: Young children often respond well to physical touch. But it should not be "hurtful" touch. Taking them by the hand, touching them on the arm, picking them up, and holding or gently restraining them are all good ways to get their attention.

Q: I spank my own children—so I guess this makes me a bad parent?

A: Part of the problem with spanking is how often it happens and the tendency to make it the only way you deal with a problem. Before you know it, spanking can quickly spiral out of control. It is easy to fall into the pattern of dealing with every problem in this way. But it is really the lazy way out. It side tracks you from doing what you really need to do, which is teaching your child skills for good behavior.

Studies show that children who experience or witness a great deal of spanking, slapping, or hitting are much more likely to become aggressive themselves. Children who are spanked frequently often hit younger children. Children who are bullied by older brothers or sisters or other children often react by bullying others.

What about temper tantrums?

Toddlers throw tantrums for many reasons—some big, some small. A square block won't fit in a round hole. Shoes feel funny, and socks don't seem to come off right. And to make matters worse, you won't let them climb on top of the kitchen table.

Toddlers have tantrums because they get frustrated very easily. Tantrums are most likely to happen when toddlers are hungry, exhausted, or over-excited.

Toddlers also have very few problem-solving skills. Most toddlers still do not talk much. They have trouble asking for things and expressing their feelings. Their ability to reason is very limited.

Preschoolers are less likely to throw tantrums. They have developed more coping skills and are able to communicate better. Still, when lunch is late or when things get frustrating, your preschoolers may begin to behave more like 2-year-olds!

Some preschoolers learn that tantrums can be used to get something they want. If caregivers give in to demands, tantrums may begin to occur with greater frequency.

School-agers sometimes react with tantrum-like behavior to situations created by school experiences. Learning to get along with friends, work as part of a team, or compete in a sport requires skills that many older kids haven't fully developed yet. Kids who have limited problem-solving skills or difficulty expressing themselves with words are likely to have temper tantrums or fits of anger. Older children can learn to recognize when they are feeling upset or frustrated and learn acceptable ways to deal with their anger.

How to handle a tantrum

Try to remain calm. Shaking, spanking, or screaming at a child only tends to make the tantrum worse instead of better. Set a positive example for children by remaining in control of yourself and your emotions.

Pause before you act. Take at least thirty seconds to decide how you will handle the tantrum. Four possible ways to deal with a tantrum include:

■ **Distract**—Try to get the child's attention focused on something else. If the child screams when you take him or her away from something unsafe (like your purse), offer something else to play with. This technique works well with toddlers.

HFCCH Chapter 9 — Guiding behavior 207

- **Remove**—Take the child to a quiet, private place to calm down. This should be a quiet "cooling down" place that is away from other children. Avoid trying to talk or reason with a screaming child. It doesn't work. Stay nearby until you see that he or she has calmed down. Then you can talk and return to whatever you were doing.

- **Ignore**—Older children will sometimes throw tantrums to get attention. Try ignoring the tantrum and going about your business as usual.

- **Hold**—Holding an "out of control" child calmly is sometimes necessary to keep him or her from hurting him- or herself or someone else. You might also say something like: "I can see you are angry right now, and I am going to hold you until you calm down. I won't let you hurt me or anyone else." Often this approach can be comforting to a child. Children don't like to be out of control. It scares them. An adult who is able to take charge of the situation and remain calm and in control can be very reassuring.

Wait until the child calms down—then talk. It's difficult to reason with a screaming child. Insist on a "cooling down" period, and follow up with a discussion about behavior. Use this opportunity to teach the child "okay" ways to handle anger and difficult situations. With practice, preschoolers and school-agers can learn:
- how to ask for help
- when to go somewhere to "cool down"
- how to try a more successful way of doing something
- how to express feelings with words (rather than hitting, kicking, or screaming)

Comfort and reassure the child. Tantrums really scare most kids. Often, they are not sure why they feel so angry and feel rather shaken when it is all over. They need to know that you disapprove of their behavior, but that you still like them.

An ounce of prevention

Tantrums are a normal part of growing up. All children will have them sometime or another. But if tantrums seem to be happening too often, you might want to consider the following suggestions:

- **Study a child's tantrums.** When and where do they seem to occur? Who is generally involved? What happens before, after, and during a tantrum? Look for patterns in behavior that can give you clues about how to avoid conditions or situations that seem to encourage tantrums.

- **Set realistic limits, and help children stick to a regular routine.** Predictable mealtimes and naptimes are particularly important. A tired, hungry child is usually one step away from a tantrum.

- **Offer real choices.** Don't ask, "Would you like to take your nap?" unless you are prepared to honor a child's choice not to nap. Instead try, "It's naptime now."

Choose your battles carefully. Say "No" to things that are really important. Avoid fighting over little things.

Give children a few minutes warning before you end an activity. Say "We are going to leave the park and go home in a few minutes" or "I wonder what we will have for a snack." It helps children get ready for change.

Help children not to "get in over their heads." Children need challenging activities but not so challenging that they experience overwhelming frustration and failure.

What about biting?

Biting is quite common among young children. It happens for different reasons with different children and under different circumstances. The first step in learning to control it is to look at why it may be happening.

Why children bite

Exploration—Infants and toddlers learn by touching, smelling, hearing, and tasting. If you give an infant a toy, one of the first places it goes to is the mouth. Tasting or "mouthing" things is something that all children do. Children this age do not always understand the difference between gnawing on a toy and biting someone.

Teething—Children begin teething around the ages of 4 to 7 months. Swelling gums can be tender and can cause a great deal of discomfort. Infants sometimes find relief from this discomfort by chewing on something. Sometimes the object they chomp on is a real person! Children this age do not truly understand the difference between chewing on a person or a toy.

Cause and effect—Around the age of 12 months, infants become interested in finding out what happens when they do something. When they bang a spoon on the table, they discover that it makes a loud sound. When they drop a toy from their crib, they discover that it falls. They also may discover that when they bite someone, they get a loud scream of protest!

HFCCH Chapter 9 — Guiding behavior   209

Attention—Older toddlers may sometimes bite to get attention. When children are in situations where they are not receiving enough positive attention and daily interaction, they often find a way to make others sit up and take notice. Being ignored is not fun. Biting is a quick way to become the center of attention—even if it is negative attention.

Imitation—Older toddlers love to imitate others. Watching others and trying to do what they do is a great way to learn things. Sometimes children see others bite and decide to try it out themselves. When an adult bites a child back in punishment, it generally does not stop the biting, but teaches the child that biting is okay.

Independence—Toddlers are trying so hard to be independent. "Mine" and "Me do it" are favorite words. Learning to do things independently, making choices, and needing control over a situation are part of growing up. Biting is a powerful way to control others. If you want a toy or a playmate to leave you alone or move out of your way, it is a quick way to get what you want.

Frustration—Young children experience a lot of frustration. Growing up is a real struggle. Drinking from a cup is great; yet nursing or sucking from a bottle is also wonderful. Sometimes it would be nice to remain a baby. Toddlers don't have good control over their bodies yet. A loving pat sometimes turns into a push. Toddlers cannot talk well. They have trouble asking for things or requesting help. They haven't learned yet how to play with others. At times, when they can't find words to express their feelings, they resort to hitting, pushing, or biting.

Stress—A child's world can be stressful, too. An inconsistent daily routine, a lack of interesting things to do, and limited positive adult attention can be stressful for children. Children also experience stressful events like death, divorce, or a move to a new home. Biting is one way to express feelings and relieve tension.

What you can do

- **Use the who, what, when, where, and how method to pinpoint the problem.** When did the biting occur? Who was involved? Where did it happen? What happened before or after? How was the situation handled?

- **Try prevention.** If you determine that the biting occurs as the result of exploration or teething, you may want to provide the child with a cloth or teething ring to gnaw on.

- **Attend to basic needs.** If a child seems to bite when tired or hungry, you may want to look at your daily routine to be sure that he or she is getting enough sleep and nourishment.

- **Provide extras of favorite toys.** If the biting occurs when two children are fighting over a toy telephone, you may want to purchase an extra toy telephone. It does not work to make very young children share. Toddlers don't have the skills to negotiate or understand another child's point of view.

- **Focus on positive time together.** If attention seems to be the main reason for biting, try to spend time with the child when he or she is doing more positive things. Snuggling up and reading a book together or rolling a ball back and forth is so much more fun than receiving a scolding.

- **Create a supportive, less stressful environment.** If the child is experiencing a stressful family or caregiving situation, you will want to make everyday life as supportive and normal as possible. Predictable meals and naptimes and extra time with a loving adult can help. Often, experiences like rolling, squishing, and pounding play dough or relaxing and splashing with water are great ways to relieve tension. In painful situations like divorce, it takes time and patience for healing to occur.

- **Teach new behaviors.** When a child bites, show the biter with your voice and facial expression that biting is unacceptable. Speak firmly and look directly into the child's eyes. For example you might say, "No! Sara, it's not okay to bite. It hurts Jason when you bite him. He's crying. I won't let you bite Jason or any other child." If the child is able to talk, you might also say, "You can tell Jason with your words that you need him to move instead of biting him. Say 'Move, Jason!'"

- **You may also want the child to help wash, bandage, and comfort the victim.** Making him or her a part of the comforting process is a good way to teach nurturing behavior. This will depend on the child and the situation.

- **Gently restraining or separating a child from others is sometimes helpful.** Insist on a "time out" or "cooling off period." Wait a few minutes until things are under control, and then talk to the child about the behavior. This works best with older children. Toddlers will have limited understanding of time out.

A final note

Biting can be an uncomfortable issue for parents. Parents of a child who is bitten often are outraged and angry. Parents of the biter may feel embarrassed and frustrated. It is important to keep the name of the child confidential, but this is understandably hard to do with a small group of children in family child care. Usually parents can figure this out. Help parents remain calm by sharing information about the causes of biting and your plans for controlling the situation. This approach can help parents put things in perspective.

Insensitivity to physical, racial, or ethnic differences

Dealing with a child who is making fun of another person's race, religion, or disability is a true challenge. Ethnic or racial slurs or personal comments about individuals with physical disabilities are examples of behaviors that need to be stopped. Such behavior embarrasses children, parents, and caregivers. Children who are teased often or victimized by inappropriate comments or actions suffer tremendously.

Young children often do not realize that this type of behavior is inappropriate. Like forbidden words, children have a tendency to pick up and use ethnic and racial slurs. For

instance, a younger child may have heard an older child or adult use words ridiculing some ethnic group or race. He or she may then try to use the same word either to imitate or to see if he or she gets the same response. Children pick up words and gestures from television too.

Racial and ethnic slurs and comments based on physical disabilities cannot be ignored. They are like verbal slaps and are too hurtful or damaging to the victim to be ignored. When caregivers witness a child saying something hurtful or disrespectful, they should immediately address the situation.

What you can do:

- **Speak directly to the child.** "It is not okay to use that word to describe Trisha. That word hurts her feelings and makes her feel sad or angry."

- **Reaffirm the value of both children.** "Her skin (religion, language, etc.) is different from yours. That makes her special and unique. You are also special. Everyone is different. Some people have white skin and some have brown. Some people have blue eyes and some have brown eyes. Some people speak different languages. Everyone is different in their own way. I care about you both."

- **Comfort and acknowledge the victim's feelings.** "I know it made you angry when Jeremy called you that name. It's okay to feel angry about that."

- **Teach appropriate words to the offending child.** Give additional information. "Trisha is African-American."

- **Model respectful behaviors for children.** Treat all children fairly and respectfully. Invite children to share information about their culture or disability as they feel comfortable.

- **Include books, toys, and materials in your program that discuss physical, racial, or ethnic differences.** Bias and discrimination often stem from ignorance and fear of the unfamiliar. You can combat destructive attitudes by purchasing books, dolls, and dramatic play props that make children aware of other races and cultures.

What about sex-related play?

Children are naturally curious about their bodies. They express this fascination and curiosity by exploring themselves and others. In older preschoolers, this kind of behavior can be redirected or explained. In younger children, however, this behavior is best ignored. Masturbation is not harmful to children and is as natural as thumb-sucking, twisting a lock of hair, or stroking a favorite blanket. Punishing, scolding, or shaming a child will only create unnecessary guilt and shame.

A positive discussion about bodies will help children develop a positive and healthy attitude. Keep discussions simple. Most children are just interested to know that boys' and girls' bodies are different and that they use the toilet in different ways. Details about reproduction or sexual behavior is not necessary at this age.

Older preschool children can be taught that our bodies are okay but some parts should be private and personal. Be careful that the child is not learning that bodies are bad or shameful. Avoid showing shock and just matter-of-factly redirect the child to something else. This approach will teach children that some behavior is inappropriate in public without being bad.

NOTE: If you suspect that play is more than simple curiosity or exploration, you may want to read more about sexual abuse warning signs (found in chapter 14). Children who demonstrate advanced sexual knowledge or actions that imitate more adult behaviors may be victims of sexual abuse.

What about toilet learning?

Learning to use the toilet is a big event in a young child's life. Most children are eager to learn how to use the "potty" and are proud of their achievement.

Toilet training/learning is easiest when children are physically and emotionally ready. This usually happens between age 2 and 3 years. Girls usually gain physical control over their bowel and bladder muscles before boys do. On the average, most girls are potty-trained by age 2 1/2 and most boys about age 3. But don't be alarmed if a child doesn't follow this pattern closely; individual children mature physically at different rates.

The secret to success is patience and timing. Emotional readiness also is important. Many bright, normal, healthy 3-year-olds may not be interested in learning to use the toilet. Learning is a full-time job for most toddlers, and learning to use the toilet may not be as important as learning to climb, jump, run, and talk. A toddler who resists toilet learning now may be ready in 3 to 6 months—often learning almost overnight.

How do you tell if a child is ready?

Check the following about the child:
- ☐ Follows simple directions.
- ☐ Remains dry for at least 2 hours at a time during the day.
- ☐ Is dry after naptime.
- ☐ Has regular and predictable bowel movements.
- ☐ Walks to and from the bathroom, pulls down own pants, and pulls them up again.
- ☐ Seems uncomfortable with soiled or wet diapers.
- ☐ Seems interested in the toilet or potty chair.
- ☐ Has asked to wear grown-up underwear.

If you left most of the items unchecked, be patient a while longer. Rushing a child through the toilet learning process will result in tears and frustration. Starting too soon may actually delay the process. Toilet learning will be easier when the child is ready.

If a child seems ready, visit with parents first. Always visit with parents about your observations and ask them if they feel comfortable with introducing toilet learning at this time. Be sure parents are willing to support the child at home in the same way to limit confusion for the child.

Ten steps to toilet learning

Step 1. Relax! A calm, easygoing approach to toilet learning works best. Learning to use the toilet takes time and each child is different. You will find that one child learns to use the toilet at age 2 and another learns at age 3 1/2. This is normal.

Step 2. Show children what they are to do in the bathroom. Toddlers love to imitate adults or older children. It is not necessary to let a child watch you use the bathroom, but you can certainly talk about what you and other children do when you use the toilet.

Step 3. Teach toddlers the words their families use for body parts, urine, and bowel movements. Make sure it's a word parents feel comfortable with—others are sure to hear it. There is nothing quite like a toddler loudly announcing in the grocery store check-out lane, "Go poo-poo!"

Step 4. Help children recognize when they are urinating or having a bowel movement. Most children will grunt, squat, turn red in the face, or simply stop playing for a moment. Children must be aware that they are urinating or having a bowel movement before they can do anything about it.

Step 5. Purchase a potty chair or a potty attachment for the toilet. You may want to let the child get used to the idea by sitting on the potty while fully clothed. The American Academy of Pediatrics suggests that parents and caregivers avoid urine deflectors because they can cut a child who is climbing on or off a potty chair. Potty attachments are preferred because potty chairs will need to be cleaned and disinfected after each use.

Step 6. Begin reading potty books to the child. Many good books have been written about learning to use the potty and may be found at your local library or bookstore. Reading a book together helps children understand the process and understand that other children also learn to use the potty. See book suggestions at the end of this chapter.

Step 7. Encourage parents to purchase training diapers or pants and easy-to-remove clothing. Just getting to the potty on time is a major task for most children. You can help make the job easier by encouraging parents to dress children in easy-to-remove clothing. Ask them to avoid buttons, zippers, and belts. Some parents prefer to use diapers at first and switch to training diapers or pants when their child is urinating in the potty several times a day.

Step 8. When a child tells you that he or she needs to use the potty, help with clothing and sit the child on the potty for a few minutes. Stay with the child. You might keep some books close by. Reading a book together helps pass the time and takes the pressure off for an immediate result.

Step 9. After 4 to 5 minutes, help the child off the potty. Give hugs and praise for a successful effort. Comment simply that the child can try again later if the effort wasn't successful. Don't be surprised if the child has a bowel movement or urinates right after begging to be taken off the toilet. This is not unusual. Accidents and near misses generally are not an act of defiance or stubbornness. It simply takes time to learn this new skill. If accidents seem to be frequent, it may be best of try toilet learning a few months later.

Step 10. Wipe the child carefully. Wipe girls from front to back to prevent infection. Teach children to always wash hands with soap and water after using the potty. Set a good example by washing your own hands.

More ideas

- If possible, plan to devote at least 3 to 4 days to begin toilet learning. Maintaining the same routine for 3 to 4 weeks also helps.

- Some caregivers find it helpful to establish a routine by putting a child on the toilet for 3 to 4 minutes right after snack time, before naps, after naps, and after meals. However, a child will not always use the potty at these times.

- If a family is undergoing major change—anticipating a new baby, moving to a new home—you may want to encourage them to wait a few months. Toilet learning is easiest when everyone can give it their full attention.

- Remind parents that it's okay to keep a child in diapers or disposable training pants for sleeping. Nighttime control generally comes many months after daytime control.

- It may be helpful to use a plastic mattress cover, tablecloth, or shower curtain between the sheet and mattress until children gain good bladder control.

- Treat accidents casually. Avoid punishing, scolding, or shaming. Give children support by keeping a positive attitude.

Cleaning up

Children often show much curiosity about bowel movements. If you find a child trying to remove fecal material from the toilet, or "finger painting" with it on the bathroom floor, try to remain calm. Explain that it's not okay to play with feces or urine; help the child clean up the mess and wash your hands and the child's with soap and water. It is generally a good idea to supervise clean-up and flushing for some time during the toilet learning process.

The big flush

Children often have one of two reactions to flushing. Either they are fascinated by it (and will do it repeatedly) or they are afraid of it. Children who enjoy flushing will delight in emptying the potty chair into the toilet, waving bye-bye, and watching everything "flush away."

Children who are fearful prefer that caregivers and parents take charge of this process. Before flushing the toilet, make sure the child is off the potty. Many children not only fear the noise and swirling water, but also think they may be flushed down, too. Reassure children that they are safe and that only body wastes and toilet paper will be flushed away.

Books for children

No More Diapers, J.G. Brooks—
A popular book with toddlers. Toilet learning is illustrated through two stories, one about Johnny and another about Susie. Simple text is used with black, white, and orange drawings.

Your New Potty, Joanna Cole—
This book tells the story of two children, Ben and Steffie, who are learning to use their new potties. Illustrated by colorful photographs. Uses adult terms for elimination.

Once Upon a Potty, Alona Frankel—
Simple text with cartoon-like illustrations. Available in both a boy's and girl's version. Comes complete with an anatomically correct doll and toy potty.

All By Myself, Anna Grossnickle Hines—
One of the few books that talks about nighttime dryness. Josie, like most children, has successfully mastered daytime control, but at night still needs help from her mother to get to the bathroom. In time she learns how to manage by herself.

Going to the Potty, Fred Rogers—
Part of the Mister Rogers Neighborhood First Experience series, this colorful book discusses toilet learning. Photographs show children of all sizes, ages, and ethnic groups.

KoKo Bear's New Potty, Vicki Lansky—
A "read together" book with cartoon bear illustrations. A useful companion to Vicki Lansky's Practical Parenting: Toilet Training.

Books for caregivers and parents

Parents Book of Toilet Teaching,
Joanna Cole

Practical Parenting: Toilet Training,
Vicki Lansky

Toilet Learning,
Alison Mack

FamilyShare...
Supporting your partners

Guiding children's behavior is one of the most challenging issues for parents. Be prepared to give advice and share resources.

The CD accompanying this chapter has fact sheets on guidance and discipline techniques, ages and stages, temper tantrums, biting, and toilet learning. Feel free to share these with parents and other family members.

Heart of the Matter

I heard a growl and felt a "paw" scratch at me as I walked by the loft. I looked down to see Lizzie frowning at me as she pawed the air. I heard a shout from the corner and looked over my shoulder to see Cayla slapping another child. I sighed. It was another typical day.

Until recently, Cayla and Lizzie had been delightful 3-year-old children. Both were a real joy to care for. Then within a two month period, both of their families informed me that they had decided to get a divorce. It seemed like the girls had changed almost overnight.

Each girl reacted differently. Cayla became very angry and hostile. She had been a favorite with the other children before, but now she lashed out. She hit other children, she took their toys. She was almost four, but now she was acting more like a 2-year-old.

Lizzie responded differently to her parents' divorce. Unlike Cayla, she didn't appear angry. And she didn't lash out at the other children, she just withdrew. Lizzie had a very active imagination. Every day, she spent the full day pretending to be either a lion or Cinderella. When she arrived each morning, she would head to the loft area, look out the loft window, and growl like a lion. She spent much of her time there. It became her castle. She stashed blankets, books, and other personal things in the corner and made the loft her own special place.

Sometimes children have very little control over their lives and the daily stress they must endure. From my observations, both families were handling the divorces as well as they could with minimum conflict, but the effect on these two children was still very traumatic. It was as if both girls were stuck in time. There seemed to be very little I could do, except be there for them every day, providing a safe, secure place to play and learn.

Gradually over about a two year period, things improved. Cayla became less aggressive and Lizzie ventured out to play more with the other children. Cinderella and the lion visited us less frequently and the loft now became more open to the other children.

The pain these two girls felt was very real. We had to live through the pain together. It was a long two years—and it taught me much patience.

Lesia

Experience Talks

Conversations with other providers

■ **Take a few seconds before you spring into action.** Unless someone is about to be seriously hurt, I always take at least 30 seconds to decide how to handle a misbehavior problem. Look at your watch. Thirty seconds is really quite a bit of time. It helps me stay in control of my own anger and make the right decision.

■ **I sometimes handle swear words with silly nonsense rhymes.** I figure that if children are learning that words have power to upset people, they also can learn that words can entertain people. Rather than acting shocked or angered, I may say something like: "Roosky, Dosy Do, Calamasue - figure that out dippsy boo!" Generally, all the children join in and the whole "shocking" episode loses its punch.

■ **When I use time out, I like to give children some control over their actions.** Rather than watching the clock or using a kitchen timer, I give the child an egg timer. I may say, "When the sand runs down you may come back and play. But if you feel that you need more time to get control of yourself, just turn it over and wait a few more minutes." This technique gives the child a chance to make a decision and encourages self-control.

■ **I make it a point to praise children at least three times a day.** Sometimes it's hard, but I can always find something good or interesting to say to a child. This technique has literally worked miracles with even my most troublesome children.

■ **I often make a game of things.** Children like challenges. So when a toddler is pestering a preschooler and driving us all crazy, I say "I wonder how we could handle this situation in a better way? Do you have any ideas?" Then we brainstorm different ways to handle the situation. And we try different things. It all becomes a grand experiment to see what works.

■ **Humor is my secret weapon.** When things get too tense and everyone is irritable, we just bend our routine a little and get silly. Dressing up backwards, telling knock, knock jokes, having puppet shows with our feet, and painting our faces with old makeup are all great techniques for lightening things up a bit.

Business matters

Contents

Where am I now?	220
Introduction	221
Registration and licensing	221
Recruiting families and marketing your business	223
Provider-parent contract	224
Child care policies	226
Record keeping	227
Child care fees	229
Your business budget	231
Tax tips	232
Contract labor/employees	237
Liability insurance	237
Resources	244
FamilyShare	244
Forms	245
Heart of the Matter	277
Experience Talks	278

Business matters—
Where am I now? What can I improve?

	Seldom 1	Sometimes 2	Often 3	Most Often 4
1. I follow state registration or licensing regulations and guidelines.				
2. I market my child care services effectively.				
3. I provide families with a written statement of my policies.				
4. I have signed agreement/contracts with each family.				
5. I keep accurate and organized records.				
6. I use accurate bookkeeping procedures for recording income and expenses.				
7. I prepare and follow an expense budget.				
8. I have liability insurance.				
9. I understand tax advantages and requirements for my business.				

Chapter 10

Business matters

Family child care is a business. Although when you first begin, it may not feel like a business. Many providers start offering child care in their home because they want to stay home and care for their own children. Often they care for a friend's or neighbor's child as well. Charging money seems like a reasonable thing to do, but the idea of child care as a real business seems too formal—and often a little scary.

Handling expenses and dealing with different families can begin to get a little complicated. Experienced providers will be the first to tell you that the sooner you learn how to deal with the business aspects of home child care, the happier you will be.

A friendly business relationship with parents will make your job much easier. Sharing written child care policies with families and asking parents to sign an agreement will save you a great deal of frustration and grief over miscommunication.

Running child care as a business will increase your income. Operating a small business is not hassle free. It requires some paperwork and some record keeping, but the trade-off is that you can make more money. It may surprise you to learn that you can take some very valuable tax deductions.

Rewards and effort go hand in hand. Becoming registered or licensed takes time and effort, but it also allows you to have access to some great training that can make your time with children much more enjoyable and easier. You will learn skills that will help you as a parent too. And you will meet other providers who share your commitment to children. Some of these providers may become lifelong friends.

Registration and licensing

In most states when you care for a number of unrelated children you will need to be certified, registered, or licensed with the state. The requirements vary from state to state, but are generally very minimal regulations put in place to ensure the health and safety of children. States that license family child care homes generally have some type of regular inspection and more stringent guidelines. States that register programs generally have a more limited inspection or no inspection at all.

Be sure you are operating legally. Even if you are not registered or licensed with the state, the number of children that you may legally care for is governed by state regulations. If you care for children other than your own above the approved number set by your state, you may be operating illegally. If a child is injured and you are operating illegally there could be serious consequences.

Accept the discomfort of having someone inspect your home. Our homes are very personal and private. However, if you are caring for other people's children in your home, they want some assurance that their children are being cared for in a safe place by someone who has experience and training. You would want the same assurance if your children were cared for in someone else's home. Registration or licensing offers parents at least a minimum level of assurance.

Being registered or licensed offers some benefits. For example you can:
- Find out about useful training that will help you in the everyday care of children.
- Link up with a network of providers, just like you, for help and support.
- Receive extra funds or bonuses in some states that support quality child care improvement.
- Receive training and funds for food reimbursement from the Child and Adult Care Food Program (CACFP).
- Receive parent referrals from child care and resource and referral agencies.
- Take significant child care related income tax deductions.

A few facts about registration and licensing

In many states there are no fees for registration or licensing. Most states do not require major changes to your home.

Typical requirements for your home might include:
- a telephone with emergency numbers posted
- medicines and cleaning supplies out of reach
- first aid supplies
- safety features, safety gates, safe wiring, smoke detectors, fire extinguisher, and outlet covers
- safe indoor and outdoor play areas and equipment
- emergency plans for tornado and fire posted and regular drills practiced

In some states you also may be required to have a fenced area for outdoor play and a required number of exits if children are cared for in a basement, remodeled garage, or upstairs second story area.

You will be required to attend some training including
- Child Abuse Mandatory Reporter Training
- Health and Safety Training
- CPR and First Aid Training
- Basic training in child development, learning activities, behavior guidance, nutrition, and business practices

You also will be required to submit your name and the names of family members and staff members for
- criminal records check
- child abuse registry check

You will be expected to keep some records on file, which may include:
- background information about children's special needs, parent's work addresses and phone numbers
- a list of persons authorized to pick up the child
- emergency information about children (doctor's names and phone numbers, medical consent form authorizing emergency medical treatment)

- physical examination report for each child in your care, updated each year with a statement of health signed by a physician
- signed and dated immunization records (or exemption) for each child
- signed physician's statement that you and your family are free of disease or disability that would prevent good child care
- certification of training relating to the identification and reporting of child abuse
- certificates or documentation for required training

You also may need to show that your program includes:
- play and learning activities for young children
- appropriate equipment and materials for children
- discipline that is not physically or emotionally harmful
- well balanced, nourishing meals and snacks

How to become a registered or licensed child care program:
To find out more about the specific registration or licensing requirements in your state you can contact your local child care resource and referral or state child care licensing agency. You also can go online http://nrc.uchsc.edu/STATES/states.htm to find your state's licensing requirements and state contact information.

Recruiting families and marketing your business

Good child care services are generally in great demand. Many family providers have no difficulty finding children. Nevertheless, if you are just getting started and building your reputation as a quality provider, you may want to consider the following ideas.

Decide first about the ages you are willing to care for. If you prefer to work with infants or perhaps older preschoolers, then you should focus on recruiting that age group. You also may want to balance the ages and gender of the children in your group. Remember that it is illegal to reject a child solely because they belong to a particular ethnic group or have a disability.

You do NOT have to accept every child or family that inquires about your services. This is your business and you can make choices. Always insist on an interview before agreeing to care for a child. During the interview you can meet, ask questions, and decide if the family and their child would be a good fit in your program. Keep in mind that it is all right to be choosy. You can read more about how to conduct an interview in chapter 2.

Talk to families that you currently serve. If you are already caring for children and have an opening, be sure to let your current families know right away. Families with young children usually know other parents who may be looking for care. Happy parents are your best advertisement.

List your services through your local child care resource and referral agency. These agencies will provide your name to parents looking for child care. In many areas this will be one of your most successful sources for marketing your services.

Join a local family child care association. Members often help each other with recruiting.

Talk to people—friends, relatives, neighbors. Many parents ask trusted neighbors, friends, and relatives for recommendations.

Advertise in local newspapers and shopping news sheets. Place notices on bulletin boards where parents will see them, like grocery stores, businesses, laundromats, shopping centers, and churches. Keep advertisements neat and simple. Use the following models if you wish.

> **Sample ad #1**
> Looking for child care? Registered provider located in NW part of town. Clean, safe, home environment; planned activities; fenced yard; nutritious meals; non-smoking. Infants and toddlers welcome, but I enjoy children of all ages. Five years of child care experience. Parent references provided. Ph 555-5555
>
> **Sample ad #2**
> Two child care openings in a cozy home setting in Southridge Heights. This is a great opportunity for families who wish to keep siblings together. I offer flexible hours for busy, working families and lots of fun learning activities for children. Piano lessons from a visiting student teacher also are available for an additional fee. Licensed provider, with 2 years experience. Ph 444-4444
>
> **Sample ad #3**
> Infant care available in licensed family child care home near downtown metro area. I am supportive of breastfeeding mothers and have specialized education and training in caring for infants and toddlers. Ph 333-3333

Identify working parents with small children in your area. Contact them personally and ask them for names of families they know.

Use community contacts. Try contacting some of the front desk staff at elementary schools, libraries, and churches and let them know of your services. Employer newsletters or bulletin boards, moving companies and real estate agencies, and hospital maternity wards or pediatrician offices are also good resources.

> **Child care resource and referral**
> A resource and referral agency maintains a directory of child care providers for families seeking child care. Resource and referrals also may offer a toy lending library, sponsor local child care provider associations, and offer consultation to parents or providers who need assistance. To locate child care resource and referral agencies in your state go to http://www.childcareaware.org.

Provider—parent contract

Many providers balk at the idea of using a contract because it seems too cold and business-like. However, the primary purpose of a contract is communication. When providers and parents put their expectations in writing, misunderstandings are easily avoided.

A contract is an agreement that defines the terms of actual care and payment between a caregiver and parents. If necessary, a contract can be used in court to seek payment of damages if the contract is broken.

Include the following basic information in any contract.
- name, address, phone of child and parents or guardians
- payment rates, fees, deposits

- time of care—days or dates
- termination procedures
- signatures of parents/guardians
- signature of provider
- date of signature

Ask yourself the following questions before you create a contract.
- What hours/days/months will I provide care?
- How much will I charge for basic child care for infants or toddlers or for a second or third child in the family?
- When will I collect fees?
- Will there be a fee for late pickups?
- Will I charge for days when children are ill or on vacation?
- Will I charge for days when I am ill, on vacation, or attending training?
- Will there be a charge for holidays?
- Will there be an extra charge for diapers or other supplies?

Once you have decided your response to these questions, you are ready to prepare a basic contract. (See sample Form A on page 245.)

Recommended practices to consider:

- **Charge by the week or by the month—regardless of whether the child has full attendance.** When a family enrolls a child, they are purchasing the right for you to care for their child during the hours identified in your agreement. If a child is ill or occasionally absent for other reasons, you very likely will not be able to fill this unexpected opening to make up missed income. You have daily expenses that you must meet even when a child is not in your care. Charging by the week or by the month is standard practice for child care centers and many home providers.

- **Require payment in advance.** You have expenses such as food and supplies that need to be purchased before the next week's activities. Asking parents to pay in advance for services also will protect you from losing income if a parent decides to suddenly withdraw their child from your program. Remind parents that they also pay for other services in advance, rent, subscriptions, health club memberships, etc.

- **Ask for advance payment of the last two weeks of care.** Although your agreement may require parents to give you two weeks notice and full payment before withdrawing their child, it is not uncommon for families to disregard this requirement. Tom Copeland, author of *Family Child Care Contracts and Policies*, recommends asking for advance payment of the last two weeks of care to ensure that you will be paid. The one disadvantage to you is that if the family is with you for a number of years, the fee you charge at enrollment is likely to be less than the fee several years later due to rate increases. However, this is a benefit to families. You may wish to point out that by paying now, they will actually be getting the last two weeks at a discount rate and not need to worry about the last two weeks.

Some families may decide not to sign an agreement requiring advance payment and will seek child care services elsewhere. This may be to your advantage. You want to serve families that will be able to pay you on a regular basis without constant reminders and challenges. Families that value your services will make the effort to pay in advance.

Review together before you sign. It is best to review contracts verbally with parents and have them sign two copies, one for each of you. You are then assured that parents were made aware of your contract expectations and had an opportunity to ask questions. (See sample Form A.)

Child care policies

Many child care professionals find it helpful to share a policy statement with parents. Such a statement lays some ground rules and helps parents understand the provider's views and practices concerning child care. Form B on page 246 is a sample child care policy statement.

The following are items you may want to consider when developing a policy statement.

Activities—What will your daily schedule be? What types of activities will you do with children?

Toys or other items from home—Will children be allowed to bring toys from home? How will you handle toys from home that might be unsafe? Who is responsible if something is damaged or lost?

Food—Will you provide snacks and meals, or will parents bring lunches? What about special treats from home? If you are licensed or registered in your state you may be eligible to participate in the Child and Adult Care Food Program, which partially reimburses you for the meals and snacks you serve to children in your care.

Administering medications—Medications can be given only with the parent's or doctor's direct written authority. This should include the name of the medication, amount to be given, time of last dose, and time to be administered. Medicines should be in the original bottle.

Emergency policy—You need permission to seek emergency medical care for a child when a parent cannot be reached. Prepare an emergency form for parents to fill out. You should have a backup person to care for the other children in case you have to take a child to the hospital. Local hospitals may have their own emergency forms and may not accept any others. Check with them first. You also will need to give families information about your emergency plans and procedures.

Illness policy—How will you handle children who become sick during the day or who arrive sick? Under what conditions will a sick child need to be taken home? Are you able to isolate contagious children (chicken pox, measles, etc.)?

Nap and rest time—Where will children rest? How long is rest time? What alternate activities will be available for short nappers?

Guiding behavior—How will you support positive behaviors? How will problem behaviors be handled? What rules will you have? It is important to discuss discipline with parents.

Clothing—What type of clothing will be needed (washable play clothes, sweater, outdoor coat, swim suit)? Is an extra set of clothing needed in case regular clothes get dirty?

Pets—Do you have pets and if so are children allowed to care for and interact with them? Are your pets vaccinated?

Smoking—Will you allow parents or other adults to smoke in your home?

Parent communication/ involvement—Are parents welcome to come at any time? When is the best time to call during the day? How will you communicate with families? Are there ways parents can be involved?

Drug or alcohol use—What will your procedure be if a parent comes to pick up his/her child and is impaired by alcohol or drugs?

Termination—Under what circumstances will you terminate service?

Record keeping

Keeping good records is important. Keeping a close eye on the money that comes in and out of your program will help you maximize your profit. After all, one of the main reasons you are in this business is to make money.

Some providers enjoy this aspect of their business tremendously. Others feel that record keeping is a hassle. Regardless of your feelings, keeping things simple and well organized will make the job easier.

Most providers find it necessary to have a separate checking account and debit/ credit card for their child care business. A business account helps them keep records more efficiently. Do not make family purchases from your business account. When you need cash for your family, write out a check to yourself from your business account and deposit it into your family checking account.

Start a new set of business files and receipts for each year. Keep all business files for at least 3 to 5 years for income tax purposes. Keep a separate file for each child, for each year.

Business files

Business files should include:
- Parent-provider child care agreement—Form A
- Child care policy statement—Form B
- Daily attendance (part-time)—Form D
- Daily attendance (monthly)—Form E
- Start-up budget—Form Q
- Annual operating budget—Form R
- Estimated cash flow—Form S
- Customer accounts—Form T
- Income summary—Form U
- Monthly expenses—Form V
- Utilities and home expenses—Form W
- Mileage record—Form X
- Time-space percentage—Form Y
- Liability insurance worksheet—Form Z
- Copies of your tax returns
- Tax forms and instruction booklets
- Warranties for child care purchases
- Receipts and cancelled checks for expenses
- CACFP records

Provider's files

Provider's files should include:
- Child care provider physical exam report (also for family members and substitutes)—Form N
- Emergency drill record—Form O
- Emergency phone numbers—Form P
- Inspection records verifying quality/safety of private sewer or water sources
- Fire safety inspection—if required by state regulations
- Pet records of examinations and vaccinations
- Documentation of training credit hours
- Information regarding professional associations

Children's files (Form AA, p. 276)

Children's records should include:
- Children's enrollment information—Form C
- Transportation and activity permission—Form F
- Special activity permission—Form G
- Emergency medical treatment release—Form H
- Child health exam record—Form I
- Medication consent record—Form J
- Child medical update—Form K
- Infant daily report—Form L
- Injury report—Form M
- Immunization record or exemption
- Correspondence with parents

Children's records

Child's enrollment information—Form C
This form (p. 249) should include the names, addresses, and phone numbers of the child, parents, and health care professionals. It also should give information regarding any special needs or requirements that a child might have. Emergency contact information and individuals who are authorized to pick up child also should be included and verified by parent signature.

Travel and activity permissions—Forms F and G
When signed, these forms (p. 253) allow the provider to arrange field trips or take the child to the store. (Parents also should be informed of any field trip several days before the date of the outing.)

Emergency medical treatment release—Form H
This form (p. 254) is signed by the parents at the time of placement and authorizes the provider to give immediate emergency care. It also authorizes medical treatment for a child in an emergency even before the parents can meet the provider at the hospital or office. Some hospitals require that this form be notarized. Check your local requirements.

Child health exam record—Form I
The physician's signed and dated report (p. 255) on the health of each child includes information regarding health history, allergies, restrictive conditions, and present health status. This information allows for proper care and safety of all children.

Medication consent release—Form J
At no time should a child be given any medication without the express written consent of the parent and the physician's prescription. Written authorization is necessary for nonprescription drugs such as Tylenol. This form (p. 259) should be filled out for each new prescription or other medically authorized treatment and for renewal of any treatment.

Child medical update—Form K
This form (p. 260) can be used for a child who already has a complete health record on file.

Infant daily report—Form L
This form (p. 261) can be used to give parents information about an infant's daily eating, sleeping, and activity schedule.

Injury report—Form M

For records and protection, it is advisable to write a report any time a child is injured, even slightly, while in a provider's care (p. 262). The report should contain information about the accident or injury and the action taken. One copy should be given to the parents and one retained for the provider's file.

Immunization record

A current immunization record (or exemption) from the child's physician also should be kept on file.

Food program

Child and Adult Care Food Program (CACFP) records should include:
- monthly menus
- meal and snack attendance records
- nutrition information
- enrollment verification form
- all agreements signed on annual basis

Where to store it all?

Many providers find that keeping these records in separate folders in a plastic file box works well. They can pull out their box and work easily at the kitchen table during naptime.

Child care fees

Because the number of children you care for is limited by law, your primary source of income will depend on how much you can charge for each child.

Fees vary a great deal from community to community. Urban areas generally have higher fees than rural areas. Areas of the country that have a higher cost of living also can generate higher fees. However, if you live in a lower income part of town you will be less likely to charge what providers do in a higher income neighborhood. In some communities family providers charge slightly less than child care centers. Communities that have a lack of quality child care create a competitive market and good providers find they can charge higher rates.

The following example shows how to estimate your annual income before taxes. Based on the care of 6 full time preschool children you could receive a gross annual income that ranged from $24,960 to $40,560. You can receive additional income each month by participating in the Child and Adult Care Food Program.

	Community A	Community B
weekly charge per child	$80	$130
× 52 weeks per year	$4,160	$6,760
× 6 children	$24,960	$40,560
Total annual gross income from enrollment fees	$24,960	$40,560

There are significant tax advantages. As a small business owner who operates a business out of your home, you also can claim a number of tax advantages, including prorated depreciation of house and furnishings and deductions of mortgage interest, utilities, and property taxes.

Factors to consider in determining your fees

Be aware of your abilities and tolerance levels. Many providers choose to care for only 3 or 4 children because that is what they are most comfortable with. Some providers prefer caring for older children, while others prefer infants and toddlers. Take time to think about the ages of children you enjoy most and the amount of income that you need to feel successful.

Many providers charge different amounts for different ages. Because infant care is hard to find and because infants do require more intensive care, providers generally charge more for infant care than for preschoolers. And fees for school-agers are usually less than for preschoolers.

Rates will vary by community. Because parents often look for child care near their own homes, fees may depend on the average income in the neighborhood, as well as the standard rate in the community. Check with your local resource and referral agency to find out what the average market rates are for your community.

Some providers give family discounts. Some charge the same rate for each child; others give a discount to families when they care for at least two of their children.

Providers can charge by the month, week, or hour. The advantages of charging by the week or month include a more stable income. For example, if a parent decides to take Friday afternoon off to take the children shopping and pays by the week, she still would be charged for that afternoon. However, if a parent pays by the hour, the provider would lose a whole afternoon of income.

Many providers prefer charging by the week because they have the same expenses regardless of the number of children. These providers also feel they have a right to a stable, predictable income. The nature of family child care does not lend itself to filling in at very short notice. The parent therefore should agree that if a provider reserves a continuous slot for their child, then the provider should be paid for full care.

Providers can choose to charge for sick days and vacation. Providers also need to decide how they will handle sick days and vacation for both themselves and their child care families. Some providers allow families one to two weeks off without charge for vacation time and up to two to six sick leave days.

You can handle your personal sick and vacation leave in two ways.

- The first way is to give yourself a few days as paid sick leave and vacation for the year and specify that information in the contract. For instance, if you want four days sick leave, you can take four days leave every year, and the parents are still expected to pay you even if their child is not in your care.

- The second way is to calculate the income you would make for days of sick leave and vacation and spread it out over the whole year. In this situation, the parents will not directly pay you for days that you are ill, but you will still receive payment because your overall fee is just a little bit higher.

Late fees are an additional source of income. Many providers charge an additional amount at a higher rate if parents pick up their children after a specific time.

Some providers also provide evening, weekend, or drop-in care. Again, the rates may differ.

Many providers request that parents supply formula, diapers, and infant food. Other providers simply charge more for infants and provide these supplies themselves.

Child and Adult Care Food Program (CACFP)

Family child care providers can choose to participate in the Child and Adult Care Food Program (CACFP). This program helps family child care providers serve nutritious meals and will reimburse them for meals and snacks that meet CACFP meal pattern requirements.

There are two different reimbursement rates. Tier I rates are for providers who have low income, live in a low income area, or serve low income children. These rates offer higher reimbursement. Providers that do not qualify for Tier I rates will be reimbursed at Tier II rates, which are lower. However, both rates can provide significant monthly income for a provider.

Providers on the Child and Adult Care Food Program receive training in nutrition, food preparation, and food safety. They also are shown how to keep records for the program. Sponsors provide this type of assistance by holding local community workshops, conducting home visits, and sending out newsletters.

A CACFP sponsor will require you to serve meals and snacks that meet the CACFP requirements. You will verify this by sending copies of your menus and a count of the number of meals served to children to your sponsor. CACFP will reimburse you for three meals or snacks per day. This means you can get money for two meals and one snack or for one meal and two snacks per child daily.

The money you receive from the CACFP is considered income for income tax purposes. All the money you spend on children's meals and snacks are tax deductions. As many family providers spend a bit more on food than they receive from CACFP, it's a good idea to keep receipts.

Public funding

Some parents are eligible for public assistance and will pay child care fees with these state subsidies. A certificate of agreement is signed on an annual basis by the provider, the parent, and the funding agency. The provider is responsible for submitting a reimbursement form to the funding agency on a regular basis (usually monthly). The payment you receive from such an agreement is still regarded as income for income tax purposes. Providers who enter into this type of an agreement should ask questions to make sure they fully understand how much they will be paid and when payment will be received.

Your business budget

How much money will you need to start a family child care business? Will you need to buy equipment or materials before you can take care of children in your home? You may already have a number of toys or supplies that you can use in your child care business, but there will be other items that you may need. Information from the chapters in this handbook on space and equipment, food and nutrition, health and safety, and routines and activities will help you decide what purchases you might need to make as you get started.

Begin by preparing a start-up budget, operating budget, and cash flow statement. These will give you an idea of what you will spend and where the money will come from for starting and operating your business. You also can determine whether the income will cover expenses and provide a profit.

A start-up budget generally includes one-time costs. You may need to purchase furniture and equipment such as shelves, high chair, crib, or diaper changing table. You also will need to purchase suitable toys for each age child. Other expenses may include installation fees, registration, licensing or legal fees. First month expenses for food and supplies also may be included. (See Form Q, p. 266.)

An operating budget helps you determine the amount of income you need to make a profit and keep your business operating. If you don't want to risk losing money, follow a budget. Be flexible because plans do change, and you have more financial security if you know where you are going to cut back (or increase income) to make up for unexpected expenses. Loss of income also can affect your budget. It is important to consider what will happen to your budget if one of your child care children moves. You also might consider how you will recover start-up expenses (loan payments, salaries, or fees). (See Form R, p. 267.)

A cash flow statement will show you how much money you will have to manage day to day expenses. Most of your income will come from fees paid by parents, but you may also have other income, for example from the Child Care and Adult Food Program. An estimated cash flow projection will help determine if your monthly income will pay monthly bills. (See Form S, p. 268.)

Tax tips

Family child care providers are eligible for some significant tax deductions. Unfortunately, many providers fail to claim all the business deductions they are entitled to because they are unaware of the rules, or they don't think it's worth their time to understand them. Most providers find they will pay less in taxes if they take advantage of all the legal business deductions they are entitled to.

It is a good idea to hire an accountant or tax preparer. Work with someone who has experience with a family child care business. It will be your responsibility to keep your tax preparer informed. Resources listed at the end of this chapter can be immensely helpful to you.

As a family child care provider, you are considered a self-employed taxpayer. You must report your business income and expenses on IRS form Schedule C Profit and Loss from Business. Nearly every provider also must fill out Form 4562 Depreciation and Amortization and Schedule SE Social Security.

It will be your responsibility to pay taxes and social security from your business income. The percentage you pay will be based on your net profit. Net profit is what is left when you subtract all your expenses (tax deductions) from your income. A complete record of all the money you spend on your child care program can help you show a lower profit, which means you pay less taxes.

Possible tax deductions
- Advertising*
- Bank service charges*
- Car expenses
- Dues and publications*
- Education*
- Food
- Interest*
- Liability insurance*
- Laundry and cleaning
- Legal and professional fees*
- Office equipment*
- Rent/mortgage
- Repairs
- Supplies (household)
- Supplies (kitchen)
- Supplies (children's)*
- Payroll taxes
- Property taxes

- Utilities and phone
- Travel, meals, entertainment
- Miscellaneous

Items with an * usually are considered strictly business expenses. All others are business/personal items.

Direct and indirect business expenses

Because many of your expenses are for items normally found in a home, your expenses are divided into two categories: direct business expenses and indirect business expenses.

Direct business expenses are bills that come solely from caring for the child care children. You will be able to deduct the full amount of these expenses when you file your taxes (toys, crib sheets, food for the children, art supplies).

Indirect business expenses are expenses shared by your home and your business (rent or mortgage, utility bills). You can deduct only a part of these expenses when figuring your taxes. Your tax preparer or family child care tax preparation books will help you figure the deduction.

Business expense records—Forms V and W

Use the Monthly expense record (Form V, p. 271) and Utility and home expense record (Form W, p. 272) to record business expenses. Keep checks and receipts to document these expenses.

Always get a receipt for all expenses and keep it. Proper record keeping of expenses begins at the moment of the purchase.

- On the receipt, record the check number if paid by check, the word "cash" if paid by cash, or credit card. Indicate on the receipt what was purchased.
- If the receipt is for both business and personal expenses, distinguish between the two by circling or coding. For example, you may have purchased picnic supplies and clothing items for your family, as well as glue, tape, and liquid starch for child care activities. Circle the items you bought for activities and keep the cash register tape.
- If there was no receipt, note the necessary information (date, store, check number, credit card, etc.) or ask for a receipt.
- Safeguard these receipts—they are like money.
- Have a regular place to put receipts (envelope in purse) until they can be filed.

Record the receipts on the Monthly expense record. Try to do this once a week or at least once a month. If the necessary information is on the receipt, the recording should be simple. If the expense was paid by check, enter the date of the check and the check number. Provide a brief description of the expense and record the amount paid. Keep all receipts to verify the Business Expense Record.

Food expenses

An important deduction for many child care home providers is food expense. Meals and snacks provided for the children can amount to a large sum. There are two ways to deduct food expenses.

Option 1: Use the standard meal allowance rate. The IRS establishes a rate each year for breakfast, lunch, supper, and snack. Instead of saving receipts to document your food expenses, you will need to keep a record of attendance and add up the total number of meals and snacks you serve and multiply them by the standard meal allowance rate. This amount will be your food deduction. Most providers choose this method because it is simple and requires less record keeping.

Option 2: Use the actual cost of food you serve. To use this method, you would need to keep detailed receipts of the actual food you purchase and serve to children. You will also need to keep all receipts of the food that you serve your own family to verify that your food purchases for child care are reasonable. Helpful instructions on using this method can be found in *Family Child Care Record Keeping Guide* by Tom Copeland, www.RedLeafInstitute.org.

Auto mileage expense—Form X

Is a personal car driven in the performance of the child care service? If so, you can take an automobile expense deduction if accurate records are kept that will substantiate the deduction. There are two methods allowed for computing the deduction:

Option 1: Keep track of actual operating expenses during the year. Actual expenses are gas, oil, lubricants, washing/waxing, tires, batteries, auto repairs, license, insurance, interest on auto loan, sales tax for car purchased during the year, motor club fees, etc. At the end of the year multiply these actual expenses times the business percentage (determined by dividing total child care business miles into total miles for all purposes for that vehicle). In addition, some depreciation is allowed. Most providers choose the alternative method of computing the deduction because of the record keeping required for the few number of miles usually driven.

Option 2: The alternative method would be to use a standard mileage rate to the business miles driven. Unless there are unusually large car expenses and an unusually high percentage of business miles that can be proven, you would most likely want to use this second, much simpler method. In any case, you must be able to document all business miles driven.

Mileage Record Form (Form X, p. 273.) For each business trip, record the date, the beginning and ending odometer reading, total miles driven, destination, and the purpose of the trip. At the end of the year, total the miles driven and use this figure for auto expense.

Time-space percentage—Form Y

In order to determine how much you can claim as a deduction for household items used for both child care and personal use, you need to calculate your Time-Space Percentage. You must apply this percentage to all items used for both business and personal use (e.g., utilities, swing set).

Use the following formula to calculate your Time-Space Percentage.

$$\frac{\text{A. Time used}}{\text{B. Total time}} \times \frac{\text{C. Space used}}{\text{D. Total space}} = \text{Time-Space Percentage}$$

1. Divide the number of hours that you use your home for business by the number of hours in a year.

For example you may have cared for children: 2,500 hours = (10 hrs per day × 5 days a week × 50 weeks)

You also may have spent time cleaning, cooking, preparing activities, or record keeping: 450 hours = (225 hrs cleaning + 50 hrs cooking + 100 hrs planning activities + 50 hrs record keeping) This total of 2,925 hrs your home is used for business divided by 8,760 hrs in a year = 0.33 (0.33 × 100 = 33%)

You should have your hours of business advertised or written in your contracts with parents. This provides the necessary proof to the IRS for your time percentage calculation.

2. Divide the number of square feet used for business (including hallways that children use, rooms they nap in, rooms that store child care supplies, etc.) by the total number of square feet in your house. For example, if you used 1,900 sq feet out of a total of 2,000 sq feet for your business, then your space percentage would be 95 percent (1900/2000 = 0.95 and 0.95 × 100 = 95%).

Many providers regularly use all of the square feet in their home for their business and their space percentage is 100 percent.

3. Multiply the percentage of time by the percentage of space. Then multiply this figure by 100 to get your Time-Space Percentage. For example, 33% of time × 95% of space = 0.33 × 0.95 = 31%.) The Time-Space Percentage should be applied to all shared business and personal time (e.g., utilities $600 × 0.31 = $186 or swing set $180 × 0.31 = $55.80). Therefore you could claim a tax deduction of $186 for utilities and $55.80 for a swing set.

Form Y sample—Calculating time-space percentage (p. 274)

A. Total number of hours/year you use your home for business	2,925
B. Total number of hours in year (8,760 hours/year)	8,760
C. Total number of square feet used for business	1,900
D. Total number of square feet in your house	2,000

$$\frac{A}{B} \times \frac{C}{D} = \underline{\ .31\ } \times 100 = \underline{\ 31\ }\%$$

My time-space % for YR (200___) is ___31___ % .

You must recalculate your Time-space percentage each year because it may change. Any change will affect your business deductions for the new year. A written weekly schedule noting times and dates for additional preparation, cleaning, or record keeping related to your business also is useful documentation.

Depreciation

It is to your benefit to calculate depreciation deductions. Although depreciation rules can be confusing and complicated, it is helpful to understand them in order to claim the maximum deduction allowed. This can help you increase your business profit.

Make a list of all the items in your home that are used for your business. Record items in your yard that are used in your business too. Estimate the value of each item at the time you began using it for your business.

You should also depreciate a portion of your house as a business expense. Keep a record of the purchase price of your home plus all the home improvements made before you went into business. Use IRS Form 4562 Depreciation and Amortization.

Federal tax forms

Income tax preparation will be easier if you keep track of your income and expenses each month. Below is a list of the federal tax forms you must fill out.

Form 4562: Depreciation and Amortization This form lets you deduct part of the cost of some items you use in your child care program. These things must last more than one year and cost more than $100 each.

Schedule C: Profit or Loss from Business or Profession

List your earnings from your business, your expenses, and the amount you pay taxes on, in this form.

Form 1040-ES: Estimated Taxes for Individuals

If you figure that you will owe the IRS more than $1,000 in taxes, you must pay your taxes every 3 months (quarterly).

Use the worksheet and payment vouchers on Form 1040-ES Estimated Tax for Individuals to pay estimated tax. The worksheet takes you through calculations that will determine how much tax you will owe by the end of the year after subtracting any withholding payment made by your spouse or by you from any other job. Estimated tax payments are made four times per year: April 15, June 15, September 15, and January 15 of the next year.

You can avoid having to fill out these estimated tax payment vouchers if you meet one of the following conditions:

1. You estimate that you will receive a tax refund for the year or that you will owe less than $1,000 in taxes by the end of the year.
2. You estimate that the total tax payments made by you or your spouse (if filing jointly) are at least equal to 90 percent of your total anticipated tax bill.
3. You had no income tax liability in the previous year.
4. You estimate that the amount of income taxes withheld from you and your spouse this year is equal to or greater than your total tax liability from the previous year. For further information see IRS publication 505 Tax Withholding and Estimated Tax.

Schedule SE: Social Security Self-Employment Tax

Self-employment tax will give you social security benefits when you retire. You must pay into this fund if your net profit is more than $400 a year.

Form W-10: Dependent Care Providers Identification and Certification

Parents who claim the Child Care Tax Credit will ask you to fill out this form. It lists your name, address, and social security or tax identification number.

Providers who do not want their social security number in circulation can easily get their own taxpayer identification number from the IRS and use this instead. Ask for Form SS-4 Application for Employer Identification Number. You will receive your identification number in the mail.

Form 1040: Individual Income Tax Return

This form ties your personal income, your business income, and your deductions together. It will show the amount of taxes you owe or the amount of your refund. If you are married you may file a joint return.

Form 8829: Expenses for Business Use of Your Home

This form addresses home expense deduction and depreciation.

Other IRS forms and publications

Form 5305 *SEP Simplified Employee Pension*
Publication 583 *Taxpayers Starting a Business*
Publication 587 *Business Use of Your Home*
Publication 334 *Tax Guide for the Small Business*
Publication 917 *Business Use of a Car*
Publication 4797 *Sales of Business Property*
Publication 8863 *Education Credits and Lifetime Learning Credits*

Contract labor/employees

Family child care providers may pay outside helpers on a regular basis to work with their child care children. If you have an employee, you must withhold social security tax and income tax and pay federal unemployment and social security tax. See IRS circular E Employer's Tax Guide for complete instructions in what tax forms to file as an employer.

An individual who comes into your home on special occasions to perform special services for you is not typically considered an employee. Expenses for independent contractors are deducted miscellaneous business expenses in Schedule C.

Liability insurance

Like other small business owners, family child care providers need adequate life, health, and disability insurance to protect their families from the loss of their income. Child care providers also face unique risks. Perhaps the most important of these risks is the financial loss that would result if the provider were found liable or responsible for the injury or death of a child or a child's parent.

If a claim were filed against you as a provider, three different types of financial losses are possible:
- medical expenses
- damages awarded to the victim or his/her family after a lawsuit
- court costs related to your defense

The most common way to protect against the liability risk is to purchase liability insurance. Most consumers are familiar with liability insurance since it is an important part of automobile and home owner's insurance coverage. Liability insurance pays attorney fees and court costs as well as damage awards. Medical payments or accident insurance pays for doctor and hospital bills and is often a part of, or required as, a companion policy to liability insurance. Yet, many home owner's insurance policies and some personal automobile insurance policies exclude coverage for claims that are related to the operation of a home-based small business. Many home owner's insurance policies specifically exclude coverage for claims related to family child care.

Options for insuring the liability risk

Family child care providers may choose from three options to prepare for the liability risk.

Option 1. Self-insure. The child care provider establishes a fund to be used in the event of a liability claim. For example, you may choose to self-insure against the risk that you will be responsible for a child's minor injury. You would then set aside money to be used for that purpose. Unfortunately, to self-insure against the risk that you will be found responsible for a serious injury or death of a child, you would need to set aside at least $500,000.

Option 2. Extend the liability and medical payments coverage of your home owner's insurance to your child care business. As mentioned earlier, virtually all home owner's insurance policies exclude child care except for the most limited operations. However, many companies do allow you to extend coverage to your family child care business if you buy an endorsement or rider in addition to your home owner's insurance. The premium for the additional coverage usually is low, but the coverage often is rather limited.

Option 3. Purchase a commercial liability and an accident insurance policy. Total premiums for both policies can range from $500 to $1,000 or more per year, but the coverage often is comprehensive.

Shopping guide for liability insurance

To explore liability and accident insurance for your child care operation, follow these guidelines:

- Evaluate your options carefully before making any decisions.
- Ask the same questions about each policy. Write down the answers so you can evaluate the policy after your conversation with the insurance agent is over. Use the worksheet at the end of this chapter (Form Z, p. 275) to record information. Obtain a copy of the policy from the agent.
- Ask questions until you are certain you understand exactly what is and is not covered by each policy. If you feel the agent you are talking with isn't knowledgeable about insurance for child care providers, ask to speak to one who is.
- Take your time to evaluate and compare policies. Resist sales pressure to make a decision before you are ready.
- Once you have reached a decision, discuss it with the parents of the children you care for. Parents should know what your insurance coverage is, especially if you include your insurance costs in the rates you charge.

Asking questions and understanding the answers

Questions about home owner's insurance

1. Is an endorsement or rider available to extend my home owner's insurance coverage to my child care business?

Many of the major companies that sell home owner's insurance make endorsements available, but some do not. If you learn that the company you currently have a home owner's policy with does not offer endorsements for child care, you have two choices. You may decide to move your home owner's insurance coverage to a company that makes child care endorsements available. Or you may purchase a separate commercial liability insurance policy.

Some companies will be reluctant to insure your home if you are providing child care services in your home. This is especially true if you do not have an endorsement to your home owner's insurance or a commercial liability policy. Your business is exposing the company to additional risks that increase the possibility of a claim against your home owner's insurance. It is in your best interest as well as the company's for you to obtain coverage. Further, if your home owner's insurance is cancelled because of a business-related accident, it may be difficult for you to get a new policy.

2. If the company offers child care endorsements, do I qualify?

Most companies and agents that sell home owner's insurance are very conservative about extending coverage to child care services. They are concerned about the potentially huge claims that could result if just one child were injured or died. As a result, many companies use a number of restrictions to limit the risks they cover.

- **Virtually all companies limit the number of children cared for by the provider.** Common restrictions are no more than three, four, or six children (usually not counting your own). If you care for more children than the policy or endorsement allows, the company could refuse your claim or cancel your coverage.

- **Some insurance companies require you to meet any applicable child care licensing, registration, or certification requirements of the city, county, and/or state in which you live.** This helps them reduce risk.

- **All insurance companies have underwriting guidelines that you must meet before a policy can be purchased.** Underwriting guidelines are conditions that must be present in the child care setting before the company will accept you as a client. For example, one company may require that a swimming pool be fenced while another company may not write the insurance if there is a pool. Other conditions that may disqualify you for coverage or make coverage more expensive include a previous history of accidents, pets in the home, an unfenced yard, unsafe playground equipment, or a wood-burning stove. An agent may visit your home to decide if you meet the company's underwriting guidelines. You also may be charged a fee for the agent's inspection.

- **All insurance companies require you to have a home owner's or renter's insurance policy with the company; you cannot purchase the endorsement alone.** If you do not qualify for an endorsement, you again must evaluate your options. You may choose to move your home owner's insurance to a company that offers an endorsement you do qualify for, or you may purchase a commercial liability policy.

3. What is and is not covered by the endorsement?

Most policies exclude or are vague about coverage of activities that take place away from the child care home. For example, an accident that occurred while at the park may not be covered by some endorsements. Some endorsements also specifically exclude claims related to serving food or giving medications. And all home owner's insurance endorsements exclude claims related to mental, physical, and/or sexual abuse.

Liability limits (the maximum claim that would be paid in any policy year) vary from company to company. Often the limit on the endorsement will match the limit on your home owner's policy. Limits should be chosen by the provider and the insurance agent based on the provider's needs.

4. Are there deductibles?

A deductible is the amount of the claim that you pay. For example, if you had a $300 medical claim with a $100 deductible, you would pay the first $100. Choose the highest deductible that you can afford. A high deductible will lower your premiums.

5. What are the premium rates?

The premium depends on the amount and type of coverage and often on the number of children. Premiums for most endorsements range from about $30 a year to $175 per year. Some policies, for example, charge one rate if you care for 3 or fewer children and another rate if you care for 4 to 6 children. Others charge the same premium regardless of the number of children. Expect higher premiums when you choose higher liability limits, when you care for 4 or more children, and when you choose lower deductibles.

HFCCH Chapter 10 — Business matters

Questions about commercial liability insurance

1. Do I qualify for the coverage?

Unlike home owner's insurance endorsements, most commercial liability policies do not directly limit the number of children in care. However, most commercial policies do require the provider to meet any applicable child care licensing, registration, or certification standards—standards that frequently do limit the number of children. Some companies require providers to belong to a specific professional child care providers' organization to qualify for coverage. Companies that sell commercial liability policies also have underwriting guidelines that providers must meet to qualify for insurance. These guidelines are similar to those for home owner's insurance. However, the company may simply charge a higher premium for a commercial policy if a risk factor such as a swimming pool or a pet is present, rather than denying coverage altogether. Other companies may not insure conditions that they consider unsafe.

2. What is and is not covered by the policy?

A commercial policy is more likely to extend coverage to activities that occur away from the provider's home. Some also specifically include coverage for accidents that occur while transporting child care children in the car. Also, commercial policies sometimes include coverage for sexual abuse claims. However, the liability limit usually is lower and is intended to pay only for legal defense costs, and not for judgments that might be awarded to a child and his/her family that you would be obligated to pay. Many commercial policies also include specific coverage for claims related to food served to a child.

Most commercial policies today are occurrence form rather than claims made form. The distinction is an important one. With an occurrence form policy, the company will follow through on claims made after the policy has expired or you have gone out of business if the injury occurred while the policy was in force. With a claims made policy, the claim must be made during the policy period.

An example will help to explain the important difference between the two types of policies. If a child in your care were injured in June of this year, only the claims you filed between June and the end of your policy year would be paid by a claims made form policy. If the policy were occurrence form, claims related to that child's injury and filed next year or even several years from now would be paid, even if you no longer had the insurance policy.

3. Must I purchase a separate accident insurance policy?

Most insurers require clients who buy a liability policy to also purchase an accident insurance policy. The insurance companies believe that a liability claim is less likely to be filed by a parent if the provider has insurance to pay the medical expenses of the injured child or parent.

4. What are the premiums? Are there deductibles?

Expect commercial liability policy premiums to range from $500 to $1000 or more per year for a $500,000 liability limit (the minimum recommended). Total premiums for both a liability and an accident insurance policy may be $1000 or more per year. Premiums usually depend on the policy limits (higher limits mean higher premiums) and the amount of the deductible (lower deductibles mean higher premiums). Some companies' premiums also may depend on the size of the home and/or the number of children cared for.

Many insurance agents may allow premium payments to be spread out over the year. A typical arrangement requires you to make a down payment and pay the remainder in two or three payments. Although $500 to $1,000 per year seems like a large sum of money, it may be well worth the price.

Depending on the number of children in your care, you may be able to increase the rate you charge by only a small amount and recover much of the insurance costs. For example, the cost of a $675 policy is about $13 a week. If you care for 6 children, that is just over $2 per child per week. And, the full cost of a commercial liability policy (as well as the cost of a home owner's endorsement) is tax deductible as a business expense.

5. How do I file a claim?

Ask to see a copy of a claim form and ask where you would send or take the form to file a claim. Ask whether the company would pay expenses directly or would reimburse you after you paid the expenses. Be certain to ask enough questions to understand the claim process before buying.

6. Where do I buy a commercial liability policy?

You may purchase a commercial policy through a local independent insurance agent (an agent who is authorized to sell insurance for more than one company). Because you may not be familiar with the companies that sell commercial policies, deciding from whom to buy the insurance is more important than usual. Insurance agents who are knowledgeable about insurance for child care providers usually can offer a choice of appropriate liability and accident insurance policies. Your state department of insurance may have a list of companies that sell liability or accident insurance to family child care providers.

Most commercial liability policies are written in the surplus lines market, often by insurance companies that are not required to meet state licensing standards. The companies may be financially sound and reputable but choose not to be licensed in a particular state. However, in a state with a guaranty fund, an unlicensed company is not backed by the fund. A guaranty fund would pay the claims of consumers if a licensed company became insolvent. Thus, as in all insurance decisions, it is important to learn all that you can about the insurance company before buying. (See question 3 in the following section.) Despite the disadvantages, companies in the surplus lines market are important because they are willing to write insurance to cover risks that other companies may not be willing to insure.

Other important questions

Whether you choose to extend your home owner's insurance coverage or buy a commercial policy, the following questions are important.

1. What are the liability and medical payments limits?

A policy limit is the maximum amount the policy will pay if there is a claim. Usually the limit is stated per claim or per person injured. There also may be an aggregate limit—a total amount the policy will pay in any one year regardless of the number of claims filed or persons injured.

Ask for rates for a minimum liability limit of $300,000 ($500,000 preferred) and a minimum accident/medical payments insurance limit of $10,000 ($20,000 preferred).

2. What is the company's financial reputation?

Check Best's Insurance Reports in your public library. Companies rated A or A+ are the strongest. If the company is not rated, check with your state department of insurance.

3. What is the company's claims and service reputation?

Ask your state department of insurance about complaints received against various companies. The department may be able to provide the complaint ratio of each company. The complaint ratio is the number of complaints reported in relation to the number of policies sold. If the company requires you to meet licensing, registration, or certification standards, the government agency that sets those standards may have information about providers' experiences with the company. If the policy requires membership in a child care providers' association, the association may know about the company's reputation. You also can check Consumer Reports for ratings of home owner's insurance companies.

4. How knowledgeable is the insurance agent?

Listen carefully to the agent's answers to your questions. Is she/he willing to work with you? Some insurance professionals are more knowledgeable than others about options for family child care providers. Look for an agent who can answer your questions and seems interested in finding the best arrangement for your situation.

5. Does my personal auto insurance policy provide coverage while I am transporting child care children?

If you transport children in your car, ask about extending your auto insurance coverage or purchasing a separate business use policy. Some commercial liability insurance policies also make available endorsements that extend coverage to autos. If your personal auto insurance policy does protect you, make sure your liability limits are adequate.

Making your choice

Even with information, your choice is not an easy one. It's not easy to decide how much insurance coverage you need, especially when the cost seems high.

Do not make the mistake of thinking you cannot afford to have insurance coverage. It is far more likely that you cannot afford not to have coverage.

Do not assume that you can avoid the need to make a decision by asking parents to sign a legal waiver of responsibility. Legal experts agree that such statements are worthless.

Do not assume that if the child's family has medical insurance you will be protected. If the child is injured while in your care, you may still be responsible for paying the medical bills.

Regardless of which insurance option you choose, most providers also can limit their liability by working to provide a safer environment for the children. Check toys and other play equipment regularly to see that they are clean and in good repair. Childproof every room. Check the condition of your front walk, steps, porch, patio, and other areas where parents enter or children play. Take first aid and

CPR courses. Establish good lines of communication with parents so you are clear about their wishes concerning the child's food, medications, limits on play activities, and general care.

Liability information adapted and updated from: Cude, B. and Volker, C. B. (1993) Liability Insurance and the Family Child Care Provider, NCR 395, Iowa State University Extension.

Glossary of insurance terms

Claims made policy—A policy for which claims are paid only if they occurred and were filed while the policy was in force.

Declarations—A section of an insurance policy that provides basic descriptive information about the insured person and/or property, the premium to be paid, the time period of the coverage, and the policy limits.

Deductible—A provision in an insurance contract stating that the insurer will pay the amount of any insured loss that exceeds a specified amount. The specified amount is the deductible.

Endorsement—An amendment or addition to the policy; also known as a rider.

Errors and omissions—Insurance for the liability of a professional for losses that occurred because of his or her errors or oversights.

Exclusion—Clauses that narrow the focus and eliminate specific coverages broadly stated in the insurance policy.

Independent agent—An agent who is authorized to write insurance for more than one insurance company.

Liability—Legal responsibility for damage or injury caused by you. The responsibility usually is financial and usually is due to negligence. Negligence occurs when there is a breach of the duty owed an individual that causes injury or damages.

Liability limits—The maximum dollar amount that the insurance company will pay for claims on the particular policy.

Licensed insurance company—A company licensed by your state; required to file rates and policies with the state; backed by the state insurance guaranty fund if the company becomes insolvent.

Occurrence form—A policy for which claims are paid after the policy has expired or you have gone out of business, if the claim occurred while the policy was in force.

Premium—The amount of money charged to a policy holder for an insurance policy.

Surplus lines insurance market—Insurance written by companies that are not licensed in your state. Unlicensed companies write policies to cover risks that licensed companies choose not to insure; usually do not have to file rates and forms with the state department of insurance; and aren't covered by the state insurance guaranty fund.

Underwriter—An employee of an insurance company who assesses the risk to the company of accepting submitted insurance applications.

Resources

The following resources are highly recommended and provide more in-depth information on taxes, contracts, and record keeping. Several resources feature a CD-ROM with customizable worksheets. They can be ordered from Redleaf Press, 450 North Syndicate, Suite 5, St. Paul Minnesota 55104-4125, phone 1-800-423-8309, www.redleafpress.org.

Family Child Care Record Keeping Guide, Tom Copeland, JD
This resource covers basic and in-depth information related to family child care record keeping. Information and illustrations are clear and understandable.

Family Child Care Tax Companion, Tom Copeland, JD
An annual publication that includes all of the tax law changes for the year and step-by-step instructions for completing federal income tax forms.

Family Child Care Contracts and Policies, Tom Copeland, JD
This important resource discusses what to include in a contract, how to prevent conflicts with parents, how to enforce and change contract terms, and how to end a contract. Sample contracts are given.

Calendar Keeper
A comprehensive family child care record-keeping system in a monthly calendar format. Includes forms for Child and Adult Care Food Program records and worksheets for tracking income, expenses, and taxes.

Family Child Care Legal and Insurance Guide, Tom Copeland, JD, and Mari Millard
An in-depth resource on insurance issues that affect family child care.

FamilyShare...
Supporting your partners

Creating a positive relationship with parents requires good communication. Giving parents a written agreement and policy statement will help parents understand your policies and respect you as a professional.

The forms in this chapter also can be found on the CD-ROM that accompanies this book. You may use them as a guide for your individual home child care business.

Form A—Parent-provider child care agreement

The following agreement is made between parent(s)/guardians(s) and provider for child care services given to:_____.
                           child's name   date of birth

Parent/guardian name:_____

Parent/guardian name:_____

Address:_____ Phone:_____

Provider's name:_____

Address:_____ Phone:_____

The terms of the agreement are as follows:

Effective date:_____ **until** _____

Hours:

Days	Sunday	Monday	Tuesday	Wednesday	Thursday	Friday	Saturday
Times							

Fees:

    Standard care:_____ per (circle one) month, week, day, hour
    Overtime rates:_____ per hour
    Standard fee payment is due one week in advance on:_____
    State Assistance $_____ per month   Parent Co-payment $_____ per month
    Overtime fee rates are due on:_____
    Additional charges $_____
    _____

    An advance payment of $_____ for the last two weeks of care is due before beginning child care.

Vacations/illness :

_____ days of non-attendance per year are allowed free of charge. All other times, including illness, will be charged the full weekly rate. Other provisions for child care must be made for the following times:

    New Year's Day   Memorial Day   Fourth of July   Labor Day
Thanksgiving and the day after   Christmas Eve   Christmas Day and December 26

Provider will take vacation _____. There will be a charge of $_____ for this time.

Termination of agreement:

Either parents/guardians or provider may terminate this agreement by giving a two-week advance notice. Payment for child care services is due for the two week notice period, whether or not the child attends the child care program. The provider can terminate the contract immediately without giving any notice if parents or guardians do not make payments when they are due.

I/we agree to abide by the written terms of this agreement.

Parent/Guardian signature _____ date _____

Parent/Guardian signature _____ date _____

Provider signature _____ date _____

Form B—Sample child care policy statement

I respect and appreciate the trust you have placed in me to care for your child. I believe parents are the most important people in a child's world, and I will make every effort to support you as a family.

I will offer the very best care that I can for your child. You can help me by keeping me informed about health concerns, favorite foods, fears, or special interests. I will share information about your child's growth and activities while in my program.

My philosophy about children and child care is reflected in the following policies.

Play and learning activities—Children learn a great deal from daily play activities. Blocks, puzzles, play dough, finger painting, sidewalk chalk drawings, singing, reading books, planting flowers in the garden, pretending to be fire fighters, or making snow angels are typical activities that we might do. I strongly believe children learn by doing and try to provide activities that are appropriate for children of different ages and interests. A weekly schedule of activities will be posted on the bulletin board.

Outdoor activities—I try to take the children outside every day for fresh air and exercise. Often we will bundle up and go outside on cold days for at least a few minutes. On warm, sunny days we may spend an hour or more outdoors. If you have special requests regarding outdoor play (such as using sunscreen, insect repellent, etc.) please let me know.

Field trips—I do take the children on walks and field trips. I always take an additional adult with me whenever we travel by car. Children are required to use seatbelts or car seats for car travel. I carry emergency contact numbers with me. You will be notified several days in advance if a field trip is scheduled.

Celebrations—I do recognize birthdays for each child. However, I ask that you not bring gifts or a cake. I provide cupcakes as a special treat for children's birthdays and will give a small gift (usually a book or other small item). We do recognize other holidays, with special food and activities, however children do not exchange gifts.

Toys and other items from home—I encourage children to bring a special "child care" friend such as a stuffed animal or doll with them to child care. A blanket for napping is also fine. However, please don't bring other items. Young children often have trouble sharing and occasionally some items with small parts may not be safe for very young children. I cannot be responsible for items if they are damaged or broken.

Clothing—Daily play and learning can get messy, especially when playing outdoors or working with art projects. Please dress your children in comfortable, washable play clothes every day. Please provide an extra set of clothing (shirt/blouse, pants, underwear, socks). Seasonal items such as swim suit, towel, mittens, boots, and snow pants also may be needed.

Form B—Sample child care policy statement (continued)

Meals/snacks—I participate in the Child Care and Adult Food Program. This means I plan nutritionally balanced, wholesome meals and snacks. I serve children a morning snack, a lunch, and an afternoon snack. Children are encouraged (but never forced) to eat a variety of foods. On occasion, the children may help me prepare special snacks or meals. Weekly menus are posted on the bulletin board.

Naps/rest time—Children in my care usually take regular naps. Infants nap as needed, and older children generally sleep in the afternoon after lunch. Even if children do not sleep, I still ask that they rest quietly.

Behavior guidance—I try to be respectful of children's basic needs. I support positive behavior by setting up child-friendly play areas and by following regular routines for eating and napping. The children are taught simple rules and manners that they can easily understand.

When children do something that is not appropriate, I redirect them to a more suitable activity. When children are arguing or out of control, I will insist on a "time out" or cooling off period. At times, I also may choose to ignore misbehavior. I work with older preschoolers and school-age children to develop problem-solving skills. I will not physically punish your child by spanking, slapping, or hitting. My goal is to help each child develop self-control and positive social skills.

Illness—Children cannot attend if they have a temperature of more than 101 degrees Fahrenheit, if they have a contagious disease, are vomiting, have diarrhea, or are not able to function well in daily activities, for example if they have a constant cough and require more supervision than I can provide without neglecting the other children. You must notify me if your child will not be attending. Parents will be notified if children become ill while in my care. Children must be picked up as soon as possible. Medications will be given only with the parent's or doctor's direct written consent. Please bring all medications in their original bottle, with written instructions indicating the last dosage given, the amount to be given, and the time to be administered. Medicine should be placed in a plastic zip bag.

Emergencies—In the event of a medical emergency, fire, or natural disaster, I will take immediate steps to ensure your child's safety and will contact you as quickly as possible. If we need to evacuate I will take the children to my neighbor's house directly across the street. If that location is not available, I will take the children to St. Andrews Church on the corner of 6th and Wildflower Lane. I maintain a list of emergency numbers. Please make sure that you keep me informed regarding current contact information. I ask that you provide me with at least one other contact if I cannot reach you.

Pets—I have a small dog, Misty, that is frequently in contact with the children. She is very gentle and affectionate with children. I believe children benefit greatly from playing with and caring for animals. Misty is vaccinated and receives regular veterinarian check-ups.

Smoking—Smoking is not allowed in my home, including outdoor areas.

Form B—Sample child care policy statement (continued)

Parent communication/involvement—I enjoy visiting with parents each morning and afternoon during arrival and departure. Please allow enough time in your schedule to update me on any information about your child that I may need to know. I also will post messages and information on our child care bulletin board, so be sure to look at it each day. Parents are welcome to visit at any time. If you have a skill or interest you would like to share with the children, please let me know. If you call during the day, please keep in mind that you may have to leave a message on the answering machine, especially if we are outside or eating. I will return your call as soon as possible.

Drug and alcohol use—If a parent comes to pick up a child and appears to have been drinking too much or is under the influence of drugs, I will call the police.

Education and training—I have an associate degree in Early Childhood Education from Red Lake Community College. I take additional continuing education training each year and from time to time will need to take a day off to attend training. I will provide qualified substitute care for your child during that time.

Termination—Service will be terminated for any of the following reasons:
- payment is late
- payment check bounces
- parent is routinely late for pick-up or drop-off
- child is extremely disruptive, e.g., excessive biting, rages, etc.

My philosophy—I am committed to providing high quality child care in a home environment. I believe family child care offers children the opportunity to learn and grow with children of different ages in a supportive, family-like atmosphere.

I believe children learn best through play and "hands-on" experiences. I strive to provide positive learning activities for each child. I also work to help each child develop self confidence and positive social skills.

I value the opportunity to work closely with each child for several years. I sincerely believe this practice provides continuity and stability for each child and allows me to better nurture and support each child as he/she grows and develops.

Form C—Child enrollment information

Child's full name:	Birth date:
Child's address:	Phone:
Name child is called:	

Parent or Guardian	**Parent or Guardian**
Name:	Name:
Home address:	Home address:
Work address:	Work address:
Home phone:	Home phone:
Cell:	Cell:
Work phone:	Work phone:

Does your child have any special needs? _____
_____

Health care professional/doctor to call if child becomes ill: _____
Address: _____ Phone: _____

Emergency contacts if parent or guardian cannot be reached:

Name: _____	Name: _____
Home address: _____	Home address: _____
Home phone: _____	Home phone: _____
Work phone: _____	Work phone: _____
Cell: _____	Cell: _____
Employer: _____	Employer: _____

The following persons are allowed to pick up my child in the event I am unable to:
_____

Anyone **NOT** permitted to pick up my child (with copy of court order if applicable):
_____

Parent/Guardian signature _____ date _____

Parent/Guardian signature _____ date _____

continued

Form C—Child enrollment information—continued

Physical Information

Allergies: _____
_____
_____

Medications: _____
_____
_____

Does your child have any unusual eating habits? likes? dislikes? (explain) _____
_____

What is your child's usual waking time? _____
   Nap time? _____ Bed time? _____

Does your child have any special problems or fears? _____
_____

Does your child have any nervous habits? How does she/he display them? _____
_____

Is your child completely toilet trained? _____
_____

Has your child had any previous group experience? _____
   What type? _____

What kind of play does he/she prefer?   ❑ books   ❑ blocks   ❑ puzzles/games   ❑ music
            ❑ outdoor   ❑ sand/water   ❑ pretend

Are there any areas where you have special concerns? _____
_____

What forms of discipline do you use with your child? _____
_____

Does your child have any pets? _____ If so, what kind and what are their names?
_____

Is there any further information that might be helpful in understanding your child?
_____
_____

Form D—Daily attendance record for part-time hours

Additional copies may be needed for more children.

Provider's name _____ **Month/year** _____ **Page #** _____

Day	1st Child (last, first name)	Time in and time out	Total hours	2nd Child (last, first name)	Time in and time out	Total hours
1						
2						
3						
4						
5						
6						
7						
8						
9						
10						
11						
12						
13						
14						
15						
16						
17						
18						
19						
20						
21						
22						
23						
24						
25						
26						
27						
28						
29						
30						
31						
	Total part-time hours used for this month:			Total part-time hours used for this month:		

HFCCH Chapter 10 — Business matters

Form E—Daily Attendance Sheet

Month _____ Year _____

Name	1	2	3	4	5	6	7	8	9	10	11	12	13	14	15	16	17	18	19	20	21	22	23	24	25	26	27	28	29	30	31

Form F—Transportation and activity permission

Transportation and activity permission

I give my permission for _____
to attend routine weekly activities away from the child care home while under the supervision of _____. These activities may be walks in the neighborhood or trips in the provider's vehicle or on public transportation to shopping areas, the library, etc.

Parent/Guardian signature _____ **date** _____

✂- -

Form G—Special activity permission

Special activity permission

I give my permission for _____ to attend activities away from the child care home.

Date of trip: _____

Departure time: _____

Arrival time: _____

Destination: _____

Persons who will be responsible for your child(ren) are: _____
_____
_____
_____

Parent/Guardian signature _____ **date** _____

Form H—Emergency medical treatment authorization

Child's full name: _____ Date of birth: _____
Name child is called: _____

I, _____ parent or guardian of the child named above give my permission to _____, child care home provider, to secure and authorize such emergency medical care and treatment as my child might require while under the provider's supervision. I also authorize the provider to administer emergency care or treatment as required, until emergency medical assistance arrives. I also agree to pay all the costs and fees contingent on any emergency medical care and treatment for my child as secured or authorized under this consent.

NOTE: Every effort will be made to notify parents immediately in case of emergency.
In the event of an emergency, it would be necessary to have the following information.

Name of Parent or Legal Guardian: _____
Address: _____
Home phone: _____ Work phone: _____ Cell phone: _____

Name of Parent or Legal Guardian: _____
Address: _____
Home phone: _____ Work phone: _____ Cell phone: _____

Doctor: _____
Doctor's address: _____
Doctor's phone: _____

Preferred hospital to contact: _____
Address: _____ Phone: _____

Person(s) to be contacted in emergency if the parents are unavailable:
Name	Home phone	Work phone	Cell phone	Relationship
_____	_____	_____	_____	_____
_____	_____	_____	_____	_____

Present medication(s): _____
Known allergies: _____
Date of last tetanus: _____ Religious preference: _____
Insurance provider: _____
Insurance number: _____

Parent/Guardian signature _____ **date** _____
Parent/Guardian signature _____ **date** _____

Form I—Child health exam record

PARENTS complete this page.

Child's name	Child's birthdate	Name of provider
		Telephone #

Parent 1 name	Parent 2 name

Child home address #1	Telephone # 1

Child home address #2	Telephone #2

Where parent # 1 works	Work address	Home phone # Work # Pager # Cellular # Home email Work email
Where parent # 2 works	Work address	Home phone # Work # Pager # Cellular # Home email Work email

In the event of an emergency, the child care provider is authorized to obtain EMERGENCY MEDICAL or DENTAL CARE even if the provider is unable to immediately make contact with the parents/guardian. During an emergency the child care provider is authorized to contact the following person when parent or guardian cannot be reached.

Parent/Guardian Signature: _____ Date _____

Alternate emergency

contact person's name: _____ Relationship to child: _____ Phone number: _____

Child's doctor's name	Doctor telephone # 1	Hospital choice
Doctor's address	After hours telephone #	Does your child have health insurance? Yes, Company _____ ID #
Child's dentist's name	Dentist Telephone # 1	Does your child have dental insurance? Yes, Company _____ ID#
Dentist's Address	After hours telephone #	☐ NO, we do not have health insurance. ☐ NO, we do not have dental insurance.
Other health care specialist name	Telephone #	Type of specialty

Form I—Child health exam record (continued)

Parent concerns   **Parent complete this page**

Tell us about your child's health. Place an ✔ in the box ❑ if the sentence applies to your child. Check all that apply to your child.

Growth
❑ I am concerned about my child's growth.

Appetite
❑ I am concerned about my child's eating/feeding habits or appetite.

Rest
❑ I am concerned about the amount of sleep my child needs.

Illness/Surgery/Injury – My child
❑ has had a serious illness, surgery, or injury. *Please describe.*

Physical Activity – My child
❑ must restrict physical activity. *Please describe.*

Medication – My child
❑ takes medication. List meds taken at home, preschool, or in child care. List the name, time medication taken, and the reason medication prescribed.

Development and Learning
❑ I am concerned about my child's behavior, development, or learning. *Please describe.*

Body Health – My child has problems with
❑ Skin, birthmarks, Mongolian spots, hair, fingernails or toenails.
Map and describe any skin markings

❑ Eyes/vision, glasses
❑ Ears/hearing, hearing aides or device, earaches, tubes in ears
❑ Nose problems, nosebleeds, runny nose
❑ Mouth, teething, gums, tongue, sores in mouth or on lips, mouth-breathing, snoring
❑ Frequent sore throats or tonsillitis
❑ Breathing problems, asthma, cough, croup
❑ Heart, heart murmur
❑ Stomach aches, upset stomach, colic, spitting up
❑ Using toilet, toilet training, urinating
❑ Hard stools, constipation, diarrhea, runny stools
❑ Bones, muscles, movement, pain with moving
❑ Mobility, uses assistive equipment
❑ Nervous system, headaches, seizures, or nervous habits (like twitches)
❑ Needs special equipment. *Please describe.*

Allergy – My child
❑ has allergies (food, medicine, fabric, inhalants, insects, animals, etc.). *Please describe.*

Parent or child care provider questions or concerns to ask health care provider:

Form I—Child health exam record (continued)

Health provider complete this page[1]

| **Date of exam:** | **Birthdate:**   **Age today:** |

| **Height or Length:**
Weight:
Head Circumference (for children under 2 yr.):
Body Mass Index (for children over 2 yr.):

Blood Pressure (start @ age 3 yr.):
Hgb. or Hct. (start @ 1 yr.):
Blood Lead Level (start @ 1 yr.):
Urinalysis: | **Date of last dental exam:**
Dental referral made today: ❏ Yes ❏ No |

Exam Results (n = normal limits) *otherwise describe*

HEENT:

Teeth:

Heart:

Lungs:

Stomach/abdomen:

Genitalia: Tanner stage:

Extremities, joints, muscles, spine:

Skin, lymph nodes:

Neurological:

Vaccines given today:

DtaP/DTP/Td

HEP B

HIB

Influenza

MMR

Pneumococcal

Polio

Varicella

Other

_____

TB testing (for high risk child only)

Referrals made today:

Sensory and developmental screening

Vision Right eye _____ Left eye _____

Hearing Right ear _____ Left ear _____

Tympanometry (attach results)

Developmental screening results:

Personal-social

Fine motor-adaptive

Language

Gross motor

Developmental referral made today: ❏ Yes ❏ No

Physician authorizes the child may receive the following medications while at child care: (include over-the-counter and prescribed):

Medication name   *Dosage*

Diaper creme:

Pain reliever:

Sunscreen:

Cough medication:

[1] The American Academy of Pediatrics has recommendations for frequency of childhood preventative pediatric health care (RE9939, March 2000) www.aap.org

Form I—Child health exam record (continued)

Health provider completes this section—Assessment Statement:

The child may participate in developmentally appropriate child care/preschool with **NO** health-related restrictions.
The child may participate in developmentally appropriate child care/preschool **with these restrictions.**
Describe all restrictions:

Health Provider *(may use stamp)*
Print name: _____
Signature _____
Provider's Type *(circle)* MD   DO   PA   ARNP
Health Care Provider Address: _____
Health Care Provider Telephone: _____
Additional Comments from the Health Care Provider:

Health Provider's Guide to Recommendations for Preventive Pediatric Health Care

Health Provider's Guide		1 mo	2 mo	4 mo	6 mo	9 mo	12 mo	15 mo	18 mo	24 mo	3 yr	4 yr	5 yr
History:	Initial and Interval	•	•	•	•	•	•	•	•	•	•	•	•
Measurement:	Height/Weight	•	•	•	•	•	•	•	•	•	•	•	•
	Head Circumference	•	•	•	•	•	•	•	•	•			
	Blood Pressure										•	•	•
Sensory Screen:	Vision	S	S	S	S	S	S	S	S	S	O	O	O
	Hearing	O	S	S	S	S	S	S	S	S	S	O	O
Developmental Screening		•	•	•	•	•	•	•	•	•	•	•	•
Complete Unclothed Physical Exam		•	•	•	•	•	•	•	•	•	•	•	•
Lab:	Hereditary/Metabolic Screen	•[3]											
	Hematocrit or Hemoglobin						• →		♦				→
	Urinalysis												•
	Lead Test						•		♦	•[4]	♦	♦	♦
	Cholesterol Screen									♦			→
	TB test[5]							♦					→
Immunizations:		•	•	•	•	•	•	•	•	•	•	•	•
Family Guidance:	Injury Prevention	•	•	•	•	•	•	•	•	•	•	•	•
	Child Car Seat Counseling	•	•	•	•	•	•	•	•	•	•	•	•
	Tricycle Helmet Counseling									•	•	•	•
	Sleep Position Counseling	•	•	•	•	•	•						
	Nutrition & Physical Activity Counseling	•	•	•	•	•	•	•	•	•	•	•	•
	Violence Prevention	•	•	•	•	•	•	•	•	•	•	•	•
	Child Development Guidance	•	•	•	•	•	•	•	•	•	•	•	•

Key: • = to be performed   S = Subjective, by history
 ♦ = to be performed for at-risk children   O = Objective, by standard testing
 → = Range in which the task may be completed

[2] If a child comes under care for the first time at any point on the schedule, or if any items are not accomplished at the suggested age, the schedule should be brought up to date at the earliest possible time.
[3] All newborns should receive metabolic screening (e.g. Thyroid, hemoglobinopathies, PKU, galactosemia) during neonatal period.
[4] Lead testing should be done at 12 & 24 months. Testing may be done at additional times for children determined at risk.
[5] TB testing for only at-risk children.

Form J—Medication consent release

Medication consent and record for _____
child's name

Parent complete this section

I give permission to administer medication to my child as stated below:

Provider complete this section

Date	Parent's signature	Name of medication/ possible side effects to watch for	To be given Date	To be given Time	Amount each dose and how given (by mouth, nose, ear, to skin)	Keep in fridge (Y/N)	Safety check – done	Time given	Initials	Date	Reaction/ notes

Safety check:
1. Child-resistant container
2. Original prescription or manufacturer's label
3. Name of child on container
4. Current date on prescription/expiration date visible and not expired
5. Name and phone number of licensed health professional that ordered medication on container or on file

Adapted from *Model Child Care Health Policies*, June 1997, by the Early Childhood Education Linkage System (ECELS), a program funded by the Pennsylvania Depts. of Health and Public Welfare and contractually administered by the PA Chapter, American Academy of Pediatrics.

HFCCH Chapter 10 — Business matters

Form K—Child medical update

Child medical update

Provider's name: _____

Provider's address: _____

I have examined _____, or have sufficient ongoing knowledge of his/her medical condition to state that this child is free of any communicable or infectious disease, and is able to participate in a child care program.

Parent/Guardian signature _____ **date** _____

Restrictions: _____

_____

Physician's signature _____ **date** _____

Physician's address: _____

Note: This form is to be used for a child beginning a second or succeeding year in this child care home.

✂- -

Child medical update

Provider's name: _____

Provider's address: _____

I have examined _____, or have sufficient ongoing knowledge of his/her medical condition to state that this child is free of any communicable or infectious disease, and is able to participate in a child care program.

Parent/Guardian signature _____ **date** _____

Restrictions: _____

_____

Physician's signature _____ **date** _____

Physician's address: _____

Note: This form is to be used for a child beginning a second or succeeding year in this child care home.

Form L—Infant daily report

Infant name: _____ **Date** _____

Parent's report about infant	Child care provider report about infant
Infant slept: ☐ Good ☐ OK ☐ Not well Infant seems: ☐ Happy ☐ Fussy ☐ Other Comments: Did the infant eat before coming to child care? ☐ Yes ☐ No Feeding times Foods Amount	**Diapering/toileting** Time Wet BM Description _____ ☐ ☐ _____ _____ ☐ ☐ _____ _____ ☐ ☐ _____ _____ ☐ ☐ _____ _____ ☐ ☐ _____ _____ ☐ ☐ _____ _____ ☐ ☐ _____ _____ ☐ ☐ _____ _____ ☐ ☐ _____ **Naptime/sleeping**　　**Today's activities** Time to sleep: │ Time awoke:　☐ Music 　　　　　　　　　　　　　☐ Reading/use of books 　　　　　　　　　　　　　☐ Tummy time 　　　　　　　　　　　　　☐ Physical activity 　　　　　　　　　　　　　☐ Outdoors 　　　　　　　　　　　　　☐ Other _____
Has infant had medication before coming? ☐ Yes** ☐ No **List the names of medicine, amount given, and time given **Reasons for medicine:	**Nutrition: Meals and snacks** Feeding time　　　　Foods　　　　Amount **Medication** Name of medicine　　Amount given　　Time given
Special requests for infant today: What time will infant be picked up and by whom?	**Infant's mood and disposition** This morning the infant was: ☐ Happy ☐ Fine ☐ A little fussy ☐ Very fussy ☐ Not well This afternoon/evening the infant was: ☐ Happy ☐ Fine ☐ A little fussy ☐ Very fussy ☐ Not well During the night the infant was: ☐ Happy ☐ Fine ☐ A little fussy ☐ Very fussy ☐ Not well
Parent signature:	Child care provider signature:

Additional instructions or comments may be written on the back of this form.

Form M—Injury report
Child injury/incident report form

Provider name: _____
Phone number: _____
Address: _____

Fill in all blanks and boxes that apply.

Child's name: _____ Gender: M F   Birthdate: _____ Incident date: _____
Time of incident: ___:___ a.m./p.m. Witnesses: _____
Name of parent /legal guardian notified: _____ Time notified: ___:___ a.m./p.m.
Notified by (name of provider): _____
Was EMS (911) or other medical professional notified? ☐ No   ☐ Yes - Time notified: ___:___ a.m./p.m.
What EMS service(s) responded or other medical professional provided advice?

Location where incident occurred: ☐ Classroom ☐ Dining room ☐ Doorway ☐ Gym ☐ Hall ☐ Kitchen ☐ Motor vehicle ☐ Office ☐ Playground ☐ Restroom ☐ Stairway ☐ Unknown ☐ Other (specify) _____

Equipment/product involved: (check all that apply) ☐ Child-proof container ☐ Climber ☐ Playground surface ☐ Medication error ☐ Motor vehicle ☐ Sandbox ☐ Slide ☐ Swing ☐ Tricycle/bike ☐ Toy (specify): _____ ☐ Other equipment (specify): _____ ☐ No equipment/product involved

*Child care provider reported to the Consumer Product Safety Commission the equipment/product involved in the injury. ☐ Yes ☐ No CPSC Telephone: 1-800-638-2772 CPSC website: http://www.cpsc.gov/

Cause of injury / incident: (check all that apply)
☐ Animal related ☐ Bite, animal ☐ Bite, human ☐ Child behavior related ☐ Choking ☐ Cold/heat over exposure
☐ Fall, running, or tripping ☐ Fall to surface: Estimated height of fall ___ feet. Type of surface: _____
☐ Hit or pushed by another child ☐ Injured by object ☐ Medication error ☐ Motor vehicle ☐ Sting, insect, bee, spider or tick bite ☐ Other (specify): _____

Describe injury/incident: Include the part(s) of body injured and the type of injury markings. For medication errors describe medication and exact circumstances of the error.

First aid/treatment given on-site (examples: cold pack, comfort, wound cleaning, bandage applied, behavior intervention):

First aid / treatment given by (name of person): _____

Medical / dental care needed day of injury/incident:
  ☐ No doctor's or dentist's treatment required   ☐ Doctor or dentist office visit same day required
  ☐ Treated as an outpatient in emergency room   ☐ Hospitalized

Signature of provider: _____ **Date:** _____

Signature of parent/person authorized by parent: _____ **Date:** _____

Complete this section with details obtained in days following event.   Date of late entry: _____
Follow-up treatment needed: _____

Reduced or limited activity required for _____ days.
Corrective action needed to prevent reoccurrence:

Signature of person making late entry: _____

Adapted for use from Iowa Dept. of Human Services and Public Health and American Academy of Pediatrics, Pennsylvania Chapter. Model Child Care Health Policies. 4th ed. Washington, D.C.: National Association for the Education of Young Children, 2002.

Form N—Child care provider physical exam report
(Provider/substitutes/family members)

Name: _____ Date: _____

Name of child care business: _____

What child care activities do you do? Check all that apply. ☐ lift or carry children ☐ infants/toddler care ☐ preschool child care ☐ school-age child care ☐ first aid duties ☐ driving ☐ playground/outdoor supervision ☐ cleaning ☐ food preparation ☐ office work ☐ I do child care in my home

Concerns and notes: *I am concerned about the following health problems.*

Health concern
☐ Allergies List:
☐ Breathing problems (asthma, emphysema)
☐ Dental problems or tooth related pain
☐ Diabetes
☐ Difficulty hearing
☐ Difficulty with vision
☐ Emotional or stress
☐ Heart or blood pressure problems
☐ Muscle, joint, or mobility problems Lifting restrictions

Health concern
☐ Neurology problems (headaches, seizures, other)
☐ Skin problems (concerns about frequent handwashing)
☐ Smoking or alcohol use ☐ I want to stop smoking
☐ Stomach or bowel problems
☐ Susceptibility to infection or illness
☐ Tuberculosis or history of positive test
☐ I have a health problem that requires work modifications: Describe:

Health care provider: The physical exam should include functional assessment of vision and hearing, with a review/exam of systems. The exam should determine health conditions that **pose a threat to the health, safety, or well-being of children** in child care, and/or **predispose the worker to occupational injury** relating to the care of children in a child care setting.

Immune status: The following list contains adolescent and adult immunizations.

Check if reviewed	Immunization*	Comments: indicate if person is immune or if vaccine was given. An adult immunization card may be used in lieu of this table.
☐	Hepatitis A* ☐ Hepatitis B	
☐	HPV* Human Papillomavirus	
☐	Influenza (annual influenza season)	
☐	Meningococcal*	
☐	MMR Measles, Mumps, Rubella	
☐	Pneumococcal*	
☐	Polio (OPV or IPV)	
☐	Shingles* (Herpes Zoster)	
☐	Td/Tdap	
☐	Varicella (chicken pox)	

* Clinicians should use the Advisory Committee on Immunization Practices (ACIP) recommendations. www.cdc.gov

Communicable disease statement
Does the person have a known communicable disease that requires modification of job duties? ☐ NO ☐ YES If yes, list the job duty restrictions.

Does the person test positive or have a history of tuberculosis (TB)? ☐ NO ☐ YES Date of positive test _____
Has the person completed TB medical diagnosis and treatment? ☐ YES ☐ NO

Health status
Does the person have known health condition(s) that requires modification of job duties? ☐ NO ☐ YES List the job duty restrictions.

Health care provider signature _____

Mailing address _____ Telephone _____

Provider type: ☐ MD   ☐ DO   ☐ PA   ☐ ARNP

HFCCH Chapter 10 — Business matters

Form O—Emergency drill record

Year_____

Month	Fire drills	Smoke alarms	Tornado drills
January	Date: Evac. time: # of children:	Date replaced batteries:	Date: Evac. time: # of children:
February	Date: Evac. time: # of children:	Date replaced batteries:	Date: Evac. time: # of children:
March	Date: Evac. time: # of children:	Date replaced batteries:	Date: Evac. time: # of children:
April	Date: Evac. time: # of children:	Date replaced batteries:	Date: Evac. time: # of children:
May	Date: Evac. time: # of children:	Date replaced batteries:	Date: Evac. time: # of children:
June	Date: Evac. time: # of children:	Date replaced batteries:	Date: Evac. time: # of children:
July	Date: Evac. time: # of children:	Date replaced batteries:	Date: Evac. time: # of children:
August	Date: Evac. time: # of children:	Date replaced batteries:	Date: Evac. time: # of children:
September	Date: Evac. time: # of children:	Date replaced batteries:	Date: Evac. time: # of children:
October	Date: Evac. time: # of children:	Date replaced batteries:	Date: Evac. time: # of children:
November	Date: Evac. time: # of children:	Date replaced batteries:	Date: Evac. time: # of children:
December	Date: Evac. time: # of children:	Date replaced batteries:	Date: Evac. time: # of children:

Form P—Emergency phone numbers

Home address _____

Paramedic _____ Police _____ Phone _____ Fire _____

Poison control _____

Child's name	Birthdate	Parents Name / Home / Cell / Work	Doctor	School	Emergency contact Name / Phone
		1 2			
		1 2			
		1 2			
		1 2			
		1 2			
		1 2			
		1 2			

Form Q—Start-up budget

Expenses*

    Facility

        Remodeling costs .... _____

    Equipment /supplies

        Office (furniture, files, etc.) .... _____

        Program (furniture, toys, paints, etc.) .... _____

        Housekeeping (cleaning supplies, etc.,) .... _____

        Installation fees (telephone line) .... _____

    Miscellaneous

        Advertising .... _____

        Food (first month) .... _____

    Legal and professional assistance

        Fees (license, permits, inspection, etc.) .... _____

        Insurance .... _____

    TOTAL .... _____

Income available .... _____

*You may not have all of the expenses listed. It will depend on what supplies you already have and the age and number of your child care children.

Form R—Annual operating budget

Expenses   **Total**

    Personnel
- Salary (pay yourself) .... _____
- Substitutes (# @ minimum wage/hr. x number of hours) .... _____

    Facilities (business portion*)
- Rent/mortgage ($ amt./mo x 12 mos.) .... _____
- Heat/gas .... _____
- Water .... _____
- Electricity .... _____
- Property taxes .... _____
- Maintenance and repairs .... _____
- Telephone .... _____
- Home insurance .... _____

    Equipment .... _____

    Supplies
- Educational materials and toys .... _____
- Household .... _____
- Office .... _____
- Postage .... _____
- Miscellaneous .... _____

    Food (meals and snacks)
- ($ amt. x no. children x no. days) .... _____

    Insurance
- Liability .... _____
- Automobile, if applicable .... _____

    Other
- Advertising .... _____
- Subscription/memberships .... _____
- Education/training .... _____
- Registration fees .... _____
- Tax preparer .... _____

    Annual payment on start-up loan ($/mo. x 12 mo.) .... _____

    Total expenses .... _____

Income

    Parent fees (** at 90% enrollment)
- (No. of children x enrollment % x $ amt./wk. x no. of weeks) .... _____

    Child and Adult Care Food Program .... _____

    Total income .... _____

* If child care income from business is entire household income, make sure personal budget costs are covered from business income.
** Since enrollment is rarely consistently 100%, a safer estimate is to start at 70% and work up to 85-90%.

Form S—Estimated cash flow forecast

Months	1	2	3	4	5	6	7	8	9	10	11	12
Expected fees*												
Carryover/ cash reserve												
+ Actual receipts												
= Total cash												
− Expenses												
= Cash balance (end of month)												

Estimated cash flow—example

Months	1	2	3	4	5	6	7	8	9	10	11	12
Expected fees*	$2,600	$2,600	$2,000	$2,600								
Carryover/ cash reserve	400	400	0	0								
+ Actual receipts	2,600	2,000**	2,000	2,600								
= Total cash	3,000	2,400	2,000	2,600								
− Expenses	2,600	2,400	2,000	2,400								
= Cash balance (end of month)	400	0	0	200								

* Expected fees: 1 infant @ $200/wk; 3 toddlers @ $150/wk. Figure 4 weeks/mo.; however, every 3 months there will be an extra week. (i.e., extra income)

**Could reflect non-payment for one toddler slot and you now have an opening to fill. The loss of just one enrolled child creates a significant loss of income and depletes your cash reserve.

Form T—Customer accounts

A Customer Account sheet provides a record of charges to and receipts from each family. A current balance of what each family owes you can therefore be maintained. It also provides the necessary information for calculating your total income at the end of the year. Start a new sheet at the beginning of each year so the records for one year can be separated easily from the records of another year.

Family name _____ Child/children _____ Calendar year _____

Address _____   _____   _____

_____   _____   Terms _____

Home phone _____   _____   _____

Parent #1/work _____   _____   _____

Cell phone _____   _____   Amount due _____

Parent #2/work _____   _____   When due _____

Cell phone _____

Notes _____

_____

_____

_____

Date	**Description of service** (daily care, drop in, late fees)	**Dates/time period covered**	**Amount due**	**Received**	**Balance**

Form U—Income summary

The Income Summary Form is a worksheet for determining total income for the year. This sheet summarizes income you have received from child care fees, Child and Adult Care Food Program, and other sources.

Calendar year _____

Child care fees	Food program	Other	Total	Year-to-date balance
Jan _____				
Feb _____				
Mar _____				
Apr _____				
May _____				
Jun _____				
Jul _____				
Aug _____				
Sept _____				
Oct _____				
Nov _____				
Dec _____				

Form V—Monthly expenses

Year-to-date total	This month's total	Balance carried forward																Date
																		Purchased from
																		Check #
																		Purchase total
																		Food
																		Supplies
																		FCC liability insurance
																		Toys
																		Equipment
																		Postage
																		Advertising
																		Substitutes
																		Other

Form W—Utilities and home expenses

Utilities | Home expenses

Month	Natural gas Date paid	Natural gas Amount	Electricity Date paid	Electricity Amount	Water Date paid	Water Amount	Trash collection Date paid	Trash collection Amount	Cable TV/Internet Date paid	Cable TV/Internet Amount	Household maintenance Date paid	Household maintenance Amount	Home insurance Date paid	Home insurance Amount	Property taxes Date paid	Property taxes Amount	Rent or mortgage interest Date paid	Rent or mortgage interest Amount
January																		
February																		
March																		
April																		
May																		
June																		
July																		
August																		
September																		
October																		
November																		
December																		
Total																		
Time/space %																		
Business expense																		

Form X—Mileage record

Calendar year: _____

Date	Beginning mileage	Final mileage	Miles driven	Destination	Purpose of trip

Form Y—Calculating time-space percentage

A. Total number of hours/year you use your home for business.......... _____
B. Total number of hours in year (8,760 hours/year)............................ _____
C. Total number of square feet used for business................................ _____
D. Total number of square feet in your house...................................... _____

$$\frac{A}{B} \times \frac{C}{D} = \underline{\qquad} \times 100 = \underline{\qquad} \%$$

My time-space % for (current year) _____ is _____.

Form Z—Liability insurance worksheet

What type of insurance do you have now? Ask your insurance agent(s):
1. What coverage is provided by my current home owner's (or renter's) insurance policy?
2. What coverage is provided by my current personal auto insurance policy?
3. What are my insurance options?

Use this worksheet to compare policies.

Questions	Policy 1	Policy 2
1. Policy type:		
Company name:		
Agent name:		
Address:		
2. How does the company limit its risks?		
• Maximum number of children?		
• License, registration, or certification required?		
• Membership in professional association required?		
• Underwriting guidelines (pools, pets, fences, etc.)?		
3. What is and is not covered by the policy?		
• Activities away from the home?		
• Transporting children?		
• Mental, physical, and/or sexual abuse?		
• Serving food?		
• Employees?		
• Giving medications?		
• Other conditions?		
4. What are the liability and accident insurance (or medical payment) limits?		
• Per claim?		
• Per year?		
5. What is the deductible?		
6. What is the premium?		
7. Is the policy an occurrence form or a claims made form?		
8. What is the company's reputation?		
What did I learn from:		
Best's Insurance Reports?		
State Department of Insurance?		
Consumer Reports?		
Government agencies?		
Professional association?		
Friends?		
My own experience?		
9. How do I file a claim?		
10. Is the agent knowledgeable and helpful?		

Reprinted with permission — Cude, B. and Volker, C. (1993) *Liability and the Family Child Care Provider,* NCR 395.

Form AA—Checklist for children's records

Records for _____
                      Child's name

Form	Completed	Date
A Agreement		
C Enrollment		
F Transportation and activity permission		
G Special activity permission		
H Emergency medical treatment release		
I Child health exam record		
J Medication consent record		
K Child medical update		
L Infant daily report		
M Injury report		
Immunization card (or exemption)		
Correspondence with parents		

Heart of the Matter

She was late—again. I felt angry. She would show up as usual, in her nice car and gym clothes and offer a heartfelt apology. Each time she explained that exercise was her salvation since her divorce. It was the only way she could deal with the stress.

I tried to understand. I knew divorce could be stressful, but I also knew her children needed her. Since the divorce they seemed restless and insecure. They were wonderful children—not a problem really—but I sensed they needed to be with her. I could tell it troubled the oldest when she was late.

The greater frustration, however, was the loss of my personal time. Her tardiness made it hard to do the things I needed to do. I needed to take a walk, prepare dinner, and go to my daughter's basketball game. And yes, I was a bit jealous. Despite her painful divorce, she seemed to have it all. She was pretty, had a well-paid job, beautiful clothes, nice car, and a health club membership. I, on the other hand, had a low income child care job, was isolated at home, wore jeans and sneakers every day of the week, drove a 6-year-old mini van, and was lucky to squeeze in an evening walk around the block.

I struggled with my feelings. I did some soul-searching. It was hard to separate out my feelings about her divorce and the impact of her lateness on me. I came to the conclusion that it was not my place to judge, but it was my place to set some boundaries. She was being inconsiderate of my time, but I could not expect her to read my mind and know what my needs were if I did not share them with her.

I revised my written policy to include extra fees for parents who were late. I also asked for the courtesy of a phone call.

I decided to approach the situation as I might do with a child who had misbehaved. In my mind, this was just another way of setting limits and boundaries. I wanted to be respectful, so I practiced what to say beforehand. I sat down with her and calmly explained the problems that were created for me personally when parents were late in picking up their children. I went through the changes in the policy and asked if she had any questions. I was kind and pleasant, but firm.

It worked. No more anger on my part. I'm just sorry I didn't do it sooner.

Lesia

Experience Talks

Conversations with other providers

■ **Don't be overwhelmed by recordkeeping.** When you look at the records you need to keep, it can be discouraging. But really it is to your benefit. It keeps you organized and by being more professional you can make more money. The tax advantages for child care home providers are amazing.

■ **I have a business form with my rates.** I send this and my policy statement to parents who call asking about care. This shows that I am a professional and take my work seriously. For parents who are price shopping this shows them that they get what they pay for.

■ **I ask parents for previous caregiver references.** I want to check to see if there were problems or concerns. This policy has helped me avoid families that tend to go from caregiver to caregiver.

■ **I keep an envelope in my purse to drop receipts into.** At the end of each week, I put them into an accordion pocket type file. Each pocket is labeled with a different expense category.

■ **Most of my expense purchases are on the weekend.** To keep myself on track, I do record keeping, file receipts, etc., every Monday at naptime.

■ **I give parents an invoice each month with amount due and due date.** Most parents have other bills like this, and I find it helps them get payments in on time. The invoice states a late fee for payments past the due date. Parents don't want to pay a late fee, and so generally get their payment in on time.

■ **I always give parents a summary statement at the end of the year for payment received.** I sign the statement and ask parents to sign it. This helps to protect me if parents mistakenly over report to IRS how much they've paid me.

■ **Sometimes parents have leftover Flexible benefit dollars (dependent care plan) at the end of the year.** When they reduce taxes by using a Flex program for child care expenses, they sometimes set aside too much. They would lose those dollars. I ask them to consider giving me those funds to purchase toys and equipment for my program.

■ **I color code everything**—forms, folders, you name it. It keeps everything much more organized.

■ **Several years ago I purchased business cards for my child care program.** It's amazing how often I find myself handing them out, and I have gotten a number of inquires from them. Even when I don't need children, I still use them. I believe in doing everything I can to help family child care providers present themselves as professionals.

Health and safety for active kids

Chapter 11

Contents

Where am I now?	280
Healthy routines	281
Cleanliness and sanitation	281
Hand washing	283
Toileting and diapering	284
Taking care of teeth	288
Creating and maintaining a safe environment	290
Coping with illness	305
Immunizations	309
Medications	309
HIV/AIDS—what you should know	310
Sudden Infant Death Syndrome (SIDS)	311
Coping with injuries and emergencies	312
FamilyShare	317
Heart of the Matter	318
Experience Talks	319

Health and safety for active kids—
Where am I now? What can I improve?

	Seldom 1	Sometimes 2	Often 3	Most Often 4
1. I check on children's health each day as they arrive and note parent concerns.				
2. I teach children simple safety rules and enforce regular handwashing.				
3. I follow the recommended steps for diapering.				
4. I use recommended practices to avoid spread of diseases or blood-borne pathogens.				
5. I use safety equipment to prevent injuries (e.g., baby gates, car seats, fire extinguishers).				
6. I have written emergency plans and practice regular drills.				
7. I maintain a current list of emergency phone numbers.				
8. I carry emergency information with me if we leave the house for any reason.				
9. I keep children's health records on file and up-to-date.				
10. I have a written illness and exclusion policy.				
11. I provide families with a written report if a child is injured and follow required state guidelines for reporting injuries.				
12. I clean my house to reduce dust mites, mold, and mildew.				
13. I check for and fix problems with carbon monoxide, radon, lead base paint, and asbestos.				
14. I do not smoke tobacco or allow others to smoke in areas where children might be exposed to smoke.				
15. I do not allow guns, firearms, or weapons of any kind in child care areas.				

Chapter 11

Health and safety for active kids

Healthy routines

Simple things like hand washing and routine cleaning can make a tremendous difference in creating and maintaining a healthy environment for the children in your care and for your family.

Cleanliness and sanitation

Cleaning, sanitizing, and disinfecting are important steps to reduce the spread of germs and illness in child care settings. Routine cleaning with soap and water removes dirt and grime from surfaces. Sanitizing removes dirt or filth and small amounts of germs. Some child care items and surfaces require the added step of disinfecting after cleaning to kill the germs on a surface.

A solution of regular household bleach and water is an inexpensive and easy way to disinfect and keep germs away from child care surfaces.

Bleach-water disinfectant
- **Tables, toilets, diaper changing surfaces, floors:**
  Mix 1 tablespoon of liquid chlorine bleach to 1 quart of water or 1/4 cup liquid chlorine bleach to 1 gallon of water
- **Dishes, eating utensils, and toys:**
  Mix 1 tablespoon of liquid chlorine bleach to 1 gallon of cool water or 1 teaspoon bleach to 1 quart of water
- Make this solution on a daily basis because it loses its strength after 24 hours
- Be sure to label the bottle and date it. Example: bleach/water solution.
- Keep out of the reach of children.

Note: Do not mix household bleach with other household chemicals such as toilet cleaners, rust removers, acids, or products containing ammonia. Mixing these chemicals with bleach may produce toxic hazardous gases.

Apply:
- Dip an object into a container filled with the bleach/water solution for 1 minute or
- Use paper towels soaked with bleach/water solution or
- Use a spray bottle
- Solution should sit on surfaces for 2 minutes then air dried or be wiped off with a clean paper towel

Other ways to remove germs
- Wash durable plastic toys that can be washed in the dishwasher.
- Wash cloth toys, linen, and bedding in the washing machine. Add 1/2 cup of chlorine bleach to the wash cycle when washing colorfast material and 1/2 cup of non-chlorinated bleach for non-colorfast material.

With adult supervision, older children will enjoy washing toys in warm soapy water. Do not allow children access to the bleach water.

Special cautions

The solution of bleach and water is easy to mix, non-toxic, safe if handled properly, and kills most infectious agents

When purchasing household bleach, make sure the bleach is labeled for household use. Household bleach typically is sold in retail stores in one of two strengths: 5.25 percent hypochlorite (regular strength bleach) or 6.00 percent hypochlorite (ultra strength bleach) solutions. Either strength of household bleach may be used.

Caution about commercial or industrial products

Products that meet the Environmental Protection Agency's (EPA) standards for "hospital grade" germicides (solutions that kill germs) often are promoted for use in child care. However, many of these products are dangerous and potentially toxic to children.

Be cautious about commercial or industrial products that advertise themselves as "disinfectants," having "germicidal action," or "kill germs"

Often these products carry a warning label on the front of the container.

Do not use products that carry a **DANGER** or a **DANGER, CORROSIVE** label warning.

Before using anything other than bleach/water for disinfecting, consult with your child care nurse consultant or regulatory licensing authority. If you choose to use an EPA-approved industrial product as a sanitizer, **carefully read the label** and **always follow the manufacturer's instructions exactly.**

Do not allow children to help you or to be in the area while sanitizing or disinfecting items and surfaces.

Source: Healthy Child Care Iowa, Iowa Department of Public Health
American Academy of Pediatrics, *Caring for our Children, National Health and Safety Performance Standards: Guidelines for Out-of-Home Child Care Programs*, Second Edition, 141 Northwest Point Blvd., Elk Grove Village, IL 60007-1098. 2002. pages 417-418.
Iowa Food Code, US Public Health Service, Food and Drug Administration, Iowa Department of Inspections and Appeals, Food and Consumer Safety Bureau. 1997. www.state.ia.us/government/

Hand washing

Washing hands can help you all stay healthy. Current health information suggests that as much as 90 percent of the virus-containing particles and bacteria on skin can be removed with good hand washing. That is a lot of protection from infection for the amount of time and effort it takes. Adults and children should wash hands regularly.

When to wash hands:
- upon arrival
- before serving or handling food
- before and after giving medication
- before and after eating
- after using the bathroom
- after changing a diaper
- after wiping noses, mouths, sores, or cuts
- after handling body fluids such as blood, mucus, or vomit
- after smoking
- after handling raw eggs, meat, or poultry
- after playing outdoors
- after touching or feeding pets or other animals

Hand Washing Dos

- **Choose liquid soaps.** A bar of soap may collect residue from the previous user, which may contain germs. Children seem to like liquid soap and may be more likely to use it every time.

- **Use warm water.** To prevent burns, however, be sure that your hot water supply does not get hotter than 120 degrees Fahrenheit.

- **Think disposable.** Recycling is great for toys and other useful household items, but when it comes to health and safety, disposable paper towels, tissues, and drinking cups will go a long way toward preventing infection and illness.

- **Wash hands for 20 seconds.** Teach children to sing the Hand Washing Song. It will help them remember to do a thorough job. Singing it twice should take about 20 seconds.

HFCCH Chapter 11 — Health and safety for active kids

- **Wash with soap and water instead of using ethanol-based hand sanitizers, whenever possible.** Hand sanitizers do not work well on soiled hands and are ineffective against Norovirus, the leading cause of gastroenteritis. Hand sanitizers contain ethanol, which is toxic if ingested. They would not be a good choice for children under 2 who may put their hands in their mouths. Keep all hand sanitizers out of the reach of children.

- **Wash infant and toddler hands too.** This often is overlooked because it is difficult to get them in the right position at a sink. A stepstool may be used to raise children to sink level, but always stay with the child. At a minimum you should use the three paper towel method described on page 285.

Hand Washing Song—
(Sing to Row, Row, Row Your Boat)
Wash, wash, wash your hands,
Play our handy game.
Rub and scrub and scrub and rub
Germs go down the drain.

Simple hand washing steps
1. Turn on warm water.
2. Wet hands with water.
3. Apply liquid soap.
4. Wash hands, rubbing hands out of running water at least 20 seconds. Rub top and inside of hands, under nails and between fingers. (Sing Hand Washing Song twice.)
5. Rinse hands at least 10 seconds.
6. Dry hands with clean, disposable paper towel.
7. Turn off water using the paper towel.
8. Throw paper towel away in a lined trash container.

IMPORTANT: If the sink being used also is used for food preparation, it must be cleaned and disinfected after each use.

Toileting and diapering

Diaper changes

Use one central place for changing diapers, preferably near a sink. The best locations will be where you can still remain close by for supervision of the other children when you are changing a diaper.

Choose a nonporous surface. The surface of the changing area needs to be nonporous so it can't absorb any contaminates, (no seams, quilting, cloth belts, or cracks), and so it can be thoroughly cleaned and disinfected. An example would be a hard plastic/laminate like countertops.

Select a surface with a raised edge. This will help keep the children from falling off.

Keep all diapering supplies and extra clothing in this area. You will need diapers, disposable wet wipes, disposable covering for the changing surface, plastic bags for soiled clothing, extra clothing, a spray bottle with soap and water and one for bleach solution or other disinfectant, disposable paper towels, and a covered, plastic lined trash container.

Avoid changing a diaper on the floor. Babies often wiggle off disposable coverings. It is very difficult to keep the floor free from contamination. This is especially important for other children who sit or crawl on the floor.

Diapering Dos

Cover diapering surface with disposable paper. Paper towels, wax paper, clean paper bags, or butcher paper are inexpensive choices for covering the diaper change surface.

Remove all wet wipes from the container ahead of time. Do this before you undress the child to avoid contaminating the container.

Have empty plastic bags ready. Use these for diapers and soiled clothing. Empty bread bags and plastic grocery sacks will cut down on odors.

Always use disposable latex gloves.

Always wipe from front of child to back. Use a new wipe each time. Be sure to clean all cracks and creases.

Remove gloves by turning inside out. This will keep contamination inside glove.

Use a covered, plastic-lined, "hands-free" trash can (step open lid). Using your hands to open the trash contaminates the can and your hands and is an easy way to transmit germs.

Limit handling of soiled cloth diapers. If reusable cloth diapers are used, put the soiled cloth diaper and its contents (without emptying or rinsing to prevent contaminating yourself) in a plastic bag to give to parents at the end of the day.

Wash the sink after every use. If the sink being used for hand washing also is used for food preparation, it must be cleaned and disinfected after each use.

Three paper towel method of hand washing

1. **Wipe the child's hands with a damp paper towel moistened with a drop of liquid soap.**

2. **Wipe the child's hands with a paper towel wet with clear water or spray with clear water.**

3. **Dry the child's hands with a paper towel.**

HFCCH Chapter 11 — Health and safety for active kids

Ten easy steps to change a diaper

NEVER leave an infant unattended on a changing table. Check to make sure you have everything you need before bringing the child to the changing table.

Step 1—Place a disposable covering on the diaper changing surface and place the child on the covered surface. Put disposable latex gloves on before picking up the child. Always keep a hand on the child.

Step 2—Remove soiled clothing. Place in a plastic bag to send home.

Step 3—Unfasten the diaper, but leave the soiled diaper under the child. Clean child's bottom with disposable wipes. Wipe front to back.

Step 4—Roll soiled diaper with used wipes inside and dispose. Remove gloves by pulling from the cuff down toward your fingertips, turning the gloves inside out as you take them off. Dispose of gloves.

Step 5—Wipe your own hands and the child's hands. Use separate wipes and dispose of wipes.

Step 6—Put on a clean diaper. Use a facial or toilet tissue to apply any necessary diaper creams. Redress child as needed.

Step 7—Wash the child's hands with soap and warm running water (preferred method). If a child is too heavy to hold for hand washing or cannot stand at the sink, use wet wipes or follow the three paper towel method.

Step 8—Return child to play area without touching anything else. Do not give child a toy or touch equipment, etc.

Step 9—Remove disposable covering and discard. Clean surface with spray bottle of soap and water, rinse and wipe with paper towel. Disinfect diapering area with bleach and water solution. Allow bleach water to stay on surface at least 2 minutes; it can air dry or be wiped after 2 minutes.

Step 10—Wash your hands with soap and warm running water. Note each child's diaper change and record on a daily sheet to give to parents.

Bathroom Safety

Decide at what age or ability level children will be allowed to use the bathroom on their own. Because there are many safety hazards; water, cleaners, make-up, soaps, medicines, electrical devices, stools to climb on, etc., children need to be supervised when in the bathroom. Even when children are older and are in the bathroom alone, check on them frequently. Do not allow children to lock the bathroom door so you can't get in if there is an emergency.

Learning to use the toilet

Learning to use the toilet will happen differently for each child. No two children will be ready at the same age.

Share information with the parents. Decide together if their child is ready to begin. It is important not to push children before they are ready. Work with parents to make the process consistent with what is happening at home.

Learning to use the toilet is easiest when children are physically and emotionally ready. This usually happens between the ages of 2 and 3 years. Girls usually gain physical control over their bowel and bladder muscles before boys do. On the average, most girls

are potty-trained by age 2 1/2 and most boys around the age of 3. But don't be alarmed if a child doesn't follow this pattern closely; individual children mature physically at different rates.

The secret to success is patience and timing. Emotional readiness also is important. Many bright, normal, and healthy 3-year-olds may not be interested in learning to use the toilet. Learning new things is a full-time job for most toddlers and toilet learning may not be as important as learning to climb, jump, run, and talk. A toddler who resists toilet learning now may be ready in 3 to 6 months, then often learns almost overnight.

Toilet Learning Dos

- **Choose a potty attachment instead of a potty chair.** A potty attachment has a smaller seat that snaps on to the regular toilet and is more sanitary. Avoid urine deflectors because they can cut the child.

- **Clean and disinfect.** If you choose to use a potty chair you must empty the chair, clean thoroughly, and disinfect between each use. Have spray bottles of soap and water and bleach water available for cleaning.

- **Keep supplies handy.** Have all supplies needed in the bathroom with you, clean diapers or pull-ups, wipes, gloves, clothing, etc.

- **Use a "hands free" plastic lined trash container.** You may need this for soiled diapers or pull-ups, wipes, and gloves. Show children how to use this type of trash container as well.

- **Assist the children as needed.** Children often need help getting on the seat, getting toilet paper, wiping, and getting off the seat. Gloves are recommended when assisting children with wiping. Your help in removing pullup diapers may help to keep things clean.

- **Wash hands.** Use a stepstool or other equipment so children can wash their hands in the sink. Help as needed. Wash your own hands.

Taking care of teeth

Tooth decay is very common in children. By second grade, an estimated 50 percent of children will have cavities. Much of this is preventable.

Children should begin to take care of their teeth at an early age. Daily care for toddlers, preschoolers, and school-agers should include eating healthy foods and brushing teeth after meals.

Tooth development

The two lower front teeth usually appear between 3 and 12 months of age. By 2 years of age children generally have at least 16 teeth. By 3 years of age children will have all 20 "primary" teeth. These teeth are very important even though they will be replaced later with permanent teeth. Baby teeth help children eat properly, assist in speech development, act as space holders for permanent teeth, and improve appearance.

Baby bottle tooth decay

Bottles should be used only to feed children, not as a pacifier or comfort. Allowing infants to have unlimited access to a bottle of milk, formula, or juice, or a sweetened pacifier will cause their teeth to decay (rot). This decay often is painful and can damage all of a child's primary teeth. Severe toothache, cavities, loss of teeth, crooked permanent teeth, and possible ear and speech problems can occur. The damage can be so severe that hospitalization may be necessary.

Prevent baby bottle tooth decay by following these rules in your home.
- Do not allow children to fall asleep with a bottle that contains milk, formula, fruit juice, or any sweet liquid.
- Discourage children from carrying a bottle around all day.
- Never dip a pacifier in any type of sweetened syrup or liquid.
- Use a bottle only to feed formula, breast milk, or water to infants. Avoid sweetened liquids such as juice or pop in a bottle.
- Teach infants to drink juice from a cup at 6 to 9 months of age.
- Discontinue the use of a bottle as soon as possible after one year of age.

Keeping teeth clean

Begin early with infants. Start cleaning an infant's teeth as soon as the first tooth appears. Wipe with a piece of gauze or a clean washcloth at first. As soon as the child adjusts to the daily routine of teeth cleaning, begin using a small toothbrush.

Build upon children's early interest in brushing. Toddlers and infants are likely to express a lot of interest in the care of teeth. They love to watch adults and older children brush and floss their teeth. This early interest can lead to good dental habits later on.

Each child should have a personal toothbrush. Label the brush with the child's name. Dentists generally recommend a small toothbrush with soft, nylon bristles. Replace worn brushes every 3 to 4 months.

Wait until the child is 2-3 to start fluoridated toothpaste. Until that time, adults should clean the child's teeth with water and a soft-bristled toothbrush. When toothpaste is used after age 2-3, adults should supervise brushing and make sure the child uses just a smear on the brush. Children should spit out and not swallow excess toothpaste after brushing.

Don't share the toothpaste tube. Instead use one of the following:
- Give each child his or her own toothpaste tube, labeled with name.
- Give each child a small paper cup with a dab of toothpaste along the rim. Each child picks up a bit of toothpaste with the tooth brush. Each child uses his or her own cup after brushing for rinsing.
- Place dabs of toothpaste along the edges of a paper plate or on wax paper.

Teach children how to brush. Children should brush their teeth in a circular motion on both the inside and outside surfaces of teeth and gums. Remind children to brush top to bottom and back to front. This habit will help ensure that all tooth surfaces are brushed. A quick brush on the tongue and a swish of water will complete the job. Whenever it is not possible to brush after eating, have children rinse out their mouths with water.

Store toothbrushes upright. Place bristle heads end up and not touching each other. If you need a holder you can make one out of a small cube-shaped box (cutoff "boutique" tissues box). Punch holes on top for each brush. An upside down egg carton also works well as a holder.

Keep brushes clean. Wash brushes at least once a week with soap and water. Washing brushes in the dishwasher may be convenient. Remember to rinse well with water.

Fluoride—Check to see if your community fluoridates its water. Fluoride helps prevent tooth decay by strengthening tooth enamel. Fluoride in drinking water can reduce tooth decay by 15 to 40 percent. If you do not have fluoride in your water, discuss with parents the possibility of using fluoride drops or tablets.

Eating healthy foods helps children keep healthy teeth. Avoid or limit sweet drinks, candy, jelly, jam, cake, cookies, sugared gelatin, and sticky fruits such as dates or raisins. When you do serve sweets, make sure that children eat them at one sitting. Eating a cookie at snack time is better than sucking on a lollipop or hard candy all afternoon.

A note about thumb sucking

Sucking is nature's way of providing children with pleasure and security. Children frequently suck their thumb even in the womb. Thumb sucking should cause little concern in the early years, and most children will gradually wean themselves from this habit. After age 5, however, thumb sucking can affect the development of permanent teeth and jaws. Children who continue to suck their thumb by age 5 should be gently discouraged from continuing this habit.

Creating and maintaining a safe environment

Homes are wonderful places to care for children, but they are full of hazards including electrical appliances, stairs, bathtubs, unsafe toys and equipment, and dozens of poisonous medicines and household cleaners.

The U.S. Consumer Product Safety Commission issues recalls for unsafe equipment and toys. If you have a question about the safety of an item, you can see a list of recalls at www.cpsc.gov.

Unintentional injuries cause the death of many children and also leave more children crippled than do diseases. Most injuries can be prevented if more care is taken. There is no golden rule to prevent injuries, but you can decrease the risks significantly by using the following checklist.

Falls and falling objects

- [ ] **Stabilize furniture.** Position tables, chairs, shelving, and other furniture so they cannot be toppled easily.
- [ ] **Screen windows.** Make sure they open from the top or have a barricade in front.
- [ ] **Check railings.** Provide secure railings on stairs, porches, decks, and lofts.
- [ ] **Equip steps.** Use tread mats or carpet to prevent slipping and a handrail that children can reach.
- [ ] **Secure carpets and rugs.** Make sure children and adults will not trip.
- [ ] **Use safety gates.** Block access to stairs and other dangerous areas.
- [ ] **Avoid baby walkers.** Walkers that can move across the floor should not be used for infants.

- ☐ **Use wide base high chairs.** These tip less easily.
- ☐ **Use high chairs with a safety strap.** It should also have a surface on the seat or lip to keep children from slipping down between the tray and the seat.
- ☐ **Have a raised edge on the changing surface.** This will help prevent children from falling off.
- ☐ **Stay within arms-reach of infant carriers.** Never leave infants on a high surface such as a table, counter, or chair.
- ☐ **Keep sides of playpens and cribs raised up—always.** Make sure crib sides cover at least three-fourths of a child's height.
- ☐ **Keep electric cords to lamps and appliances out of reach.** Tape to floor or wall, or move furniture in front of cord and outlet.
- ☐ **Keep unused rooms, such as a basement or attic, locked.** This will prevent children from being in areas where they should not be.
- ☐ **Make sure all doors to rooms and closets can be unlocked from both sides.** This will allow you easy access.
- ☐ **Place heavy items (like an iron or skillet) out of a child's reach.** Make it a practice to turn handles toward the back of the stove.
- ☐ **Teach children safe and unsafe areas for climbing.** Shelves or counters are not for climbing.
- ☐ **Wipe spills from floors immediately.** Keep paper towels close by.
- ☐ **Make sure your electric garage door has a spring back - safety feature.** This causes the door to go back up when it touches an object or person in the way.
- ☐ **Never use climbers indoors on hard surfaces.** Carpet over concrete, asphalt, wood, or other hard surfaces is not adequate protection from falls.

Poison

- ☐ **Keep trash covered and out of reach.** Hazardous items should go into a trash can protected by a safety latch.
- ☐ **Provide a tobacco-free environment for children.** Tobacco products are poisonous when eaten.
- ☐ **Keep perfumes and cosmetics in high cabinets with safety latches.** Do not leave on counters, dressers.
- ☐ **Keep all vitamins and drug products in high cabinets with safety latches.** Do not leave on counters.
- ☐ **Keep purses and diaper bags out of reach.** They often contain items that could be toxic.
- ☐ **Keep bleach water spray bottles out of children's reach.**
- ☐ **Do not store common household items within reach of children:** alcoholic beverages, cleaning supplies, cosmetics, pet supplies, medicines, vitamins, gasoline, paint thinner, fertilizer, weed killer, and other poisons in areas used by children.

- [ ] **Store hazardous products in their original containers.** Do not transfer them to used food or beverage containers or to a food storage area.
- [ ] **Keep hand sanitizers out of the reach of children.** Hand sanitizers can be toxic if eaten or licked.
- [ ] **Do not use insect poisons, rat poisons, or weed killers where children are present.** Keep them locked up. Dispose of leftover poisons immediately.
- [ ] **Follow directions and caution warnings on drugs, cosmetics, and chemicals.**
- [ ] **Make sure that walls, furniture, and toys have lead-free paint only.** Avoid purchasing any items that contain lead. Check to make sure there is no peeling paint on walls or furniture.
- [ ] **Have your home checked for radon—** an odorless gas that seeps through the soil into homes. Inexpensive test kits can be purchased at most hardware stores. Call your Cooperative Extension service for more information.
- [ ] **Check private water supplies annually** with a laboratory analysis. Check for bacteria and nitrates.
- [ ] **Check toys and materials to make sure they contain nontoxic, nonpoisonous materials.** Look for the "CP" or "AP" seal signifying safe art material for children.
- [ ] **Teach children not to taste things** like berries, roots, plants, pills, tablets, or liquids without your permission.
- [ ] **Remove all indoor and outdoor plants that might have poisonous parts.** See list in this chapter.
- [ ] **Install a carbon monoxide detector.** Check batteries annually.

Choking and suffocation

- [ ] **Make sure toys have no small parts** that could be broken off and swallowed.
- [ ] **Use balloons only with close adult supervision.** Pop and dispose of balloons immediately after use.
- [ ] **Do not allow children under 3 to play with any toy that is less than 1 1/4 inch in diameter** (about the size of a half dollar).
- [ ] **Make sure that mesh-sided playpens have holes no larger than 1/4 of an inch.**
- [ ] **Remove hanging crib toys** when infants are able to pull themselves up.
- [ ] **Remove plastic wrap on crib mattresses.** Make sure crib sheets fit snugly.
- [ ] **Do not feed children under 4 nuts, hard candies, popcorn, pretzels, or raw carrots.** Cut hot dogs or sausages into small bites and NOT round slices.
- [ ] **Teach children to chew their food well** and to eat only when sitting down.
- [ ] **Put infants on their back when sleeping** in a crib or a playpen and NEVER on an adult bed, waterbed, thick rug, pillow, or beanbag.
- [ ] **Remove rockers, recliners, and gliders from areas where children may be crawling.** Position furniture to avoid pinched fingers or head entrapment.

- ☐ **Store all plastic bags out of reach of children.**
- ☐ **Do not store clothing in dry cleaning bags** that are accessible to children.
- ☐ **Remove doors or lids from old freezers,** refrigerators, and cars and car trunks.
- ☐ **Remove latches and lids from toy chests.** Install a slow closing hinge and make sure the chest has ventilation holes.
- ☐ **Do not allow children to use or play with objects that have long cords.** This includes pacifiers with strings attached, long telephone cords, old jewelry, necklaces, and long scarves.
- ☐ **Tie hanging cords on draperies or blinds up high** and out of reach.
- ☐ **Install clotheslines out of reach of children.**
- ☐ **Use only safety gates that have a straight topped edge** and a rigid mesh screen. Do not use old accordion style safety gates.
- ☐ **Make sure stair railings and crib rails are no more than 2 3/8 inches apart.**
- ☐ **Make sure crib mattresses fit tightly** with no more than two finger widths in the gap between mattress and crib frame.

Burns, electrical shock, or fire

- ☐ **Do not heat bottles in the microwave.**
- ☐ **Stir all microwave heated foods** and check for "hot spots" before serving to children.
- ☐ **Keep pots and pans on the back side of the stove** where children can't reach them. Turn handles to the back.
- ☐ **Set the water heater in your home to a temperature of 120 degrees** Fahrenheit or less.
- ☐ **Cover unused electrical outlets** with safety caps.
- ☐ **Avoid burning decorative candles.**

- [ ] **Block electrical outlets** when possible with some type of barrier or furniture.
- [ ] **Fit Ground Fault Circuit Interrupters (GFCI) on electrical outlets** in kitchens, bathrooms, and outdoor areas to prevent risk of electrical shock when in contact with water.
- [ ] **Keep electrical cords for appliances** (irons, toasters, radios, TV, etc.) out of reach.
- [ ] **Place stereos, VCRs, DVD players, computers, and other electrical equipment up high** and out of reach.
- [ ] **Avoid running cords under rugs**, over hooks, through door openings or in other areas that would be a hazard.
- [ ] **Replace used and worn electrical cords and equipment.**
- [ ] **Store lighters and matches out of reach.**
- [ ] **Use screens or barriers around fireplaces,** wood stoves, heaters, radiators, hot water pipes, or furnaces or steam-producing vaporizers.
- [ ] **Never leave children alone in a room with an open fire**, heater, or hot stove.
- [ ] **Install smoke detectors** and test them every month.
- [ ] **Keep an approved fire extinguisher** in a secure area and make sure it's charged.
- [ ] **Store combustible materials away from furnaces, stoves, or water heaters.**

Drowning

- [ ] **Never leave children alone in the bathtub or swimming pool or with water play.**
- [ ] **Keep toilet lids closed.**
- [ ] **Empty mop buckets, ice chests, or pails of water immediately** after use. (Children can drown in 2 or 3 inches of water.)
- [ ] **Do not allow children to play near garden ponds, storm sewers, or excavations.**
- [ ] **Protect, cover, and childproof wells and cisterns.**

Cuts and punctures

- [ ] **Keep all sharp objects out of reach** (cooking knives, silverware, cooking utensils, scissors, razors, plastic wrap boxes, glass bottles or drinking glasses, knitting needles).
- [ ] **Do not allow children to play with sharp tools** or around lawn mowers and power saws.
- [ ] **Mark glass windows and doors with decals or tape** so they are more visible. If possible, install safety glass.

Car safety

- [ ] **Use seat belts and car seats** when traveling by car.
- [ ] **To avoid a burn, cover car seats and boosters** with a towel or sheet when not in use.
- [ ] **Keep purses, diaper bags, and other dangerous items out of reach.**
- [ ] **Teach children to sit calmly and quietly** while in a car or bus. Leave toys that encourage active behavior at home or in the trunk.
- [ ] **Never leave children alone in a car.**
- [ ] **Do not allow children to play near or behind a parked car.**
- [ ] **Teach children to look both ways when crossing the street** and to hold the hand of an adult. Use the same cautions for parking lots.

Outdoor safety

- [ ] **Never leave children alone outside.**
- [ ] **Teach children not to play near the street** and to ask for help if toys roll into the street or driveway.
- [ ] **Require children to use helmets** with bicycles, skateboards, or rollerblades.
- [ ] **Children should not wear helmets when playing on playground equipment.** This can be a choking hazard.
- [ ] **Use safety straps in strollers to secure children.** Do not put children who are not sitting up well in wagons with low sides.
- [ ] **All outdoor play areas should be fenced**, especially those near a street, parking lot, pond, well, or railroad track.
- [ ] **Electrical appliances, such as air conditioners, in the play area should be fenced** so children cannot reach them.
- [ ] **Secure or remove gas grills** from outdoor play areas.
- [ ] **Keep gates closed and install child-proof latches.**
- [ ] **Lock storage sheds, barns, and garages.**
- [ ] **Check play area routinely** for trash, sharp branches, tools, lawn equipment, or animal feces.
- [ ] **Regularly inspect surface and playground equipment** for broken, worn, or missing parts. Remove, repair, or replace items immediately.
- [ ] **Cover sand box when not in use** so animals won't use it as a litter box. Check frequently for cleanliness.
- [ ] **Provide some shade in the play space**, either from natural sources like trees or from a tent, awning, or other simple shelter.
- [ ] **Place metal equipment (such as platforms and slides) in the shade** to prevent burns. A slide that faces north will receive the least direct sunlight.
- [ ] **Place equipment that has moving parts, such as swings, on the outside of the play area** and teach children to stay away from the front and back swing area.
- [ ] **Keep outdoor play equipment at least 6 feet away** from pavement, fences, trees, buildings, walkways, or other play equipment.
- [ ] **Make sure the surface area under play equipment is impact absorbing** (such as sand, pea gravel, or wood chips). Refill material as needed. Grass and dirt are not considered protective surfacing because they do not give upon impact.
- [ ] **Surface materials should be a minimum of 12 inches deep** for equipment up to eight feet high. The material should extend at least six feet beyond the edge of stationary equipment. For swings, surfacing should extend in back and in front, two times the height of the suspension bar.
- [ ] **Do not install loose fill surfacing over hard surfaces** such as concrete or asphalt.
- [ ] **Provide guardrails or barriers** for platforms or ramps over 30 inches high.
- [ ] **Cover all protruding bolts or screws** with plastic safety caps.
- [ ] **Close hooks** completely on swings.
- [ ] **Never attach ropes or cords of any kind to play equipment.** This includes jump ropes, clotheslines, pet leashes, etc.
- [ ] **Safely anchor permanent outdoor equipment**, such as swing sets or climbers.
- [ ] **Preschoolers, ages 2 – 5, and children ages 5 – 12 are developmentally different** and need different equipment located in separate areas to keep the playground safe and fun for all.

Insect repellent

- **When using insect repellent, apply it to your own hands and then rub it on the child.** Do not apply insect repellent to a child's hands, mouth, or eye areas. Only use a small amount around the ears. Do not apply to any irritated areas or scraped skin. Get parents' permission before using.
- **For children under 2 years of age, repellents should contain no more than 10 percent DEET.** The chemical is absorbed through the skin and can cause harm in higher concentrations. Products containing up to 30 percent DEET are safe for children over 2 years of age. The concentration of DEET varies greatly from product to product. So, it is very important to read the label carefully of any repellent you purchase.
- **Insect repellents containing 10 percent DEET provide protection**, but require reapplication every 1-2 hours to remain effective.
- **Remove insect repellent by washing with warm water and soap** when the child comes indoors and before the child eats.

Sunscreen

- **Sunscreen should not be used on babies under six months old.** Babies under six months should be exposed to the sun as little as possible.
- **Coat children's skin liberally and evenly.** Rub in well. If babies or toddlers are squirmy, apply the sunscreen to your hands first.
- **Apply the sunscreen at least 30 minutes before going outside**, and reapply every 2 hours. If the children are playing in the water or sweating a lot, reapply more often.
- **Don't forget hands, ears, nose, lips, and the area around the eyes.** Zinc oxide on the nose and ears can provide extra protection. An SPF 15 lip balm should be applied to the lips, and toddlers may enjoy applying it themselves. UV-blocking sunglasses will help protect the vulnerable eye area.
- **Wash children's hands and faces before they eat.**

Pets

Having a pet to talk to and to touch can be a great psychological benefit to children, especially to shy youngsters. But there also can be risks involved.

Furry animals (especially cats) may pick up and transport fungus spores through their coats. Children petting the cat can transfer these spores to themselves. Children may get bitten if a pet is mishandled.

Pets to avoid in group care settings
- **Pet turtles** can pass on salmonella (an intestinal infection) and are, therefore, not recommended.
- **Birds of the parrot family** (a budgie or parakeet, love-bird, etc.) can transmit an airborne respiratory illness to humans. Keep them away from rooms where the children will play or sleep.
- **Cats' litter boxes** are a problem too. Young children are apt to put just about anything in their mouths, and cat feces may contain parasites that can be transmitted to humans. If they were to touch anything that came into contact with cat feces they could become infected. Most infections are mild, but if a pregnant woman becomes infected, it can cause birth defects in the unborn child (toxoplasmosis).

The benefits of pets far outweigh the risks in most cases, as long as you follow these precautions.

Reduce possible hazards to children by following these simple precautions:

- **Tell prospective parents about your pets at the interview.** Parents will know if the child is allergic to or afraid of animals.
- **Wash hands after touching animals.** Teach the children to wash their hands after touching animals. This is especially important before eating.
- **Keep your pets clean.** Because dogs and cats use their tongues to clean themselves, try to discourage pets from licking the children and vice versa.
- **Empty kitty litter boxes daily.** If you are pregnant, have someone else do this job.
- **Cover sandboxes.** Keep sandboxes covered when not in use to prevent cats from adopting them as litter boxes.
- **Keep your pets healthy.** Keep animals free from internal and external parasites. (Fleas can bite children too.) Make sure pets receive all their shots, including distemper and rabies shots (for cats as well as dogs).
- **Clean up after pets.** Keep yard free of animal feces. Dogs and cats with roundworm can give it to children if the children step in it and have a cut or sore on their feet.

Poisonous Plants

Children learn a great deal from planting seeds, watching plants grow, and smelling flowers. They love to touch plants and sometimes even taste them. Encourage children to look at but not touch or eat anything without asking an adult first. Some of the most common and attractive plants contain highly poisonous substances. See plant list on the following pages. This is not intended to be a complete list. For more information you can go to http://chppm-www.apgea.army.mil/ento/PLANT.HTM

Common name	Scientific name	Poisonous parts
House plants		
Caladium	Caladium, xanthosoma	entire plant
Castor Bean	Ricinus communis	all parts
Dumbcane	Dieffenbachia sequine	entire plant
Elephant's Ear	Colocasia antiquorum	entire plant
English Ivy	Hedera helix	leaves and berries
Mother-in-law	Sansevieria trifasciata	leaves
Mistletoe	Phoradendron	berries
Philodendron	Philodendron	entire plant
Pothos	Scindapsus aureus	entire plant
Rosary Pea	Abrus precatorius	red and black seeds
Holly	Ilex	berries
Calla lily	Zantedeschia aethiopica	leaves
Vegetable garden plants		
Potato	Solanum tuberosum	green spots on shoots, sprouts, leaves & stems
Tomato	Lycopersicon esculentum	green parts
Rhubarb	Rheum	large coarse leaf
Flower garden plants		
Autumn Crocus	Colchicum autumnale	entire plant
Azalea	Rhododendron	entire plant
Bird of Paradise	Poinciana	pods
Bleeding Heart or Dutchman Breeches	Dicentra cucullaria	leaves, roots
Christmas Pepper	Capsicum annuum	entire plant
Christmas Rose	Helleborus niger	rootstocks, leaves
Chrysanthemum	Chrysanthemum	leaves and stems
Daffodil	Narcissus	bulbs
Delphinium /Larkspur	Delphinium	seeds, young plants
Four-o'clocks	Mirabilis jalapa	roots and seeds
Foxglove	Digitalis purpurea	entire plant extremely poisonous
Hyacinth	Hyacinthus orientalis	bulbs
Hydrangea	Hydrangea macrophylla	flower bud is most poisonous
Iris	Iris versicolor	leaves, rootstocks
Jonquil	Narcissus jonquilla	bulbs
Lily-of-the-Valley	Convallaria majalis	leaves, white bell-like flowers, roots
Morning Glory	Convolvulus sepium	seeds
Narcissus	Narcissus	bulbs
Nicotiana	Nicotiana	leaves
Oleander	Nerium oleander	entire plant
Peony	Paeonia	roots
Snow on the Mountain	Euphorbia marginata	leaves, stem, milky sap
Star-of-Bethlehem	Ornithogalum umbellatum	bulbs, flowers
Sweet Pea	Lathyrus	seeds, peas
Tulip	Tulipa	bulbs
Yellow Oleander or Be-Still-Tree	Thevetia nereifolia	entire plant

Common name	Scientific name	Poisonous parts
Ornamental plants		
Daphne	*Daphine mezereum*	bright red berries
Golden Chain	*Laburnum anagyroids*	bean-like seed capsules
Lantana	*Lantana camara*	green berries
Mountain Laurel	*Kalmia latifolia*	entire plant
Rhododendron	*Rhododendron*	entire plant
Wisteria	*Wisteria*	pods or seeds
Yellow or Carolina Jessamine	*Gelsemium sempervirens*	entire plant, nectar
Yew	*Taxus*	entire plant
Wild plants		
Rosary Pea	*Abrus precatorius*	red and black seeds
Holly	*Ilex*	berries
Calla lily	*Zantedeschia aethiopica*	leaves
Belladonna	*Brugmansia × candida*	entire plant
Bittersweet	*Solamum dulcamara*	berries
Indian hemp	*Cannabis sativa*	entire plant
Jack-in-the-pulpit	*Arisaema triphyllum*	entire plant
Jimsonweed	*Datura stramonium*	entire plant
Monkshood	*Aconitum*	entire plant
Nightshade	*Solanaceae nigrum*	leaves and unripe berries
Poison hemlock, ivy, oak, sumac		entire plant
Trees and shrubs		
Apple	*Maltus sylvestris*	seeds
Black Locust	*Robinia pseudoacacia*	bark, foliage, young sprouts
Boxwood	*Buxus sempervirens*	entire plant
Buckeye	*Aesculus*	sprouts, nuts
Cherry	*Prunus*	twigs, leaves, bark, fruit stones
Chinaberry Tree	*Melia azedarach*	berries
Elderberry or Black Elder	*Sambucus canadensis*	shoots, leaves, bark, roots
Horse Chestnut	*Aesculus hippocastanum*	young sprouts, mature nuts
Jerusalem Cherry	*Solanum pseudocapsicum*	entire plant
Magnolia	*Magnolia*	flower
Oak	*Quercus*	acorns, young shoots, leaves
Peach	*Prunus persica*	leaves, twigs, seeds
Privet	*Ligustrum vulgare*	entire plant

Indoor Air Quality

The air that people breathe inside their homes often is more polluted than the outdoor air in even the largest cities. Young children especially are affected by indoor air pollution. Children who spend long hours breathing polluted air are more likely to develop respiratory problems, allergies, and asthma. They also face serious long-term health problems.

See the following sections for ways to identify potential sources of indoor air pollution and to reduce the pollution.

Mold and mildew

Mold and mildew thrive in damp, dark spaces. They can cause eye, nose, and throat irritations.

Prevent excess moisture and humidity levels in the home by:
- Installing exhaust fans vented to outdoors in kitchens and bathrooms.
- Venting clothes dryers to the outdoors.
- Reducing or eliminating humidifier use.
- Emptying water trays in air conditioners, dehumidifiers, and refrigerators frequently.
- Insulating basement walls to prevent condensation during summer.
- Putting a plastic cover over dirt in crawl spaces to prevent moisture from coming in from the ground. Ventilate crawl spaces.

Remove mold and mildew:
- Use a dehumidifier or air conditioning to remove excess moisture from the air.
- Increase ventilation. Run fans to circulate the air.

- Clean and dry, or remove, water-damaged carpets.
- Scrub off mold and mildew with a chlorine bleach solution (1 tablespoon of liquid chlorine bleach to 1 quart water).

Dust mites and animal-related allergens

Dust mites are very tiny animals too small to be seen that live in your home. They eat dead skin cells called dander that are regularly shed by people and pets. Pet dander and cat saliva also can cause problems. Your air conditioner and furnace will distribute these contaminants throughout the home.

To reduce these allergens:
- **Clean the house regularly** to reduce the number of allergy-causing agents.
- **Reduce humidity levels.** Damp conditions usually lead to greater numbers of dust mites.
- **Vacuum when children are gone.** Vacuuming can stir up dust mites temporarily, so wait until the children have gone to vacuum and have someone else vacuum if you are allergic to dust mites.
- **When possible use a damp cloth on floors, rather than a broom.** This will pick up dust mites rather than blowing them around.
- **Use central vacuum systems.** If possible use central vacuum systems that are vented to the outdoors.
- **Clean your air ducts.** Get air ducts cleaned by a trained professional. Poor cleaning techniques can stir up contaminants and circulate them throughout the house.

Lead-based paint

Household dust in older homes often contains lead that gets on children's hands and toys. Eating lead-based paint chips or inhaling lead dust can cause learning and behavior problems for children.

Protect children under your care by taking the following steps:

- **Check for peeling paint.** Look inside and outside your home. Check windowsills, the space between storm windows, inside windows, and outdoor play areas.
- **Keep children away from areas that have chipped paint.** Keep paint chips picked up. Place in plastic bags for disposal in landfill.
- **Wet mop all surfaces.** Wet mop all floors and wet-clean woodwork, windowsills, and other painted surfaces once or twice a week, using an all-purpose wood cleaner.
- **Wash children's hands throughout the day.**
- **Wash toys often and pacifiers at least daily.**

Radon

Radon is a cancer-causing natural radioactive gas that you can't see, smell, or taste. It is found in many soils across the nation and can seep into homes undetected. Radon is the leading cause of lung cancer among nonsmokers. Children may be especially susceptible to radon, because of their higher respiratory rates and developing lungs.

Testing for radon is especially important for family child care homes— especially those that care for children in basements. Testing is the only way to find out if you have a radon problem. Every home should be tested.

- Purchase a short-term radon detector kit for $10 to $20 from a local hardware store. They also are available online.
- Follow instructions on the detector package for monitoring radon levels. The detector usually is left in place for two to seven days.
- Mail the detector to the testing laboratory identified on the package.
- Wait for test results to be returned.
- If the test shows radon levels above 4 pCi/L, the EPA suggests that action be taken to reduce radon levels.
- Contact a trained professional to reduce the radon problem.
- Retest the home after treatment has been completed to see that radon levels have been reduced below the 4 pCi/L action guideline.

Tobacco smoke

Secondhand smoke increases the risk of lung cancer in nonsmokers. Very young children exposed to smoking at home are more likely to be hospitalized for bronchitis and pneumonia.

To reduce these serious health risks:
- Stop smoking and discourage others from smoking.
- Ask smokers to smoke outdoors.
- Keep smokers away from sleeping areas at all times. Children need to have clean smoke-free sleeping surfaces.
- Keep cigarettes, cigarette butts, and all tobacco products away from children. Tobacco is poisonous when eaten.

Asbestos

Until the 1970s, asbestos was contained in many types of home building products and insulation materials. The mere presence of asbestos in the home is not hazardous, but if asbestos materials are disturbed, they may release fibers into the air. Breathing high levels of asbestos fibers can lead to an increased risk of lung and chest cancer and lung diseases.

To reduce exposure to asbestos:
- Regularly check materials that contain asbestos for signs of wear or damage. Materials that may contain asbestos are pipe and furnace duct insulation, resilient floor tiles, ceiling tiles, and soundproofing materials. Tears or abrasions may release asbestos fibers into the air, which will then be circulated through the central heating and cooling system.
- Do not disturb asbestos materials that are in good condition.
- Supervise children's play in areas that contain asbestos, especially if their play might damage the material by hitting, rubbing, or handling it.
- Don't dust, sweep, or vacuum debris that may contain asbestos. Clean with a wet mop.
- Don't use abrasive pads or brushes on power strippers to remove wax from asbestos flooring.
- Do not make holes of any kind in asbestos materials. Don't saw, sand, scrape, or drill holes in any asbestos materials.
- Obtain professional advice before remodeling, removing, or cleaning up asbestos.

Carbon monoxide

Carbon monoxide is a colorless, odorless, highly poisonous gas. It may be released into the home through unvented kerosene and gas heaters, leaking chimneys, faulty furnaces, and automobile exhaust from attached garages. Carbon monoxide can cause fatigue, dizziness, nausea, and death. Infants and pregnant women can be especially sensitive to carbon monoxide exposure.

Inexpensive carbon monoxide detectors are now available. These detectors are similar to a smoke detector and will alert you if the carbon monoxide level is high.

To prevent carbon monoxide poisoning:
- Do not use unvented heaters inside the home.
- Never use a gas stove or oven to heat your home.
- Have a trained professional inspect, clean, and tune up heating system (furnaces, flues, and chimneys) **each year.** Repair any leaks.
- Watch for heavy moisture condensation on windows and walls that could indicate high levels of carbon monoxide. Immediately call the gas utility company or a heating contractor to inspect your home.
- Do not warm up or idle a car inside the garage.

Formaldehyde

Formaldehyde is a chemical that is widely used in carpeting, permanent press fabrics, furniture. It also is used in pressed wood products such as inexpensive modular furniture that can be purchased from discount stores. Often this furniture is used for children's rooms. The smell of formaldehyde will generally decrease as products age. Some people can develop chemical sensitivity after exposure to formaldehyde, causing watery eyes, throat irritations, nausea, breathing difficulties, and asthma attacks.

To reduce formaldehyde exposure:
- Avoid the use of pressed wood products and other formaldehyde-emitting goods.
- Open a window or turn on a fan for ventilation after installing new carpeting or bringing other formaldehyde sources into the home.
- Use air conditioning and dehumidifiers to maintain moderate temperatures and reduce humidity levels.

Water Quality

Water quality is an increasing concern. Homes with a private water supply should have an annual laboratory analysis to check for bacteria and nitrates. When private water supplies are determined unsuitable for drinking, use commercially bottled water or water treated through a process approved by your health department.

Coping with illness

Health care issues for children vary greatly from those of adults. Several aspects of health care in children require planning and decision-making on your part.

Illness policy

A written illness policy tells families what your procedures and policies are if their child becomes ill. This policy should consider:
- whether the illness is contagious
- whether the child is running a high fever or vomiting
- whether you have an arrangement that allows you to keep a sick child isolated
- whether you would be able to take the child to the doctor or hospital if necessary and the parent was unavailable
- whether you could give proper care to the sick child and still care for the other children

Illnesses—how to respond

Be aware of the different signs of illnesses and be able to decide if it is mild, severe, or life-threatening so you can provide timely care.

Start each day with a health check

- Look for the following signs each morning during arrival: paleness, fever, unusual tiredness, rash, sores, runny nose, watery eyes, hoarseness, or coughing.

- Ask parents and child for more information about how the child is feeling.
- If you don't feel the child is well enough for child care, remind the parent of your illness exclusion policy. (See chapter 10 for more information.)

When to exclude child from care

Sometimes it is best for children to stay home and not come to child care. Consider including the following as good reasons for excluding a child from care.

- The child does not feel well enough to participate in routine activities.
- The child requires more care than you are able to provide without compromising the health and safety of the other children.
- The illness is any of a specific list of diagnosed symptoms or conditions for which exclusion is recommended.

Most health professionals recommend that children with the following illnesses or symptoms be excluded from child care.

- Fever (101 degrees Fahrenheit or higher) along with behavior change or other signs of illness such as sore throat, rash, vomiting, diarrhea, earache
- Signs of serious illness, uncontrolled coughing, wheezing, continuous crying, difficulty breathing
- Vomiting (2 or more times within 24 hours)
- Body rash with fever
- Diarrhea—uncontrolled runny, watery, or bloody stools
- Sore throat with fever, swollen glands or mouth sores with drooling

Specific diseases that usually require exclusion

Children with the following diseases can return to child care after a specific course of treatment. Follow recommendations of the child's doctor. An exception to this would be when the illness is no longer contagious, but the child does not feel well enough to participate in regular activities or requires more attention than you can provide during normal care.

- Aseptic meningitis
- Bacterial meningitis
- Chicken pox
- Haemophilus influenzae Type B
- Hepatitis A
- Herpetic gingivostomatis
- Impetigo
- Measles
- Mumps
- Pertussis (whooping cough)
- Pinworm
- Purulent conjunctivitis (pink eye)
- Ringworm
- Rubella
- Scabies (until 24 hours after treatment)
- Shigella
- Shingles
- Strep throat
- Tuberculosis

Fortunately many of today's treatments and medications for these illnesses are fast-acting and highly effective. Frequently children can return to child care after treatment has been started. Check with your health care professional to verify when it is safe for the child to return.

If a child becomes ill in child care

Call Emergency Medical Services (EMS) 911 immediately if:

- You believe the child's life is at risk or there is a risk of permanent injury.
- The child is acting strangely, much less alert, or much more withdrawn than usual.
- The child has difficulty breathing or is unable to speak.
- The child's skin or lips look blue, purple, or gray.
- The child has rhythmic jerking of arms and legs and a loss of consciousness (seizure).
- The child is unconscious.
- The child is less and less responsive.
- The child has any of the following after a head injury: decrease in level of alertness, confusion, headache, vomiting, irritability, or difficulty walking.
- The child has increasing or severe pain anywhere.
- The child has a cut or burn that is large, deep, and/or won't stop bleeding.
- The child is vomiting blood.
- The child has a severe stiff neck, headache, and fever.
- The child is significantly dehydrated: sunken eyes, lethargic, not making tears, not urinating.

After you have called EMS, call the child's parent.

Some children may have urgent situations that do not necessarily require ambulance transport but still need medical attention. The box on the next page lists some of these more common situations. Parents should be informed. If you or the parent cannot reach the physician within one hour, the child should be brought to a hospital.

Get medical attention within one hour for:
- Fever of 101 degrees or more in any age child who looks more than mildly ill.
- Fever in a child less than 2 months (8 weeks) of age.
- A quickly spreading purple or red rash.
- A large volume of blood in the stools.
- A cut that may require stitches.
- Any medical condition specifically outlined in a child's care plan requiring parental notification.

Probable signs of communicable illness: Call parents, ask them to take the child to the doctor, and isolate the child until treated.
- redness, swelling of eye, eye drainage
- unusual spots or rashes with fever or itching
- sore throat
- crusty, bright yellow, gummy skin sores
- diarrhea (more than 2 loose stools a day)
- vomiting (more than 2 times a day)
- yellow coloring of skin and whites of eyes
- clay-colored stools or tea-colored urine.

Possible signs of communicable illness: Watch child closely and discuss signs with parents.
- earache (check for fever or discharge)
- headache
- itching of scalp; check for head lice nits and if present, isolate until treated
- fever less than 101° Fahrenheit
- unusual behavior
- runny nose (check color and smell; check temperature if discharge is yellow with odor)

While you are waiting for parents to pick up an ill child.
- Maintain good supervision, but separate child from other children as much as possible.
- Remove and sanitize toys he or she has been playing with.
- Continue to observe for new or worsening symptoms.
- Write down symptoms and actions taken in the child's file.

Source: *Caring for Our Children, National Health and Safety Performance Standards: Guidelines for Out-of-Home Child Care Programs.* Washington, D.C.: American Public Health Association and American Academy of Pediatrics (1992).

How to handle a fever

Use a digital thermometer to measure fever:
In the arm pit—Infants and toddlers
By mouth—Children older than 4 years

Fever is defined as having a temperature of 101 degrees Fahrenheit or higher
(**Note: Glass and mercury thermometers** are no longer recommended by the American Academy of Pediatrics for use with children. **Forehead or pacifier thermometers** are not considered to be reliable.)

DO offer cool fluids or fruit juice popsicles.

DO offer a lukewarm wash cloth or sponge to rub on face or body.

DO give Tylenol if you have a medication administration policy and written permission from parents and/or health provider.

DO call parents for emergency assistance if temperature increases or does not respond to the above measures.

DON'T give aspirin to children under age 12 unless prescribed by a health care provider. Aspirin in children is associated with Reyes syndrome, which can cause death.

DON'T cover with heavy blankets.

DON'T use ice packs or alcohol rubs.

HFCCH Chapter 11 — Health and safety for active kids

Department of Health and Human Services • Centers for Disease Control and Prevention

Recommended Childhood Immunization Schedule Ages 0-6 United States 2007

Age Vaccine	Birth 1 month	2 months	4 months	6 months	12 months	15 months	18 months	19-23 months	2-3 years	4-6 years
Hepatitis B	1st dose	2nd dose			3rd dose					
Rotavirus		1st dose	2nd dose	3rd dose						
Diphtheria, Tetanus, Pertussis		1st dose	2nd dose	3rd dose		4th dose				5th dose
Haemophilus influenzae type b										
Option 1		1st dose	2nd dose	3rd dose	4th dose					
Option 2		1st dose	2nd dose		3rd dose					
Pneumococcal		1st dose	2nd dose	3rd dose	4th dose				Certain risk	high groups
Inactivated Poliovirus		1st dose	2nd dose		3rd dose					4th dose
Influenza					yearly					
Measles, Mumps, Rubella					1st dose					2nd dose
Varicella					1st dose					2nd dose
Hepatitis A					2 doses				HepA series	
Meningococcal									Certain risk	high groups

Source: http://www.cdc.gov/vaccines/

The Recommended Immunization Schedules for Persons Aged 0–6 Years are approved by the Advisory Committee on Immunization Practices (http://www.cdc.gov/nip/acip), the American Academy of Pediatrics (http://www.aap.org), and the American Academy of Family Physicians (http://www.aafp.org).

Immunizations

Make sure children are up-to-date on all immunizations and physical check-ups. This will help prevent serious diseases such as diphtheria, tetanus, whooping cough (DPT), measles, mumps, rubella (MMR), polio (OPV), Haemophillus influenzae meningitis (HiB), and hepatitis B (HBV). A current schedule can be found at http://www.cdc.gov/vaccines/.

Some parents may prefer to have a signed immunization exemption.

Medications

Note the following ways to store and give medicines to children.

- **Have the parent or legal guardian fill out and sign a Medication Release Form** for each medication. (See chapter 10)
- **Give only medicine (prescription or over-the-counter) that is in the original container.** It should be labeled with the child's name, correct dosage, and the name of the pharmacy that supplied the medicine.
- **If you have any questions about how to give the medicine, contact the parents.** A pharmacist will not give out information on the child but may be able to help with other questions, such as storage, timing, etc.
- **Store medications properly.** When refrigeration is required, store in a separate covered container to prevent contamination of food and other medications. All medications should be stored out of children's reach.
- **You need parental permission to give the following medications.** Medical permission is NOT required. Wash hands beforehand and afterwards.
  - Antihistamines
  - Nonaspirin pain relievers and fever reducers
  - Cough medicine
  - Decongestants
  - Anti-itching creams
  - Diaper ointments and powders
  - Sunscreen
- **Use an accurate medicine dropper or dosage spoon.** Regular silverware spoons are NOT acceptable for measuring medicine.
- **Stop giving medication if you observe side effects.** Inform parents and/or a medical professional.
- **Keep a record of each dosage of medicine** that you give any child. Note child's name, medication, dose, date, and time of day.

HIV/AIDS—what you should know*

It is possible that you may knowingly or unknowingly care for a child with HIV infection. You should be aware that:

HIV is known to be spread only five ways

- through unprotected anal, vaginal, or oral sexual intercourse
- through shared needles or syringes contaminated by HIV-infected blood during recreational drug use, tattooing, body piercing, steroid injections
- through a blood transfusion
- from a pregnant woman to a fetus or to a newborn by nursing
- through infected blood to an open cut or sore

HIV is not spread by

- casual contact
- insects
- through air or water

HIV and children

- It is possible for a child to have an HIV infection and show no signs of illness.
- It is not possible to tell if a child has an HIV infection without a medical diagnosis.

- Children with AIDS will have periods of wellness and illness.
- HIV-infected children can get the same infections as uninfected children. Because a child with HIV has a weakened immune system, these infections can be more frequent, more severe, and harder to cure.
- Examples of common infections include infections of the ears, sinuses, lungs (pneumonia), blood (sepsis), urinary tract, bladder, intestines, and skin, as well as fluid around the brain (meningitis). The presence of these illnesses does not mean the child has HIV/AIDS.
- HIV-infected children also can have swollen glands, breathing problems, fever, poor weight gain, and slow development.
- Some children may have a low immune system and not have HIV/AIDS.
- Only about one-third of infants born to mothers who are HIV-infected also will be infected.
- Children with HIV infection generally develop AIDS at an early age, approximately 50 percent by the first year and 82 percent by 3 years of age.

Your legal responsibility

- Generally, under federal and most state antidiscrimination laws, it is illegal to refuse to accept a child into your program because he or she may be HIV-infected.
- Notifying parents of other children about the presence of a child who is or may be HIV-infected violates confidentiality and is illegal.

Universal precautions

Be prepared to protect yourself and others.
It is important to protect yourself and others against blood-borne illnesses such as Hepatitis B or AIDS. You can become infected with these

*Sources: *Serving Children with HIV Infection In Child Day Care*, Donna Pressma & L. Jean Emery, Child Welfare League of America, 1991.
Caring for Our Children, National Health and Safety Performance Standards: Guidelines for Out-of-Home Child Care Programs, American Academy of Pediatrics, 2002

diseases if blood or body fluids containing blood from an infected person enters your body through your skin via a cut, a needle stick, or a bite wound; through skin that is chapped, scraped, or otherwise broken; or through a mucous membrane, such as a blood splatter to your eyes, nose, or mouth.

Take precautions. It is important to protect your body from exposure to these substances, rather than concentrating on who may become or currently is infected. People who have these diseases often show no symptoms.

Provide a barrier between you and all blood or body fluid by:
- Wearing disposable latex gloves.
- Using paper or fabric to control bleeding. Use thick amounts of toweling to apply pressure to a wound.

Clean contaminated surfaces:
- Wear disposable latex gloves to clean up any spilled blood or body fluids.
- Use freshly diluted bleach (1/4 cup of chlorinated bleach per gallon of water) to clean soiled surfaces.

Dispose of waste properly:
- Put all paper products and gloves into a plastic bag that is closed with a twist tie or zipped shut.
- Place sharp items in a hard container before disposal.
- Remove gloves by pulling from the cuff down toward your fingertips, turning the gloves inside out as you take them off. Place gloves in a plastic bag.

Wash hands properly. Use handwashing steps cited earlier in this chapter.

Source: Caring for Our Children, *National Health and Safety Performance Standards Guidelines for Out of Home Child Care Programs*, American Academy of Pediatrics, 2002

Sudden Infant Death Syndrome (SIDS)

What is Sudden Infant Death Syndrome (SIDS)?

SIDS is the sudden, unexplained death of an infant younger than one year old.

It is the leading cause of death in children between one month and one year of age. Most SIDS deaths happen when babies are between 2 months and 4 months of age.

What causes SIDS?

No one knows for sure what causes SIDS.

Factors that seem to contribute to SIDS are
- Putting babies to sleep on their stomachs
- Keeping the room too warm
- Overheating from clothing or crib bedding
- Being exposed to secondhand smoke

What you can do to reduce the risk of SIDS

■ **Always place babies on their backs to sleep.** Babies who sleep on their backs are less likely to die of SIDS than babies who sleep on their stomachs or sides.

■ **Use the back sleep position every time.** Babies who usually sleep on their backs but who are then placed on their stomachs, like for a nap, are at very high risk for SIDS. So it is important for babies to sleep on their backs every time, for naps and at night.

- **Place baby on a firm sleep surface, such as a safety-approved* crib mattress covered with a fitted sheet.** Never place a baby to sleep on a pillow, quilt, sheepskin, or other soft surface.

- **Keep soft objects, toys, and loose bedding out of baby's sleep area.** Don't use pillows, blankets, quilts, sheepskins, or pillow-like bumpers in a baby's sleep area. Keep all items away from the baby's face. Make sure nothing covers baby's head.

- **Avoid letting the baby overheat during sleep.** Dress baby in one-piece sleeper and keep the room at a temperature that is comfortable for an adult.

- **Consult with parents about using a pacifier when placing baby down to sleep**, but don't force the baby to take it. (Wait until breastfeeding babies are at least 1 month old before using a pacifier.)

Tummy time is awake time

Babies do need some tummy time. Place babies on their stomach when they are awake and someone is watching. Tummy time helps a baby's head, neck, and shoulder muscles get stronger and helps to prevent flat spots on the head.

Source: Back to Sleep Campaign
Mail: 31 Center Drive, 31/2A32, Bethesda, MD 20892-2425
Phone: 1-800-505-CRIB (2742)
Fax: (301) 496-7101
National Institute of Child and Health Development
Internet: http://www.nichd.nih.gov/sids

*For more information on crib safety guidlines, call the Consumer Product Safety Commission at 1-800-638-2772 or visit their Web site at http://www.cpsc.gov.

Coping with injuries and emergencies

First aid kits

Accidents do happen despite the best prevention efforts. A well-stocked first aid kit is an absolute must in a family child care program. Store items in a tightly sealed container within reach of adults, but out of the reach of children. Contents should be arranged in an orderly fashion and restocked after each use.

Suggestions for supplies in first aid kit

- [ ] adhesive strip bandages
- [ ] sterile gauze squares 2 to 4 inches
- [ ] rolled sterile gauze
- [ ] adhesive tape
- [ ] elastic wrap (Ace wrap)
- [ ] thermometer
- [ ] scissors, tweezers, and a needle
- [ ] triangular bandages (rectangle cloth for sling)
- [ ] safety pins
- [ ] disposable latex gloves (at least 2 pair)
- [ ] rubber bulb syringe like turkey baster (to rinse out wounds)
- [ ] sterile eyewash, such as a saline solution
- [ ] clean cloth
- [ ] soap
- [ ] cotton-tipped swabs
- [ ] antiseptic solution or towelettes (hydrogen peroxide)
- [ ] petroleum jelly or other lubricant (for body parts stuck in tight places)
- [ ] pen, pencil, and note pad
- [ ] small plastic cup
- [ ] plastic bags for ice or a commercial cold pack (store in freezer)

- [ ] ice cubes or frozen bags of vegetables stored in the freezer
- [ ] first aid handbook
- [ ] plastic bags for throwing contaminated materials away

Medications

- [ ] over-the-counter antibiotic ointment
- [ ] anti-diarrhea medication
- [ ] over-the-counter oral antihistamine (Benadryl, others)
- [ ] non-aspirin pain relievers (never give aspirin to children)
- [ ] over-the-counter hydrocortisone cream
- [ ] special items for specific emergencies and health problems that are prescribed by a doctor for a specific child (asthma inhaler, auto-injector of epinephrine—EpiPen [bee sting kit])
- [ ] syringe, medicine cup, or dosage spoon

Travel first aid kit

You should also have a travel first aid kit to take with you outdoors and on field trips. Minimum suggestions include

- [ ] assorted bandages
- [ ] antiseptic wipes to clean scrapes
- [ ] wet wipes
- [ ] disposable gloves
- [ ] antibiotic ointment
- [ ] facial tissues
- [ ] special medicines needed by specific children (inhalers, EpiPen [bee sting kit], etc.).

Car emergency kit

- [ ] photos of children, in case you are separated
- [ ] cell phone and charger that uses the accessory plug in your car dashboard
- [ ] emergency phone numbers
  - doctor and pediatrician
  - local emergency services
  - emergency road service providers
  - regional poison control center
  - children's family contact numbers
- [ ] small first aid kit
- [ ] small, waterproof flashlight and extra batteries, or wind-up, battery free flashlight
- [ ] candles and matches for cold climates
- [ ] sunscreen
- [ ] mylar emergency blanket
- [ ] portable radio (wind-up, battery free)

Home disaster kit

- [ ] first aid supplies
- [ ] medication
- [ ] portable radio (wind-up, battery free or with extra batteries)
- [ ] toilet paper
- [ ] paper towels
- [ ] disposable diapers

- ☐ wipes
- ☐ re-sealable plastic bags
- ☐ extra bedding and blankets
- ☐ bottled water—1 gallon per child/adult per day
- ☐ 24-hour emergency supply of non perishable food
    - small cans of fruit
    - fruit or vegetable juice boxes
    - cans of tuna
    - pudding cups
    - peanut butter
    - cereals
    - crackers
    - nonfat dry milk
- ☐ disposable bowls and eating utensils
- ☐ manually operated can opener
- ☐ games or stuffed animals for children
- ☐ a telephone that does not rely on electricity and plugs directly into a wall phone jack
- ☐ emergency phone numbers (including a long distance emergency contact number for parents if they can't be reached locally)
- ☐ signed permission cards from parents to transport children in an emergency

Give your kits a checkup

- Mark your calendar to check your first aid kits at least every three months.
- Check to be sure the flashlight batteries work.
- Replace supplies that may have expired.

First aid training and cardiopulmonary resuscitation (CPR) is critical for anyone who cares for children. A child's life may depend on you doing the right thing in an emergency. Classes can be found in the phone book or by contacting your nearest hospital. Classes will need to be repeated on a regular basis so you keep current about what to do in an emergency.

Emergency telephone numbers

Post a list of emergency telephone numbers near the phone. When accidents happen, there may not be time to locate these numbers in the telephone book. See the following page for an example of emergency numbers that should be listed.

Emergency Medical System (EMS) – 911

_____

Poison control center _____

Fire _____

Police _____

Doctor/health consultant _____

Hospital _____

Child abuse reporting hotline

_____

Suicide prevention hotline

_____

Electric company _____

Gas company _____

Heating and cooling repair service

_____

Plumber _____

Water company _____

Neighbor or substitute caregiver

_____

_____

_____

Most communities are served by a 911 emergency number. Teach this number to older children. Parents' home and work numbers also should be listed by the phone. You also should have contact information for each child's physician and a responsible person who can be contacted when a parent cannot be reached (see sample forms in chapter 10).

Emergency/disaster procedures

You should have a plan in the event of an emergency or disaster. Share your plans with parents. Practice your responses and include the children in your drills. Know when you should evacuate and when you should stay put.

Emergency and disaster plans should include procedures for

- transporting an ill or injured child to a hospital
- arranging for care of remaining children
- quickly removing children (fire, gas leak, etc.)
- seeking protective shelter within your home (weather conditions, etc.)
- moving the program temporarily (floods, structural damage, etc.)
- keeping the children in your care for several days (if emergencies keep parents from coming to pick up their children)

Keep emergency contact information up-to-date and easy to get to. Include:

- Contact information of children's families
- Local emergency responders

Share your emergency procedures with parents

- Include phone numbers they can call if they can't reach you
- Post emergency plans by primary and secondary exits
- Include a diagram or map that shows the exits, outside meeting place, and alternate shelter (with address and phone number)

HFCCH Chapter 11 — Health and safety for active kids 315

Practice procedures regularly with the children

- Practice drills at least twice a year
- Some states have requirements on how often emergency drills must be practiced
- Check with your state agency that oversees child care for other regulation requirements

Review your plans on a yearly basis

- Make sure that all previous arrangements for assistance (where to go if there's a fire, temporary site for care if you must evacuate your home, where you might get supplies during an emergency, back-up transportation, etc.) are still options
- Be sure to notify parents of any changes

Sample emergency plan—fire
1. Grab emergency numbers by the door.
2. Exit with children.
3. Pull younger children in wagon by the door.
4. Go to neighbor's house across the street.
5. Call 911.
6. Call parents.
7. Remain with children until parents arrive.

Sample emergency plan—storm or tornado
1. Go to the basement with the children.
2. Sit in a protected area with children.
3. Provide children with pillows and blankets to cover heads.
4. Listen to weather radio in emergency kit stored in basement.
5. Wait for clearance from weather service.

More information on emergency preparedness for child care programs is available at the Better Kid Care Web site at http://betterkidcare.psu.edu. Example planning forms, sample letters to parents, and sample agreements to use with people and/or agencies that have agreed to support your program in an emergency situation can be downloaded from the Web site.

FamilyShare...
Supporting your partners

Daily communication with families about health and safety is so important. Parents need to work, and often will bring their child to child care with a slight fever or a runny nose. You will need to be clear about your rules for when children need to stay home.

If you excluded all children who were slightly ill, you would hardly ever have anyone in child care. On the other hand, sick children spread illness to other children. And if you become sick and unable to care for children, everyone loses.

Make sure your health policies are written in your policy statement. (See chapter 10 for more information.)

Heart of the Matter

Okay, now I was getting scared. I had looked everywhere. Behind every door, in all the closets—absolutely everywhere. Twice. Even three times. There weren't that many places to hide in the house. He simply wasn't here.

I glanced at the clock. It had been at least seven minutes. I had been calling and he hadn't responded. This wasn't like him to hide like this. He was 6 years old—he knew better. We had been outside. Everyone came indoors. I was sure of it. I counted. I always count. That's what child care people do—we count. All the time we count. Even in our sleep—we count kids.

Where could he possibly be? Maybe he didn't come inside. Maybe I was wrong. My mind raced. Maybe he wandered off. Maybe someone took him—it happens.

I stepped outside and called his name. I looked behind the shrubs and behind the hedge. I could feel my heart pounding. I was so worried. Worried, and angry!

I collapsed in the patio chair. Tears were coming. What should I do next? How long should a child be missing before you call the police? And how would I feel when they found him. Of course they would find him—and I would be so embarrassed, because of course, he was here all along. Only he wasn't and he isn't. He's gone. I had to call the police. There wasn't any choice.

I stood up and turned to go back inside. Just then, I heard something. I looked back. A pine cone fell.

I looked up. At the very top of the pine tree, I glimpsed something yellow. I moved closer to the tree. Yellow shorts. Yellow shorts, in the very top of a 30 foot tall pine tree. I called out his name. He didn't reply. But slowly, very slowly, he began to climb down.

Inch by inch, limb by limb --until he was safe in my arms. Tears were streaming down his face. I could see from his eyes that he had been terrified. Afraid of coming down and probably afraid of me too. Punishment enough, I guess.

We both sighed with relief—and went inside for snack.

Lesia

Experience Talks

Conversations with other providers

■ **I store medicines that must be kept in a refrigerator in a small tackle box that I keep locked.** This makes them inaccessible to the kids.

■ **I never tell children that medicine tastes like candy.** I don't want them to get the wrong idea and try to eat a bottle of it.

■ **When we practice a fire drill, I have the older children hold hands.** I keep a wagon by the door to haul my two infants away from the house.

■ **I have my two school-agers help me do a routine safety check on the first week of each month.** I also have them demonstrate the Stop, Drop, and Roll method for fires. This not only teaches them the importance of safety, but they enjoy it so much that they never let me forget.

■ **I always keep a ring of emergency information 3 x 5 cards and release forms on a hook by the door.** I have this information in my files, but I know that in an emergency it will just be easier for me to grab them off the hook—especially in case of a fire. I also take the cards with me when I go to the playground or on a field trip.

■ **I keep a sign on bright orange card stock that says: 911 please send for help.** On the back it has my address, telephone number, and personal emergency contact information. My older school-age kids know that if something should happen to me, they are to call 911 or take the card and run next door to my neighbors for help.

■ **Occasionally I get down on my knees and literally crawl through my house looking for safety hazards.** I have never failed yet to find something that could be a potential hazard. It's amazing what I can find down on a child's eye level.

■ **Frozen sponges or small frozen bags of vegetables (especially peas) can make a great ice pack in a pinch.**

■ **If part of a splinter is sticking out of the skin, try putting tape over the splinter and then pulling it off.** Many times this will pull the splinter out without using a needle or tweezers. This works well if the child has many thorns from a cactus or other plant.

Nutrition power: Choices with kid appeal

Contents

Where am I now? 322
Eating is one of life's greatest pleasures 323
Make smart choices from every food group 323
Show and serve children correct portion sizes 324
Take time to savor meals and snacks 324
Participate in the Child and Adult Care Food Program (CACFP) 325
Appropriate serving sizes for children 326
Snack suggestions—Mix and match 327
Colors of vegetables, fruits, and beans 328
Sample menus 329
Ages and stages of eating 333
Make mealtimes pleasant 334
Make mealtimes easier 334
Make meals appealing 335
Prevent unhealthy attitudes about food 335
Food safety 336
Money-saving food tips 338
Read the label 340
Is sugar OK? 343
How much fat should children have? 343
What about the "overweight" child? 345
Should children shake the salt habit? 346
What about fiber? 346
Special diets 347
Feeding infants 349
Heart of the Matter 355
FamilyShare 356
Experience Talks 356

HFCCH Chapter 12 — Nutrition power: Choices with kid appeal

Nutrition power: Choices with kid appeal—
Where am I now? What can I improve?

	Seldom 1	Sometimes 2	Often 3	Most Often 4
1. I use Child and Adult Care Food Program guidelines.				
2. I plan menus to use recommended number of servings from each food group.				
3. I serve recommended portion sizes.				
4. I plan menus with variety so that different foods are offered throughout the week.				
5. I plan meals with different colors and textures.				
6. I know how to adjust meals and menus to meet the individual needs of children (age, ability, special diets, culture, etc.).				
7. I know how to support and work with mothers who breastfeed infants.				
8. I know how to serve infant foods.				
9. I follow the basic principles of food safety.				
10. I make sure children wash their hands before preparing foods, setting the table, eating, and after eating.				
11. I encourage children to help with preparing and serving food.				
12. I provide child-size eating utensils and dishes.				
13. I provide child-size tables, chairs, booster chairs, and high chairs.				
14. I encourage children to try new foods.				
15. I allow children to choose what they want to eat from the foods I serve.				
16. I sit and eat with the children to show them good eating habits and manners.				
17. I use meal and snack times to teach children new skills and encourage learning.				
18. I share information with families about what, when, and how well children are eating.				
19. I work with families to make decisions about infant feeding and introduction of foods.				

Chapter 12

Nutrition power: Choices with kid appeal

Eating is one of life's greatest pleasures

Good nutrition, growth, health, and learning go together. Good nutrition is especially important for young children because they grow so quickly. Understanding the basics of healthy food planning will make it easy for you to serve nutritious foods that children enjoy.

Cooking and enjoying meals together creates wonderful memories for children. The healthy habits and life skills they develop in early childhood can last a lifetime.

Make smart choices from every food group

The daily food choices you provide for children can have a positive impact on their health today, tomorrow, and in the future. Children's bodies need a variety of nutritious foods daily to get all the nutrients necessary for good health. One useful resource is the *Dietary Guidelines for Americans*, 2005 (6th edition), which includes the following five recommendations:

Make half your grains whole

Choose whole-grain foods, such as whole wheat bread, oatmeal, brown rice, and lowfat popcorn, more often.

Vary your veggies

Include a variety of colors and types over several days, including:
- Dark green: spinach and broccoli
- Orange: carrots and sweet potatoes
- Starchy: corn and potatoes
- Dry beans and peas: pinto beans, black beans, lentils
- Other vegetables: tomatoes and onions

Focus on fruits

Eat fresh, frozen, canned, and dried fruit. Include 100 percent fruit juice as well but in smaller amounts and less frequently.

Get your calcium rich foods

Drink and eat milk and milk products, such as yogurt and cheese. Children ages 2 – 6 should have 2 cups of milk daily.

Go lean with protein

Choose lean protein sources, such as lean meat, poultry, and fish. Experiment with more dry bean and pea-based foods.

Show and serve children correct portion sizes

Child care providers and parents are often advised to serve food "family style" in large bowls on the table. Children are encouraged to serve themselves from the family size bowls. This helps children become more independent and more in control of what and how much they eat.

However, knowing how much to put on a plate is often confusing to young children. Even adults struggle with this, perhaps because many are most familiar with very large or "super-size" portions offered by restaurants. Nutritionists now recommend that adults provide more guidance on portion size.

Young children need to see proper portion sizes on their plates. You can help children learn appropriate portion sizes. Assist children with measuring out child-size portions. The chart on page 326, gives appropriate serving sizes for toddlers, preschoolers, and school-age children. Over time children will learn how to serve themselves the correct portion size. If a child decides he/she needs more of a particular food, second helpings are certainly okay.

Ban the "clean plate club." Children should not be taught to finish eating everything on their plates. They need to learn to listen to their bodies and stop when they are full.

Take time to savor meals and snacks

Make mealtime a highlight of the day. Take time for conversation and fun, as well as food. Talk about children's families, talk about activities of the day, talk about the food you are eating. Discuss colors, shapes, and sizes of foods. Talk about where food comes from. The choices for good conversation are endless.

Make it last. Children have short attention spans, but most can sit and eat for about 15 minutes, especially if you are talking with them and having fun. No meal should last less than 15 minutes. The stomach needs about 20 minutes to get the message to the brain that it is satisfied. If food is eaten in less than 15 minutes, it is likely a child will not feel satisfied. On the other hand, if the same amount of food is made to last 20 minutes or longer a child will feel satisfied.

Let's talk about food

Don't limit your conversation about food to just colors and shapes. Stretch children's imaginations and build their vocabularies by introducing the following words as you cook and eat together.

Bitter	Eye-catching	Irresistible	Red	Steaming
Bland	Firm	Juicy	Refreshing	Sticky
Bright	Flaky	Leafy	Rich	Strong
Brittle	Flavorful	Lean	Ripe	Sugary
Bumpy	Fleshy	Lumpy	Rough	Sweet
Chewy	Fluffy	Luscious	Round	Sweet-smelling
Chilly	Fragrant	Mashed	Salty	Tangy
Chunky	Freezing	Mellow	Savory	Tart
Clean	Fresh	Mild	Scrumptious	Tasty
Coarse	Frosty	Milky	Sharp	Tempting
Cold	Fruity	Moist	Shiny	Tender
Colorful	Fuzzy	Mouth-watering	Showy	Thick
Cool	Gooey	Mushy	Slick	Toasted
Creamy	Gorgeous	Peppery	Slurpy	Warm
Crisp	Green	Pink	Smooth	Wet
Crumbly	Hard	Plump	Soft	Wrinkled
Crunchy	Hearty	Popping	Sour	Yummy
Curly	Heavy	Prickly	Sparkling	Zesty
Delicious	Hot	Pulpy	Spicy	
Dry	Icy	Raw		

Source: http://www.fns.usda.gov/tn/

Participate in the Child and Adult Care Food Program (CACFP)

CACFP is funded by the United States Department of Agriculture (USDA).

What CACFP can do for you:
- Help you pay for meals and snacks you serve to children
- Teach you how to plan and serve nutritious meals
- Ensure parents that their children are receiving nutritious meals
- Help you get to know other providers who provide child care

What is required. You will need to:
- Prepare and serve meals that meet CACFP guidelines
- Keep records of your weekly menus
- Keep records of the children you serve
- Practice good food safety
- Attend training about food and nutrition
- Submit your records to a local CACFP agency for reimbursement

To locate a local CACFP agency: contact your county extension office or local child care resource and referral agency.

Appropriate serving sizes for children

Children 1 - 12 years
Child and Adult Care Food Program
(Post where meals are prepared and served.)

	Ages 1-2	Ages 3-5	Ages 6-12 [4]
Breakfast			
Milk	1/2 cup	3/4 cup	1 cup
Juice or Fruit or Vegetable [1]	1/4 cup	1/2 cup	1/2 cup
Grains/Breads [2]	1/2 serving/slice	1/2 serving/slice	1 serving/slice
or cereal, cold dry	1/4 cup*	1/3 cup**	3/4 cup***
or cooked cereal	1/4 cup	1/4 cup	1/2 cup
Snack (Select 2 of the 4 components listed)			
Milk	1/2 cup	1/2 cup	1 cup
Juice or Fruit or Vegetable [1]	1/2 cup	1/2 cup	3/4 cup
Meat or Meat Alternate	1/2 ounce	1/2 ounce	1 ounce
or egg (large)	1/2	1/2	1/2
or cheese	1/2 ounce	1/2 ounce	1 ounce
or cheese food, cheese spread	1 ounce	1 ounce	2 ounces
or yogurt	1/4 cup	1/4 cup	1/2 cup
or cottage cheese	1/8 cup	1/8 cup	1/4 cup
or cooked dry beans/peas	1/8 cup	1/8 cup	1/4 cup
or peanut butter (nut or seed butter)	1 Tbsp.	1 Tbsp.	2 Tbsp.
or nuts and/or seeds [3]	Not recommended	Not recommended	1 ounce
Grains/Breads [2]	1/2 serving/slice	1/2 serving/slice	1 serving/slice
or cereal, cold dry	1/4 cup*	1/3 cup**	3/4 cup***
or cooked cereal, rice, pasta	1/4 cup	1/4 cup	1/2 cup
Lunch or supper			
Milk	1/2 cup	3/4 cup	1 cup
Meat or Meat Alternate	1 ounce	1 1/2 ounces	2 ounces
or egg (large)	1	1	1
or cheese	1 ounce	1 1/2 ounces	2 ounces
or cheese food, cheese spread	2 ounces	3 ounces	4 ounces
or yogurt	1/2 cup	3/4 cup	1 cup
or cottage cheese	1/4 cup	3/8 cup	1/2 cup
or cooked dry beans/peas	1/4 cup	3/8 cup	1/2 cup
or peanut butter (nut or seed butter)	2 Tbsp.	3 Tbsp.	4 Tbsp.
or nuts and/or seeds [3]	Not recommended	Not recommended	1 ounce
2 Vegetables and/or fruits to total [1]	1/4 cup (total)	1/2 cup (total)	3/4 cup (total)
Grains/Breads [2]	1/2 serving/slice	1/2 serving/slice	1 serving/slice
or cooked rice, noodles or pasta	1/4 cup	1/4 cup	1/2 cup

[1] Juices must be full strength 100% juice. For snack, juice cannot be served when milk is the only other component. Juice may contribute up to half the fruit/vegetable at lunch and supper. Only one serving of juice per day is recommended.

[2] Use whole grain, enriched or fortified breads, cereals, or pasta.

[3] Caution, children under 5 should not be served nuts. Older children may have up to 1 ounce of nuts or seeds at any one meal.

[4] The minimum quantities listed must be served. Children may be served larger portions based on their individual food needs. Programs serving migrant children may claim meals through age 15 and At Risk Afterschool Snack Program and homeless shelter participants may be served through age 18.

* 1/4 c or 1/3 oz, whichever is less, **1/3 c or 1/2 oz, whichever is less, *** 3/4 c or 1 oz, whichever is less.

Tbsp. = Tablespoon, Cup=measuring cup

Snack suggestions—Mix and match

Children can get one-fourth to one-third of their day's calories or energy from snacks, and many children eat 2 to 4 snacks daily. Nutritious snacks are an important part of a healthy diet.

A healthy snack should include foods from at least two of the following component groups:

Component 1	Component 2	Component 3	Component 4
Grains and breads	**Vegetables and fruits**	**Milk**	**Meat and meat alternatives**

Bagel
Banana bread
Biscuit
Breadstick
Bread, whole grain or enriched
Brown rice
Bulgur (cooked)
Cereal pieces, low sugar
Cinnamon roll
Cinnamon toast
Cookies
Cornbread
Crackers, animal
Crackers, graham
Crackers, oyster
Crackers, whole grain
English muffin
Flatbread, whole grain
Granola
Grits
Muffins
Pasta
Pita bread
Pretzel, soft
Pumpkin bread
Raisin toast
Tortillas
Vanilla wafers
Waffle square
Zucchini bread
	*Carrot sticks
	Cauliflowerets, slightly cooked, chilled
	*Celery sticks
	*Celery stuffed with peanut butter or cheese
	*Cucumber slices
	Green beans, cooked and chilled
	Green peas in the pod
	*Green or red pepper pieces
	Mixed vegetable juice
	Salads
	Tomato juice
	Tomato
	Vegetable soup
	Zucchini pieces
	
	Apple juice
	*Apple rings
	Apple rings, peeled
	Applesauce
	*Apple wedges
	Apple wedges, peeled
	Apricots, fresh or dried
	*Baked apple, unpeeled
	Banana chunks
	*Cherries
	Fruitsicles, frozen
	Fruit slushes
	*Grapes, seedless
	Melon pieces
	Nectarine, fresh
	Orange juice
	Orange sections
	Peach pieces, fresh or canned in light syrup
	Pear pieces, fresh or canned in light syrup
	Pineapple chunks, canned in own juice
	Pineapple juice
	Plums, fresh or canned
	Prunes, dried
	Raisins
	Strawberries
	Tangerine segments
		Buttermilk
		Lowfat milk
		Lowfat flavored milk
		Skim milk
		Whole milk
			Beef
			Cheese
			  American,
			  Cheddar,
			  Monterey Jack,
			  Mozzarella,
			  Swiss
			Chicken
			Cottage cheese
			Egg, deviled
			Egg, hard-boiled
			Fish
			Ham
			Lunch meats
			Peanut butter
			Pork
			Sausages
			Tofu (not CACFP creditable)
			Turkey
			Yogurt

*Caution: These foods may cause choking in children under the age of 4 or 5.

Colors of vegetables, fruits, and beans

Choose foods of different colors to add variety to meals. You also can use this list to select 3-4 foods for fun "taste-tests" with children. This is a great way to introduce new foods.

White	Yellow	Orange	Red	Blue/Purple	Green
Applesauce	Acorn squash	Apricots	Apples	Belgian endive	Apples
Beans, garbanzo	Apples	Cantaloupe	Beans, black	Blackberries	Asparagus
Beans, navy	Banana	Carrots	Beans, kidney	Black currants	Avocado
Cauliflower	Butternut squash	Mango	Beans, pinto	Blueberries	Beans, lima
Garlic	Corn	Nectarines	Beets	Eggplant	Bok choy
Ginger	Grapefruit	Oranges	Cherries	Grapes	Broccoli
Hominy	Lemons	Papaya	Cranberries	Plums	Brussels sprouts
Jicama	Peppers, bell	Peaches	Onion	Prunes	Celery
Mushrooms	Pineapple	Peppers, bell	Peppers, bell	Purple cabbage	Chayote squash
Onions	Star fruit	Pumpkin	Pink/red grapefruit	Purple grapes	Chinese cabbage
Parsnips	Summer squash	Sweet potatoes	Plums	Purple peppers	Collard greens
Pears	Yellow tomatoes	Tangelos	Radicchio	Raisins	Cucumbers
Potatoes	Yellow watermelon		Radishes		Grapes
Shallots			Raspberries		Green beans
Turnips			Red grapes		Green cabbage
			Red onions		Green onions
			Red pears		Green peas
			Red potatoes		Honeydew
			Rhubarb		Kale
			Strawberries		Kiwi fruit
			Tomatoes		Lettuce
			Watermelon		Lima beans
					Limes
					Mustard greens
					Okra
					Parsley
					Pears
					Peppers, bell
					Snap peas
					Snow peas
					Spinach
					Swiss chard
					Zucchini

Sample Menu: Week 1
Provider name _____ Month _____ Year _____

Menu children 1-12 years* of age

Meal Patterns	Day 1 ___ date	Day 2 ___ date	Day 3 ___ date	Day 4 ___ date	Day 5 ___ date
Breakfast • Bread or bread alternate (including cereal) • Juice or fruit or vegetable • Juice or fruit or • Milk, fluid • Other foods	• Bran muffin (I) • Mandarin oranges (A) (C) • 1% or skim milk	• Raisin bran (I) • Banana slices (F) • Orange wedges (C) (F) • 1% or skim milk • (Egg and cheese) (extra)	• Egg/cheese English muffin (whole wheat) (I)) • 1% or skim milk • Scrambled eggs (I) (extra)	• French toast sticks • Apricots (A) • 1% or skim milk	• Whole wheat toast • Fresh peach slices (C) • 1% or skim milk • Scrambled eggs (I) (extra)
AM Snack (Select two of these four components) • Milk, fluid • Juice or fruit or vegetable • Bread or bread alternate • Meat or meat alternate	• Water • Grapes (F) • Triscuit crackers	• Apple juice • Paint A Face (N) (Tortilla w/peanut butter, cereal, raisins)	• Cherry juicy juice (C) • Soft pretzel (I)	• 1% or Skim milk • Baked potato wedges (C) • Shredded cheese	• Water • Banana Stack (N) (Banana slices (F), Ritz crackers, peanut butter)
Lunch • Meat or meat alternate • Vegetable or fruit • 2nd Vegetable or fruit • Bread or bread alternate • Milk, fluid • Other foods	• Goulash (I) (HM) (hamburger and macaroni) • Carrots (A) • Red/green apple slices (F) w/ Cinnamon sprinkle (F) • Garlic toast • 1% or skim milk	• Bean burritos (B) (I) • Shredded lettuce (F) • Chopped tomato (F) (C) • Guacamole (F) • Whole grain tortilla • 1% or skim milk	• Teriyaki chicken (I) • Honeydew (C) (S) (F) • Summer squash (C) (S) • Rice brown/white mix • 1% or skim milk	• Tuna salad • Fresh spinach salad (A) (C) (F) (I) • Cantaloupe (A) (C) (F) (S) • Whole grain pita bread (I) • 1% or Skim milk	• Ham (I) and bean soup (HM) • Watermelon (A) (C) (F) (S) • Celery sticks (F) • Cauliflowerettes (F) (C) • Whole grain corn muffin • 1% or skim milk
PM Snack (Select two of these four components) • Milk, fluid • Juice or fruit or vegetable • Bread or bread alternate • Meat or meat alternate	• 1% or Skim milk • Peanut butter cookies (HM) (made with half whole wheat flour)	• Water • Broccoli Trees (A) (C) (F) • Red (A) and green pepper slices (F) • Cottage cheese dip	• 1% or Skim milk • Three-bean Salad (N) (Kidney beans wax beans, green beans) (B) (I)	• Water • Fruit Kabobs (N) (Kiwi, grapes, banana) (C) (F) • Cheese fingers	• 1% or Skim chocolate milk • Pumpkin bar (HM)

Use these codes: (N) Nutrition activity, (A) Vitamin A food, (B) Cooked dried beans or peas, (C) Vitamin C food, (I) Iron food source, (S) Seasonal food, (F) Fresh, (HM) Homemade
*Toddlers, 1-2 years of age, should receive whole milk and may require texture modification or substitutions of some foods to avoid choking.
Food-related book(s) to read to the children: *The Very Hungry Caterpillar* by Eric Carle and *Growing Vegetable Soup* by Lois Ehlert.

Sample Menu: Week 2
Provider name _____   Month _____ Year _____

Menu children 1-12 years* of age

Meal Patterns	Day 1 ___date___	Day 2 ___date___	Day 3 ___date___	Day 4 ___date___	Day 5 ___date___
Breakfast • Bread or bread alternate (including cereal) • Juice or fruit or vegetable • Milk, fluid • Other foods	• English muffin • Kiwi (C) (F) (S) • 1% or skim milk	• Cinnamon/raisin toast • Fruit punch-Juicy juice (C) • 1% or skim milk	• Total cereal (A) (C) (I) • Banana (F) • 1% or skim milk	• Waffle • Cantaloupe (A) (C) (F) • 1% or skim milk	• Whole wheat toast • Fresh peach slices (C) • 1% or skim milk • Scrambled eggs (I) (extra)
AM Snack (Select two of these four components) • Milk, fluid • Juice or fruit or vegetable • Bread or bread alternate • Meat or meat alternate	• 1% or skim milk • Graham crackers	• Water (extra) • Plum slices (F) (A) • Strawberries (F) (C) (S) • Blueberry muffin (HM)	• Water (extra) • Salad in a bag (N) (lettuce, tomato, carrot, broccoli, cucumbers) (A) (C) (F) • Breadstick	• Water (extra) • Salsa • Whole wheat tortilla • Scrambled eggs (I)	• Water (extra) • Banana Dog (N) (1/2 banana (F), 1/2 whole wheat bun, peanut butter)
Lunch • Meat or meat alternate • Vegetable or fruit • 2nd Vegetable or fruit • Bread or bread alternate • Milk, fluid • Other foods	• Chicken taco (I) (shredded chicken) • Refried beans (B) (I) • Shredded lettuce and chopped tomato (F) (C) • Corn or whole grain wheat tortilla • 1% or skim milk	• Baked fish sticks • Oven fried sweet potatoes (A) • Cabbage salad (C) • Whole wheat roll • 1% or skim milk	• Ham slice (I) • Macaroni and cheese (HM) (macaroni, half whole grain) • Mixed vegetables • Pears • 1% or skim milk	• Chili (HM) (B) (I) (hamburger, beans, and tomato) • Carrot sticks (A) (F) • Celery sticks (F) • Fresh pear slices (C) (F) • Crackers • 1% or skim milk	• Egg salad (I) • Apricot halves (A) • Jicama sticks (F) • Green beans (C) • Whole grain pita bread (I) • 1% or skim milk
PM Snack (Select two of these four components) • Milk, fluid • Juice or fruit or vegetable • Bread or bread alternate • Meat or meat alternate	• Grape juice (C-if fortified) • Deviled egg (I)	• Water (extra) • Warm whole grain pita wedges (I) • Hummus (B) (I)	• Water (extra) • Fresh pineapple (C) (F) • Wheat crackers	• Water • Merry-go-round (N) (apple-circle (F), animal crackers peanut butter)	• 1% or Skim • Oatmeal cookie (HM)

Use these codes: (N) Nutrition activity, (A) Vitamin A food, (B) Cooked dried beans or peas, (C) Vitamin C food, (I) Iron food source, (S) Seasonal food, (F) Fresh, (HM) Homemade
*Toddlers, 1-2 years of age, should receive whole milk and may require texture modification or substitutions of some foods to avoid choking.
Food-related book(s) to read to the children: *Pancakes, Pancakes!* by Eric Carle.

Sample Menu: Week 3
Provider name _____ Month _____ Year _____

Menu children 1-12 years* of age

Meal Patterns	Day 1 ___ date	Day 2 ___ date	Day 3 ___ date	Day 4 ___ date	Day 5 ___ date
Breakfast • Bread or bread alternate (including cereal) • Juice or fruit or vegetable • Milk, fluid • Other foods	• Whole wheat toast • Peaches • 1% or skim milk	• Cheerios (I) • Blueberries (C) (S) • 1% or skim milk	• Whole grain bagel (I) with cream cheese • Berry juicy juice (C) • 1% or skim milk	• Oatmeal • Banana (F) • 1% or skim milk	• Whole wheat toast • Nectarines (A) (C) (F) • 1% or skim milk
AM Snack (Select two of these four components) • Milk, fluid • Juice or fruit or vegetable • Bread or bread alternate • Meat or meat alternate	• Water (extra) • Quesadillas (whole grain tortilla) Melted cheese refried beans (B) (I)	• Water (extra) • Animal crackers • Yogurt	• 1% or skim milk • Cinnamon-sugar whole wheat toast	• 1% or Skim milk • Baked potato wedges (C) • Shredded cheese	• Water • Banana Stack (N) (Banana slices (F), Ritz crackers, peanut butter)
Lunch • Meat or meat alternate • Vegetable or fruit • 2nd Vegetable or fruit • Bread or bread alternate • Milk, fluid • Other foods	• Spaghetti (HM) (I) (ground turkey) • Broccoli (A) (C) • Apricots (A) • Whole grain pasta • 1% or skim milk	• Turkey mini sub (I) (shaved turkey, lettuce, tomato, cheese) • Pear slices (F) • Orange smiles (C) (F) (S) • Half hoagie bun • 1% or skim milk	• Taco salad (B) (I) (hamburger, black beans, cheese, tomatoes, romaine lettuce) • Mexican corn • Mango (A) (C) (F) (S) • Whole grain taco chips • 1% or skim milk	• BBQ chicken legs (I) • Peas and carrots (A) • Winter squash (A) (S) • Whole grain corn bread squares (HM) • 1% or skim milk	• Cheeseburger (I) • Baked beans (B) (I) • Watermelon (A) (C) (F) (S) • Lettuce leaf (F) • Tomato slices (F) (C) • Whole grain bun • 1% or skim milk
PM Snack (Select two of these four components) • Milk, fluid • Juice or fruit or vegetable • Bread or bread alternate • Meat or meat alternate	• Water (extra) • Tangerine (C) (F) (S) • Zucchini or banana bread (made with half whole wheat flour) (HM)	• Water (extra) • Mouse Faces (N) (Raisins-eyes, Apple-smile (F), Banana-nose (F) Carrot coins-ears (A) (F) Tortillas, Peanut Butter)	• Water (extra) • Whole wheat crackers • Ham (I) and cheese cubes	• Water (extra) • Grapes (F) • Kiwi wedges (F) (C) • Mini bagels	• Tomato juice (A) (C) • Fish crackers

Use these codes: (N) Nutrition activity, (A) Vitamin A food, (B) Cooked dried beans or peas, (C) Vitamin C food, (I) Iron food source, (S) Seasonal food, (F) Fresh, (HM) Homemade

*Toddlers, 1-2 years of age, should receive whole milk and may require texture modification or substitutions of some foods to avoid choking.

Food-related book(s) to read to the children: *Eating the Alphabet: Fruits and Vegetables from A-Z* by Lois Ehlert.

Sample Menu Form

Provider name _____ Month _____ Year _____

Menu children 1-12 years* of age

Meal Patterns	Monday date ____	Tuesday date ____	Wednesday date ____	Thursday date ____	Friday date ____
Breakfast • Bread or grain • Juice or fruit or vegetable • Milk, fluid • Other foods					
AM Snack (Select two of these four components) • Milk, fluid • Juice or fruit or vegetable • Bread or grain • Meat or meat alternate					
Lunch • Meat or meat alternate • Vegetable or fruit • 2nd Vegetable or fruit • Bread or bread grain • Milk, fluid • Other foods					
PM Snack (Select two of these four components) • Milk, fluid • Juice or fruit or vegetable • Bread or grain • Meat or meat alternate					

Use these codes: (N) Nutrition activity, (A) Vitamin A food, (B) Cooked dried beans or peas, (C) Vitamin C food, (I) Iron food source, (S) Seasonal food, (F) Fresh, (HM) Homemade

*Toddlers, 1-2 years of age, should receive whole milk and may require texture modification or substitutions of some foods to avoid choking.

Food-related book(s) to read to the children:

Ages and stages of eating

Swings in behavior and growth rate are common for young children and will influence their eating choices.

1 to 2 years
- Has appetite drop as growth slows
- Learns to drink from cup, usually is weaned
- May cut back to about 2 cups of milk daily
- Learns to bring food to mouth with spoon
- Likes to feed self but will likely need some help
- Copies others and will eat many family foods
- Is cutting teeth and may have difficulty chewing
- Has acute taste buds and can detect slight differences in foods
- Develops likes and dislikes; likes sweet foods
- Likes to touch and play with food; responds to food texture
- Learns to say "No" and becomes more independent

2 to 3 years
- Has much improved muscle control; can use spoon and fork easily
- Often desires and requests desserts and sweets
- Will wait a little for requests to be filled
- Usually will eat raw vegetables but may refuse salads

Source: *Raising Healthy Kids, Food for 'Me Too,'* Litchfield R. (2004), Iowa State University Extension PM1257

- Finds green vegetables more acceptable
- Can make simple either/or food choices: "Would you like a peach or pear?"

4 to 5 years
- May return to food jags or go on food "strikes"
- Is influenced by others: other children, television ads, teachers, etc.
- Likes plain cooking and foods separated on the plate
- Dislikes most mixed food dishes and gravies
- By age 5, often has fewer demands and will accept food available
- Has a gradual increase in appetite

6 to 8 years
- Continued influence by others: children, television ads, teachers, etc.
- Shows more interest in trying new foods
- Enjoys preparing simple foods and snacks without adult direction
- Enjoys reading and following simple recipes
- Wants to use real kitchen tools and utensils—not child-size or plastic
- Appetite continues to increase with growth

Make mealtimes pleasant

The following tips can help the children who eat with you develop positive attitudes toward food and the meal experience:

Make mealtimes pleasant. Show your enthusiasm for good foods. Children will feel more comfortable if you sit with them and share the same meal.

Help children learn skills. Children can set the table, spread jam or butter on bread, stir batter, pour milk from a small pitcher.

Remember that eating is a social time. Children should be seated around a table so they can talk with and observe one another.

Plan fun food activities to encourage children to try new foods. Read a book about the new food and then serve the new food as a snack when children are hungry. Getting children involved in preparation also will boost self-confidence.

Make mealtimes easier

Provide child-size furniture. Some providers use a child-sized table for meals; others arrange chairs, high chairs, and booster seats around the family table.

Use serving utensils that help serve the right size portions of food. Utensils should be easy to handle. Tongs, smaller serving spoons, and scoops work well.

Use plastic squeeze bottles. Children can squeeze jellies, peanut butter, mustard, mayonnaise, catsup, and other spreadable ingredients onto foods.

Try using serving utensils of a single color to help children identify cooking and serving utensils from eating utensils. It's easier for children to remember not to lick the red spoon. If you can't find colored plastic utensils, you can mark serving utensil handles with vinyl tape. This tape lasts a long time and stays on well in the dishwasher.

Provide child-sized utensils for eating. Small spoons are essential. A plate with edges or a small, shallow bowl allows children to scoop up their food more easily.

Serve finger foods frequently. Foods such as small meat or cheese cubes, vegetable sticks, and fruit chunks teach coordination to children. Finger foods are a good way to introduce new foods.

Learning eating skills can be messy in the beginning. Encourage children to help you clean up spills. Placing a drop cloth or old shower curtain on the floor also can make cleanup easier. Have paper towels and a sponge handy. A spill is not a catastrophe.

Make meals appealing

Consider food temperature. Most children do not like very hot or very cold foods.

Consider food texture. Vary textures—crunchy, crisp, smooth, creamy. Children often dislike lumpy or stringy foods. Avoid over cooking vegetables.

Consider food color. Serving foods of different colors makes a meal more interesting and appealing.

Serve foods of different shapes. Choose round crackers, or cherry tomatoes. Cut sandwiches into triangles. Serve square chunks of cheese and apple wedges.

Balance food flavors. Consider foods with sweet, salty, sour, tart, spicy, and mild flavors.

Include some "well liked" foods in every meal. Choose healthy foods that are familiar to children.

Introduce new foods with familiar foods. Introduce only one new food at a time.

Serve a new food several times. The more chances children have to try a new food, the more likely they are to accept it. Offer the new food first to a child who enjoys trying new things. Other children will follow this child's lead.

Go easy on fruit juice. Fruit juice is a healthy choice, but should not be offered in unlimited quantities. When children eat or drink too much of only a few foods they may miss the nutrients they need from other foods.

Prevent unhealthy attitudes about food

Food jags are normal; **never force a child to eat.** It is normal for children to eat a lot one day and almost nothing the next. If you offer choices from each of the food groups every day, children will adjust and eat appropriate amounts over several days. Deciding how much to eat at a given meal or snack is the child's job. Your job is to serve a variety of nutritious, tasty foods.

Expect some waste. It is good for children to naturally stop eating when they are full. Serving small child-size portions will help cut down on leftover food.

Avoid bribing or rewarding children for trying new foods. These techniques make children believe that new foods are undesirable.

Never use food as a punishment or reward. Withholding food can make children anxious that they will not get enough food, thus causing overeating. Using foods like sweets or special treats as a reward teaches children that some foods are better or more valuable than others.

Respect and value cultural eating differences. Introduce children to foods from different cultures. Encourage children and families to share stories about their various cultures.

---

5 Rules for good table manners
1. Wash hands first
2. Take the food you touch
3. Take turns talking
4. Say please and thank you
5. Clean up when you are finished

Prevent choking

Do not serve these foods to children under the age of 4 years
- Marshmallows
- Large chunks of meat
- Nuts, seeds, and peanuts
- Raw carrots (in rounds)
- Fish with bones
- Hot dogs (whole or sliced in rounds)
- Hard candy
- Popcorn
- Whole grapes (cut them in half)
- Ice cubes

Food safety

Safe storing, preparing, and serving of foods are as important as serving a balanced diet. Many children and adults get sick from eating food that is not properly handled. Follow food safety guidelines carefully whenever you buy, store, prepare, or serve food.

Food safety guidelines

Food purchasing
- Use inspected meats.
- Use pasteurized milk.
- Use pasteurized 100% juices.
- Do not buy or use leaking or bulging cans of food.

Food storage
- Put away frozen and cold foods promptly after purchasing.
- Rinse fruits and vegetables before use. Even prepackaged, pre-washed foods like lettuce, spinach, and carrots can still carry harmful bacteria.
- Store foods in covered containers in the refrigerator.
- Place thermometers in a visible location in refrigerators and freezers. Check the temperature frequently.
   a) Keep refrigerator temperature between 32 degrees – 40 degrees F.
   b) Keep freezer temperature at 0 degrees F or less.
- Clean dry food storage areas, refrigerator, and freezer frequently.
- Store foods and cleaning supplies in separate cupboards.
- Store cleaning supplies in a cupboard that is locked.

> **10 safety rules for kids who cook**
> 1. Wash hands with soap and water before eating or cooking.
> 2. Use a clean work surface.
> 3. Use clean utensils—no licking!
> 4. Keep cold foods cold—put in the fridge until needed.
> 5. Always wash fresh fruits and vegetables.
> 6. Throw away foods that fall on the floor.
> 7. Sneeze or cough away from the food.
> 8. Use only plastic knives and ask permission first.
> 9. It's adults only with plug-in appliances.
> 10. It's adults only at the stove/microwave.

Preparing meals

- Wash hands often with soap and water.
- Wash and sanitize counters and tables before and after use.
- Wash and sanitize cutting boards before using and after each use for different foods.
- Wash utensils before using them to work with a different food. Use a different utensil for cooking raw meat.
- Wash and sanitize can openers after each use.
- Do not change diapers in areas where you prepare, store, and serve foods.
- Keep pets in another room or outside when meals are being prepared and served to children.
- Put frozen meats into a pan before placing them in the refrigerator to thaw. Never thaw on the kitchen counter.
- Cook meats thoroughly. Use a food thermometer to be sure.
  - Steaks and roasts: beef, veal, and lamb – 145 degrees F
  - Ground pork, beef, veal, and lamb – 160 degrees F
  - Whole poultry (take measurement in thigh) – 165 degrees F
  - Fin fish – 145 degrees F or until the flesh is opaque and separates easily with a fork.

Serving meals

- Serve foods on a plate or napkin or in a bowl rather than directly on the table.
- Use serving utensils such as larger spoons or tongs. Teach children not to lick serving utensils.
- Discard cracked or chipped plates, cups, and bowls.
- Give children clean utensils and napkins if these items are dropped during meal service.
- Store unserved foods immediately. Discard leftovers on children's plates. Do not re-serve.

Dishwashing

- If a dishwasher is used, the rinse temperature should be 180 degrees F to sanitize dishes.
- To wash and sanitize dishes without a dishwasher:
  1. Rinse or scrape.
  2. Wash in hot sudsy water.
  3. Rinse in clear water.
  4. Sanitize dishes by:
     a) submerge for 1 minute in a solution of 1 tsp. bleach per quart of water, **or**
     b) submerge in 170 degree water for at least 30 seconds.
  5. Air dry. Do not towel dry dishes.

Garbage

- Throw out leftovers from children's plates.
- Cover garbage and use liners.

Clean and sanitize surfaces.

- **For disinfecting tables and floors** use a fresh bleach solution of one tablespoon of bleach per 1 quart of water or ¼ cup per 1 gallon of water. Pour this mixture in a spray bottle, mark it "Bleach Spray," and date it.
- **For sanitizing dishes, utensils, and toys** use a milder fresh bleach solution of 1 teaspoon of bleach to 1 quart of water.
- See chapter 11 for more information about cleaning and sanitizing surfaces.

Teach children to wash hands

Careful hand washing is one of the best ways to stop germs from spreading. Here are some ways to share the message.

Talk about all the things hands do: clap, make clay figures, build sand castles, pet animals, carry food to your mouth. Hands are very busy and must always be washed with soap and water before handling food.

Let children look at their hands with a magnifying glass. Remind them that dirt and germs can hide in the lines, cracks, and wrinkles. They might see dirt, but they won't see germs—they're too small.

Simple hand washing steps
1. Turn on warm water.
2. Wet hands with water.
3. Apply liquid soap.
4. Wash hands, rubbing hands out of running water at least 20 seconds. Rub top and inside of hands, under nails and between fingers. (Sing Hand Washing Song twice.)
5. Rinse hands at least 10 seconds.
6. Dry hands with clean, disposable paper towel.
7. Turn off water using the paper towel.
8. Throw paper towel away in a lined trash container.

IMPORTANT: If the sink being used also is used for food preparation, it must be cleaned and disinfected after each use.

Hand Washing Song—
(Sing to Row, Row, Row Your Boat)
Wash, wash, wash your hands,
Play our handy game.
Rub and scrub and scrub and rub,
Germs go down the drain.

Money-saving food tips

Spend food money wisely. Feeding children every day can be expensive. If you plan carefully and buy food on sale and in season, you can give children nutritious meals with less cost. Participation in the Child and Adult Care Food Program can lower your expenses for food.

Plan menus at least one week at a time. Having weekly menus makes your life less stressful, because you don't have to think about what to prepare at the last minute. Menus also can help you save money by helping you buy only what you need.

Make a grocery list before shopping. Do not go shopping when you are hungry. You will plan meals more wisely if you shop soon after a meal.

Choose healthy foods children enjoy. Avoid serving foods children will not eat.

Limit purchases of sweets, fats, and salty foods. Do not buy expensive snacks such as potato chips or cookies.

Buy necessary food items on sale. Most stores advertise sales in newspapers and online. Many stores and companies offer coupons online as well.

Use bulk cheese in main dishes such as casseroles. Cheese can be served for breakfast as well as for snacks and lunch.

Use eggs. They are economical. Creamed, scrambled, baked, poached, deviled, and hard-cooked eggs can be served for snacks and lunch, as well as breakfast.

Buy fresh fruits and vegetables in season. Purchasing food such as apples in autumn, when they are seasonally available, can save you a great deal of money. Many foods are available in markets year around, but out of season foods are shipped in from distant areas, often from other countries, and can be quite expensive.

Buy locally. Buying foods locally can sometimes save you money and will help you stay with seasonal foods. Local farmers' markets often offer many items.

Limit purchases of perishable foods to amounts that you will use. Buy large quantities of nonperishable foods on sale—if you will use them.

Buy whole grain or enriched breads and cereals. Buy bulk rice, pastas, and bulgur wheat.

Check prices to see if day-old bread is economical. Your community may have an outlet where day-old bakery goods are sold.

Compare store or generic brands. They are usually a few cents cheaper and cost less per serving than comparable nationally advertised products.

Double your recipe. Cook soups and spaghetti sauce in large amounts, cool, and freeze meal-size portions.

HFCCH Chapter 12 — Nutrition power: Choices with kid appeal 339

Read the label

"Nutrition Facts" food labels are required on almost all packaged foods. These food labels can help you make wise food choices and plan a healthy diet.

By reading the new label, you can find:

❶ Serving size
Start at the serving size and the number of servings in the package. The serving size identified on the package determines all the nutrient amounts listed on the label.

It is important to pay attention to the serving size, including the number of servings in the package. Compare this to how much YOU actually eat.

❷ Caloric Intake
Look at the calories and calories from fat. Calories are a measure of how much energy is in a serving of food. Children ages 1-3 need 1,300 calories a day. Children ages 4-6 need 1,800 calories per day.

Eating too many calories per day is linked to overweight and obesity; it doesn't matter if the calories are from protein, carbohydrate, or fat.

❸ – ❹
Macronutrients and Micronutrients
The Nutrition Facts Panel includes a number of nutrients that are important for your health. These have been separated into two main groups: macronutrients (#3 on sample label) and micronutrients (#4 on sample label).

❸ Macronutrients
Total fat, saturated fat, and cholesterol are required on the Nutrition Facts Panel. Some products, usually margarines and oils, also include polyunsaturated and monounsaturated fat. When comparing foods, look at the Nutrition Facts Panel and choose the food with the lower amounts of saturated fat and trans fat.

Carbohydrates included on the Nutrition Facts Panel are total carbohydrate, dietary fiber, and sugars. Carbohydrate is an important source of energy for the body. A minimum intake is 130 grams of total carbohydrate daily.

Dietary fiber is the part of plant foods that the body cannot digest. Lack of dietary fiber has been linked to increased risk of certain types of cancer, heart disease, diabetes, and obesity. Nineteen grams per day for children 1-3 years and 25 grams per day for children 4-8 years is recommended.

❹ Micronutrients
Vitamins and minerals, called micronutrients, are optional on the Nutrition Facts Panel. Children often don't get adequate amounts of vitamin A, vitamin C, calcium, and iron. Eating recommended amounts of these nutrients can improve their health and help reduce the risk of some diseases and health concerns.

❺ % DV Guide
The % Daily Value helps you determine whether the nutrients (fat, sodium, fiber, etc.) in a serving of food contribute a little or a lot to your daily intake. The % DV is the percent of the recommended daily amount of a nutrient in a serving of food.

Serving size ❶

Calorie intake ❷

Macronutrients ❸

Micronutrients ❹

Nutrition Facts
Serving Size 1 cup (228g)
Servings Per Container 2

Amount Per Serving

Calories 260   Calories from Fat 120

% Daily Value*

Total Fat 13g	**20%**
Saturated Fat 5g	25%
Trans Fat 2g	20%
Cholesterol 30mg	**10%**
Sodium 660mg	**28%**
Total Carbohydrate 31g	**10%**
Dietary Fiber 0g	0%
Sugars 5g	
Protein 5g	

Vitamin A	4%	•	Vitamin C	2%
Calcium	15%	•	Iron	4%

* Percent Daily Values are based on a 2,000 calorie diet. Your daily values may be higher or lower depending on your calorie needs:

	Calories:	2,000	2,500
Total Fat	Less than	65g	80g
Sat Fat	Less than	20g	25g
Cholesterol	Less than	300mg	300g
Sodium	Less than	2,400mg	2,400mg
Total Carbohydrate		300g	375g
Dietary Fiber		25g	30g

Calories per gram:
Fat 9 ▪ Carbohydrate 4 ▪ Protein 4

❺ **% DV Guide**

❻ **Footnotes**

% DVs are based on a 2,000 calorie diet. The general guide is: 5% DV or less is considered a low source of the nutrient, while 20% DV or more is considered a high source of the nutrient.

❻ **Footnotes**
The statement, "Percent Daily Values are based on a 2,000 calorie diet" must appear on all Nutrition Facts Panels.

Seasonal Fruits and Vegetables*

Fall	Winter	Spring	Summer
September **October** **November**	**December** **January** **February**	**March** **April** **May**	**June** **July** **August**
- Apples - Broccoli - Brussels sprouts - Cabbage - Cauliflower - Celery root - Chicory - Chinese cabbage - Cranberries - Cucumbers - Dates - Eggplant - Fennel - Grapes - Greens - Lettuce: head or iceberg - Mandarin oranges - Mushrooms - Nuts - Okra - Pears - Peppers, chili - Peppers, sweet - Persimmons - Pomegranates - Pumpkin - Quince - Shallots - Spinach - Squash, winter - Star fruit - Sweet potatoes - Turnips	- Avocados - Broccoli - Brussels sprouts - Cabbage - Cauliflower - Celery root - Chicory - Chinese cabbage - Dates - Fennel - Grapefruit - Greens - Lemons - Mandarin oranges - Oranges - Pears - Spinach - Sweet potatoes - Tangerines - Turnips	- Asparagus - Avocados - Basil - Beans - Beets - Berries - Broccoli - Cabbage - Chinese cabbage - Cucumbers - Lettuce: head or iceberg - Mangoes - Okra - Oranges - Papayas - Peas - Peppers, chili - Peppers, sweet - Radishes - Rhubarb - Shallots - Spinach - Summer squash - Turnips	- Apricots - Basil - Beans - Beets - Blackberries - Blueberries - Boysenberries - Carrots - Cherries - Collards - Corn - Cucumbers - Dates - Figs - Grapes - Green beans - Limes - Mangoes - Melons - Nectarines - Okra - Peaches - Pears - Peppers, chili - Peppers, sweet - Plums - Raspberries - Summer squash - Tomatoes - Watermelon

*Adapted from United States Department of Agriculture (USDA)
http://www.fns.usda.gov/tn/

Is sugar OK?

Sugar has little nutritional value. Eating too much sugar can cause tooth decay and weight problems. Even very young children can be affected.

The following suggestions can help you avoid some of these problems.

Reduce added sugar. Substitute fruit, vegetables, cheese, or unsugared cereals as snacks.

Buy fruit juices carefully. Buy only pure, 100 percent fruit juice. The fruit punches, cocktails, or juice drinks often advertised as breakfast beverages are high in sugar, and may have unneeded artificial flavorings and colors as well. These products do NOT fulfill nutritional requirements for fruit and do not count in the CACFP.

Sweeten cereals and drinks yourself. You also can make your own gelatin desserts and puddings. Packaged foods contain lots of sugar. You have more control over the amount of sugar a child gets if you make your own.

Limit candy, cake, cookies, ice cream, and soft drinks. These foods should be served only occasionally.

Use plain yogurt. Add your own fruit instead of buying sweetened, flavored yogurt.

How much fat should children have?

Fat consumption affects many health aspects and is closely related to blood cholesterol levels.

Fats should not be limited in the diets of children under 2. Infants need cholesterol and fat for growth and brain development.

After age 2, children need only about 30 percent of their calories from fat. But fat and cholesterol intake should not be severely limited. Children ages 2-6 should have about 4 tsp. of oil each day. Children ages 7-13 years may have 5-6 tsp. of oil.

| Applying the Guidelines to Calorie Recommendations* ||||
Age	Total Calories[1]	Grams of Fat	Grams of Saturated Fat
2-3			
Boys	1000-1400	33-47	11-16
Girls	1000-1200	33-40	11-13
4-8			
Boys	1400-1600	47-53	16-18
Girls	1400-1600	47-53	16-18
9-13			
Boys	1800-2200	60-73	20-24
Girls	1600-2000	53-67	18-22
14-18			
Boys	2400-2800	80-93	27-31
Girls	2000	67	22

[1] Calorie ranges are based on low active lifestyle according to energy levels for proposed Food Guide Pyramid food intake patterns. Low active lifestyle is defined as physical activity equivalent to walking about 1.5 to 3 miles per day at 3 to 4 miles per hour, in addition to the activities of independent living.

* Source: American Heart Association: http://www.americanheart.org/presenter.jhtml?identifier=1088

Cholesterol values for children ages 2 to 19*

Total Cholesterol (mg/dL)	LDL Cholesterol (mg/dL)	Risk	Action
Less than 170 mg/dL	Less than 110 mg/dL	low	eat a healthy diet and be physically active
170 – 199	110 – 129	moderate	eat a healthy diet and be physically active
200 or more	130 or more	high	eat a healthy diet, be physically active, and consider drug treatment

* Source: American Heart Association: http://www.americanheart.org/presenter.jhtml?identifier=1088

Tips for reducing cholesterol and fat

Avoid cooking food in large amounts of butter, margarine, or oil. Many vegetables can be lightly steamed with water or chicken broth instead.

Decrease fat in recipes or substitute other ingredients. For example you can use applesauce instead of oil when making muffins.

Tips
- Monitor cholesterol intake with a goal of less than 300 mg per day.
- Encourage 5 servings of vegetables and fruits daily.
- Encourage 6-11 servings of whole grain and other grain food daily.
- Encourage consumption of adequate amounts of fiber.
- Substitute foods high in saturated fat with foods high in mono- and polyunsaturated fats.

Types of fats

Choosing foods low in saturated fat helps reduce total and LDL (bad) cholesterol levels. Most saturated fat comes from animal sources and is usually solid at room temperature.

While no more than 30 percent of total calories should come from all fats, no more than 10 percent should be from saturated fat.

Trans fats are formed by hydrogenation—turning liquid fats into solid fats at room temperature. Hydrogenation helps increase the shelf life of a product, but too many trans fats in the diet can increase cholesterol levels. Limit products with high trans fatty acids such as crackers, fried foods, cookies, bakery items, candy, and other snack foods.

Polyunsaturated fats are considered heart healthy because they help lower cholesterol. Cooking oils such as soybean, corn, safflower, and sunflower are all polyunsaturated fats and are recommended over saturated and trans fats.

Monounsaturated fats are heart healthy too because they lower cholesterol, particularly the LDL (bad) cholesterol. Olive, canola, peanut, almond, and walnut oils are all types of monounsaturated fats and are recommended over the other fats.

What about the "overweight" child?

One in two children is at risk of being overweight. The number of overweight children (ages 6-11) has almost quadrupled in the past four decades: the number of overweight adolescents (ages 12-19) has tripled.

Overweight children are likely to have serious future health problems. Overweight children are 43.5 times more likely to have at least three cardiovascular risk factors. One in three American children born in 2000 will become diabetic unless food consumption is reduced and exercise is increased.

African–American and Mexican American children are at even greater risk. Both genetics and environment contribute to problems and are shared by the entire family.

The power of advertising. Children are strongly influenced by what they see and hear. Parents and caregivers compete with 10,000 food commercials and $13 billion in advertising directed specifically toward children annually.

Making healthy choices is challenging. Fast food and convenience food tend to provide more calories, fat, carbohydrate, added sugars, sugar-sweetened beverages, and less fiber, milk, fruits, and non-starchy vegetables than other meal choices.

It is important to remember that children come in all sizes. Children who are large or small for their age may be teased by their playmates. It is important for them to know they are loved and accepted, whatever their size.

You can help children feel good about themselves and maintain a weight that is right for them. Here are a few ideas.

- **Weight loss diets are not appropriate for children.** It is best to offer overweight children a variety of healthy food, correct portion sizes, and opportunities to be active. Following these practices will help children grow into a more normal weight.

- **Offer children a variety of nutritious foods at planned meal and snack times.** Join children in eating a variety of foods, and look for opportunities to discuss the different food groups and the importance of eating foods from all of them.

- **Plan meals and snacks at regular times.** Planned times for eating help children develop good eating patterns and teach them good food behaviors in social situations. Children who are fed regularly do not worry about not being fed and have regular sources of energy.

- **Teach children how to learn when they are hungry and full.** Feed infants when they are hungry, not simply because they cry. Learn their cues for hunger. Allow toddlers to leave food on their plates, even if you believe they have not eaten enough. If a child asks for a second helping, serve a small portion, even if you believe the child has eaten enough. Include low-calorie foods in meals and snacks, and offer these foods when children ask for more.

- **Show children a healthy lifestyle.** Children like to imitate adults. Be enthusiastic about many foods. Help children find physical activities they enjoy.

Find a balance between food and physical activity

Eating healthy is only one part of maintaining a healthy weight. Children and adults need physical activity too.

Set a good example by being physically active during your time with and without children. After work go for a walk or ride a bike.

Establish a routine by setting aside time each day as activity time.

Children and teenagers need 60 minutes of activity every day on most days of the week.

Should children shake the salt habit?

Americans eat too much salt. We shake it on at the table, add it when we cook, put it in canned foods in large amounts, and cure and pickle foods with it. Salt is everywhere.

Children learn to like salty foods. They are generally given little salt during the first year of life, but gradually increase salt intake as they learn to eat new foods.

Children who are given foods with no added salt do not miss it. The body needs sodium (from salt), but children need only a small amount of salt.

Adding salt to foods regularly can cause problems later in life. Some adults are "sensitive" to sodium, and eating salty foods raises their blood pressure. These people also may have kidney problems. While not all adults have this problem, there is no way to know which people will be "sodium-sensitive." It is easier to teach children to eat foods without added salt than to teach adults to give up the salt they have learned to need.

Help children avoid the salt habit

Keep the salt shaker off the table. If salt is not easily available, children will not learn to shake it on their food.

Salt foods lightly. Reduce or omit the salt altogether. Sodium is present naturally in some vegetables, milk, and meats.

Limit salty foods. Foods such as pickles and cured meats (ham, bacon, sausage), salty snacks (potato chips, pretzels), and condiments (catsup, mustard, and steak sauce) are high in salt. Limit them.

Read labels. Choose foods with less salt. Many canned and frozen prepared foods are high in salt.

What about fiber?

Dietary fiber is important to children for several reasons. It:
- promotes normal bowel movements
- helps prevent diet-related cancer
- helps reduce serum cholesterol concentrations and risk of coronary heart disease
- helps prevent overweight and the risk of diabetes

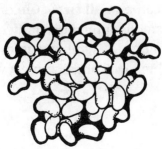

Fiber content of kid-appeal foods

Fruits	Grams
Apple, 1 medium	3
Applesauce, 1/2 cup	2
Banana, 1 small	2
Grapes, white, 10 small	1
Orange, 1 medium	3
Orange juice, 1 cup	<1
Juicy Juice®, 1 cup	0
Raisins, 1/4 cup	2

Vegetables	
Carrot, 1 medium	3
Corn, 1/2 cup	3
Potatoes, baked, without skin	2
Potatoes, baked, with skin	3.5
Potatoes, french fried, 10 pieces	2

Cereals and grain products	
Captain Crunch®, 3/4 cup	1
Cheerios®, 1 cup	1
Granola bar, 2	2
Mini wheats, frosted, 1 cup	6
Oatmeal, cooked, 1 cup	6
Pancakes, 1 4-inch cake	<1
Wheaties®, 1 cup	3
White bread, 1 slice	<1
Whole wheat bread, 1 slice	2

Snack foods	
Corn chips, 1 ounce	1
Ice cream bar, 1	0
Oreos®, 3	1
Potato chips, 1 ounce	1
Pudding, 1/2 cup	0
Ritz bits®, 14 pieces	1
Triscuits®, 7	4
Twinkies®, 2	<1

Protein foods	
Cheese, 1 ounce	0
Chili with beans, 1 cup	7
Egg, scrambled, 1	0
Peanut butter, 2 tablespoons	2
Hot dog, beef and pork, 1	0
Macaroni and cheese, 1 cup	2.2
Spaghettios®, 1 cup	1

No endorsement of companies or their products is intended, nor is criticism implied of those not mentioned.

Adequate intake for dietary fiber among children and adolescents are listed below [based on Dietary Reference Intakes (DRI) released by the Food and Nutrition Board and Institute of Medicine; see also http://books.nap.edu/books/0309085373/html/299.html].

Adequate intake for young children
1-3 years 19 g/day of total fiber
4-8 years 25 g/day of total fiber

Dietary fiber intake should be gradually increased by consuming more fruits, vegetables, legumes, cereals, and whole grain products. One serving of most fruits and vegetables provides 1 to 4 grams of fiber. The skins, edible seeds, and fibrous flesh of fruits and vegetables contain most of their dietary fiber. Whole grain breads usually contain 2 or more grams of fiber per serving. The fiber content of cereals varies greatly; check labels and choose cereals with more than 2 grams of fiber per serving—such as wheat-bran based and whole wheat cereals. Cheese, milk, eggs, and meat contain no fiber.

Special diets

Sometimes children will have special dietary requirements. It is a good idea to post weekly menus so parents will be aware of the meals you offer. Ask parents about food needs and family eating patterns when you enroll their child. Enrollment is the time to decide whether or not you can fulfill a particular child's food needs.

Allergies

Discuss food plans and eating habits with families when you first enroll each child. Some children are allergic to certain foods or may not be able to tolerate even the smallest amount used as an ingredient in other foods.

Food allergies are not uncommon. Cow's milk is a problem for some infants and young children. Other common sources of allergic reactions are wheat products, nuts, and eggs. Some young children have trouble with high fiber foods.

Dietary supplements sometimes will be needed. There are health conditions such as anemia or diabetes that may be treated with a special diet or dietary supplements. You need to know about these problems and follow medical recommendations. Rely on parents to explain the routines and food needs, but be sure you can call a physician or dietitian when you have questions.

Cultural or religious beliefs and food

Occasionally, a family's religious beliefs will prohibit or demand certain foods or foods at certain times. You should be informed about these special practices and be prepared for them.

Families also may request certain foods that reflect their cultural background. You may want to include some of these foods in your menus. Eating familiar foods will help children feel welcome and that they belong. Other children also may be interested in eating new foods, especially if you explain a little about the cultural background or practices. Even more ideal would be to have a parent bring food, visit, or help the children prepare a special food. Your local librarian may be able to help you locate children's books or cookbooks with pictures to share with children to help them understand about foods from different cultures.

Vegetarian diets

Families who follow a vegetarian diet may request that you alter meal patterns for their children. These requests will vary, however, as some families may eat dairy products, eggs, some poultry, or fish while others avoid these products altogether.

Vegetarians must eat more food at times to get proper nutrients. Since small children cannot eat large amounts of food, milk, cheese, and eggs must be added to their vegetarian diets.

A vegetarian child care menu that follows the guidelines of the Food Guide Pyramid and the Child and Adult Care Food Program might include the following menu.

Sample vegetarian menu

Breakfast:
Oatmeal
Milk
Toast
Orange juice

Morning snack:
Applesauce
Graham cracker

Lunch:
Whole wheat roll
Cheese omelet
Peas
Milk
Banana slices

Afternoon Snack:
Peanut butter on whole wheat bread

Feeding infants

Infants need special feeding care. Parents and caregivers must work closely to ensure consistent care in this most important growth period. Parents should establish a regular routine of feeding their baby according to the recommendations of a pediatrician.

Talk to parents often about the feeding of their infants. Keep feeding recommendations and any changes in those recommendations signed by parents and filed with the infant's records.

Breast milk or formula feeding

Babies grow more rapidly in the first year of life than at any other time. Babies double their birth weight in the first 4 months of life and birth weight triples by the first birthday.

Infants need the same nutrients as children and adults: protein, carbohydrates, fat, water, vitamins, and minerals. Infant foods also must contain enough calories to allow normal growth and development at this critical time.

Parents may choose to breastfeed their infants or to provide commercial infant formulas. Either type of feeding contains the calories and nutrients infants need for the first 4 to 6 months. Infant formula should be iron fortified. Mothers who choose to breastfeed will express their milk using a pump and will bring the milk in to be fed to baby in a bottle. Appropriate amounts of either frozen breast milk or commercial formula may be brought to a child care provider each day. You also may choose to provide the formula as part of your service.

Feed whenever baby seems hungry—usually about every two hours. Avoid putting a baby on a strict schedule. Babies grow rapidly and hunger needs change quickly.

Hold baby when you are feeding. Babies need to feel safe and secure. Breastfed babies need to eat frequently. Expect to feed infants approximately every 2-3 hours.

Always hold an infant for feeding. Babies can easily choke. If an infant falls asleep while feeding, and an adult is not present to remove the bottle, milk may remain in the mouth during sleep. The sugar naturally found in this milk can cause cavities in new or forming teeth. Teeth with cavities may hurt or break, making it difficult for a child to chew.

Avoid letting infants or toddlers carry bottles. They easily can fall and injure themselves. Children who carry bottles may share sips with other children. By sharing sips, they also may share infections.

HFCCH Chapter 12 — Nutrition power: Choices with kid appeal

Breastfeeding— How you can help

Some mothers may wish to continue breastfeeding while their children are in child care. They may choose to adjust their work schedule so they can come and nurse the baby at your home, collect and store breast milk for you to use while they are away, or use formula during the day, but continue nursing at home. The following information about breastfed babies can help you if you happen to care for one.

Be supportive and understanding. Breastfeeding is an important way for mothers to bond with their babies. It also offers important advantages for babies. Breastfed babies usually
- are sick less often
- spit up less
- have less constipation
- have less odor in stools

Provide a quiet, comfortable space for nursing mothers. Some mothers may ask you if they can come to your home and nurse the baby at mealtime. They also may wish to nurse their baby before they go home. Breastfeeding mothers may feel quite comfortable nursing the baby while visiting with you and the other children, or they may wish to go to a quiet corner or another room.

Breast milk will last up to 48 hours in the refrigerator. Label all bottles with baby's name and date. Breast milk will last up to one month in the back of a freezer that stays at zero degrees. Be sure milk is labeled with name and date. Use older milk up first.

Breastfed babies need to eat frequently. Expect to feed infants approximately every 2-3 hours.

Occasionally, breastfed babies may have trouble accepting the bottle. This may be because babies suck the breast nipple and the bottle nipple in different ways. A breast-shaped nipple may help solve this problem. A long, soft nipple may help the younger baby get more milk. An older baby may take a "sippy" cup with a narrow plastic spout on the lid.

Be sure to shake breast milk that has been refrigerated or frozen and thawed. Breast milk is not homogenized, and the cream separates out and rises to the top.

Breast milk does not look like cow's milk or formula. In spite of its thin appearance and blue color, breast milk is rich and nutritious. Thawed milk often has small pieces of fat floating in it that makes it look curdled. Warming and shaking the breast milk gently will help fat dissolve.

Watch for 6-8 wet diapers during the day. This indicates that baby is getting enough food.

Frequent daily stools that are loose are normal for breastfed babies in the first 2 months. Stools look like cottage cheese and mustard.

Label all infant feedings with the baby's name and date. Ask parents to label bottles before bringing them. Have labels and a marker on hand in case they forget.

Store bottles of commercial infant formula in the refrigerator. Store frozen breast milk in the freezer until feeding time. Then thaw it in the refrigerator or under cool, running water. Do not warm bottles on the stove, which may cause the milk to curdle.

Do not warm bottles in the microwave. Uneven heating may cause hot spots, which can burn baby's mouth. Cover all bottles during storage.

Wash hands carefully with soap and water before preparing any infant feeding. Do not touch nipples with your fingers.

Prepare commercial infant feedings according to instructions. Add the right amount of water to ensure that the infant gets adequate calories and nutrients.

Throw away any breast milk or formula left in a bottle after feeding. If too much seems to be going to waste, record the amount usually used and prepare a smaller amount. You also may ask parents to save breast milk in smaller bottles.

Clean reusable bottles and nipples thoroughly after each use. Bottles and nipples may be washed in a dishwasher in very hot water or washed by hand and boiled for five minutes before refilling.

Breast milk and infant formula are the only foods recommended for the first 4 to 6 months of life. Vitamin and mineral supplements usually are not necessary and should be given only when recommended by a physician.

Beginning solid foods

Introduce solid foods at 4 to 6 months. Although breast milk and infant formula continue to be an important part of baby's diet through 12 months, solid foods may be introduced at 4 to 6 months. These foods provide extra calories and nutrients for the older baby.

Wait for the baby to develop these skills before you start. At 4 to 6 months, babies learn to control head movements and to keep food in their mouths rather than pushing it out with their tongues. They also learn to sit up, making feeding with a spoon possible.

Talk with parents first. Parents should take the lead on introducing new foods. You will want to work with them to introduce the same food at the same time.

Start slowly. Only 1 or 2 spoonfuls of food are needed in the beginning.

Introduce one new food at a time. Add another new food after 4 or 5 days. Waiting allows the baby to get used to new flavors and allows you to identify foods that may cause allergic reactions.

If baby rejects food, try offering it again. Babies sometimes need to try a new food several times before developing a taste for it.

Which foods first?

Start with rice cereals. Rice is less likely than other grains to cause an allergic reaction. Make sure the cereal is iron fortified. Mix it with breast milk or infant formula to provide a good balance of protein, carbohydrate, and fat and to serve as a source of iron.

Vegetables may be introduced after cereals, at about 7 months. The baby may begin to make chewing motions at this time. At this stage, cereal may be made with less formula or breast milk, and mashed vegetables may be added to encourage chewing.

Fruits should be introduced after vegetables. Use single ingredients such as applesauce. Combination baby foods, such as fruit desserts cannot be counted for the Child and Adult Care Food Program (CACFP).

Babies with one or two teeth can eat some lumpy foods. Some babies chew very well even without teeth. Foods served to the other children may be offered to the baby. Easily mashed foods, such as potatoes and carrots, bananas, or canned fruits, work well. Remember, though, that babies do not need added sugars or salt.

Offer soft finger foods as soon as a baby can grasp. Any food that will not fall apart between the plate and mouth is appropriate as a finger food. Finger foods are messy at first, but the mess will decrease with practice. (Examples are: soft banana slices or tender cooked carrots.)

Meat, egg yolks, and small amounts of cheese may be added to baby's diet starting at 8 months. Babies should not be given egg whites before the first birthday.

Wheat is not recommended before 8 months. Many infants are sensitive to wheat. Waiting until 8 months will help to avoid a potential allergic reaction.

Honey and corn syrup are not recommended before 12 months. Some honey and corn syrup contain botulism spores. These are not harmful to children and adults but may produce poisons that can be fatal to babies. Infants' digestive systems cannot destroy these spores.

Formula, breast milk, juices, and water may be given from a cup after 10 months. Hold the cup and serve only small amounts of liquid. Only an adult should feed an infant. By the first birthday, the baby should be able to handle the cup alone.

Special concerns

Avoid serving foods that may choke an infant. Serve only foods that are soft or that will soften in the mouth. Avoid raw carrots, nuts, popcorn, unpeeled fruits and vegetables, hard candies, pickles, hot dogs, and other hard foods.

Be careful when warming baby's foods. Mix food well and check temperature. Microwaving may leave hot spots in the food, so that one spoonful of food may be cold, while the next spoonful may burn baby's mouth. Hot spots can cause serious burns. Never heat bottles in a microwave. Heat bottles in warm water in a container or under running water.

Serve baby food in a bowl, rather than directly from baby food jars. Throw away leftover food after the meal. The baby's saliva can spoil the food.

Remember that contact with your skin will contaminate the infant's food. Do not touch the nipple or rim of the cup. Do not put a spoon with strained food onto your arm to test temperature and then into the baby's mouth. Do not stick your finger into the jar of baby food or test it with the tip of your tongue. Test the food temperature by dripping a sample onto your wrist or inner elbow.

If you are in CACFP, refer to their infant meal pattern guidelines and infant reimbursable food list for information on specific foods and appropriate amounts.

Discuss feeding infants with your CACFP sponsor, and remember that you must have on file a medical exception if other than the required foods are to be reimbursed. Remember that infant formula and cereals should be iron fortified. Fruit juices should be 100 percent juice.

The chart below shows age-appropriate foods for infants and foods to avoid.

Age	Foods good for baby	Foods to avoid
0 to 4 months	Breast milk Infant formula	Cow's milk Solid foods
4 to 6 months	Breast milk Infant formula Water Iron fortified cereals	Cow's milk Sugar or honey Meat Eggs Powdered soft drink mix
6 to 9 months	Breast milk Infant formula Water Cereal Unsalted mashed vegetables Unsweetened fruits and juices Finger foods	Cow's milk Honey or sugar Sweets Eggs Meat Powdered soft drink mixes Soft drinks Salt Spinach and beets Wheat based cereals
9 to 12 months	Breast milk Infant formula Water Unsweetened cereal Unsalted vegetables Unsweetened fruits and juices Cheese and yogurt Finger foods Breads and crackers Lean meats Egg yolks	Cow's milk 2% or skim milk Honey or sugar Candy or sweet desserts Sugar-coated cereals Powdered soft drink mixes Soft drinks Popcorn Whole peanuts Coffee or tea Whole eggs or whites

Although the following CACFP meal pattern specifies breakfast, lunch, supper, and snack, this may not match each baby's pattern. Babies seldom accept rigid eating schedules and may need to eat every 2 to 4 hours. Babies should be fed when hungry, "on demand," or "on cue."

Sample menus for infants			
Age of baby	**Breakfast**	**Lunch and supper**	**Snack**
Birth through 3 months	4-6 fluid ounces (fl oz) breast milk [1,2] or formula [3]	4-6 fluid ounces (fl oz) breast milk [1,2] or formula [3]	4-6 fluid ounces (fl oz) breast milk [1,2] or formula [3]
4 months through 7 months	4-8 fluid ounces (fl oz) breast milk [1,2] or formula [3] 0-3 Tbsp. Infant cereal [3,4] (optional)	4-8 fluid ounces (fl oz) breast milk [1,2] or formula [3] 0-3 Tbsp. Infant cereal [3,4] (optional) 0-3 Tbsp. fruit and/or vegetable [4] (optional)	4-6 fluid ounces (fl oz) breast milk [1,2] or formula [3]
8 months through 11 months	6-8 fluid ounces (fl oz) breast milk [1,2] or formula [3] 2-4 Tbsp Infant cereal [3] 1-4 Tbsp fruit and/or vegetable	6-8 fl oz breast milk [1,2] or formula [3] and 2-4 Tbsp Infant cereal [3] and/or 1-4 Tbsp meat, fish, poultry, egg yolk, cooked dry beans or peas; or ½-2 oz cheese; or 2-8 Tbsp. cottage cheese; or 1-4 oz cheese food, or cheese spread; and 1-4 Tbsp fruit and/or vegetable	2-4 fluid ounces (fl oz) breast milk [1,2] or formula [3] or fruit juice 0-1/2 slice of bread [4,5] or 0-2 crackers [4,5] (optional)

[1] Breast milk or formula, or portions of both may be served (ask parent's wishes); however, it is recommended that breast milk be served in place of formula from birth through 11 months.

[2] For some breastfed infants who regularly consume less than the minimum amount of breast milk per feeding, a serving of less than minimum amount of breast milk may be offered, with additional breast milk offered if the infant is still hungry.

[3] Infant formula and dry infant cereal should be iron fortified.

[4] A serving of this component is required only when the infant is developmentally ready to accept it.

[5] Fruit juice must be full-strength.

[6] Bread, crackers, and bread alternatives must be made from whole-grain or enriched meal or flour.

Heart of the Matter

My "Cooking with Kids" workshop was over. Almost everyone had left. I moved over to the "cooking table" to clean up. We had made fruit kabobs today—always a popular item. I speared a leftover piece of kiwi and a chunk of pineapple with a pretzel stick. I reflected on the workshop as I munched.

This had been a talkative group. We had a lively discussion about the appropriateness of using food for art. There were strong feelings on this issue. Some felt that we should never play with food or use it for art, because it is disrespectful of low income families who may not have enough to eat. One woman was especially passionate about global hunger. But others felt that using food for art helps children develop an appreciation for it. They also felt it was a safer option than other materials, because young children like to put things in their mouth. Chocolate pudding as finger paint for toddlers seemed to be a favorite activity.

I could see both sides. Making fruit and vegetable prints with children is one of my all time favorite activities. It introduces our "fast food, French fries" kids to the beautiful designs found in natural foods. But when I worked with low income children in Head Start programs, I chose not to use food in this way. It just didn't feel right.

"Can I speak with you for a moment?" I turned. A woman who had been fairly quiet in the workshop was now standing behind me. She smiled. "I just wanted to share with you my thoughts about the food for art discussion." I nodded and sat down to listen.

"You see, it's not just low income kids who go hungry," she said. "I grew up in a middle class neighborhood. We had a nice house and nice cars, but we seldom had food. My mother was an alcoholic. She went grocery shopping on and off. It was often feast or famine. My dad worked a lot and wasn't around much. As a kid I remember standing in the kitchen, looking in a refrigerator that had nothing but butter, sour milk, and some moldy lettuce. That happened a lot. My sister and I lived off of crackers and what little we could find in the cupboard. Many nights we went to bed hungry. I remember, in first grade we made pasta necklaces. I brought mine home and tried to cook it."

She smiled weakly, "To this day, I find myself hoarding food. I am always afraid I will not have enough. My sister struggles with an eating disorder." She paused. "I just wanted to be sure that in your next workshop, you share this story with others. People need to know that this is not just an issue for low income families."

As I reflect back on her story and the discussion that day, the lesson learned is to teach children about the tremendous value food has in our lives. Regardless of how we use it, we must celebrate it and treat it with respect.

Lesia

FamilyShare...
Supporting your partners

Eating good food offers many ways to involve families in child care. Invite families to visit for lunch occasionally. You might also ask them to share a favorite family dish with the children. During holidays or special times children enjoy preparing food gifts to share with families.

Many providers are well known for their good cooking. Be prepared to have parents ask for recipes of their children's favorite dishes.

Share with families your "healthy eating practices" and encourage them to do the same at home. Post menus so they will know what their children are eating. Parents of infants will want to know about their child's eating patterns.

Experience Talks
Conversations with other providers

- **I always try to have a quiet activity before eating.** This helps children relax and settle down.

- **We always start and end every meal with a song or fingerplay.** This makes our meal feel more family like and teaches children to have good manners.

- **We go around the table and share "good news" as we eat.** Children talk about each other, their families, silly things they did, and fun things they want to do. This helps them develop language skills and polish the art of conversation.

- **We play soft music at snack and mealtimes.** This really helps make mealtimes more enjoyable. It also makes the transition to naptime easier.

- **Children sometimes have trouble with measuring spoons.** Bending the handle of metal measuring spoons or serving utensils helps children dip and scoop more easily.

- **Every Friday we set the table with a tablecloth and put flowers on the table.** In summer we use fresh flowers; in winter we use dried or silk flowers. Children look forward to this as a special occasion.

- **Each child makes his or her own placemat.** We use construction paper, markers, old wallpaper books, and recycled greeting cards. I cover each placemat with clear adhesive shelf paper to protect it.

- **I offer slightly frozen vegetables or chilled fruits to children who are teething.** These cool snacks seem to soothe young children. Orange slices are favorites.

- **I use happy, teachable moments to introduce new foods.** I make it a point never to introduce a new food to a child who is not feeling well or who is sleepy.

Children with disabilities

Contents

Where am I now?	358
Introduction	359
Important things you should know about disability laws	360
Good news! The Individuals with Disabilities Education Act (IDEA)	360
Heart of the Matter	361
General ideas to help children with disabilities	362
Specific ideas to help children	363
Signs of concern	367
Talking with parents about a concern	369
Heart of the Matter	372
FamilyShare	373
FamilyShare handout	374
Experience Talks	376

Children with disabilities—
Where am I now? What can I improve?

	Seldom 1	Sometimes 2	Often 3	Most Often 4
1. I recognize common signs of developmental delay or concerns.				
2. I know how to talk effectively with parents about a developmental concern.				
3. I know how to provide families with continued support as they seek to learn more about a disability.				
4. I understand how laws like the Americans with Disabilities Act (ADA) affect my program.				
5. I know how to find and contact Individuals with Disabilities Education Act (IDEA) services for young children.				
6. I work with families and consultants to support and implement an Individualized Family Service Plan (IFSP) and/or an Individualized Education Program (IEP).				
7. I know how to modify activities and play areas for children who have visual disabilities.				
8. I know how to modify activities and play areas for children who have hearing disabilities.				
9. I know how to modify activities and play areas for children who have mental disabilities.				
10. I know how to modify activities and play areas for children who have social-emotional disabilities.				
11. I know how to modify activities and play areas for children who have physical disabilities.				

Children with disabilities

Chapter 13

Occasionally you may be asked to care for a child with a disability. The disability may be already identified when the parents come to you, or it may be noticed after the child becomes a part of your program.

In many cases children with disabilities can be cared for easily in a regular child care setting. Family child care programs are well suited for this situation because they already maintain a flexible program to meet the needs of multi-age groups. For example, if a 4-year-old child with Down's Syndrome has the developmental skills of a 2-year-old, you probably would not have to make many changes in your program. Instead you would provide many of the same activities for this child as you would for other 2-year-olds in your program.

Children with disabilities are like all children. They need to be physically comfortable and to feel loved and secure. They also need opportunities to play and learn. Often, these children are not so different. They may need more time to learn and practice skills. They may need more praise and encouragement to gain the skills typical for their age group.

Everyone benefits. Children with disabilities benefit greatly from being with other children and from receiving consistent care from a caring adult over a period of years. Children without disabilities also benefit by learning how to assist, help, and respect a child who may have abilities different from their own.

Important things you should know about disability laws

It is illegal to charge parents more for the care of a disabled child or to discriminate against someone with a disability.

The Americans with Disabilities Act (ADA) requires reasonable modifications in policies, practices, and procedures in order to accommodate individuals with disabilities. A modification is not required if it would fundamentally alter the goods or services of a child care setting. Architectural barriers must be removed if "readily achievable." The term "readily achievable" means that it can be accomplished easily and carried out without much difficulty or expense. Auxiliary aids and services must be provided unless that creates an "undue burden." "Undue burden" means significant difficulty or expense.

So, for example, making minor changes to toys or equipment would probably not be an "undue burden," but hiring a full-time staff person for extra assistance would alter the basic structure of a family child care program, and would most likely be considered an "undue burden."

Every child is unique, with or without disabilities. Most likely you already make small changes every day to meet the needs and interests of your children without disabilities. Making small changes to meet the needs of children with disabilities is not much different. You may be pleasantly surprised to learn that such changes often benefit all the children in your program.

Good news! The Individuals with Disabilities Education Act (IDEA)

There are now services for children with disabilities that can provide screening and consultation. The Individuals with Disabilities Education Act (IDEA) is a law ensuring services to children with disabilities. Under this act, infants and toddlers with disabilities (birth-2) and their families may receive help through early intervention services in each state. These are often called IDEA part C services.

Watch your words

Choose your words carefully when you talk about children with disabilities. It is better to use the word disability than the word handicap. And in fact many people like to speak in terms of children with "different abilities" rather than "disabilities."

When you speak about a specific disability remember to say it in a way that you name or describe the disability rather than label the child.

Rather than say: "I have a Down's Syndrome child" say "I care for a child who has Down's Syndrome." The first example tends to make others think of the disability first, the second example seems to say that the disability is just one characteristic of the child.

Rather than say "I care for a deaf child" say "I care for a child who doesn't hear well." The second example is better because children typically have a range of hearing loss. Every child is unique and every disability impacts a child's life a little differently.

Teach children in your child care program how to speak respectfully as well.

Heart of the Matter

Peter was two years old and he had Down's Syndrome. I really didn't know what to expect when he came to my program. He was very little and petite—even for a toddler. I was fascinated to discover that in many ways he had better skills than the other 2-year-olds. For example, he easily could button his shirt and zip his pants. He was potty trained long before the other boys. He could use his fingers to do all kinds of things that most toddlers couldn't begin to do. Actually he was much less trouble than the other toddlers. I was amazed.

I learned that his mother had consulted a specialist when he was just a baby and worked hard to learn how to help him develop the skills he needed. I began to see just how much difference it could make if a child got help early on.

As time passed the other kids began to gradually move beyond his abilities. However, they never seemed to realize that he was not developing in the same ways they were. He was just Peter, their friend. They continued to think of him as a younger child. Because my child care program had children of different ages, Peter could grow and develop a little slower but at his own pace.

Lesia

Families may request an evaluation and assessment. This is free of charge. Qualified specialists know how to work with young children to discover if a child has a problem or is developing within normal ranges. If it is determined that a child (birth-36 months) is eligible for further assistance, parents will meet with a team of specialists to develop a written plan for providing early intervention services. This plan is called the *Individualized Family Service Plan*, or IFSP.

Children ages 3-21 receive IDEA part B services. For these children, an *Individualized Education Program* (IEP) is developed. An IEP is a written statement of an educational program designed to meet a child's individual needs. Every child who receives special education services must have an IEP. The IEP sets reasonable learning goals for a child and states the services the school district or other qualified specialists will provide for the child.

Family child care providers may be asked to serve on the team that creates the IFSP or IEP. Early intervention services for the child are supposed to occur in the child's natural setting whenever possible. This could mean that a specialist may come to your home to assist the child or could perhaps teach you skills that would help the child.

Families can locate early intervention services and assistance in their state by calling the National Dissemination Center for Children with Disabilities (NICHCY) at 1-800-695-0285 or by locating state resources at http://www.nichcy.org/states.htm or Spanish version http://www.nichcy.org/spanish.htm

General ideas to help children with disabilities

Children with disabilities usually will have some specific needs but the following are some general ways you can help.

Modify toys and equipment.
Simple changes often can be made to regular toys. For example, a child may have difficulty with stacking rings. Simplify the game by removing every other ring. For a child who has difficulty holding a bottle, cover the bottle with a cloth sock so little hands can grasp it better.

Plan together.
Parents, consultants, and caregivers need to set goals together. You should ask to be included in planning for the child so you can discuss activities, exercises, and support needed to reach goals. Your time with the child is very important. Goals should be simple and should match the abilities of the child. Always discuss your ideas and plans with the family. Together you can support the child to reach his/her full potential.

Make slight changes in your home.
Slight adjustments in your home may make the time that a child with special needs spends with you easier and more enjoyable for all. A quiet, private space for play may help an overactive child. A child with poor vision may benefit from an extra lamp in the play area. Removing a rug that slips will help a child who has trouble walking.

Model appropriate behaviors.
Children with disabilities are sometimes timid about playing with others. You can show them how to play with others by being a play partner yourself. For example, you might play a game or pretend to go shopping together. As the child becomes more comfortable, you can invite other children to join your play activity.

Teach specific words and skills that will show how to find a playmate and be a playmate.
Learning how to look directly at another child when speaking or to say "May I play?" are big steps for some children.

Teach non-disabled children how to talk and play with children who have a disability.
Talk to the children about what to do. For instance, a gentle touch on the shoulder of a child with a hearing impairment, or a direct look at him/her while talking are effective ways of getting the other child's attention.

Look for strengths as well as needs.
Avoid becoming too focused on a child's disability. Treat each child as a whole person. Provide activities that will support a child's strong points. Every child needs to feel successful and capable.

Consult with parents, health care professionals, and early childhood specialists.
Ask parents to sign a release so specialists can provide specific information and suggestions for working with a child who has disabilities. Do not be afraid to ask questions. Parents sometimes take it for granted that caregivers will know what to do.

Specific ideas to help children

The following suggestions will give you some ideas for how to help children with specific disabilities. Parents, health professionals, and consultants also can give you other ideas. Keep in mind that some children will have more than one disability. Each child is unique, so you will need to try different things to see what works best.

Visual Disabilities	What you can do.
Children who cannot see well are sometimes delayed in their physical and motor skills. Often they will not be able to locate or pick up small objects that have been dropped. They may spill things or bump into things. Helping children understand about space and size will further their development. Children who cannot see well often learn well through other senses, such as hearing and touching.	**Make it easy to move around.** ■ Arrange your house for safe and free movement. Keep doors and cabinets closed. ■ Place sound-making objects (clocks, wind chimes, radio) in different parts of the house to help children learn their way around. ■ Help children use textures throughout the house: tile, carpet, wood, glass windows, plastered walls, marble counter top, to locate different areas of the house. ■ Keep space organized so children can find things easily. ■ Establish specific areas for play activities and routines and try not to change them often. Help a child become familiar with your room arrangement. **Make it easier to see.** ■ Use good lighting to help children see better. ■ Provide toys and materials in contrasting colors. For example, it is easier to see objects in blue and yellow than objects in similar shades of red and orange. ■ Label items with larger letters and symbols. ■ Tape raised cardboard labels of toy symbols on toy shelves so children will know where to return toys during cleanup. ■ Use blocks that have a different color for each size. **Use words and speak out loud more.** ■ Read aloud stories that predict what will happen next. You also may wish to choose stories that offer interesting descriptions of actions or objects. ■ Use electronic "talking books" or books recorded on tape or CD. ■ Expand the child's learning by talking him or her through an activity. Use descriptive words such as long, short, over, under, big, and little. Whenever possible, provide real experiences that show these important ideas. For example, you might offer the child two balls and say, "The ball in your hand is big. Feel how big it is. But the ball in my hand is small. Would you like to touch it?" **Teach other children to:** ■ Call the child with visual disabilities by name to get his or her attention. ■ Use more words to describe what they want. For example, instead of saying "Come over here to play." They should say, "Come over to the playhouse and play dolls with Maddie and me."

| **Visual Disabilities** | **What you can do.** |

- Say the names of objects such as phone, hat, or car rather than this, it, or that.
- Describe their art activities or block buildings in words. For example, "This bridge is three blocks wide."

Encourage learning through touch.
- Use sand and water play, collages, play dough, and finger painting as everyday learning activities.
- Look for toys and books with raised numerals, letters, or designs that children can touch and explore.
- Encourage children to build with blocks horizontally. Children can feel shapes and lay blocks end-to-end or in different patterns without the frustration of falling blocks.
- Follow up read-aloud stories with concrete experiences. For example, after reading *The Three Little Pigs*, encourage children to feel the difference between straw, sticks, and bricks.
- Cut out symbols, shapes, letters, and numbers from sandpaper or cardboard. Guide fingers over these shapes as you discuss them.
- Show children how to make rubbings by coloring over an interesting texture.

| **Hearing Disabilities** | **What you can do.** |

Children who cannot hear well need opportunities to listen and learn how to speak. Some children may be able to hear a little and others may not be able to hear at all.

Children can develop important language skills with practice. Provide activities that encourage communication and language development.

Balance these with activities that require very little verbal interaction. Art activities and block play offer good opportunities for satisfying play without heavy demands on language or communication.

Cut down on background noise.
- Turn off the radio, dishwasher, and TV when you are doing an activity.
- Use carpets, rugs, drapes, and pillows to absorb excess sound.

Provide visual cues.
- Make eye contact before you start to speak. A gentle tap on the shoulder usually will get a child's attention.
- Talk in a normal voice. Use gestures and facial expressions to clarify your message.
- Label shelves with a picture of toys to make cleanup easier.
- Learn basic sign language and teach it to all the children.
- Use pictures to show hand washing steps or steps of a recipe during cooking activities.

Adapt learning activities.
- Provide earphones or set up a special area where a tape recorder can be played at a higher volume.
- Teach children in your program to use gestures and sign language.
- Encourage a child who doesn't hear well to talk about what he or she is doing. Use who, what, where, why, or how questions.
- Use stories, songs, and fingerplays to increase language skills. Repeat favorite rhymes and songs to encourage confidence and improve learning.

Mental Disabilities	What you can do.
Children with mental disabilities generally will go through typical developmental stages, but sometimes at a much slower rate. Taking the time to identify what problems a child comes across during play will give you many ideas for how to adapt toys and learning activities.	**Keep things simple.** - Choose activities that match the child's mental age and abilities. - Break activities into small steps. - Give one instruction at a time. - Use the same words when giving each instruction. - Practice activities over and over. - Shorten activities to match the child's attention span. **Demonstrate how to do things.** - Show and tell a child how to do something by guiding hands and body through the motions of an activity. - Provide opportunities to play near a child who is doing a similar activity. This can give the child with mental disabilities some ideas on how to use and explore the same materials. **Adapt learning activities.** - Make sure there are obvious differences in size, shape, and color when sorting or classifying objects. Subtle differences between red and maroon or circles and ovals can be confusing. - Limit the number of art materials or toys to avoid overwhelming the child with choices. - Use materials such as play dough or blocks that can be used by children of all ages. - Announce ahead of time when an activity is about to change or end. - Give simple tasks or instructions to make moving to the next activity easier.
Social and Emotional Disabilities	**What you can do.**
Children with behavioral disabilities often display one of three types of extreme behavior: withdrawal, aggression, or excessive activity. Each type of behavior may require a different type of adult support. Children with behavioral challenges need consistent daily schedules and dependable interactions with others.	**Provide adult guidance and support.** - Provide regular schedules and routines. - Invite a withdrawn child to join others in an activity by watching others. As the child becomes more comfortable, demonstrate how to play with materials or toys. Encourage the child to play along with you. - Watch for signs of aggressive behavior and intervene quickly. - Teach problem-solving skills. - Help children plan or organize an activity. For example, if a child wants to play "fire fighter," you might make suggestions that can help him or her organize props and invite other children to play. - Provide a cozy, quiet space for times when a child needs a break from other children or activities.

Social and Emotional Disabilities	What you can do.
Children often have difficulty moving from one activity to another.	**Adapt activities.** ■ Provide activities that will help the child feel capable. Avoid activities that can be done only a certain way. ■ Watch for periods when children are more calm and in control. Use these times to present a new activity. ■ Keep stories and group activities short to match attention spans. Seat the child near you and away from distractions such as a nearby toy shelf. ■ Avoid giving children too many toys or activities to choose from. ■ A squeezable, figet toy may help during storytime. **Guide transitions.** ■ Announce cleanup time and other transitions ahead of time. ■ Assign a specific task to the child during the transition. For example, rather than ask a child to clean up, ask him or her to pick up the "red" toys.
Physical Disabilities	**What you can do.**
The type and amount of assistance and support needed by children with physical disabilities will vary for each child. Make your plans based on input from the parents, the consultants, and the child. Playmates are usually eager to assist children with disabilities. While you need to applaud and encourage helping behaviors, a child with physical disabilities also needs encouragement to do as much as possible on his or her own. This may mean that tasks and chores could take a little more time, but self confidence and independence are fostered by encouragement and patience.	**Make it easy to move around in play areas.** ■ Provide heavy, stable furniture and equipment that are not easily knocked over. ■ Remove rugs that can be tripped over or tape them down. ■ Arrange furniture and equipment to allow for a wide aisle. ■ Provide a safe place for walkers, crutches, or canes so other children do not trip over them. ■ Work with parents to find comfortable ways for a child to sit. A corner with two walls for support, a chair with a seat belt, or a wheel chair with a large tray across the arms are three possibilities. ■ Make objects more steady. For instance, tape paper, mixing bowls, or wood blocks to the table or floor so they remain in place as the child paints, draws, stirs, or hammers. **Adapt learning activities.** ■ Provide objects that can be used for grasping, holding, transferring, and releasing. Objects should be age appropriate. For example, a bean bag made from dinosaur fabric is much more appropriate for a 5-year-old than a rattle or a baby toy. ■ Provide materials of different textures such as play dough, fabric swatches, ribbon, corrugated cardboard, and sandpaper to encourage the sense of touch. ■ Plan activities to encourage exercise and movement of all body parts. Work with parents and specialists to give special exercises for the child depending on his or her needs. ■ Add tabs to books for turning pages. ■ Tape foam or place tape on crayons and markers to make them easier to grip. ■ Keep items contained. Roll a ball inside a hoola-hoop placed on the floor. Play with blocks on a cookie sheet or a tray with raised edges.

Signs of concern

Because you work with children of all ages and are familiar with typical ages and stages, you are in a unique position to notice if a child does not seem to be developing normally. If you think a child may have a developmental delay, it is very important to discuss it with the parent right away.

Children develop very quickly. If there is a serious concern, it is best not to take a "wait and see" approach. Getting professional help early for children can make a tremendous difference in their quality of life and later development.

Watch for some of the following signs that may point to a developmental problem. Sometimes you may see only a few signs. In other cases you may see many more. Regardless, it is always best to encourage parents to have things checked out if there is a concern.

The resource information included on the CD can help you locate Web sites with more detailed lists of warning signs and can help families locate assistance for evaluation and assessment.

Visual Disabilities	Signs of concern
	■ sometimes or always crosses one or both eyes ■ has eyes that won't focus ■ avoids bright lights ■ blinks or rubs eyes a lot ■ stumbles or falls a great deal, trips over small objects ■ covers one eye ■ tilts head to side or to front ■ squints or frowns a great deal ■ complains of dizziness, headaches, or nausea after doing intense work ■ is unable to locate and pick up small objects that have been dropped ■ may turn face away when being talked to; this may not mean inattentiveness, but rather the child may have better peripheral (side) vision ■ prefers contrasting colors or large pictures ■ holds books or objects very close to face ■ has unintended spills or knocks things over frequently (e.g., food, toys)
Hearing Disabilities	**Signs of concern**
	■ does not respond when spoken to ■ does not startle at loud noise ■ does not turn to sound ■ does not wake up in response to sound ■ may respond to very loud sounds, but not softer normal sounds ■ coos or gurgles, but does not progress to saying words ■ does not talk very much or at all ■ talks, but is impossible to understand

Hearing Disabilities	Signs of concern
	- leaves out many sounds when talking - talks in a monotone voice - seems unable to follow verbal directions; often says "huh" or "what"—requires repetition - interrupts conversations - seems unaware that others are talking - may hold head so that one ear is turned toward speaker - alert and attentive only to things that can be seen
Mental Disabilities	**Signs of concern**
	- has short attention span - is easily distracted - has difficulty with transitions - prefers to play with younger children - is afraid of trying new things - has difficulty in problem-solving - does not remember things well - may not be able to transfer learning to a new situation - speaks and uses language like a much younger child
Social and Emotional Disabilities	**Signs of concern**
	- doesn't smile, laugh, or make happy faces - does not babble or make baby noises, or stops making such noises - doesn't point, reach or wave by 12 months - doesn't speak by 16 months - stops or refuses to speak at any age - withdraws or stays quiet and passive most of the time - regresses to babyish behavior whenever stress occurs - cries a great deal, seems depressed and unhappy, laughs seldom - shows extreme fear and anxiety - doesn't seem to recognize basic feelings of happiness, sadness, anger, or fear - always reacts in the same way, such as crying or hitting - may not want to be touched - eats non food items - shows excessive activity, restlessness, or inability to stick with something - shows agitation such as screaming or pacing - uses aggressive behavior to deal with most situations - does repetitive, self stimulating acts (like rocking back and forth, etc.) - injures self often with head banging, self biting, eye poking, or pulling own hair

Physical Disabilities	Signs of concern
	■ has unusually tight muscle tone (resists sitting up or bending knees) ■ has unusually loose muscle tone (cannot hold head up after 3 months) ■ does not reach for toys ■ has difficulty releasing objects voluntarily ■ has poorly developed hand or finger coordination ■ does not reach across the body during play ■ reaches only with one hand, even when feeding self ■ doesn't put hands out to catch self if falling ■ has difficulty picking up small objects ■ stumbles and trips frequently ■ has poor balance

Talking with parents about a concern

Sharing a concern about a child's development with a parent is never easy. Yet it is important to do—and the earlier the better. Identifying a disability and getting help right away can make a real difference for both child and family.

If a parent comes to you with a concern, listen respectfully. Take a few days to watch the child and see if you can observe the same things.

If you need to bring up a concern with a parent, show the same respect. Allow them some time to see if they can observe the same things you are sharing with them.

Here are some suggestions:

Choose a time and place where you can talk alone. Share your thoughts in person; this is not a conversation to have on the phone. If you are still responsible for children during this time, ask another adult to supervise the children.

Make sure both you and parents have enough time to talk. This should not be done in a hurry as a parent is rushing out the door to work. You may want to schedule this conversation ahead of time.

You might say, *"Mary, I often have regular chats throughout the year with parents to get to know them better, talk about how their children are adjusting to child care or just general things we need to touch base on. It's time to schedule a chat with you. I wonder if you would have time this week to drop by in the afternoon?"*

Be prepared for strong emotions.
Parents often sense there may be a problem, but have been afraid to talk about it. Often they may not know how to put their concerns into words. Sometimes they are not familiar with normal ages and stages and are unsure about things they may have noticed. This is especially true for young parents who may not have other children.

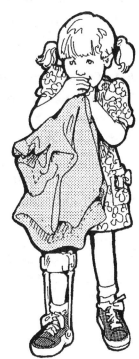

HFCCH Chapter 13 — Children with disabilities

Parents also may be worried that if there is something wrong, you will no longer want to provide child care for their child.

Be caring, supportive, and respectful. Some parents may be relieved to visit with you, others may be defensive or scared. Showing warmth and respect will help parents trust and listen to what you have to share.

Begin by saying something positive about the child. You might point out several things you really like about the child—their smile, their curiosity, their love of puzzles. Or you might mention something positive the child did recently such as helping a friend or learning a song.

Say something positive about the child's relationship with the parent. When things go wrong, parents sometimes tend to blame themselves. It helps to reassure them that they are good parents.

You might say, *"Mary, Sara seems to have a real interest in puzzles. She is so skilled at them. Tell me have you worked with her on this? ... I can tell that you seem to have a real interest in helping Sara grow and develop."*

Ask if the parents have concerns or questions about how their child seems to be developing. Quietly and respectfully ask them to share what they have noticed. Who, what, when, where, and how questions will help you gather more information and help parents focus on the issue.

You might say, *"I wonder if you have had any concerns about Jason being able to understand what you say?"* Or *"Have you noticed if Sara seems to be having a hard time hearing loud noises or people talking? Tell me what you have noticed."* You might also say, *"How long has this been happening? When does this seem to happen? What happens next? Has anyone else noticed this? Where does this seem to happen most?"*

Share your own observations and concerns. Do this only after the parent has had a chance to talk. Share the Ages and Stages information in this book or other developmental checklists so parents will have something to look at. If it makes you feel more comfortable, practice what you will say beforehand.

Choose your words carefully. Rather than say, *"I think Sara might be deaf,"* give specific examples and describe what you have seen. You might say, *"I noticed the other day a gust of wind blew the door shut. It made a loud bang and scared all of us, but Sara didn't even flinch. And last week, I kept calling her to come to the lunch table and she didn't seem to hear me."*

Avoid using labels or technical terms. Remember you are not trying to present yourself as an expert. It is not your job to identify the specific disability. It is a very scary thing for parents to hear that someone may think their child has a disability. Keep it simple. Use words that describe only what you have seen.

You might say, *"I've noticed that Sara doesn't seem to hear loud sounds"* or *"Jason seems to bump into things a lot as if he has trouble seeing,"* or *"I miss hearing Megan babble and smile like she did when she was a baby."*

Keep your eye on the goal. Your goal is to encourage the parents to get a professional evaluation for their child so that any concerns can be checked out.

You might say, *"It never hurts to check things out. Think about how relieved you will be to find out for sure. And if it does turn out that there is a problem, getting help now will make a big difference."*

Stress the importance of checking things out right away. It is very common for parents to need a few days to think about and understand what you have shared. They often feel doubtful, confused, and scared. If they seem unable to take action, reassure them of your support. Remind parents that if there is a problem, getting help early can keep things from getting worse. Early help can make a big difference for a child's later development.

Be ready to offer information and resources. Be prepared to guide the parent through the next steps to get an evaluation or help for the child. The first step usually is to have the child's doctor assess the situation. Your local school system should also be able to direct you to local services available to evaluate young children for developmental delays. Resource information on the accompanying CD can help you locate state and local services. Have contact information and Web site information on hand. If a parent does not have access to the Internet, print off information and have it ready to share.

Continue your support. When parents find out that their child has a disability, they often are in shock. They often go through a period of grieving. They may become depressed or angry. The range of emotions they experience may make it hard for them to complete everyday tasks.

It is possible they may even consider removing the child from your care because they don't want to face the issue. Sometimes this happens. Continue to be understanding, listen, and offer help.

Trust yourself. As someone who cares for children every day you are in a unique position to notice when a child may be experiencing problems. Sharing your concerns respectfully with parents shows that you really care about their child. Even if parents seem to resist your efforts at first, they will most likely be grateful later for your concern.

Heart of the Matter

"I need to talk to you about something." Brent's mother pulled me aside. "Have you noticed anything wrong with Brent? Does he play with the other kids okay? I'm worried that he's not talking enough."

It was late in the day. I was trying to get everybody out the door and on their way home. I listened absentmindedly to her questions as I picked up a bunch of toys left on the floor. I reflected for a moment. It was true that Brent was quiet and spent most of his time watching the others kids play. But I told myself that this was not unusual for a child that had just turned three. Many 3-year-olds play alongside other children. They learn a lot by watching. It takes time for them to learn the back-and-forth type of play that 4- and 5-year-olds have. Brent didn't talk a lot, but I didn't see that as too unusual either. He had always been quiet. I hurriedly reassured her that he was fine and wondered why she seemed so worked up over this.

Several mornings later she came to the door and was shaking with emotion. She shared that she had taken Brent for a screening test and discovered he had a great deal of hearing loss. She was angry that I had not recognized this problem. And she was furious that I had dismissed her concerns earlier. She told me she had decided to withdraw both Brent and his older sister from my child care program.

I was stunned. This was my first experience with a child who had hearing loss. I felt unsure of myself. Had I just been too busy to see that something was wrong? I had grown very fond of both children and hated to lose them, but Brent's mother was determined to take her children elsewhere. She was so very angry.

Looking back, I learned several things from this experience. The first was that I needed to educate myself about the warning signs for disabilities. I didn't know the first thing about hearing loss, and probably never will know a great deal, but I should have been able to notice a few signs. The second was that I should never dismiss a parent's concern or question about his or her child. I resolved that next time I would be more respectful.

I missed Brent and his sister Lara and was deeply sorry to lose them.

Lesia

FamilyShare...

Supporting your partners

Reaching out for help can be overwhelming for parents. Some professionals they meet will be very helpful, but others will not be. Many programs and services have waiting lists, so patience and persistence may be needed before families can get answers. Your guidance and support can make a big difference.

The FamilyShare handout on the next two pages gives useful tips for parents. Photocopy this or print off the handout from your handbook CD and share it with parents.

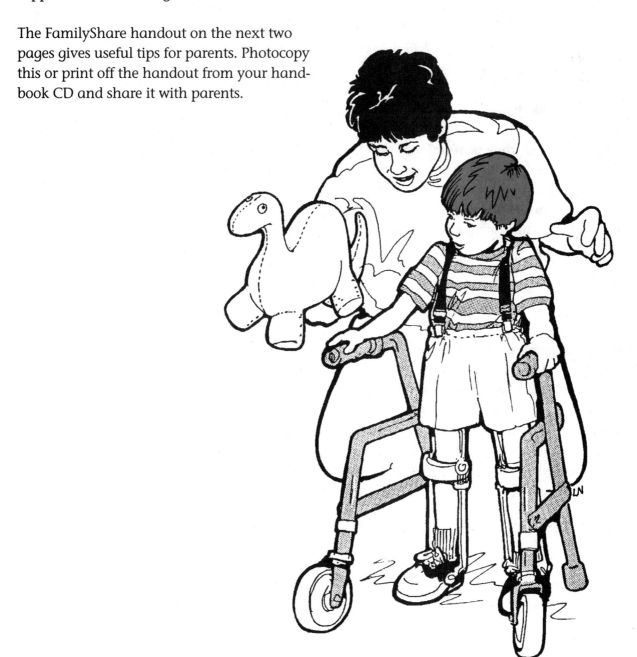

HFCCH Chapter 13 — Children with disabilities   373

\# FamilyShare...

"I have a serious concern about how my child is developing. What do I do now?"

If you have a concern, it is important to get it checked-out right away. If things turn out to be okay, then you can sigh with relief. You will know that you did the right thing as a parent.

But if there is a problem, getting help early may keep things from getting worse and can make a huge difference for both you and your child.

There are services to provide help for families whose children may be experiencing problems with their development. These services can begin as early as the birth of your child.

The following suggestions may be helpful to you.

1. **Visit your health care professional and be specific about your concerns.**
   Write down what you have noticed. Include who, what, when, and where information such as when it started, how often it seems to happen, and where it happens. Something that happens once is usually no big deal, but something that happens often and has been going on for a while is cause for concern.

   - "My child does not respond to loud sounds."
   - "She doesn't smile or look at me anymore."
   - "He bumps into things all the time and seems to have trouble seeing."

2. **Insist on a developmental screening or evaluation.**
   If your health care professional can't or does not want to conduct a screening, ask for a referral to a professional who can and will do one. During the last few years, many professionals have been trained to recognize and provide services to children with disabilities beginning at birth. Families can request a free evaluation and assessment from a qualified special education consultant. There are also parent support groups in every state that can help answer some of your questions.

3. **Don't be shy—ask lots of questions.**
   If you don't understand an explanation ask for it to be explained again. If the explanation is not clear, continue to ask. Ask for words and information to be put in writing. Be sure you fully understand what the results mean and what needs to happen next. You might say,

   - *"I am feeling overwhelmed right now and need you to repeat what you just said so I can clearly understand it."*
   - *"Can you give me a little more detail?"*
   - *"Sorry, but I am not familiar with that word, could you write it down?"*
   - *"I would like to read more about this. Please give me a handout or a Web site for more information."*

   Families can locate early intervention services and assistance in their state by calling the National Dissemination Center for Children with Disabilities (NICHCY) at 1-800-695-0285 or by locating state resources at http://www.nichcy.org/states.htm or Spanish version at http://www.nichcy.org/spanish.htm

4. **Keep moving forward.**
   If a referral for help is made, be sure you follow through with it. It is normal to be in shock, but don't allow yourself to get stuck. If you meet professionals who are not helpful, find someone else who will help you.

5. **Be an advocate for your child.**
   Insist on the best possible services for your child. There are laws in place to ensure that you get the help you need. Your child is depending on you.

6. **Find a support group.**
   A local parent support group or an online support group can be a tremendous help to parents. It is okay to just listen. You are not alone. Other parents can suggest services and professionals that have been helpful and give tips for how to deal with problems.

7. **Stay involved with your child.**
   Sometimes parents pull away from a child with a disability. It just seems too much to handle. While it is true that your relationship with your child will change as you learn new ways to deal with the disability, your child is still your child and will continue to need your love, attention, and affection.

Experience Talks
Conversations with other providers

■ **The first time I cared for a child with a disability, I was very nervous.** But it worked out just fine. I had to make a few changes, but honestly I forgot that she had a disability much of the time. She was just Valerie—one of the kids.

■ **I have cared for several children with disabilities.** Sometimes it has worked well and other times it has not. Each child and each situation is different. The most challenging for me was caring for a child with a behavioral disability. I found that caring for a child with a physical disability was easier for me personally.

■ **The hardest situation for me was when I began to suspect that one of my child care kids had a hearing problem.** I had to discuss it with his parents and they just didn't want to accept that there might be a problem. After we worked through that and they got help, everything was much easier. The specialist they worked with also gave me a lot of tips and suggestions—so it has been a team effort.

■ **Over the last 10 years, I have cared for two different children with Down's Syndrome** and have just loved it. Both were just delightful, happy kids and brought real joy to my child care home. Both of them loved to sing. I am not very musical, but frankly it didn't matter. We danced and sang to our hearts' content. Nobody cared if we sang off key.

■ **Sometimes it makes parents nervous to enroll their child in a child care program that has a child with a disability.** I just try to be very matter-of-fact and give them information. I stress that the child with the disability is much more like the other kids than she is different. I encourage them to spend a little time with us before making their decision.

■ **I think parents respect me more professionally because I care for a child with a disability.** They recognize that I have had to learn some special skills to do what I do. I think they are impressed that I have made the effort and understand that I would do the same for their child.

■ **My situation is a bit different, because the child with the disability is my own child.** I needed to stay home with my son and providing care to other people's children seemed to be the answer to having a career too. I only care for three other children, because I wanted to make sure I could give everyone the attention they needed. It has worked out well, because the child care children have been like brothers and sisters. I think they also have benefited from growing up with a child who has a disability.

■ **Sometimes life brings you real surprises. I never imagined I would care for a child with a disability.** But I did and it was an experience I wouldn't trade the world for. It was not always easy but it gave me a very different view about life. Watching this child grow and develop helped me come to terms with my own abilities and shortcomings.

Child abuse and neglect

Contents

Where am I now?	378
Introduction	379
Who abuses or neglects children?	379
Recognizing child abuse	380
Reporting child abuse or neglect	387
Tips to help victims of abuse and neglect	392
FamilyShare	394
Heart of the Matter	395
Experience Talks	396

Child abuse and neglect—
Where am I now? What can I improve?

	Seldom 1	Sometimes 2	Often 3	Most Often 4
1. I can identify common signs of physical abuse.				
2. I can identify common signs of emotional abuse.				
3. I can identify common signs of sexual abuse.				
4. I can identify common signs of neglect.				
5. I understand how to talk with children about suspected abuse.				
6. I understand my responsibility as a mandatory reporter to report suspected abuse or neglect.				
7. I know how to report child abuse or neglect.				
8. I know how to help lower the stress level in children during the time they are in my program.				
9. I share information with families about stress management and model appropriate ways to guide young children's behavior.				

Child abuse and neglect

Every year thousands of children suffer from child abuse and neglect. As someone who works every day with young children and families, you are in a position to offer help and support. Registered or licensed early childhood professionals are required by law to report abuse. As a professional, you can join others to advocate for increased help and support for young children.

Who abuses or neglects children?

Abusers of children can be parents, siblings, friends, relatives, or adults who work with children. People who abuse children can be rich or poor. They can be uneducated or well-educated. About one-third of abusers have been abused as children themselves. But the majority of abused children do not grow up to be abusive parents, especially if they did not experience long-term abuse.

There is a difference between short-term abuse and long-term chronic abuse. Abuse that happens once or only a few times often is related to stressful events. Long-term abuse and sexual abuse of children are the result of much more complex problems and are much harder to understand.

Unrealistic expectations. Often adults who abuse children do not understand normal child development. They may expect very young children to be quiet or to sit still for long periods of time. They may not understand that young children need naps and to eat at regular times. They may be frustrated because babies cry a lot. A large number of child abuse cases occur with children under the age of two.

Stress and crisis. Parents of infants and toddlers rarely get enough sleep. Young parents usually have limited income. They struggle with the high costs of diapers, child care, and medical expenses. If stress builds, they may find themselves less patient and may turn in frustration against their children. Children with disabilities are especially at risk because they place extra demands on parents and caregivers.

Lack of supervision. Often children are placed in unsafe situations with little or no adult supervision. Basic needs for food or shelter can be neglected. Children are also at risk for abuse from siblings.

Substance abuse and family violence. Families who struggle with drugs or alcohol often neglect children. Children may be left unsupervised, go hungry, or may be exposed to drugs or alcohol themselves. Violence in the home often places children in danger as well. Even if children are not physically harmed, they can suffer a great deal from watching a loved one harmed.

Both the abuser and the abused child need help. In most cases, people who are abusive or neglectful truly love their children. They simply get caught up in a cycle of frustration and violence and lose control. They often don't know how to change their behavior.

Recognizing child abuse

The first step in helping abused or neglected children is learning to recognize the signs or symptoms. The presence of a single sign does not prove child abuse is occurring in a family; however, when these signs appear repeatedly or in combination you should take a closer look at the situation and consider the possibility of child abuse.

The following are some signs often associated with particular types of child abuse and neglect: physical abuse, neglect, sexual abuse, and emotional abuse. It is important to note, however, that these types of abuse are more typically found in combination than alone. A physically abused child, for example, often is emotionally abused as well, and a sexually abused child also may be neglected.

Signs of physical abuse*

Consider the possibility of physical abuse when . . . .

the child:	the parent or adult caregiver:
■ Has unexplained burns, bites, bruises, broken bones, or black eyes. ■ Has fading bruises or other marks noticeable after an absence. ■ Seems frightened of the parents and protests or cries when it is time to go home. ■ Shrinks at the approach of adults. ■ Reports injury by parent or another adult caregiver.	■ Offers conflicting, unconvincing, or no explanation for child's injury. ■ Describes the child as "evil," or in some other very negative way. ■ Uses harsh physical discipline with the child. ■ May have a history of abuse as a child.

* This information was adapted, with permission, from *Child Welfare Information Gateway*, www.childwelfare.gov/can/identifying and *Recognizing Child Abuse: What Parents Should Know*. Prevent Child Abuse America © 2003, www.preventchildabuse.org

Physical abuse**

Things you should know

Physical abuse injuries are often the result of harsh or inappropriate discipline. Abuse may include shaking, throwing, or striking a child. More severe examples might include burns, bites, pokes, cuts, welts, bone fractures or twisted limbs, or injury to internal organs and brain tissue.

Young children frequently fall down and bump into things. Such accidents may result in injuries to elbows, chins, noses, foreheads and other bony areas. However, bruises and marks on the soft tissue of the face, back, neck, buttocks, upper arms, thighs, ankles, backs of legs or genitals are likely to be caused by physical abuse. Another sign to look for is bruises at various stages of healing, as they indicate more than one incident.

The most common cause of death related to child abuse is head injury or shaken baby syndrome (SBS). This often happens when a frustrated parent or adult shakes a crying baby. Infants have large heavy heads and weak neck muscles. When an infant is shaken, the movement bounces the brain back and forth within the skull, rupturing and tearing blood vessels, nerves, and brain tissue.

Most victims are less than a year old, and about 50 percent die. Symptoms of shaken baby syndrome include extreme irritability, lethargy, poor sucking or swallowing, breathing problems, seizures, vomiting, unequal pupil size, pale or bluish skin, inability to lift the head, and inability to focus the eyes or track movement.

Children who survive often have permanent damage including blindness, hearing loss, seizures, developmental delays, speech and learning difficulties, and paralysis.

Changing diapers or helping children go to the toilet may reveal bruises or burns that are normally covered by clothing. Abusive parents are consciously or unconsciously aware that the signs of their abuse need to be concealed, and tend to dress their children in long sleeves or long pants.

Injuries to the abdomen or the head often go undetected unless there are internal injuries. Injuries to the abdomen can cause swelling, tenderness, and vomiting. Injuries to the head may cause swelling, dizziness, blackouts, retinal detachment, and even death. In particular, black eyes in both eyes at the same time could be a sign of bleeding in the brain.

** Adapted with permission from: Koralek, Derry (1992). "Caregivers for Young Children: Preventing and Responding to Child Maltreatment" User Manual Series: National Center on Child Abuse and Neglect. U.S. Department of Health and Human Services Administration on Children Youth and Families.

Behavioral signs of physical abuse—

In addition to the physical signs of abuse, the child might also exhibit behavioral signs. Some examples include:

"Jackie" (3 years old) runs to get her blanket whenever she hears another child crying. She clutches her blanket and rocks back and forth saying, "No hitting, no hitting."

"Daniel" (2 1/2 years old) usually is picked up by his mother. When his father comes to get him, he screams and hides behind his care provider's legs. Earlier that day his provider overheard him playing with dolls and saying, "I told you no wet pants. Now I beat your butt."

"Peter" (3 1/2 years old), who had been a very affectionate child, resists his caregiver's offers to tuck him in at naptime or refuses to sit in her lap to hear a story.

"Kathy" (4 years old) causes havoc all morning by repeatedly grabbing toys from the other children. She spends the afternoon in the book corner by herself, and keeps stroking her blanket.

Six-month-old "Miguel" lies quietly in his crib when he wakes up. He looks around the room, but does not cry or attempt to get his caregiver's attention.

Signs of neglect*

Consider the possibility of neglect when . . .

the child:	the parent or adult caregiver:
■ Is frequently absent from child care or school.	■ Appears to be indifferent to provide care.
■ Begs or steals food or money.	■ Seems uninterested or depressed.
■ Lacks needed medical or dental care, immunizations, or glasses.	■ Behaves irrationally or in a bizarre manner.
■ Is consistently dirty and has severe body odor.	■ Is abusing alcohol or other drugs.
■ Lacks sufficient clothing for the weather.	
■ Abuses alcohol or other drugs.	
■ Says there is no one at home to provide care.	

* This information was adapted, with permission, from *Child Welfare Information Gateway*, www.childwelfare.gov/can/identifying and *Recognizing Child Abuse: What Parents Should Know*. Prevent Child Abuse America © 2003, www.preventchildabuse.org

Child neglect**

Things you should know

Child neglect is a failure to provide for children's basic needs. Neglect can be physical (hunger or inadequate clothing in cold weather), medical (refusal to seek health care when a child clearly needs medical attention), educational (failure to enroll a child of school age), or emotional (chronic or extreme spouse abuse in the child's presence).

Neglect tends to be on-going and chronic. Severe neglect often results in death, particularly in the case of very young children. Look for patterns when you suspect neglect. Do the signs of neglect occur rarely or frequently? Are they chronic (occurring almost every day), periodic (happening after weekends, vacations, or absences), or episodic (seen twice during a specific event).

Behavioral signs of neglect—

Five-year-old "Andrea" tells her provider that she is tired that morning because her 6-month-old brother, Max, woke her up. She says, "My mommy wasn't home yet, so I made Max a bottle and gave it to him. Then he finally went back to sleep."

"Geraldine" (4 years old) tells her caregiver that she is very hungry because she didn't have any breakfast. When asked why she didn't eat, Geraldine says that her father took her breakfast away from her because she spilled a glass of milk on the floor.

"David" (4 months old) arrives at his family child care home with a severe diaper rash. The family child care provider lets his mother know about the rash and asks for permission to use some ointment that will heal David's skin and protect it from further irritation. The mother says, "If you've got to put that greasy stuff on, go ahead." The provider uses the ointment all week and the rash goes away. She gives the mother the tube to take home and use over the weekend. On Monday morning David arrives with the rash again. This pattern is repeated over a 4-week period.

** Adapted with permission from: Koralek, Derry (1992). "Caregivers for Young Children: Preventing and Responding to Child Maltreatment" User Manual Series: National Center on Child Abuse and Neglect. U.S. Department of Health and Human Services Administration on Children Youth and Families.

Signs of sexual abuse*

Consider the possibility of sexual abuse when . . .

the child:	the parent or adult caregiver:
■ Has difficulty walking or sitting. ■ Suddenly refuses to participate in physical activities. ■ Reports nightmares or bed wetting. ■ Experiences a sudden change in appetite. ■ Demonstrates bizarre, sophisticated, or unusual sexual knowledge or behavior. ■ Becomes pregnant or contracts a venereal disease, particularly if under age 14. ■ Runs away. ■ Reports sexual abuse by a parent or another adult caregiver.	■ Is unduly protective of the child or severely limits the child's contact with other children, especially of the opposite sex. ■ Is secretive and isolated. ■ Is jealous or controlling with family members.

* This information was adapted, with permission, from *Child Welfare Information Gateway*, www.childwelfare.gov/can/identifying and *Recognizing Child Abuse: What Parents Should Know*. Prevent Child Abuse America © 2003, www.preventchildabuse.org

Sexual abuse**
Things you should know

Sexual abuse includes a wide range of behavior: fondling a child's genitals, intercourse, rape, sodomy, exhibitionism, and commercial exploitation through prostitution or pornography. Sexual abuse may begin with inappropriate touching (fondling) and progress to more intensive or traumatic forms of sexual abuse (intercourse, rape).

Sexual abuse is often a secret. Sometimes children report sexual abuse immediately after the incident. At other times, the abuse goes on for months or even years before the child reports it or before it is discovered by someone else.

Children often do not report because they are afraid. Children do not usually report the abuse because of threats by the perpetrator to harm the child or the child's parent. In some cases, perpetrators tell children they will be harmed by monsters or other creatures that young children are typically afraid of. The abuser often knows how to manipulate children and promises them gifts of attention in exchange for playing sex games.

The physical signs of sexual abuse include some that a provider might notice while caring for young children. For example, while helping the child use the bathroom, a caregiver may notice a child's torn, stained, or bloody underclothing or bruises or bleeding in the child's external genitalia, vaginal, or anal area. If a child says that it hurts to walk or sit, or if he or she complains of pain or itching in

** Adapted with permission from: Koralek, Derry (1992). "Caregivers for Young Children: Preventing and Responding to Child Maltreatment" User Manual Series: National Center on Child Abuse and Neglect. U.S. Department of Health and Human Services Administration on Children Youth and Families.

the genital area, a caregiver should take note and watch to see if it is a recurring condition.

Young children who have been sexually abused also may exhibit behavioral signs of the abuse. They may show excessive curiosity about sexual activities or touch the breasts and genitals of adults.

Some children who have been sexually abused are afraid of specific places, such as the bathroom or a bed. Sexually abused children also may act out their abuse using dolls or talking with other children about sexual acts. Such premature sexual knowledge may be a sign that they have been exposed to sexual activity.

There is, however, a great deal of controversy regarding the use of dolls, particularly anatomically correct ones, and whether demonstrations of interest in genitalia by young children should be construed as an indication of sexual abuse. Therefore, caregivers should not encourage a child to demonstrate what might have happened to them using dolls unless they have received adequate training to conduct such assessments.

Behavioral signs of sexual abuse—

Five-year-old "Marci" displays precocious sexual behavior. Her provider often observes her masturbating when she is off by herself. One afternoon, her caregiver heard her asking one of the boys if he would show her his penis. On another occasion, the provider saw her laying the dolls on top of each other. Marci whispered to one of the dolls, "I promise not to hurt you."

A provider is helping "Jason" (age 4) get to sleep at naptime. For several weeks, Jason has been having a hard time settling down. When he does fall asleep, he sometimes wakes up crying about monsters. Today, he turns to his caregiver and says, "I've got a secret, but I can't tell you what it is."

"Nancy" (3 1/2 years old) is wiggling around in her seat a lot. Her caregiver asks her if she needs to go to the bathroom. Nancy says, "No, it's not that. My bottom hurts where Gary poked me." Gary is her 15-year-old brother.

Signs of emotional abuse*

Consider the possibility of emotional abuse when . . .

the child:	the parent or adult caregiver:
■ Shows extremes in behavior, such as overly compliant or demanding behavior, extreme passivity, or aggression. ■ Is either inappropriately adult (parenting other children, for example) or inappropriately infantile (frequently rocking or head-banging, for example) ■ Is delayed in physical or emotional development. ■ Has attempted suicide. ■ Shows a lack of attachment to the parent.	■ Constantly blames, belittles, or berates the child. ■ Is unconcerned about the child and refuses to consider offers of help for the child's problems. ■ Openly rejects the child.

* This information was adapted, with permission, from *Child Welfare Information Gateway*, www.childwelfare.gov/can/identifying and *Recognizing Child Abuse: What Parents Should Know*. Prevent Child Abuse America © 2003, www.preventchildabuse.org

Emotional abuse**

Things you should know:

Emotional abuse includes blaming, belittling, or rejecting a child; constantly treating siblings unequally; or persistent lack of concern for a child's welfare. It also includes bizarre or cruel forms of punishment (for example, locking a child in a dark closet).

Emotional abuse is hard to identify because the signs are rarely physical. The effects of mental injury, such as lags in physical development or speech disorders, are not as obvious as bruises and cuts. Sometimes children exhibit behavior such as facial tics, rocking motions, and odd reactions to a person in authority. Other effects might not show up for many years.

Although emotional abuse does occur alone, it often accompanies physical or sexual abuse. Emotionally abused children are not always physically abused, but physically abused children often are emotionally abused as well.

Behavioral signs of emotional abuse—

Each time he comes to pick up "Nathan" (5 years old), Mr. Wheeler makes fun of his son's efforts. Typical comments include: "Can't you button that coat right? You never get the buttons to line up with the holes. You look like an idiot." "What's that a picture of? Is that the only color you know how to use?" "Can't you climb to the top of the climber yet? All the other kids climbed to the top. What's the matter with you? Are your legs too short?"

"Yolanda" (3 years old) was so busy playing with her friends that she wet her pants instead of using the toilet. Her mother, who had just arrived, notices her wet pants and says sternly,

"Well Yolanda, I see that you aren't just playing house. You really are a baby. Only a baby would wet her pants."

** Adapted with permission from: Koralek, Derry (1992). "Caregivers for Young Children: Preventing and Responding to Child Maltreatment" User Manual Series: National Center on Child Abuse and Neglect. U.S. Department of Health and Human Services Administration on Children Youth and Families.

Reporting child abuse or neglect

When you work with families and care for their children day-after-day you are in a good position to identify abuse or neglect problems that may arise within a family. Identifying problems and getting help for families early on is important—the sooner the better.

Talking with children about suspected abuse or neglect

Sometimes you will be able to make a report about suspected abuse just from your observations. But other times, it may necessary to talk with a child to gather more information.

Use the following guidelines when talking to a child about suspected abuse or neglect.

Help the child feel safe
- Choose a place that is quiet, familiar, and non-threatening.
- Make sure you can talk uninterrupted, for as long as needed.
- Tell the child that you believe him/her and that you are going to contact people who can help.

Show respect for the child.
- Allow the child to show his/her injuries only if he/she wishes to do so.
- Do not insist, and never press the child to remove clothes.
- Don't display horror or shock.
- Don't show disapproval of parents or the child.
- Believe the child, especially if she or he reports sexual abuse. It is rare for a child to lie about sexual abuse.

Choose your words very carefully.
- Listen more, talk less.
- Use terms and language that the child can understand.
- Seek only information you need to justify a report. The child will need to tell the story to a trained investigator later.
- Ask open-ended questions and do not suggest answers. For example, it would be appropriate to say, "That bruise looks like it hurts. Tell me how that happened." It would be inappropriate to say, "Did you get that bruise when someone hit you?"
- Avoid "why" questions. Children usually have limited understandings about why they are abused and often feel it is their fault.
- Avoid probing for answers or supplying the child with terms or information.

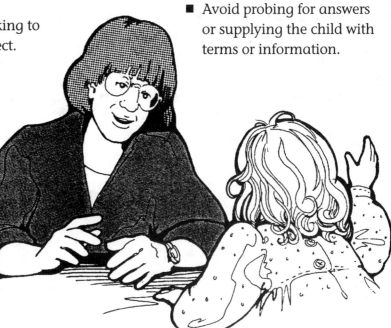

Several major child sexual abuse cases have been dismissed in court because it was felt that the adults who first interviewed the children inappropriately influenced or biased them.

Who should report?

Anyone who suspects child abuse or neglect. We all are responsible for the well-being of children. Anyone can call the national hotline (1-800-4achild) anonymously, report a concern, or ask a question.

Mandatory reporters. Each state requires adults who work in certain professions to report abuse. Typically health professionals, educators and school personnel, child care providers, and law enforcement officials are considered mandatory reporters. Mandatory reporters can be held legally responsible if they do not report suspected abuse and a child is injured or dies.

If you are a registered or licensed child care provider you are required by state law to take mandatory reporter training. Check with your local child care resource and referral office or state department of social services for more information.

Reports are confidential. Names of reporters are not revealed to the person being investigated during the investigation. Professional social service staff investigate reports of suspected abuse in a confidential and professional manner. However, in the unlikely event of a court case you may be asked to testify.

When to report

Report immediately if a child is in danger. Take action and dial 911 if a child could be seriously hurt.

Report concerns by phone within 24 hours if your concerns are serious, but you do not feel the child is in immediate danger. It is easier to remember details and information that happened just a few hours ago. But if 24 hours passes, it is still okay to call in. The important thing is to do it.

Report when a concern keeps happening over and over. Sometimes we don't notice things until they have happened several times. Trust your instincts. If you feel uncomfortable about something, write down what you are seeing. Even short, brief notes can be helpful in filing the report and can provide useful information to a child abuse investigator.

Don't wait for absolute proof. Although it is important to take notes to confirm what you are seeing, waiting for absolute proof may put the child at serious risk. You also are legally responsible if the child should be injured further or dies.

Report again if help is delayed. If you notice continued abuse or neglect after your report, call in your concerns again and again if needed. Agencies that deal with child abuse reports often are understaffed. Many children have been injured or have died after a report was made, because trusted adults assumed the problem was being dealt with. Have the courage to speak up, as often as needed, until you are sure of a child's safety.

Where to report

Dial 911, for immediate help. If immediate protection of the child is needed, call your local law enforcement.

Dial 1.800.4.A.CHILD – USA® National Child Abuse Hotline. To find your local or state hotline number or to ask questions, contact the National Child Abuse Hotline. Your local child care resource and referral agency, county extension office, or public library also can give you local contact information.

What to report

Have the following information on hand when reporting:

About the child:
- child's name, age, and address
- parent's name and address
- names of others who might be involved
- child's present location
- names and ages of other children in household

About the concern:
- what you observed or heard—description of the injury or condition
- where it happened—description of location and address
- when it happened—dates and times you noticed injury or condition
- who was involved—victim and suspected person responsible for abuse, if known
- what action has been taken thus far to treat, shelter, or otherwise assist the child

Reporter information:
- reporter's name and location and the relationship to the child
- names of other mandatory reporters who have knowledge of the suspected abuse
- abuse reports can be made anonymously, however in order to follow up with additional information, callers are encouraged to identify themselves.

Additional information:
- any history of abuse in the home
- presence of weapons, fierce pets, illegal activity
- language problems, or disabilities that would require special handling by the investigator, such as needing an interpreter, etc.
- any information that indicates the difference in age and size between the victim and the possible perpetrator; the greater the difference, the more likely it is that the abuse has occurred rather than normal activities for growing up, such as childhood fighting and sexual play.

HFCCH Chapter 14 — Child abuse and neglect

What happens after you report?

First, it must be decided if the information provided justifies an investigation. If so, an investigation is started right away. In some states, action is taken within a 24-hour period. But, it may take 30 to 60 days to complete an investigation.

Emergency services can be provided while the investigation is pending.

You have the right to:
- call an investigator if you are concerned about the progress of the investigation.
- report again if evidence of suspected abuse continues.

You also may wish to ask what additional information would be required for an investigation. Call again, if additional information becomes available.

Investigation
The investigation must determine
- if abuse or neglect occurred
- the degree of the abuse or neglect
- the cause of abuse or neglect
- the name, age, and condition of every other child in the household

If the report is confirmed, the caseworker must determine if the child will be safe at home. A decision also must be made on how best to protect the child in the future. Only a small percentage of children must be removed from their homes. At times, the person responsible for the abuse is removed from the home as a condition for the child to remain in the home.

Assessment and treatment
Depending on the situation, families will be linked to resources and professionals who can assist them. This may involve working with a counselor or mentor to improve parenting skills. It also may mean helping families reduce stress by locating help for basic needs such as food, clothing, utilities, or housing.

Confidentiality
It is sometimes necessary for investigators to consult with child care providers when assessing the family and in planning treatment. Child care professionals often have information in records or personal knowledge concerning the child and the family's skills and abilities. This information can be very helpful in setting realistic treatment goals and objectives for the families.

In providing this information, individuals must be conscious of the rights of children and parents. Great care must be taken to ensure the confidentiality of information and to share it only with those persons officially involved in the case.

Dealing with a child abuse situation can be very stressful. It can be very tempting to discuss it with family, friends, neighbors, or other child care providers. However, sharing of information should be strictly limited and kept confidential.

Typical concerns regarding reporting child abuse and neglect**

Concern	Response
"The parents seem like very angry people. What if the parents come after me?"	Although there may be a few exceptions, most abusive parents lack the social skills to face adults, especially those whom they perceive to be in positions of authority. This inability to confront adults is one of the reasons why their children are vulnerable to being harmed. An occasional parent may yell or threaten a reporter, but that usually is as far as it goes.
"I have no right to intervene in a family's affairs."	All state laws give you the right to protect a child by reporting your suspicions of child abuse and neglect. It is the only way the child and family can begin receiving the help they need.
"Will the child be hurt by parents or primary caregivers when they learn a report of suspected abuse has been filed against them?"	If you have fears that the family will flee or that the child might be harmed, include this information in your report of abuse. Based on the information you provide, the investigator will take measures to protect the child.
"Their cultural practices are different from mine. I have no right to impose my child rearing beliefs on them."	The definitions of child abuse and neglect included in state laws apply to all families residing in a state or community. These laws do not provide for exceptions when by legal standards, culturally accepted child-rearing practices are abusive or neglectful.
"I've known this parent for years. I just can't believe that she would sexually abuse her children. There must be some other explanation."	Adults who abuse or neglect children come from all kinds of backgrounds and are not always easy to identify. You must trust your observation skills and your knowledge of the physical and behavioral signs of child maltreatment. Also remember that you are not accusing any one person in your report; you are reporting the condition of a child or children that you suspect was caused by child abuse or neglect.
"What effect will a child abuse investigation have on my child care business?"	Remember that the investigation is confidential, so it isn't public knowledge. Parents are unlikely to tell others that the investigation is going on because it is very personal to them.
"I might be sued by the parents for making a false report."	Mandatory reporters are immune from civil or criminal liability for making a report in good faith (where knowledge or reasonable suspicion exists) even if it is not substantiated by the investigator. Even if someone does sue you, the court will dismiss the case when they find out you are a mandatory reporter.
"What happens to me if I don't report?"	Willful failure to report is a misdemeanor. If a mandatory reporter fails to report suspected abuse, the person can be held liable in civil court if the child is injured or dies later.

**Adapted with permission from: Koralek, Derry (1992) "Caregivers for Young Children: Preventing and Responding to Child Maltreatment" User Manual Series: National Center on Child Abuse and Neglect. U.S. Department of Health and Human Services Administration on Children Youth and Families.

Report because you care

Recognize your feelings. It can be hard to report a concern. If the parents of the abused or neglected child are friends or neighbors, it may be really hard to admit that abuse may be going on. You may feel afraid, or tempted to ignore the problem. You also may feel you can avoid reporting by reaching out to parents and helping to solve the problem. It is very common to have all of these feelings.

Understand that the child's safety and well-being should come first. Child abuse can be a very complex problem. Many family members who abuse children may be very loving to their children in other ways. It can be confusing. It is not your job to fully understand everything that is going on; it is your job to protect children by reporting a concern.

Report to help families get much needed support. Professionals who work with child abuse reports are trained to know how to help families. In some cases, this may mean removing the child from the home, but often it means helping the family with basic needs or parenting skills.

Protect yourself legally. If a child is injured or dies, you can be held legally responsible. Child care providers are mandatory reporters and are legally required to report concerns of child abuse and neglect. It is the right thing to do.

Tips to help victims of abuse and neglect

Child care providers can have a tremendous impact on the life of a child. The following suggestions will help you respond effectively to children who have been abused or neglected or who are undergoing stress in their daily lives.

Realize that you can make a difference. You may not be able to change the stressful conditions that children must deal with at home, but you can offer them a safe, comfortable, and accepting place to be while they are in your care.

Greet each child warmly every day. That transition from parent to provider is an important one. Often mornings are extremely stressful for families. Children often are yelled at, hurried, and given breakfast in the car. A warm smile or hug as a child walks in the door can go a long way to help a child feel accepted and wanted.

Be there for children. Put aside your own frustrations about the past and worries about the future. There is very little you can do to solve your life problems while you are working. Being there for the children means that you will be an active, in-control caregiver.

Spend time with each child every day. Even if it is just for a few minutes, get down on the child's level; make eye contact, listen, and watch.

Provide a quiet place to be alone. A quiet place to spend some time alone should always be available for children who may need to escape for a while. A cozy corner with a few pillows or a special space under a table works well.

Follow a predictable routine. Allow for flexibility and teachable moments, but try to stick to a consistent routine so children know what to expect each day. Plan your day so it balances active and quiet activities, organized projects, and free play.

Avoid putting children in high pressure situations. Children get stressed when they are expected to perform before a group or complete a task they don't have the skills for.

Learn to value each child's special self. Remember that children learn to value themselves through the eyes (and words) of others. What you say (or don't say) to a child has tremendous impact.

Model acceptable behaviors. Children under stress have difficulty picking up on cues from caregivers and peers. Telling a child to do something is not good enough. You may need to show or model the correct behaviors. ("Tell Josie with words that you want the truck" often needs to be followed with the caregiver saying, "I'll pretend to be you—Josie, may I please play with that truck?")

Respect children's needs for personal space. Children under stress (even aggressive children) often feel threatened by others and need more personal space. Avoid crowding children into one area.

Provide opportunities for children to comfort themselves. Many children find comfort in repeating activities over and over. Often they will show behaviors you might see in younger children, such as thumb sucking or rubbing the edge of a blanket. Security objects such as a doll, teddy bear, or blanket should not be kept from a child who is under stress.

Avoid unexpected touching of a sexual abuse victim. An unexpected touch may cause a child to have sudden unpleasant memories. Over time, as you build trust, a child may feel comfortable giving you permission to touch a shoulder or give a gentle hug. Find ways to help children experience "healthy" touching.

Be aware of nonverbal behaviors. Be aware of the child's body language. Watch carefully for signs of restlessness or frustration and be prepared to offer assistance, change the activity, or redirect the child.

Avoid over stimulation. Put away toys that are not being used. Reduce the noise level by introducing a quiet activity. Slow down the activity (roll a ball to a child instead of chasing a child with the ball).

Provide many open-ended activities that involve no possibility of failure. Sand and water play, play dough, or painting are good examples of materials that can be used in many different ways.

Allow children to show younger behaviors. Children under stress often are overwhelmed and may move backward to more familiar behaviors you would normally see in a much younger child. If a 5-year-old has difficulty interacting with peers, he or she may feel much more comfortable playing with others and watching from a distance, much as a 3-year-old would.

If a 4-year-old seems to be acting much like a 2-year-old, kicking and biting, you may need to structure the child's activities like that of a 2-year-old—short term, low frustration level, soothing experiences, such as water play or play dough.

Create situations in which the child can share feelings. Help the child talk about feelings. Give him/her words for feelings. For example you might say, "I can see you are tired and sad." Let the child know you understand and accept such feelings. As long as the child is not in danger of further abuse, treat what the child tells you as confidential.

Be honest with the child without being discouraging. Help the child find any information that might increase understanding. Children's books often are wonderful resources.

Share your strength and support. Let the child know that you are working on the problem together.

Be understanding and respectful of parents. Avoid expressing anger or morally judging the child's parents, particularly in the child's presence.

Help children understand the problem in simple terms. During a crisis, children often struggle to understand. You can help by explaining the situation in terms that the child understands.

Alert parents to a child's concerns. Parents need to know when their child is hurting. You may help the child by steering the parent toward sources of help without betraying the child's confidence and without putting the parents on the defensive by becoming angry or by moralizing.

FamilyShare...
Supporting your partners

You play an important role in the prevention of child abuse. Many parents do not have family or support nearby to discuss parenting issues. Talk openly with parents about how you deal with stress and guidance issues with children. Whenever possible model appropriate ways to talk with children. Suggest simple activities that parents can do with children at home.

Spending just a few minutes each day listening and talking with parents can go a long way to making a real difference in a child's life. Be sure to share some of the parenting handouts and resources on the accompanying CD that comes with this book.

Heart of the Matter

My first experience with child abuse was caring for a child whose parents had been turned in for abuse by someone else. Social services helped place the child in my care.

I wish I could say that I made an immediate difference in this child's life, but the truth is it was a challenge. Dan (not his real name) had some very violent and aggressive behaviors. Although I didn't allow toy weapons, he was constantly pretending to shoot someone or wrestle them to the ground.

Dan rarely sat still and became easily frustrated with even very simple tasks. To my amazement this 4-year-old seemed to be completely unaware of how to use crayons or markers. He used books only to make a "pretend" fire in the block area. Scissors were thrown in frustration across the room. During the first few months, I followed him around making sure he did not hurt anyone. It was exhausting.

Yet despite this, I grew to like him. He was bright and curious. And he also could be very kind, particularly with the younger ones.

Dan's parents were struggling with learning new parenting skills. I was not told a lot of detail about their circumstances, but I felt they truly loved their son and were sincerely trying to turn things around. We talked every day. They seemed to cling to any positive comment or story I had to share.

I noticed he loved play dough, water play, and blocks. So I began encouraging him to learn new skills in those areas. I gave him cooking tools to use with play dough so he could cut, shape, and sort. We used lots of plastic dinosaurs in water play and in the block area. We "taught" those "mean" dinosaurs how to be "nice" to each other and get along.

We took lots of pictures of block buildings and play dough sculptures, so Dan would have something to share with his parents. We also made a book together using a sturdy photo album. Each page had photos of Dan playing with his friends. We wrote words below each picture. This book was treasured and did not end up in the "pretend" fire.

Over time Dan changed into a well-behaved, remarkable young boy. It didn't happen overnight, but several years later it was hard for me to remember what he had been like before. I felt very confident that things were going to be okay with him and his family.

Lesia

Experience Talks
Conversations with other providers

■ **In my state, I am required to participate in mandatory reporter training.** Frankly, this is not my favorite type of training. But I know it is important. I have never had to report child abuse, but I'm glad I know how to do it if I should ever have to.

■ **I haven't had to make a child abuse report on any of the families or children in my program, but I have used it to report on a neighbor who was abusing his wife and children.** This was very scary for me, but it really helped that I had learned something about abuse and the report process. Now things are much better for the wife and her kids. I'm really glad that I took action.

■ **Unfortunately I have had to report a sexual abuse situation.** At first I was having a hard time believing this could happen to one of my child care children. The family seemed really nice. But it was true—the abuse really did happen. I was not given a lot of details about the situation and things got a little crazy before it was all over. The dad moved out of the house and social services stepped in to help mom and the other kids.

■ **The really hard thing about family child care is that you don't have another adult to talk things over with if you think you might be seeing some signs of abuse.** I kept seeing some bruises on one of my child care kid's legs. At first I thought, "well—kids will be kids" and "all children have bruises." But they kept happening so often, I decided to report it and have it checked out. And it was abuse. I wonder what would have happened if I hadn't reported when I did.

■ **I often wonder if emotional abuse is worse than physical abuse.** I have had parents who constantly seem to yell and criticize their children. I can see it really affects the way children see themselves. I struggle with whether to report this or not. I think it is much easier to report if you see physical signs of abuse.

■ **I once turned in a family for child abuse and it turned out to be a medical condition instead.** The family was upset about being cited for child abuse, but the good news was that they did get medical help.

■ **I have lost a family over a child abuse situation.** I reported them and although they were not told who turned them in, they suspected me. They did change child care and I lost both children. Losing the income so suddenly was a blow, but I am glad I did it.

■ **I live in a small town and people tend to look the other way when they see parents abuse their child.** Taking mandatory reporter training has helped me realize that it is not okay to pretend abuse is not happening. Getting along with others in a small community is important, but never at the risk of allowing children to be hurt.

Taking care of yourself

Chapter 15

Contents

Where am I now?	398
Introduction	399
Making changes—setting goals	399
Are you taking care of your health?	400
What is stress?	400
Coping with stress	401
Time management	403
FamilyShare	405
Coping with special child care stressors	406
26 Great suggestions to reduce stress in child care programs	408
Heart of the Matter	412
Experience Talks	413

Taking care of yourself—
Where am I now? What can I improve?

	Seldom 1	Sometimes 2	Often 3	Most Often 4
1. I set realistic goals for myself.				
2. I reach my goals.				
3. I nourish my body with healthy food.				
4. I drink 6 to 8 glasses of water each day.				
5. I exercise for 30 minutes each day.				
6. I get 8 hours of sleep each night.				
7. I wash my hands regularly.				
8. I have a strong support system of family, friends, and community.				
9. I ask for help when I need it.				
10. I seek out other providers for support.				
11. I recognize my personal signs of stress.				
12. I regularly use at least one relaxation method to release daily physical tension.				
13. I do something fun and enjoyable every day.				
14. I have an enjoyable "nonwork"-related hobby.				
15. I am a skilled problem solver.				
16. I use at least three methods to reduce the stress level of my child care home.				
17. I use good time management skills.				
18. I take regular vacation days to relax and refresh myself.				

Chapter 15

Taking care of yourself

Your health and well-being are one of your most valuable assets. Imagine for a moment what your life would be like if you lost your good health. Sometimes health problems hit us suddenly, such as when we are injured in an accident. But more often our health declines slowly as we neglect to take care of ourselves. This slow decline is not so noticeable from day-to-day and can sneak up on us. When health problems do arise we feel surprised, overwhelmed, and may have great difficulty recovering our good health.

You must take care of yourself in order to care for others. Giving children your best, means being your best. If you take care of yourself, you will have more energy and be more attentive to the children's needs.

Caring for yourself starts with valuing yourself. You recognize and value children as unique, special individuals. Extend that recognition to yourself as well. Be aware of your shortcomings; but celebrate and build on your strengths. When you can like and accept yourself as you are, you can be sure you will keep on going and—growing.

Making changes—setting goals

As you identify different ways to care for yourself, you may find it helpful to set some goals. The following tips will help you move forward:

1. **Write it!**—post it where you can see it; journal about your progress.

2. **Value it!**—identify the positive benefit of meeting your goal.

3. **Visualize it!**—every day; picture yourself meeting your goal.

4. **Evaluate it!**—is it doable?

5. **Divide and conquer it!**—break large goals into manageable smaller goals.

6. **Schedule it!**—set realistic deadlines and post them on a calendar.
7. **Troubleshoot it!**—spot potential problems that may keep you from reaching your goal.
8. **Problem-solve it!**—identify actions you can take to prevent or address possible problems.
9. **Just do it!**—Be persistent; all positive results require effort.
10. **Review it!**—check your progress on a regular basis.
11. **Celebrate it!**—rejoice and honor each small success.

Are you taking care of your health?

People who value themselves pay attention to their health. Good health is basic to feeling good about yourself. You know the drill: eat right, exercise, get enough sleep; but do you do it? Decide now to improve your health habits.

Set at least one small goal to improve your health habits.

How do you show a feeling of self-worth?

- Nourish your body with healthy food.
- Exercise regularly.
- Get enough sleep at night.
- Wear comfortable clothing and shoes.
- Practice healthy habits such as hand-washing.
- Limit the use of substances that may harm your health.
- Get regular health check-ups.

What is stress?

We experience stress anytime we feel overwhelmed. Stress can be the result of a major tragedy or upheaval—such as a family death, divorce, or being fired from a job. Stress also can be the result of daily "hassles." Both can affect your sense of well-being.

Your body creates extra energy to protect itself when you are stressed. This additional energy can build up and create an overload. You may feel a physical reaction to stress such as a headache or a rapid heart beat. Many people often have an emotional response as well. You may feel nervous, anxious, or even depressed.

The stress checklist

Stress can affect you physically, mentally, emotionally, and socially. The following list of symptoms includes some typical reactions to stress. It can help you focus on ways to manage stress. Check any symptoms you've noticed lately in yourself. Add any symptoms that are not on the list.

Physical
___ headaches
___ feeling tired
___ problems sleeping
___ weight change
___ colds
___ stomach upsets
___ pounding heart
___ frequent accidents
___ teeth grinding
___ restlessness
___ increased alcohol, drug, and tobacco use
___ tightening up and aching of neck and shoulders

Mental
___ forgetfulness
___ dull senses
___ poor concentration
___ not getting much done
___ negative attitude
___ confusion
___ feeling sluggish or indifferent
___ no new ideas
___ boredom

Emotional
___ anxiety
___ the "blues"
___ mood swings
___ bad temper
___ impatience
___ crying spells
___ irritability
___ depression
___ nervous laugh
___ worry
___ easily discouraged
___ need to eat, even when not hungry

Social
___ isolation
___ resentment
___ loneliness
___ lashing out
___ clamming up
___ lowered sex drive
___ nagging
___ fewer contacts with friends
___ using people

Look over the symptoms you've checked and circle those that occur often or regularly.

Study your list. Which symptoms cause you the most concern? Are you always aware when they are happening to you?

Do you see a pattern in your symptoms? Are they mostly physical? Do they usually involve other people?

Identify ways you can prevent or reduce stress. Set one small, short term goal to begin changing something that concerns you.

Coping with stress

Stress is a natural part of life. It's a bit like the weather—everybody experiences it, but only some of us adequately prepare for it. We deal with weather by preparing for both the expected and unexpected. We adjust our clothing, bring an umbrella, and winterize our car. We need to prepare the same way when dealing with stress.

How we prepare for and react to stress can make a big difference in how we experience stress. We can't make stress go away completely, but there are effective ways to reduce stress and bring balance to your life. The following information can give you some ideas to relax, build a support network, manage your time effectively, and work more professionally.

Easy relaxation techniques

Belly breathing
This technique needs to be learned because most of us have learned to breathe from our chest. Belly breathing is a natural way of breathing and a good stress-reducing habit. Sit or lie comfortably in a relaxed position. As you breathe in slowly, let your belly expand. Think of it as a balloon that you are filling with air. As you exhale, let the air out of your "balloon" slowly. Place your hands on your stomach and feel it rise and fall as you breathe.

Tension releaser
Try to touch your ears with your shoulders. Hold for a count of four. Then let your shoulders drop. Now rotate each shoulder separately toward the rear. Do each shoulder 5 to 10 times. Then do both shoulders together.

Stretches
These are great exercises for releasing back tension.

Stretch your arms above your head and clasp hands. Standing in one place, breathe outward and turn from your waist to the right. Inhale as you turn back to center. Exhale as you turn to your left. Inhale as you turn back to center. Repeat 6 times.

Stand with your hands on your hips. Swivel your hips clockwise to the right 6 times. Swivel your hips counter clockwise 6 times.

Bend down slowly until you can almost touch the floor. Using your right hand draw an imaginary circle around your left foot. Using your left hand draw an imaginary circle around your right foot. Repeat several times, then slowly rise back to standing.

Neck massage
Sit down, close your eyes, and relax. Massage the back of your neck, concentrating on the part that feels tense. Cup your thumbs at the front of your neck and massage on both sides of your spinal column, letting your head fall limply back against your rotating fingers. Use your fingers to massage around your hairline and under your jaw and cheekbones. Gently draw a line up and down the side of your nose with one finger. How do you feel?

Centering
Get into a relaxed position and breathe through your nose, easily and naturally, with eyes closed. As you breathe out, think "one." As you breathe in, think "one." Continue for 10 to 20 minutes, but don't watch a clock. Just think "one." If your mind wanders, gently pull it back to thinking "one" every time you exhale or inhale. After 10 to 20 minutes of this activity, sit quietly for a few minutes with your eyes closed. Then for a few minutes more, sit with your eyes open. Don't worry about doing it "right." Relaxation will happen if you let it. Do this once or twice daily.

Building a support system

What does your support network look like? Grab a pen or pencil and find out.

1. Write your name in the center of the circle.

2. In the first ring from the center, write the names of the people you confide in and depend on most for emotional support.

3. In the second ring, list those people you are not as emotionally close to as first circle members, but who still might be helpful to you.

4. In the third and outermost ring, list people or agencies you have little personal involvement with, but who could provide you with help if you needed it.

Evaluate your support network
Now that you've taken a look at your personal support network, ask yourself the following questions:

- Do I feel satisfied with the number of members in each circle of support within my support network?

- Do I need/want to add to my support network?

- Do I feel satisfied with the quality of relationships in each circle of support? Are my needs for emotional support being met?

Support system

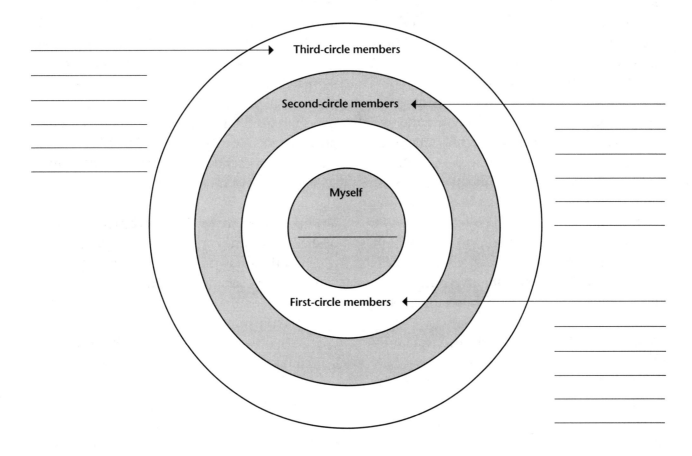

- Do I need/want to strengthen some friendships in my first and second circles?
- Do I need to discover more about possible support in my community to build a third circle of support?
- Are there people in any of the circles who have a negative influence on me? If so, can the relationships be changed or accepted?

Strengthen family support

Strong family relationships often provide the base for strong social support. If you find that your family support is weak, encourage family members to talk about their joys, needs, and sorrows and to appreciate each other. Spending quality time together can help strengthen your family support too.

Time management

Time management does not mean being busy all of the time. It means using your time the way you want to use it. Time management is really self-management. Each of us has 24 hours each day that we can spend as we choose.

Recognize your many roles. Family child care providers are whole people. They are parents, spouses, friends, community members, and business people. Learning to manage time means learning how to determine what is important to you and balancing it within each of these roles. One good way to manage time is to figure out the number of roles you play and the goals and tasks for each role. For example you might list your roles as self, wife, mother, cook, housekeeper, child care provider, business manager, community member.

Schedule your tasks by role and responsibility. Identify tasks that are important to each role and schedule them on a weekly calendar. As a cook, you might schedule one evening for meal planning and a daily time to prepare meals. As a wife, you might schedule a quick call to your husband each day to chat for a few minutes. As a businessperson, you might plan for an hour to update your expense records. As a mother, you might pencil in a reminder to tuck a "love note" into your child's lunch box.

Balance your "to do" priorities. Most time management methods focus only on the "working hours." The above method treats individuals as whole people with whole lives, and helps to schedule personal and family needs as well as work needs. If you see that one role has far more tasks than others, it is time to review your priorities. The main idea for successful time management is to keep things in balance.

Get a good start. Plan the night before for snacks, beverages, and lunches. Lay out clothes for family members who must go to work or school the next day. Gather books, homework assignments, and other work items and put them by the door. Ask other family members to help with these tasks.

Develop routines. Establish times of the week for doing the laundry, shopping, etc. Caring for children all week and trying to do all of your housework on the weekends can be very tiring. Scheduling one chore each day of the week can free up a block of personal time just for you.

Make a master shopping checklist. Child care providers do not have a lot of time or freedom to make constant trips to the grocery store. Organize your master list by sections such as fruits and vegetables, meat and dairy, canned goods, beverages, snack foods, cereals and bakery items, paper goods, cleaners, health items. Make copies of your checklist and post one each week on the refrigerator or inside a kitchen cabinet door. This one practice can save you a lot of money and time.

Group similar tasks. Save precious weekend and evening time by completing similar errands in the same part of town during the same trip. Try scheduling health check appointments on the same day. Take advantage of stores that offer one-stop services including groceries, dry-cleaning, mailing and postage, banking, and movie rentals in one location.

Limit multi-tasking. Grouping tasks together and completing them in sequence is a good idea. Doing too many things at the same time is not. Decide which tasks are most important and focus on a few tasks at a time.

Avoid crowds and busy times. Crowds, lines, and busy peak times rob you of your time. Plan to avoid them. Carry a book with you, just in case you are delayed.

Take advantage of your mood and energy level. We all have a time during the day when we feel more energetic. For some of us it is in the morning, for others it is late afternoon or evening. Pay attention to your energy level and use your "best" time to get more done.

Coordinate personal care and health needs in advance. Check your calendar often for commitments and appointments. For regular monthly appointments, schedule them at the same time each month so you will remember them.

Use your phone to save time. Call ahead to check on availability of products or services. Call to get directions and to determine opening and closing times of stores.

Shop online. You can save a lot of money by comparison shopping online. Even if you choose to purchase items locally, take advantage of on-line services that give product information and evaluations.

Family Share...
Supporting your partners

When you make a decision to take care of your health in a way that will affect families, it is a good idea to share that information with them. You may assume that families realize you need a vacation or an afternoon off. Some will and some will not.

You can explain your needs and be a good role model for them. You might say:

"One challenge for family child care providers is the lack of regular daily breaks, sick leave, or a lunch hour. So that I can be my best for the children, I need to take some regular time off to take care of my health and refresh myself."

If you arrange for a substitute, be sure to give notice ahead of time. Also give families the substitute's qualifications and background information. It is also a good idea to introduce them ahead of time. You might say:

"Alisa Jackson, my neighbor, will be caring for the children for several hours every Friday afternoon. Alisa has two grown children of her own and is great with kids. She has taken first aid and CPR. Alisa has visited us before, so the children are comfortable with her. Alisa will be here Thursday afternoon at pick-up time, so you can meet her."

You may find that some families will be very understanding. Other families may not. As long as you have explained things clearly and handled things as professionally as possible, there is no need to feel guilty. You know in your heart that taking care of yourself is one of the best things you can do for the children.

HFCCH Chapter 15 — Taking care of yourself

Coping with special child care stressors . . .

While the rewards of child care are tremendous, caring for children presents special challenges that contribute to stress and burnout. The following are some examples of those challenges:

Stressor	How to cope . . .
Children often are unpredictable. It's hard to keep your cool when a toddler drowns your favorite house plant in apple juice or dumps your measuring cups in the toilet.	▪ Learn to pause before you react—or over react. ▪ Say to yourself, "Is this really important? "Major disasters may deserve tears, but small problems only deserve a chuckle." ▪ It helps to keep your sense of humor. "This will make a great story later on."
Children of different ages have very different needs. Caring for children in your home often means caring for children of different ages at the same time. Although there are some clear advantages to this practice, it can be a real challenge to juggle the needs of an infant, a toddler, a preschooler, and a school-age child.	▪ Learn what to expect from each age group. ▪ Plan activities that match children's skill level and understanding. ▪ Encourage children to help and teach each other. ▪ If there is an age group that seems more of a problem for you, limit the number of children you accept of that age.
Caring for children requires quick action and decision making. Think quick! What takes priority – an infant with a dirty diaper, a hungry preschooler, a biting toddler, or a school-ager who is about to miss the bus? Each day child care providers must make hundreds of decisions to keep children safe, healthy, and focused on learning.	▪ Safety should always take priority. Think prevention. Walk through your house and look at it as if you were a child. ▪ Ask yourself: What trouble could a curious child get into? ▪ What can I do to make my home safer?
Children are noisy and loud. Whether happy or sad, children make noise and are often very loud. Giggles, shouts, sobs, bouncing balls, and stomping feet can really wear on your nerves.	▪ Try to balance active activities with quiet activities. For example, after children go outside to run and play, come inside for a quiet reading time. ▪ Reduce other household noise. Turn off the TV. Close the door to the laundry room. ▪ Play soothing music to set the stage for quiet play.

Stressor	How to cope . . .
The results and rewards of your work are often long term. In some jobs, you can measure your success each day. Working with children does have its everyday joys, but the end result of your patience and caring may not be evident until many years later. It is sometimes difficult to remember that your work provides a strong beginning for a child to become a mature, caring, and competent adult.	■ Recognize that your work will have a lasting impact. Think back to influential people in your own life. ■ Identify the things they did that made a difference in your life. ■ Identify the way they made you feel. ■ Think about how you can use your experiences to make a difference in the lives of the children and families you serve.
Working with parents can be hard sometimes. Communication, late payments, and failure to pick up children on time are just a few of the problems you might face.	■ Learn not to judge. Many people we meet are going through some type of struggle, even though it may not be obvious. ■ Set reasonable expectations. Parents of young children are generally young themselves. They rarely get a good night's sleep. They struggle with lower incomes, cranky bosses, and cars that break down. It's all a part of serving and working with imperfect human beings. ■ Develop realistic policies that will help you manage late payments and other challenges. Enforce the policies and move on.
Limited income must cover both your salary and the costs of caring for children. Child care is not a highly paid profession. State regulations and recommended practices limit the number of children you can care for at any one time. The fees parents pay must provide you with income and an adequate supply of food, toys, and equipment. Providers are always faced with the difficult task of "making do."	■ Believe in the value of your service and pay yourself well. Check what other providers are charging in your area and set your fee at the upper range. If you truly do provide excellent service, parents who value their children will pay for it. ■ Buy quality toys and equipment—even if it means fewer items. Stick with the classics: blocks, good books, etc.
Children are with you only for a short while. Most caregivers have a genuine affection for children and invest a great deal of love and care into their relationship. Yet, this relationship is often short term because children outgrow child care or move away.	■ Recognize that children will leave and prepare for it. Take pictures and keep a photo album. ■ Mail children notes and cards to recognize birthdays and special events and plan to do this after they leave as well. Find other ways to keep in touch.

Stressor	How to cope . . .
Providing child care in your home can be lonely work. Children can be great company, but adults need other grown-ups as well. The isolation from other adults may be hard.	■ Explore ways to connect with other providers or adults. A short phone call can make a big difference. ■ Schedule a daily "walk and talk" with a friend after work.
Vacations and sick days are hard to arrange. Families depend on you. When you are sick or need to take a day off, it can throw them into a crisis. Knowing this means that you may not take off the time you need.	■ Make sure parents know they need to have a back-up plan if you are sick. Put this in your written policies. ■ Schedule a 3-day weekend mini-vacation every season and a longer vacation during the year. Let parents know well in advance of your plans, so they can arrange for other care.

26 Great suggestions to reduce stress in child care programs

How do people cope with stress successfully? How do caregivers prevent daily hassles from turning into burnout? Here are some suggestions for both your personal and professional life:

1. Follow a reasonable routine or schedule. Routines help provide a sense of purpose and balance to our lives. Children and adults need regular eating times, resting times, and a balance of quiet and active play. A consistent routine makes life a bit more predictable and creates a strong sense of security for children. Children who feel secure and comfortable generally have fewer behavior problems.

2. Arrange your home so you can comfortably "cover" it with your attention at all times. Close rooms where children could get into trouble when you cannot see what they are doing. Arrange furniture and activity areas so that you can watch children closely. Putting breakable or "no-touch" things out-of-sight and out-of-reach will greatly reduce stress.

3. Create a pleasant work environment. Child care providers spend long hours in their homes. It's important that they enjoy their surroundings. Regardless of where you live, there are many little things that you can do to make your home more enjoyable. Simple changes such as a vase of flowers on the kitchen table or a new hand towel in the bathroom can make a difference. Rearrange the furniture or put on a new coat of paint to change things dramatically. Playing soothing music at different points in the day can soothe the soul of many a cranky child.

4. Simplify and de-clutter. Over the years we often collect and keep too much stuff. Things that were once useful to us may no longer be needed. Items that require too much dusting or maintenance create stress and distract us from more important things in our lives. Children need our attention. If you don't have the energy for a yard sale, make it a goal to take a few things each month to your local charity.

5. Tidy up before the mess becomes chaos.
Children are naturally playful, curious, and – messy. Toys and "found treasures" quickly pile up. If you can't put up with clutter and mess on a daily basis you are in the wrong business. However, it is true that too much disorder creates chaos and unhappy children. When you can't walk through the play area, and toys are getting stepped on and broken, things have gone too far. Make it part of your routine to spend 1-2 minutes, several times each day keeping things tidy. Children can help you with this task. You will be amazed at how much difference a two minute cleanup time can make.

6. Do little things for yourself every day.
Try to take in life's little pleasures each day. Take a few minutes to enjoy each morning's sunrise. Wave "hello" and greet a favorite neighbor. Enjoy a cup of coffee. Savor the quietness as children lay sleeping. Make a point of noticing what is really important to you. Help children notice these things too.

7. Set short-term goals. Most of us have dreams or goals. Try to set one short-term, realistic goal for yourself, and plan how you will reach it. Decide how you will do it and set a time line for yourself.

8. Relax and wind down. One of the disadvantages of caring for children in your home is that you can't just shut the door and leave your work at five, like most other workers. Create a ritual to bring the child care part of your day to a close. This can be as simple as drinking a cup of tea on the front porch or taking a short bike ride around the block. The regularity of the act, however, can help you wind down and signal to your family that you are now ready to spend time with them.

9. Balance your strengths and limitations.
Often our greatest strength is also our greatest weakness. Great organizers sometimes have trouble being flexible. Good speakers often have trouble listening. Artistic or creative thinkers may scorn rules and routines. Look closely at your strengths and weaknesses. Look for the "down side" and "up side" in every quality. If a particular characteristic seems to be getting you into trouble, try to find a balance that you can live with.

10. Develop a sense of humor. Humor is a talent than can be learned. Perhaps you know someone who always seems to have a good sense of humor. If you take the time to study this person a little, you may discover that humor is based on attitude and a different way of looking at things. Next time you feel discouraged or angry, look for humor in the situation.

11. Schedule alone time. Everyone needs a few minutes alone each day. Spend at least 15 minutes each day listening to music, sitting in nature, or taking a warm bath. Give yourself permission to just "be"—no need to plan, think, or talk.

12. Practice gratitude. Look for the blessings in your life and be thankful for them. Sometimes the smallest things, like a bird singing, can help you set the stage for your whole day. Remind yourself of the special reasons you chose child care as a profession. Looking for the positives and minimizing the negatives can enrich your life.

13. Treat yourself the way you would like others to treat you. Have you ever noticed how people seem to be drawn to others who respect and take care of themselves? Self-respect is a personal quality that is quiet but powerful.

14. Nourish your body. There is a difference between nourishing your body and eating. You want more for your body than just calories to get you through the day. Nourishing your body means you are eating wholesome, healthy food, giving your body what it needs to do its very best both today and years from now. Make changes one at a time and slowly. Soon you will be feeling better and well nourished for a lifetime.

15. Move, move, and move again. The human body was made to move in many different ways. Movement and activity throughout the day not only reduce stress but can give you energy. They can also improve your immune system and keep you healthy. If exercising vigorously after a day of caring for children feels overwhelming to you, consider a leisurely walk, tai chi, or a few yoga stretches. Keep everything in balance—try a variety of stretching, mild weight lifting, bicycling, swimming, dancing, or jogging.

16. Take "time out." Child care providers are busy people and often claim that it is impossible to take a break during the day. Without another adult for back-up, the standard 15-minute break in the morning and afternoon just doesn't happen. Yet, like the children they care for, providers do need breaks and time to be alone too. Try the following idea. Take "one minute" for yourself several times each day for quiet thought and relaxation. One minute may not sound like a very long time, but just try sitting quietly for one whole minute. It's amazing how 60 seconds can slow things down and give you a fresh perspective on things. Try to think about something pleasant such as a recent chat with a friend or your upcoming vacation. The one minute that you take for yourself offers you a mini break, a time-out.

17. Take a vacation. Everyone needs a longer "time-out" every now and then. Explain in your policy statement that you will take an annual vacation and at least one vacation day each season. Schedule vacations far in advance and let families know they will need to find other care during that time. Recognize that this will be an inconvenience for families and don't feel guilty about it. Scheduling vacations is always a challenge—all businesses have to deal with this.

18. Problem solve. When things are going crazy and kids are bouncing off the wall, providers often find themselves reacting to one crisis after another. Clear thinking is difficult if not impossible. It helps to take a deep breath, step back, and see if there is a better way of handling things. Use the "who, what, when, where, and why" method. Who seems to be involved, what is happening, when is it occurring, where does it take place, and why does it seem to be happening? A fresh look at an old situation can sometimes reveal new ideas and solutions.

19. Show integrity and admit your mistakes. No one is perfect and we all have slip-ups from time to time. Guilt can be a real stressor. Avoid saying "If only I had . . . ." When you make a mistake or wrong someone, apologize, make amends, let go of the past, and move on.

20. Evaluate your expectations. If you find yourself stressed because others are unwilling to meet your expectations, stop and ask yourself if those expectations are realistic. If not, make a few changes. If you do think your expectations are reasonable, it may be that you have not communicated them well. Families often will not understand your needs and wishes if you don't tell them. You can avoid a great deal of frustration and resentment by clearly stating your expectations. Often it helps to both say expectations out loud and put them in writing.

21. Resolve conflict. Everyone has conflict from time to time. However if it goes unresolved, it begins to fester and increases anger and frustration. When possible it is best to resolve only one issue at a time. If successful, you can build on your success and move on to the next conflict. Start by asking the other person to help you understand his/her point of view. Summarize what you think you heard. Ask the other person if your summary was accurate. Then share your view. Work together and come up with a solution.

22. Avoid stressful people and stressful situations. Fine-tune your personal radar and feelings. Steer clear of certain people or situations that make you feel uncomfortable.

23. Connect with others. It often helps to talk about your day. Some parts of your day you can share with your family, but it really helps to link up with other providers as well. Check with your child care resource and referral or local licensing agency to see if there is a local provider group you can join. Many providers are finding support through online discussion groups. The KIDCARE online discussion group is sponsored by Cooperative Extension and the National Network for Child Care (NNCC). To subscribe go to www.nncc.org.

24. Change your perspective—watch your stress talk! It is easy to get weighed down with day-to-day problems. You may find yourself complaining inwardly to yourself. Making negative statements to ourselves over and over can get to be a bad habit and soon affects our whole outlook on life. If you find this happening to you, start looking for the positives in your life. Practice saying positive things to yourself: "I am confident," "I have good people skills," and "I am a good problem solver." Changing your perspective can make a tremendous difference in how you deal with stress.

25. Master your personal finances. Financial problems can be a big burden to shoulder. Debt and money worries are very stressful and can affect your work. Decide to learn what you can do to reduce personal financial problems. A great Web site with easy to understand information about consumer credit, children and money, home ownership, insurance, saving and investing, retirement planning, legal topics, and finance calculators and tools is found at www.extension.org.

26. Get a hobby. Studies show that a "non-work"-related hobby can significantly reduce burnout. Find something you enjoy and get involved.

Heart of the Matter

There are hundreds, if not thousands, of articles that have been written about reducing stress and taking care of yourself. But somehow it is always easier to read about how to reduce stress than it is to actually make it happen. I don't think I am alone in this.

I have never met an early childhood provider who didn't struggle with this issue. We give so much of ourselves to children. We work long hours, wipe drippy noses and smelly bottoms. We teach children how to read and count and how to be kind to each other. We feel immense pride knowing we are helping to shape the future, but also feel a heavy burden from the tremendous responsibility. We give and give and give–and at times wonder if we have anything left to give.

Books on stress mention slow, deep breathing as one technique that will calm things down and bring things back into perspective. We are told that breathing symbolizes balance in our lives. We are told to take slow, gentle breaths – breathing in and breathing out.

It occurred to me recently that maybe we spend far too much time breathing out and not enough breathing in. In other words, we spend far more time taking care of others than allowing ourselves to be cared for. We neglect to build relationships that can nurture and support us. Many of us find it very hard to accept the gifts of kindness and joy we receive each day. We quickly deplete our reserves and ability to give back.

We need to receive care and love often. If we are to reach some balance in our lives we need to receive as often as we give—like breathing in and breathing out.

I am learning to accept the gifts in my life. And that is the key. Often the gifts are there right in front of us, but we fail to embrace them. A hug from a child, a beautiful sunrise, a call from a friend, a kind word from a parent are all gifts that we can receive that will fill us up and allow us to give back. Like breathing in and breathing out.

Lesia

Experience Talks

Conversations with other providers

■ **I've learned to follow the motto "Wherever you are, BE THERE."** I discovered that I was living too much in the past, feeling bad about mistakes that I had made, or living too much in the future, worrying about what was going to happen. The result was that I was never emotionally available for the children or my family. Now I take one day at a time.

■ **I've made a real effort to simplify my life.** I'm normally a pack rat, but I've found a great sense of freedom from cleaning closets, cabinets, and drawers. Don't be afraid to get rid of things! I think twice about buying anything now. I ask myself—is this a want or a need? It is amazing how little we really need. This has greatly reduced all those little stresses. No longer do I fight to get the utensil drawer open. Fewer clothes results in less washing and mending. "Less clutter and less dusting" has become my motto! I feel much more peaceful.

■ **I've seen the nasty results of burnout and I don't want to go down that road.** I fight burnout by hiring a regular substitute to come in so I can take an hour or so to run errands or go out to eat with a friend. I always tell parents ahead of time when I will have a sub and tell them a little about her background and qualifications.

■ **I learned quickly that school-age children like "real projects" so I give them routine tasks to help out.** Each week my school-agers help me make play dough, mix paint, and prepare Jell-O and fruit salad. I give them opportunities to lead an activity with the younger children. One child has learned songs and fingerplays to sing with the kids; another loves to read to individual children.

■ **I make a game of seeing how much exercise I can get during the day.** I keep a couple of pound weights on hand and do a few arm curls often. I organize a race around the yard and run with the kids. At naptime I do sit ups before I stretch out on the sofa to read and relax. During bad weather, I turn on some lively music and we all dance.

■ **I use a pedometer and step my way to better health.** I clip it onto my belt each morning and then try to get 10,000 steps each day. I glance at the steps I have as the last child goes out the door. If I haven't reached 10,000 I go for a short walk around the block before dinner. Before I started using this, I would feel a little cranky about having to go up and down the stairs and chase the kids all the time. But now I look at it a different way. I love my active job! It keeps me on the move and helps keep me fit.

■ **I've found it is really easy to eat a healthier diet since I joined the Child and Adult Care Food Program.** Basically, I just eat the same foods that the children do. I'm modeling good health habits for them and am taking care of myself at the same time.

■ **I rest when the children are resting.** It's tempting to use the time to get some housework done, but I need time to relax. I'm an

HFCCH Chapter 15 — Taking care of yourself 413

avid reader, and naptime is my time to read a good book or look through a magazine, while I quietly supervise the children.

■ **I needed a mentor.** Through my child care resource and referral agency, I located several experienced caregivers whom I can call for guidance and support. After I had a year or so of caring for children, I offered to mentor new caregivers. Helping new caregivers get started has been a wonderful experience. I don't always know the answers to every question, but I can help them with some problems. I also have developed some wonderful friendships.

■ **No time to clean—join the club!** Just because you are home all day with kids doesn't mean you have a lot of time on your hands to cook and clean. If you are doing your job well, you are really spending your time with the children. I sit down on Sunday afternoon and plan meals and weekly errands. I also assign chores to my family members. Do they gripe?—yes! But I remind them they would have to do chores regardless of whether I work at home or elsewhere. Chores are a part of life and responsibility builds character.

■ **Breakfast, snack, lunch, snack, dinner—it never ends in child care.** The very best investment I ever made was to purchase a crock pot and a rice cooker. I keep them going constantly. You will not believe how much time and money it will save you. An added benefit is that it makes your house smell wonderful. Often when I see children who are no longer in my care, they almost always mention the great smells coming from my kitchen. What a wonderful memory for children to have of their childhood!

■ **Turn off the TV!** I know it is tempting to have it on, even if it's just to hear an adult's voice, but the noise and the impact it will have on the children will only add to your stress. I learned long ago to master the VCR and DVD player. If I can do it, anyone can. When the children all go home, I relax and watch uninterrupted. Let me repeat that—uninterrupted! It is also a great incentive to watch these shows later while I am on the treadmill—and I need all the incentive I can get!

■ **I once heard the phrase "If you can't make it, fake it."** The idea is, even if you are feeling really down or grouchy, go ahead and at least appear to be cheerful. Just doing so will help; people respond better to you and help you get a new perspective on things. I went through a tough time recently and was really having trouble getting through the day. I tried the "If you can't make it, fake it" idea and amazingly it worked. It is surprising how just setting your mind to something can make a difference.

■ **Everything has trade-offs.** We are taught by TV and media to believe that we can have it all. We are led to believe that we can have perfect jobs and perfect lives. But the truth is that there are always trade-offs—there are no perfect jobs. Child care providers work long hours, but unlike many others, they get to enjoy their home. Working with children is stressful, but frankly I prefer it to the stresses of working with adults. A crying child makes me crazy, but a giggle and a hug warms my heart like nothing else.

■ **I used to take pride in my multi-tasking ability.** Now I try to focus on one thing at a time and really pay attention to it. Rather than worry about the activity I have planned for tomorrow, I focus my time on the children today. I'm more in tune with them and they seem more delightful and well-behaved. Everyone wins.

■ **My husband comes home for lunch three days a week.** He takes over and feeds the kids lunch. The children like having him around and it gives me a much needed break.

Growing as a professional

Contents

Where am I now? 416
Introduction 417
Consider your professional image 418
Professional ethics 418
Be prepared for work 419
Evaluate your work 419
Family feedback request 420
Continue your education 421
Heart of the Matter 422
Professional Development Record (PDR) 423
Experience Talks 424

Growing as a professional—
Where am I now? What can I improve?

		Seldom 1	Sometimes 2	Often 3	Most Often 4
1.	I maintain a clean, well groomed appearance.				
2.	I focus more on child care responsibilities during the time children are in my care than on personal or family needs.				
3.	I refer to myself as an early childhood professional.				
4.	I use qualified substitutes to care for children when I am ill or on leave.				
5.	I understand and practice ethical conduct.				
6.	I read articles and books to learn more about the early childhood field.				
7.	I meet my state registration or licensing requirements.				
8.	I participate in state quality initiatives to improve the quality of my program.				
9.	I ask families to evaluate my performance.				
10.	I set short-term and long-term goals for my professional growth.				
11.	I know where to go to receive more information about training and formal education.				
12.	I participate in training and education to improve my skills and knowledge.				
13.	I keep a personal record (class title, topic, date, training agency, # hrs of credit) of training requirements and classes or workshops I have completed.				
14.	I am a member of one or more early childhood professional groups.				
15.	I mentor and support other child care professionals.				
16.	I am an advocate for children and families.				
17.	I meet national accreditation requirements, e.g., NAFCC.				
18.	I participate in formal education for early childhood or related area. (GED, CDA, AA, BS, MS)				

Chapter 16

Growing as a professional

Do you consider yourself a professional? Some family child care providers don't feel professional because they work out of their home. Others don't view caring for young children as a "real job." But these are mistaken ideas. You may be surprised to learn that the early childhood profession has a long history supported by national organizations. And in today's world many professionals in many different fields work out of their home.

The work you do with children is very important and has a tremendous impact on the future. The first step in helping others respect your work is for you to show you value it. Believe in yourself and take pride in your work as a professional.

Refer to yourself and your business in professional terms—always. Use terms such as "child care provider," "early childhood educator," "early childhood professional," "family child care professional," etc. DO NOT call yourself a "baby sitter" or refer to your child care business as "baby sitting." Politely correct other people when they misname you, so they understand that your service is a high quality career and that you are proud of it.

Smile and say pleasantly, "I prefer to be called a family child care professional, rather than a baby sitter. I not only nurture children, but I teach them as well. Family child care is a nationally recognized profession. If you are interested, I would be happy to tell you more about the important work I do."

HFCCH Chapter 16 — Growing as a professional 417

Consider your professional image

What do parents and children see when they look at you? Child care providers work long hours. It is tempting to throw on last night's sweats, as you rush to greet children early in the morning. But if you wish to earn the respect of parents, it is important to consider your appearance.

Clothes and jewelry are important too. You will be on your feet a lot, so good shoes are a must. Clothes should be comfortable, washable, and stain resistant. Because you will be bending over and lifting children a great deal, you also will want to avoid low necklines, bare midriffs and low rise pants. Jewelry also should be limited —for your own safety. Children like to pull on long dangling earrings or necklaces.

Keep a change of clothing handy. Kids can be messy. If the baby spits up on you, you will want to change your shirt before parents arrive at the end of the day.

Each morning give yourself a quick check:

- ❏ Is my hair combed?
- ❏ Do I have clean hands and nails?
- ❏ Are my teeth brushed?
- ❏ How is my breath?
- ❏ Are my clothes professional, comfortable, and clean?
- ❏ Are my shoes comfortable and supportive?
- ❏ Have I removed any jewelry that can be pulled or easily damaged?

Professional ethics

What does it mean to be ethical? In simple terms, parents want to know:
- Are you honest?
- Can we trust you?
- Will you be respectful of our family values?
- Will you be an advocate for our child?
- Will you keep information we share with you confidential?
- —And above all else, will you keep our child safe from harm?

Parents trust you with the care of their child—often without knowing very much about you. They are relying on you to be a professional who follows a professional code of ethics.

The National Association for the Education of Young Children (naeyc.org) has developed a professional code of ethics that offers principles for responsible behavior and guidelines for resolving ethical dilemmas that occur in early care and education.

The National Association for Family Child Care (nafcc.org) has adopted the NAEYC code of ethics and recommends that all family child care professionals become familiar with this document. You can view the code of ethics at http://www.naeyc.org/about/positions/PSETH05.asp.

Be prepared for work

Just as with any job, you need to prepare for work. On a daily basis this means having the materials and equipment you need for daily activities with the children. A weekly schedule for meals and activities will keep you on the right track. A few hours planning and organizing the week ahead will make a tremendous difference.

Over the long term you will want to prepare yourself in other ways. Read about child development. Learn how to choose the right activities for each age child. Get to know each child and plan for individual needs. Get acquainted with families immediately and maintain positive relationships with them.

Network with other providers. Seek out other child care professionals who can share their expertise with you. As you become more experienced, offer to help new providers.

Evaluate your work

Seek feedback. Let families know that you want to improve your program. Provide a questionnaire at least once a year. Parents will be impressed to know that you value their input.

Review your work. Use the checklists in this book. Keep a journal of your observations, questions, and thoughts. Review this personal journal occasionally and note your growth as a professional.

Enjoy your work. Be proud of your commitment to one of society's most precious tasks. As a child care professional, you are in a position to know children well and guide them individually. You can help and support their families as you share your knowledge and insights.

Family feedback request

Dear Families, Date_____

Each year I take time to reflect on my child care program and consider what I can do to improve my services.

I greatly value your input. Please rank the following areas and give me your suggestions.

	Needs improvement ☹	OK 😐	Works well 🙂	Comments or suggestions
Daily schedule				
Arrival				
Learning activities				
Toys, materials, and equipment				
Health and safety				
Meals and snacks				
Guidance and discipline				
Outdoor activities				
Parent communication				
Departure				
Other comments:				

Continue your education

Watch for opportunities to learn more about child care. Workshops, evening courses and sessions, educational television, and child care newsletters and publications are good sources for further learning. Child care resource and referral, cooperative or university extension service, community colleges, and other education agencies offer free or low cost training and information.

Keep a record of your training and education. This will be very useful to you if you need to document training for state licensing or registration. Use the professional development record (PDR) provided in this chapter.

Keep a professional development portfolio. Portfolios are a good way for you to document your professional growth. Keep training certificates, a professional development record, and educational transcripts. You can share this with parents or prospective future employers later on. You also may want to save conference brochures and articles on ideas you want to know more about.

Join a professional association. The National Family Child Care Association (www.nfcca.org) and the National Association for the Education of Young Children (www.naeyc.org) are two organizations that provide support and training for child care professionals. Both organizations have state affiliate groups that provide conferences and training.

Earn your Child Development Associate Credential (CDA). As you seek additional training, you may wish to consider earning a national Child Development Associate Credential (CDA). Either community based non-credit training or college courses can be used to meet the training requirements. Earning your credential can be the first step toward more formal education. For more information contact the Council for Professional Recognition at 800-424-4310 or (www.cdacouncil.org.)

Consider working toward an early childhood degree. You may want to consider classes at your local community college or university. Check for online courses, too. Taking classes can be a little scary for some, but it will improve the quality of care you provide. It can be a great way to connect with other early childhood professionals. Many states have programs that offer tuition scholarships to early childhood professionals (e.g., the T.E.A.C.H program). Check with your local child care resource and referral or county extension office.

Heart of the Matter

It took a long time for me to feel comfortable with early childhood as a profession. I was a straight A student in school—a scientist working on a graduate degree in plant physiology. I was good at what I did and very proud of being one of the few women scientists in my field. Then I had a baby and my world changed overnight.

Infant care in our community was virtually non-existent. What I could find was very scary. My grandmother offered to help care for my daughter and I juggled my schedule between work, school, and home. Soon I was caring for my daughter and other children. I literally stumbled into this new profession, and to my surprise found myself enjoying my new work.

Ever the good student, I began to read everything about early childhood I could get my hands on. I discovered a wealth of resources and training that helped me improve my skills as a provider and as a parent. And believe me, learning how to guide and discipline young children was much more of a challenge than organic chemistry.

Eventually, I went back to school and earned a degree in my new field. As the months turned into years, I began to feel more comfortable and confident.

Nevertheless, I still panicked whenever anyone would ask me what I did. My self esteem was still wrapped up in my earlier identity as a scientist. In my head and in my heart, I knew that what I was doing with children was extremely important. But I knew that society did not value this worthy new role I had stumbled into. I had to do a lot of soul-searching.

Finally, I realized that society would never value early childhood, if we as early childhood professionals did not value it ourselves. So it was up to us. I had chosen to work in this incredibly important field, guiding and shaping our world's very future. Nothing could be more challenging or more rewarding than working with children.

Lesia

Professional Development Record (PDR)

Name: _____

Address: _____

County: _____

Phone: _____

	Title of Training	Educational Organization	Instructor	Dates Month	Dates Day	Dates Year	# of Hours of Training
1.							
2.							
3.							
4.							
5.							
6.							
7.							
8.							
9.							
10.							
11.							
12.							
13.							
14.							
15.							

HFCCH Chapter 16 — Growing as a professional

Experience Talks
Conversations with other providers

■ **Frankly, it took me a few years to begin feeling like a professional.** It takes time—at least for some of us! As I took a few classes and learned more about child development, I began to feel more confident. I also began to see the difference I was making in children's lives. Now I am proud to call myself an early childhood professional.

■ **I work hard to present myself as a professional.** Casual comfortable clothes are a big plus in my job, but I'm careful about my appearance. I never want to come across as a slob.

■ **One of the biggest rewards of this profession is talking with other providers.** Only they truly know and understand what you are dealing with each day. I have made some life-long friends by joining a local early childhood professional association.

■ **I keep a "professional notebook" to share with parents interested in my program.** It helps us get off on the right step. In this notebook, I include pictures of learning activities I do with the children. I share my professional development record and certificates I have earned from workshops and classes. I also keep a photocopy of the National Association for Family Child Care Web site. I want them to know that family child care is a nationally recognized profession.

■ **I can't stress enough how important it is to keep an organized record or file of your training.** Of course you need this documentation for registration or licensing, but you may be surprised at how you can use it in other ways. Sometimes there are opportunities for scholarships or additional funding from your state or local community. It also can help if you decide to move on to another job. Future employers want to see that you are interested in professional growth.

■ **Challenge yourself a little.** It is very easy to slip into the habit of seeking training only on your favorite topics. Arts, crafts, and reading are favorites of mine. But recently I took a great workshop on outdoor science. It has been wonderful to have some new activities for the kids. I now have a new favorite.

■ **Once a year, I take time to reflect on my professional development.** I look back at the challenges I faced this last year and at my successes. I make note of any training I took. Then I set some goals for myself for next year. I write my goals down and make a note on the calendar to review them every three months to monitor my progress. I don't always achieve every goal, but this approach keeps me focused.

■ **You are your own boss and it is up to you to recognize yourself as the valuable employee you really are.** Give yourself a professional development day and send yourself to some worthwhile training. Or make arrangements to visit another provider to see how another program operates. At the very least, give yourself an occasional treat for the good work that you do.

Notes

Notes